CONTESTED OBJECTS

Contested Objects breaks new ground in the interdisciplinary study of material culture. Its focus is on the rich and varied legacy of objects from the First World War as the global conflict that defined the twentieth century. From the iconic German steel helmet to practice trenches on Salisbury Plain, and from the 'Dazzle Ship' phenomenon through medal-wearing, diary-writing, trophy collecting, the market in war souvenirs and the evocative reworking of European objects by African soldiers, this book presents a dazzling array of hitherto unseen worlds of the Great War.

The innovative and multidisciplinary approach adopted here follows the lead established by Nicholas J. Saunders' *Matters of Conflict* (Routledge 2004), and extends its geographical coverage to embrace a truly international perspective. Australia, Africa, Italy, Germany, France, Belgium and Britain are all represented by a cross-disciplinary group of scholars working in archaeology, anthropology, cultural history, art history, museology, and cultural heritage. The result is a volume that resonates with richly documented and theoretically informed case studies that illustrate how the experiences of war can be embodied in and represented by an endless variety of artefacts, whose 'social lives' have endured for almost a century and that continue to shape our perceptions of an increasingly dangerous world.

Nicholas J. Saunders is Senior Lecturer at the University of Bristol and Honorary Reader at University College London. He is currently investigating First World War battle-zone landscapes in Belgium and Jordan. His recent publications include *Trench Art* (2003), *Matters of Conflict* (Routledge 2004), and *Archaeology and the First World War* (2007).

Paul Cornish is a Senior Curator in the Imperial War Museum's Department of Exhibits. Since the turn of the century he has become increasingly involved in the study of the material culture of conflict – particularly in relation to the First World War. He is the author of several papers on the subject, as well as a book: *Machine Guns and the Great War* (2009).

CONTESTED OBJECTS

Material memories of the Great War

*Nicholas J. Saunders and
Paul Cornish (editors)*

Routledge
Taylor & Francis Group

LONDON AND NEW YORK

First published 2009
by Routledge
2 Park Square, Milton Park, Abingdon, Oxon, OX14 4RN

Simultaneously published in the USA and Canada
by Routledge
711 Third Avenue, New York, NY 10017

First issued in paperback 2013

Routledge is an imprint of the Taylor & Francis Group, an informa business

Typeset in Garamond 3 by
Swales & Willis Ltd, Exeter, Devon

British Library Cataloguing in Publication Data
A catalogue record for this book is available from the British Library

Library of Congress Cataloging in Publication Data
A catalog record for this book has been requested

ISBN 13: 978–0–415–45070–6 (hbk)
ISBN13: 978-0-415-85293-7 (pbk)

IN MEMORY OF ITALO HELLMANN
(1941–2007)

CONTENTS

CONTENTS

CONTENTS

LIST OF FIGURES

The following were reproduced with kind permission. While every effort has been made to trace copyright holders and obtain permission, this has not been possible in all cases. Any omissions brought to our attention will be remedied in future editions.

LIST OF CONTRIBUTORS

Marco Balbi is President of the Società Storica per la Guerra Bianca, and coordinator of Progetto Archeologia della Grande Guerra, Buccinasco (MI), Italy.

Sonia Batten is a graduate student at the Centre for First World War Studies, Departments of Medieval and Modern History, University of Birmingham, UK.

Dr Jonathan Black is Senior Research Fellow in History of Art, Dorich House Museum, Kingston University, London, UK.

Graham Brown is an Archaeological Field Investigator with English Heritage, Swindon, UK.

Martin Brown is an Environmental Advisor for Archaeology with Defence Estates, Ministry of Defence, Tilshead, UK.

Paul Cornish is Senior Curator in the Department of Exhibits and Firearms, Imperial War Museum, London, UK.

Dominiek Dendooven is a researcher at the In Flanders Fields Museum, Ypres, Belgium.

Mark Dennis is Curator of the Library and Museum of Freemasonry, Freemasons' Hall, London, UK.

Marc Dewilde is a heritage researcher in archaeology at the Vlaams Instituut voor het Onoerend Erfgoed, Kortemark, Belgium.

David Field is an Archaeological Field Investigator with English Heritage, Swindon, UK.

Dr Paola Filippucci is Lecturer in Social Anthropology at Murray Edwards College, University of Cambridge, UK.

Professor Paul Gough is Executive Dean of the Faculty of Creative Arts, and Pro-Vice Chancellor at the University of the West of England, Bristol, UK.

Fabio Gygi is a postgraduate student in the Department of Anthropology, University College London, UK.

Gulya Isyanova is an independent researcher who lives in London, UK.

Alan Jeffreys is Curator in the Department of Exhibits and Firearms, Imperial War Museum, London, UK.

Dr Catherine Moriarty is Principal Research Fellow, Faculty of Arts, University of Brighton, UK.

Daniel Phillips is an independent researcher, who lives in Hitchin, Hertfordshire, UK.

Matthew Richardson is Curator of Social History, Manx National Heritage, Douglas, Isle of Man.

Dr Nicholas J. Saunders is Senior Lecturer in the Department of Archaeology and Anthropology, University of Bristol, UK.

Dr John Schofield is currently Head of Military Programmes with English Heritage, Swindon, UK, Part-time Lecturer in Archaeology at Southampton University, UK, and Visiting Fellow in Archaeology and Anthropology at the University of Bristol, UK.

Roger Smither is Keeper of the Film and Photograph Archives, Imperial War Museum, London, UK.

Dr Richard Waller is Associate Professor of History and International Relations in the Department of History, Bucknell University, Lewisburg, Pennsylvania, USA.

FOREWORD

In September 2001, just a few days before the Al-Qaeda attack on New York's World Trade Center, University College London and the Imperial War Museum held the first in a series of conferences focused on the interdisciplinary study of twentieth- and twenty-first-century conflict. The aim was to establish a secure footing for the investigation of material culture and memory through a hybrid approach that embraced anthropology, archaeology, cultural history, military history, art history, cultural geography, and museum and heritage studies.

Our choice of the term 'conflict' rather than 'war' was an acknowledgement of the distinctive civilian aspect of modern industrialized wars, and the increasing violence of the twentieth and twenty-first centuries aimed specifically at civilians, in the Balkans, the Middle East, Africa and beyond, in bitter ethnic, religious and political struggles. Little could we have known how tragically appropriate this inclusive approach and choice of words would prove to be. In the wake of '9/11', the world is a changed place, where shocking and bloody violence against civilians (and often in unmilitarized civilian landscapes) appears to have become equal to, if not more frequent, than acts of aggression between those in uniform in more traditional war zones.

Both of us, in our distinct but increasingly conjoined worlds of academia and museums, had identified a rising specialist and public interest in twentieth-century conflict, and in what the investigation of material culture could tell us about the individual experience of war and its aftermath through studying what anthropologists refer to as 'the social lives of objects'. It seemed to us that there needed to be an intellectual centre of gravity for a global and cross-disciplinary community of scholars who specialized in different aspects of modern conflict, and whose work centred on some aspect of materiality. From the beginning, we wished to draw upon all available expertise, but not to privilege any particular discipline.

It was decided, for reasons of our own interests and expertise, and the role of the First World War in ushering in industrialized conflict on a global scale, that the first two conferences should focus on the conflict of 1914–18, but that subsequently a thematic and pan-twentieth- and twenty-first-centuries approach would be adopted.

It was always our intention that these conferences should leave a permanent record in the form of publications. To this end, the first conference was published by

Routledge in 2004 as *Matters of Conflict: Material Culture, Memory and the First World War* – edited by one of us (NJS). The international interest generated by the conferences and this initial volume manifested itself by many investigators expressing the desire to publish their own research in publications dedicated to twentieth-century conflict-related themes as well as through more traditional avenues.

Contested Objects is in part a response to this enthusiasm, and originates from the second conference held at the Imperial War Museum in 2004. This conference, and others that followed, was consciously interdisciplinary. The resulting publication shows obvious differences in approach between historians, archaeologists and anthropologists – differences that have been only partially muted by the editorial process in an attempt to illustrate the benefits of empirical and theoretical interplay between academic disciplines.

There is also, we believe, an essential rightness in the fact that these conferences were held in Britain's foremost repository of the material culture of conflict. Nevertheless, it is important to point out that the Imperial War Museum has not yet, in any corporate sense, achieved full awareness of the significance of its collections as artefacts of material culture. Since the early days of the museum, the collections have been used almost exclusively as a medium through which history can be explained. Despite their importance in this respect, we believe that re-engaging with the museum's unique corpus of conflict-related objects from a broadly anthropological perspective opens up exciting new opportunities for research. In addition, the IWM's collections offer a unique depth and breadth as raw material for a material culture studies approach, as is evident from the contributions of the museum's staff to the 2004 conference and this volume. What is true for the Imperial War Museum also holds, we believe, for many other war museums (large and small) around the world – many of which are the repositories of objects and memories that have lain dormant for the best part of a century.

INTRODUCTION

Nicholas J. Saunders and Paul Cornish

This volume aspires to an international outlook, both in the geographical origins of its contributors and of their chosen subject matter. We regard this as an essential response to current developments in the study of the First World War (and, of course, to the conflicts of the twentieth and twenty-first centuries more widely). Only in recent years has the study of the Great War of 1914–18, so fundamental to our understanding of subsequent history, begun to escape from a state of national and doctrinal compartmentalization.

In Britain, the historiography of the First World War was dominated throughout the twentieth century by the argument concerning Britain's role in the conflict (see Bond 1991). Were the huge losses justified? Were they avoidable? This debate has produced successive waves of 'revisionism' since the 1930s. Many excellent historical studies (and polemics of dubious value) resulted, but, however compelling their conclusions, these works have made scant impression on the public perception of the war – a perception which originates not in academic study but in television documentaries, novels, visits to battlefields and cemeteries and, fundamentally, a kind of 'folk memory' rooted in the testimony of those who served in the war and returned. The power of views originating in personal experience, memory, imagination and exposure to selective and fictional accounts is evident, and has to be acknowledged in efforts to gain a more accurate and nuanced understanding of the ways in which modern conflict affects us today, and is transmitted to future generations.

In recent years, a further shift has occurred in Great War historiography (see Winter and Prost 2005). The cultural ramifications of the war have come under the scrutiny of cultural historians such as Modris Eksteins (1989), Joanna Bourke (1996) and Jay Winter (Winter 1995). Others have called for a re-appraisal of the impact of the violence, hatred and grief engendered by the war (Audoin-Rouzeau and Becker 2002). A shared quality of many of these new approaches has been their international outlook. Epitomizing this approach, Hew Strachan (2001) has commenced publication of his combined military, social and economic history of the war – a landmark publication written from an avowedly global perspective.

Simultaneously, the First World War has become the subject of anthropological and archaeological investigation – not least because it remains so ambiguously 'recent' in the European imagination – hovering on the border where oral history, military history and cultural history meet individual and collective memories:

> Great War objects live on in peoples' homes, in museums, and in salesrooms, and its legacies permeate the tortuous politics of identity, via nationalism and ethnicity, across Europe and beyond. The war exists also in the conjoined worlds of tourism and heritage, with ever-increasing numbers of visitors to its battlefields and museums, especially along the old Western Front of Belgium and France.
>
> (Saunders 2007: v)

Hitherto, the landscapes and material culture of the war had only ever been in the background of the innumerable military histories of the conflict.

Anthropology and Great War material culture

Anthropologically, the study of Great War material culture has forged new empirical and theoretical approaches to the study of conflict and identity, nationality, faith, memory, landscape, memorialization, heritage, museums and tourism. Specifically, it has focused on documenting and analysing material culture – exploring the cultural biographies of distinctive kinds of objects, from memorabilia (Thierry 2001) to 'trench art' (Saunders 2003a), battle-zone landscapes and their civilian counterparts (Saunders 2001; Schofield 2004; Chielens et al. 2006), religion (Becker 1998), war memorials (Black 2004; Kidd 2004; King 1998) and tourism (Lloyd 1998). Yet, while these and related issues form the basis of this discussion, another virtually unexplored dimension of the war demands what some might regard as a more traditionally anthropological response.

The Allied armies were international in composition, and thus multi-ethnic and multi-faith (see Dendooven and Chielens 2008). On the Western Front alone, the war involved British, French, Belgian and German soldiers, as well as American, Russian, Australian, New Zealand, South African and Canadian troops. Furthermore, non-white indigenous peoples from across the world took part, such as African-Americans, African-Caribbean peoples (Howe 2002; Smith 2004), men from African tribal societies (see Chapter 6), Native Americans (Britten 1997), Hindus (Omissi 1999), Sikhs (Anon. 1999), Maoris, Vietnamese ('Annamites'), and Chinese (Bailey 2000). Each group represented a society with distinct ideas, beliefs and practices concerning not just the nature of conflict, but of life, death and the treatment and commemoration of the dead as well. So far, none of these indigenous groups has received a sustained anthropological investigation in terms of their relationships with what was called at the time 'The Great War for Civilization' – a phrase which has become ironic, yet has always been replete with Eurocentric and colonialist preconceptions and attitudes that elided the contributions and sensitivities of those non-Europeans who fought and died during it.

Anthropological studies of material culture and landscape have been a major influence on recent attempts to understand the Great War and its aftermath. Arguably the most important theoretical contribution has been to force an acknowledgement that the materialities of conflict are not restricted to obvious wartime items such as weaponry, ammunition, uniforms, devastated buildings and defensive structures. While these cannot be ignored, we must look also at personal belongings, memorabilia, souvenirs and the architecture and objects made during the post-war era as well as during the war, from war cemeteries to museums, whole (reconstructed) towns to individual monuments (see Brandauer 2007 for a pioneering case study from Austria). Most of all, perhaps, we must reassess the battle-zone landscapes within which all these features are located, and thus investigate issues of media representation, heritage and the burgeoning tourist industry that inevitably (and increasingly) reshape their physical nature and reconfigure their meanings (see Gough 2006).

Objects

The objects of the Great War have a curious and unique character. More than any other kind of matter they seem to exist (physically and metaphysically) in a seemingly infinite number of cultural and personal worlds simultaneously, and so can appear as worthless trash, cherished heirloom, historical artefact, memory item or commercially valuable souvenir depending on those who own or observe them. They can be rusting mud-covered artefacts excavated from the earth, treasured mementos in peoples' homes, captioned exhibits in museum displays, exquisitely polished objects in private collections or commodities for sale in militaria fairs and on the Internet (Fabiansson 2004; see also Chapter 9).

Some, like the little-investigated 'trench club', are impromptu weapons that contain within their savage design and purpose unique insights into social classes and attitudes of the soldiers who used them, and equally of the prejudices of museum curators who selectively displayed them decades after the war (Chapter 3). Others are arguably more terrifying in that they haunt the mind. Gygi's (this volume) analysis of the social life of the German steel helmet reveals how an object designed for wartime protection became entangled in a web of contested copyright, transformed into an epitomizing metaphor for the steely character of the German soldier, and the terror of the Third Reich, before finding its way via the Hells Angels and Star Wars to modern Iraq.

Different kinds of objects encode a more emotional and individual message (sometimes contesting with official rules), such as the Commonwealth War Grave Commission's headstones inscribed with their sometimes heart-rending, sometimes formulaic 'language of grief' (Chapter 11). Equally insightful, if far more fragile, are personal diaries. These can tell not only of a long dead soldier's experiences in war, but may become transformed by subsequent generations of the same family, who see in their writing, and the feel in their textured surfaces, visceral connections and affinities with their own ancestors who created them in life and death circumstances (Chapter 14). As with war medals, whose social valuations and uses varied over time (Joy 2002; see also Chapter 7), it is often the long tumultuous afterlife of these objects that bestows cultural value as an index of their personal associations.

The same is true for that most common but visually loaded object of material culture – the postcard. As Filippucci (Chapter 15) shows, postcard images of the pre-war landscape of the Argonne region of France are manipulated – almost wielded – with commemorative precision to recall a past that no one now living can remember. These images elide the damage and suffering of the war (yet are curiously underscored by them), recalling layers of memory (and myth) than can still sometimes be glimpsed in the region today in jarring scenes where a building, crossroads or duck pond has survived and instantly links a 90-year-old past with the present.

What is clear from these examples is that the Great War does not stand alone as a single indisputable legacy that we are only now discovering – it is a heritage that we are all creating and shaping as we come into contact with new and different under-standings and presentations of its physical remains, and of the personal experiences embodied in them.

The constantly evolving meanings of Great War objects, and the slippery and ambiguous concepts that lie behind them, challenge our ability to know how to formally represent them in museums. Many war museums continue to take the line of least resistance, exhibiting weapons and uniforms in the traditional military history way – yet, as we have seen, in so doing they tell one story but miss many more that lie sealed within the object. The problematical issue is that Great War objects, unlike those in other kinds of museums, are not valued and appreciated for their age, their rarity, their technical virtuosity, their beauty or even their serendipitous survival. Most Great War objects have no such intrinsic worth – their significance comes from their associations, not only with other similar items, but with experiences, memories, imagination and a wealth of historical documentation.

A bullet carved into a crucifix after being dug out of a wound (Saunders 2003b), a metal matchbox cover, an identity tag, a woollen blanket, an army boot, a corroded roll of barbed wire, a fragment of carved wood or chalk, or a hundred other everyday objects from a soldier's life connect directly to a (sometimes well-documented) human life. The very ordinariness of these often mass-produced objects is matched only by their unusual (sometimes extraordinary) qualities of connectedness – as Cornish (Chapter 1) shows for war trophies in the Imperial War Museum.

Such objects, as Dendooven (Chapter 4) illustrates, can also be fragments rather than whole items, and can travel along strange trajectories before they end up in an exhibition, intersecting peoples' lives across the world for generations. It is a revealing and powerful fact that those who send back to the In Flanders Fields Museum at Ypres objects acquired in that town by their distant relatives during the war feel that somehow they are returning home, that a debt is being repaid, and that the old soldier will now be remembered forever through the professionally curated and displayed object.

Landscapes

Landscapes are cultural artefacts, tied irrevocably to a sense of place and notions of identity, and subject to changing attitudes towards war and memory. As artefacts, Great War battle-zones were seen, imagined and represented in a host of ways at the time by soldiers and, separately, by the media. The cultural schema of what was and what was not acceptable or required for understanding the landscape changed in newspapers and magazines throughout the war (Beurier 2004) and is shown in detail for the stylized panoramic sketches made by British artists at the front (Chapter 16). Here, above all, images of landscape were designed not to represent actuality, but to increase the effectiveness of killing the enemy, and avoid being killed oneself.

Today, places in the landscapes of the Somme in France and Belgian Flanders that were 'empty' a few years ago have become the focus of well-attended commemorative events – such as that which takes place annually on 1 July at the Lochnagar Crater near La Boiselle on the Somme. Such developments are, in part, an acknowledgement that First World War battle-zone landscapes are some of the most expensive real estate in the world in terms of their cost in human lives and suffering (Saunders 2001).

In assessing landscape, we are drawn inexorably into another field of anthropological inquiry – that which investigates the sensorial domains of battle-zones. The physical and psychological intensities of human experiences of industrialized war produced a different view of the world, if not a new world entirely, for many soldiers. In this universe of mud, trenches, dugouts, deafening artillery bombardments, night raids, choking gas and blind advances across no-man's-land, it was often impossible to see anything at all, and so sight was replaced by other kinds of sensory experience, such as smell, sound and touch (Howes 1991: 3–5; Eksteins 1990: 146,150–1; Classen 2005). Industrialized war had created a new landscape of the senses that was captured time and again in diaries, memoirs, novels, and war poetry.

In his 1917 war novel, *Under Fire*, the French soldier-author Henri Barbusse drew on his own experiences of this new sensorial terrain in describing an infantry attack: 'There is no whistling through the air. Amid the huge pounding of the guns, one can clearly perceive the extraordinary absence of the noise of bullets around us.'(Barbusse 2003: 225). Wilfred Owen, the English war poet, had a darker experience. Writing to his mother after just three weeks in the trenches, he observed 'I have not seen any dead. I have done worse. In the dank air, I have perceived it, and in the darkness, felt.' (Wilfred Owen, quoted in Das 2005: 7).

On the battlefields of the Great War, and for the first time in human history, the literal fragmentation of human bodies and the earth (by artillery barrages and machinegun fire) was on such a vast scale that reality itself was pulverized. The result was a surreal world – a landscape of darkness, sound, touch and smell, where seeing was impossible or lethal. Soldiers were often reduced to crawling and slithering, feeling and smelling their way around. Their knowledge of the world came not from sight, but through tactile sensations – the 'haptic' way of knowing the immediate environment. Perhaps for this reason, soldiers' experiences (and writings) of Great War battlefields were often less concerned with vision than touch – feeling their way through a haptic landscape (Das 2005: 23). It is hardly surprising that the fear of mud (with its metal splinters, diseases, effluents and fragments of other men) sucking the body down to a suffocating death was one of the most common nightmares suffered by soldiers (ibid.: 37). In the Great War, it often seemed, the land had become the ravenous monster of ancient myth and medieval superstition.

Great War archaeology

Archaeologically, dugouts, hospitals, bomb craters, tunnels, ruined villages, battle-field graves, weaponry and associated war debris and innumerable kilometres of trenches have all become the focus of investigation over the past two decades or so (e.g. Adam 2006; Desfossés 1999; Desfossés et al. 2002, 2005; Saunders 2002, 2007; Price 2004; also Chapters 17 and 18). It is as if the idea of an archaeology of the Great War – at once so recent and so distant – has finally come of age, offering new information and insights into the tragic cost in human lives and suffering that the war created.

Running through all the varied aspects of this new kind of archaeology like an electric current are the lives of real people – recent ancestors, not distant ones (see Chapter 18; Fabiansson 2007; Saunders 2003b). Unlike the human remains of deep prehistory, these individuals have names, signatures and faces, and their letters, photographs and objects seem to announce a new and very anthropological kind of archaeology – that of the recent historical past in time of war.

Great War archaeology itself, is, of course, a hybrid. It draws on industrial archaeology, whose strata are saturated with mass-produced artefacts of the twentieth century, and borrows from historical archaeology, informed as it is by a wealth of written documents on every conceivable aspect of the conflict. It is also, and fundamentally, social archaeology and public archaeology, in that it excavates peoples' lives, and represents them to audiences that themselves remake the war in their own imaginations from fragments of knowledge, experience and memory. Great War archaeology is all of these and more, for it deals with new worlds brought into being at terrible cost between 1914 and 1918 – worlds that have transformed themselves ever since, within which we still live today, and with whose legacies we still struggle, in Bosnia, Gaza, Iraq and beyond.

The course of Great War archaeology along the old Western Front has differed in France and Belgium. In France, Regional Archaeological Services operate as part of the local Direction régional des affaires culturelle (DRAC). Their responsibility is for their region's total archaeological heritage, from prehistory to recent times. In other words, French archaeologists have been excavating First World War remains for decades not because of any proactive policy to do so, but solely as a consequence of their wider duties. Nevertheless, isolated finds of bodies, and more extensive excavations at the Actiparc site near Arras and elsewhere, added not only to practical experience, but also led to remarkable discoveries of Great War material culture and communal battlefield graves (Desfossés et al. 2002, 2005).

In Belgium, it was only in 2002 that professional archaeologists became officially involved with investigating Great War remains when they were asked by the government to assess the route of a projected extension to the A19 motorway across the old Ypres Salient battlefields (Dewilde et al. 2004; Chapter 17; de Meyer and Pype 2004). Hitherto, excavations had been carried out by a number of amateur groups such as 'The Diggers' and the 'Association for Battlefield Archaeology in Flanders'.

The differences between French and Belgian archaeologists in their relationships with the developing archaeology of the First World War are professional, cultural and legal, and intimately tied to the development of traditional archaeology in each country. Nevertheless, as Great War archaeology develops, so too does the realization that the artefacts are not only national and international heritage, but that they can also become the centrepiece of a new museum exhibition that in turn becomes a 'must see' stop on a battlefield tour, and thereby potentially aid the economic regeneration of certain regions. Great War archaeology is thus caught in a spider's web of war history, war heritage and tourism, and further entangled with issues concerning authenticity and the ethics of collecting and exhibiting war objects. In these situations, the symbiosis and synergy between archaeological excavation and an anthropological approach to the material culture of war becomes increasingly evident.

The excavation of First World War sites along the old Western Front, unlike so much of traditional archaeology, is a memory-making activity. Excavators, landowners, heritage specialists and tourists struggle to imagine today's verdant woods and fields as monochrome images of Hell, just as returning refugees in 1919 struggled to see devastated landscapes as fertile pastures and farms (Saunders 2002: 107). The tension between modern archaeology's scientific objectivity, the intensity of emotions involved, and the all but inevitable momentum towards commemoration at such locations, reveals Great War archaeology as a uniquely interdisciplinary endeavour – an undertaking that is inextricably caught up with anthropological ideas of material culture and landscape.

This vision of interdisciplinarity has also informed more recent engagements with Great War archaeology beyond the Western Front. In Britain, increasing attention has been paid to the industrial infrastructure of the war (e.g. Cocroft 2000: 155–96), the facsimile landscapes of training trenches (Chapter 20), and the remains of the iconic Zeppelin airship raids of 1917 (Faulkner and Durrani 2008).

Further afield, high altitude warfare in the Italian Alps (Chapter 19) and in the Austrian–Italian Dolomites (Brandauer 2007) has been investigated from archaeo-logical and anthropological perspectives which themselves have taken a wide-ranging bottom-up view of material culture. The social transformation of Great War materialities in Africa have been investigated by Waller (Chapter 6), and in southern Jordan new investigations have yielded unique insights into the relationships between the Great War, the Great Arab Revolt, the Hejaz Railway and the nature of conflict landscapes (Faulkner and Saunders, in press).

It is this unique combination of event, recollection and representation that this volume seeks to document and to understand. The challenges facing a material culture-based investigation of the First World War, and of twentieth- and twenty-first-century conflict more widely, are considerable, as they mix and juxtapose materiality with spirituality, experience with memory and science with emotion. We believe that the ultimate goal of such an approach speaks for itself – a transformation in our understanding of modern conflict, its varied legacies and its potent lessons.

These developments bring us back to the cross-disciplinary genesis of the UCL/IWM conferences, and of this volume. At the point where the Great War finally recedes from living memory, its study is undergoing a sea change – one that is an integral part of new ways of looking at the material culture of modern wars and their relationships with modernity. We hope that this volume will play its part in carrying these developments forward.

Nicholas J. Saunders, University of Bristol
Paul Cornish, Imperial War Museum, London
January 2009

References

Adam, F. (2006) *Alain-Fournier et ses compagnons d'arme*. Metz: Editions Serpenoise.

Anon. (1999) 'Sikhs in the Salient'. *In Flanders Fields Magazine* 1 (1): 16.

Audoin-Rouzeau, S. and A. Becker (2002) *1914–1918: Understanding the Great War*. London: Profile Books.

Bailey, P. (2000) 'From Shandong to the Somme: Chinese indentured labour in France during World War I'. In Anne J. Kashen (ed.) *Language, Labour and Migration*, pp. 179–96. Ashgate.

Barbusse, H. (2003) *Under Fire*. London: Penguin.

Becker, A. (1998) *War and Faith: Religious Imagination in France, 1914–30*. Oxford: Berg.

Beurier, J. (2004) 'Death and material culture: the case of pictures during the First World War'. In Nicholas J. Saunders (ed.) *Matters of Conflict: Material Culture, Memory and the First World War*, pp. 109–22. Abingdon: Routledge.

Black, J. (2004) '"Thanks for the Memory": war memorials, spectatorship and the trajectories of commemoration 1919–2001'. In Nicholas J. Saunders (ed.) *Matters of Conflict: Material Culture, Memory and the First World War*, pp. 134–48. Abingdon: Routledge.

Bond, B. (ed.) (1991) *The First World War and British Military History*. London: Clarendon Press.

Brandauer, I. (2007) *Menschenmaterial Soldat: Alltagsleben an der Dolomitenfront im Ersten Weltkrieg 1915–1917*. Innsbruck: Golf Verlag.

Britten, T.A. (1997) *American Indians in World War I: At Home and at War*. Albuquerque: University of New Mexico Press.

Chielens, P., D. Dendooven and H. Decoot (eds) (2006) *De Laatste Getuige: Het oorlogslanschap van de Westhoek*. Tielt: Lanoo.

Classen, C. (ed.) (2005) *The Book of Touch*. Oxford: Berg.

Cocroft, W.D. (2000) *Dangerous Energy: The Archaeology of Gunpowder and Military Explosives Manufacture*. Swindon: English Heritage.

Cornish, P. (2004) '"Sacred relics": objects in the Imperial War Museum'. In Nicholas J. Saunders (ed.) *Matters of Conflict: Material Culture, Memory and the First World War*, pp. 35–50. Abingdon: Routledge.

Das, S. (2005) *Touch and Intimacy in First World War Literature*. Cambridge: Cambridge University Press.

de Meyer, M. and P. Pype (2004) *The A19 Project: Archaeological Research at Cross Roads*. Zarren, Belgium: Association for World War Archaeology (AWA) Publications.

Dendooven, D. and P. Chielens (2008) *World War I: Five Continents in Flanders*. Tielt: Lanoo.

Desfossés, Y. (1999) 'Préserver les traces: l'archéologie et la Grande Guerre aujourd'hui'. *Noêsis: Revue Annuelle d'Histoire* 2: 37–51.

Desfossés, Y., A. Jacques and G. Prilaux (2002) 'Actiparc: premier bilan de l'operation d'archéologie preventive'. *Histoire et Archéologie du Pas-de-Calais* XX: 3–26.

—— (2005) *Archéologie en Nord-Pas de Calais: l'archéologie de la grande guerre*. Villeneuve d'Ascq: DRAC Nord-Pas de Calais. Service régional de l'Archéologie.

Dewilde, M., P. Pype, M. de Meyer, F. Demeyere, W. Lammens, J. Degryse, F. Wyffels and N.J. Saunders (2004) 'Belgium's new department of First World War archaeology'. *Antiquity* 78 (301) Project Gallery (see http://antiquity.ac.uk/ProjGall/Saunders).

Eksteins, M. (1989) *Rites of Spring: The Great War and the Birth of the Modern Age*. London: Bantam.

Fabiansson, N. (2004) 'The internet and the Great War: the impact on the making and meaning of Great War history'. In Nicholas J. Saunders (ed.) *Matters of Conflict: Material Culture, Memory and the First World War*, pp. 72–89. Abingdon: Routledge.

—— (2007) *Das Begleitbuch zu Ernst Jünger 'In Stahlgewittern'*. Hamburg: Verlag E.S. Mittler & Sohn.

Faulkner, N. and N. Durrani (2008) *In Search of the Zeppelin War: The Archaeology of the First Blitz*. Stroud: Tempus.

Faulkner, N. and N.J. Saunders (in press) 'War without frontiers: the archaeology of the Great Arab Revolt'. In A. Peacock (ed.) *The Frontiers of the Ottoman World*. Proceedings of the British Academy. Oxford: Oxford University Press.

Gough, P. (2006) 'Beaumont-Hamel: The recovery, construction, and reconstruction of a site of national memory'. *Stand To!* 75: 13–19.

Howe, G.D. (2002) *Race, War and Nationalism: A Social History of West Indians in the First World War*. Oxford: James Currey.

Howes, D. (1991) 'Introduction: "To Summon All the Senses"'. In David Howes (ed.) *The Varieties of Sensory Experience*, pp. 3–21. Toronto: University of Toronto Press.

Joy, J. (2002) 'Biography of a medal: people and the things they value'. In J. Schofield, W.G. Johnson and C.M. Beck (eds) *Matériel Culture: The Archaeology of Twentieth Century Conflict*, pp. 132–42. London: Routledge.

Kidd, W. (2004) 'The Lion, the angel and the war memorial: some French sites revisited'. In Nicholas J. Saunders (ed.) *Matters of Conflict: Material Culture, Memory and the First World War*, pp. 149–65. Abingdon: Routledge.

King, A. (1998) *Memorials of the Great War in Britain: The Symbolism and Politics of Remembrance*. Oxford: Berg.

Lloyd, D.W. (1998) *Battlefield Tourism: Pilgrimage and the Commemoration of the Great War in Britain, Australia and Canada, 1919–1939*. Oxford: Berg

Omissi, D. (1999) *Indian Voices of the Great War: Soldiers' Letters, 1914–18*. London: Palgrave Macmillan.

Price, J. (2004) 'The Ocean Villas project: archaeology in the service of European remembrance'. In Nicholas J. Saunders (ed.) *Matters of Conflict: Material Culture, Memory and the First World War*, pp. 179–91. Abingdon: Routledge.

Saunders, N. J. (2001) 'Matter and memory in the landscapes of conflict: the Western Front 1914–1999'. In B. Bender and M. Winer (eds) *Contested Landscapes: Movement, Exile and Place*, pp. 37–53. Oxford: Berg.

—— (2002) 'Excavating memories: archaeology and the Great War, 1914–2001'. *Antiquity* 76 (291): 101–8.

—— (2003a) *Trench Art: Materialities and Memories of War*. Oxford: Berg.

—— (2003b) 'Crucifix, calvary, and cross: materiality and spirituality in Great War landscapes'. *World Archaeology* 35 (1): 7–21.

—— (2007) *Killing Time: Archaeology and the First World War*. Stroud: Sutton.

Schofield, J. (2004) 'Aftermath: materiality on the home front, 1914–2001'. In Nicholas J. Saunders (ed.) *Matters of Conflict: Material Culture, Memory, and the First World War*, pp. 192–206. Abingdon: Routledge.

Smith, R. (2004) *Jamaican Volunteers in the First World War: Race, Masculinity and the Development of National Consciousness.* Manchester: Manchester University Press.

Strachan, H. (2001) *The First World War, Vol. 1: To Arms!* Oxford: Oxford University Press.

Thierry, J.-P. (ed.) (2001) *Petites histoires de la Grande Guerre: les objets insolites de l'historial*, pp. 45–61. Péronne: Historial de la Grande Guerre.

Winter, J. (1995) *Sites of Memory, Sites of Mourning: The Great War in European Cultural History.* Cambridge: Cambridge University Press.

Winter, J. and A. Prost (2005) *The Great War in History: Debates and Controversies, 1914 to the Present.* Cambridge: Cambridge University Press.

1

'JUST A BOYISH HABIT'. . .?

British and Commonwealth war trophies in the First World War

Paul Cornish

Taking trophies in war is a practice as old as warfare itself. Celtic warriors would seek to collect the severed heads of their foes; Roman generals paraded in triumph behind the captured nobility and temple goods of their defeated enemies. In more recent times, much blood has been spilt in attempts to seize or defend regimental standards. Monuments and medals have been cast from the metal of captured guns. Here, I will discuss the continuation of such practices during the First World War, in particular by the forces of Britain and its Dominions. Furthermore, the wealth of memoirs and other personal records of the Great War will permit an investigation of the collecting of trophies by individuals.

First, it is necessary to define 'trophy', as opposed to 'souvenir'. Essentially a trophy can be defined as something seized by force from the enemy. It may be a purely symbolic item; it may have a practical (or military) value, or even a monetary value. Virtually always it will be in some way redolent of the enemy from whom it was taken. However, for the purposes of this analysis, it will not include items scavenged from the battlefield. There was in fact an 'immense vogue' among British troops for collecting artillery shell nose-caps' (Anon 1919: 46; see also Richards 1964: 92; Coppard 1969: 62). However, these were picked up from the battlefield, not captured from the enemy.

As contemporary diarists, letter writers and chroniclers were not interested in categorizing such activities, their work shows no analytical precision in separating the trophy from the souvenir. Both terms appear to be used almost indiscriminately. A member of 37th Division, writing in the division's 'chronicle' under the pseudonym 'Gwinell', stated

> This war will undoubtedly go down to posterity as the 'War of Souvenirs'.
> The souvenir habit is, I suppose latent in all of us, and it only needed a really
> good war like this bring it bubbling to the surface.
>
> (Anon 1919: 46–7)

However, the 'souvenirs' which he proceeds to discuss includes trophies seized from the Germans, as well as items purchased from local people, shell nose-caps and objects which would now be defined as 'Trench Art' (ibid.; and see Saunders 2003: 129–33).

For the purposes of this chapter, trophies will be divided into two main categories: 'public' – trophies which passed through official channels and were intended for public display; 'personal' – trophies acquired by individuals.

Public trophies

The practice of publicly displaying captured enemy war material was well established by 1914. To do so satisfied a number of desires: victory was plainly announced – you cannot capture enemy guns while retreating (see Vance 1995: 48); civilian morale was likely to be bolstered; and (by no means a lesser consideration) the *esprit de corps* of the unit responsible for the capture of such trophies was enhanced. The letters, diaries and memoirs of British soldiers contain frequent references to the capture of such trophies. Graham Greenwell, an officer with 1/4 Oxfordshire & Buckinghamshire Light Infantry, wrote to his mother (on 17 March 1917) 'We captured two little German machines for bomb-throwing, which are being despatched to Oxford' (Greenwell 1972: 163). The following year, Colonel A.C. Borton was delighted to include the following news in his diary, regarding guns captured in Palestine by 2/22nd London Regiment, commanded by his son: 'He says his captured Turkish guns are to come home as a present to BERMONDSEY!' (Slater 1973: 154).

Interestingly, both of these references date from a period when the regional associations of British Army regiments were becoming increasingly diluted by a policy of sending new drafts of men from areas outside their traditional recruiting area. Officers, however, where they served with their own regiment, generally attempted to sustain the original regimental identity. They did so not only out of sentiment, but also as a way of enhancing the morale of their soldiers. A fine example of regimental tradition expressed in the form of a trophy is recorded by Rowland Fielding, in a letter to his wife in July 1916:

> I saw a big 'minenwerfer' [German trench mortar] very cunningly concealed in a deep excavation. A piece of paper was attached to it, with the following words: 'Captured by the Minden boys'; i.e. the Suffolk Regiment, a battalion of which attacked at that point.
>
> (Fielding 1929: 88)

Not only was the Suffolk Regiment claiming merit for the capture of the mortar in question, but its officers did so by a reference to the Regiment's most famous action – at the Battle of Minden, in 1759.

Such marking of trophies extended even down to individual companies. After a successful action in April 1917, Graham Greenwell wrote that 'Our captured [machine] guns are fine trophies, and I have already had them stamped "Captured by 'B' Company 1/4 Oxford and Bucks Lt. Infty." They will go to Oxford at the end of the war.' (Greenwell 1972: 175). Infantry formations were not the only type of unit to wish to obtain trophies expressive of their achievements. As late as the spring of 1919, the Wing Commander of 65th Wing RAF wrote to the Officer Commanding 204 Squadron: 'I have applied for one German ARCHIE [i.e. anti-aircraft] GUN, from the 6th French Army, as a remembrance of the work done by your Squadron when working with them' (NA AIR 1/1084/204/5/1714 Letter 31/3/19 from DAE to GOC RAF France.)

On occasion, major items of captured equipment could bear the marks of more than one unit. The series of inscriptions and motifs added to the German A7V tank captured at Villers Brettoneux by 26th Battalion, Australian Imperial Force, is a case in point. They ranged from the badge and name of the battalion and the name of the salvage unit that recovered it, to individual names of men who handled the tank in the rear areas (Whitmore 1989: 52–3). One such trophy, a huge German railway gun captured at the Battle of Amiens (8 August 1918), became a source of some controversy. The Australian 31st Battalion effected its capture, but, in the wake of the continued Allied advance, the gun received a large painted inscription stating that the gun had been captured by the British 4th Army (of which the ANZAC Corps was a component). A thorough investigation was made of the circumstances of the gun's capture – an insightful example of the contested nature of war material involving notions of identity and ownership – before it was finally transported to Australia for public display (AWM Archive).

Captured weapons were employed by all the combatant powers to symbolize the success of their troops in the field, generally being displayed in their capital cities. In London, a large number of German guns were placed in The Mall (IWM Photos Q31243–Q31251) (Figure 1:1). Such trophies also acted as an aid to raising money from the public. The Imperial War Museum sent out items from its collections to various British cities during 'War Weapons Week' in the summer of 1918. Its secretary Charles Ffoulkes, quoted in *The Times*, stated that the collections could still be drawn upon for local exhibitions having as a 'sole object the raising of funds for war charities, or other purposes directly conducive to the successful prosecution of the war. The public response to the direct appeal of actual and tangible souvenirs of the war has been very marked' (*The Times*, 6 June 1918). The same article referred to the success of a British tank used for money raising, but went on to suggest that

> A captured gun, grimed with the mud of France or Flanders, a heavy *minenwerfer* that perhaps a month ago was shelling a British first line trench, a machine-gun that may have 'held-up' half a battalion till its team were bayoneted by the vanguard of our advancing infantry, make an even more effectual appeal.
>
> (ibid.)

Smaller trophies were also used to raise money. The Imperial War Museum's collections feature a captured Austrian bayonet, bearing a Serbian inscription, which was sold in aid of the work of the Red Cross in alleviating the suffering of the latter

Figure 1:1 A public display of captured German guns in The Mall, London. (© and courtesy of the Trustees of the Imperial War Museum, IWM Q 31244)

country (IWM WEA 159). The Red Cross also benefited from the sale of pieces of German airships that had been shot down. Again, the Imperial War Museum has several examples (IWM EPH 4653).

After the war, many trophies were issued to individuals and communities who had shown particular endeavour in fundraising or war-work. The Imperial War Museum possesses five German rifles that bear plaques on their butts noting that they were presented to private individuals in recognition of their work raising money for war charities (IWM FIR 7104–5, FIR 7344, FIR 7348, FIR 7868). In Canada, German heavy guns were offered as prizes during a Victory Loan drive in 1919 (Vance 1995: 49).

Recruitment was another area in which trophies were held to be efficacious. In the late summer of 1918, with British manpower resources coming under intense strain, the Irish Recruiting Council requested trophies suitable for displaying in 'about ten shops in different parts of Ireland'. They asked for 'a truckload of selected trophies, not too bulky in size, such as rifles, bomb throwers, flame throwers, helmets, damaged machine guns etc.' (NA NATS 1/258. Letter 26/8/18 P Lloyd-Greame). Interestingly, a subsequent attempt to get this consignment increased failed, due to the fact that 'no more could be spared & so much of what they had being claimed by units & consequently could not be sent out of the country' (NA NATS 1/258 Memo 5/9/18 Maj. Garnett).

Even before the end of the war, the Army Council had set up a board to oversee the distribution of officially sanctioned trophies. A letter to the Treasury in January 1919 gave an assurance that there was an already functioning

> Departmental Committee to deal with all the questions relating thereto, and to watch the interests of the Imperial War Museum in consultation with the museum committee. The normal procedure is for guns and other trophies sent to this country from France and other theatres of war, to be claimed as having been captured by certain units. If the claims of these units are substantiated the commanding officers are given the opportunity of determining whether the trophies should be presented to the Regimental Depot, the Imperial War Museum, or some City, Borough, etc.
>
> (NA T1/12438)

The trophies were free gifts, but towns and cities had to defray the cost of transport. The Treasury did, however, agree to fund the transportation of trophy guns to Colonial countries (NA T1/12438).

Therefore, in addition to adorning Regimental Headquarters and augmenting the collections of the Imperial War Museum (see Cornish 2004), trophies were publicly displayed by municipal authorities, at town halls, in parks and as adjuncts to war memorials. Such foci of civic pride appear to have been particularly popular in the Dominions. In Australia, 'State Trophy Committees' were set up to supervise the distribution of captured weapons, a number of which have survived to this day (CDVA 2000). Others were pressed into service under the threat of Japanese invasion in 1942. Indeed, there were enough German machine-guns to make it worthwhile to have them rechambered for .303 inch ammunition (Skennerton 1989: 54–7), an ironic transformation of weapons reconfigured as trophies of the First World War back into working weapons during the Second. In Canada, according to Jonathan Vance:

> Hundreds of Canadian communities clamoured for a trophy to place in their park or schoolyard, but not out of a recognition that technology had played the most important part in the war. German field guns and mortars were craved for precisely the opposite reason, because they proved that Canada's citizen-soldiers had overcome the enemy's engines of war. For Victor Odlum, who commanded the 11th Infantry Brigade for the last two years of the war, the captured guns served as 'physical and tangible reminders of the courage, fortitude and skill of Canada's sons'. The public display of German trench mortars, howitzers and field guns was intended to remind townspeople, not that such machines had taken over the war, but that they were no match for Canada's citizen-soldiers.
>
> (Vance 1997: 147)

Canada eventually received many thousands of trophies, including 900 artillery pieces and 4,000 machine-guns (Vance 1995: 50). In both Canada and Australia it is evident that civic and institutional pride dictated that all concerned were intent on acquiring the largest and most impressive trophy possible (Vance 1995: 51; CDVA 2000).

Personal trophies

A study of battlefield trophies taken by individuals reveals an altogether more complex set of relationships between man and material than those governed by official regulations. Here one has to accept that the very definition of what constitutes a 'trophy' becomes blurred. Although excluded from this study, it is clear that enemy shell nose-caps or fuses were widely appreciated as a worthy form of battlefield souvenir. Likewise, items taken from the dead bodies of the enemy were accepted as a valid form of trophy – even if the men acquiring them had taken no direct part in the killing process. These traits are exemplified by George Coppard, a machine-gunner, who recalled that he initially collected, and then 'jettisoned', a heterogeneous collection of souvenirs:

> German fuse tops, funny-shaped bits of shrapnel and a rusty saw-edge bayonet were among this collection of old iron. Why I had been torturing myself with this agonising load I don't know – just a boyish habit of collecting something out of the ordinary I suppose.
>
> (Coppard 1969: 62)

Later he graduated to more portable and valuable items:

> Collecting military badges from the dead was indulged in by many Tommies. I wore a broad leather belt that was covered with them, and I regret that I parted with it for five francs. Today, such a belt might fetch a tidy sum in a London sale room.
>
> (Coppard 1969: 89)

These items are now often referred to as 'Hate Belts' (Kimball 2004: 46, 55 plate 3.15).

Above all, it is clear that, certainly among enlisted men, the desire to acquire trophies was endemic. Indeed, some officers evidently perceived it as a threat to discipline. In April 1917, the Commanding Officer of the 15th Durham Light Infantry included the following warning in his operational orders:

> Many instances have accrued of men searching for souvenirs instead of instantly consolidating their position and in consequences being unready to meet the enemy's counter-attack. It is therefore to be distinctly understood that any officer, NCO or man in possession of any such souvenir, will be tried by court-martial.
>
> (Thompson 2005: 11)

References to such 'souvenirs' and the circumstances of their acquisition appear frequently in contemporary diaries and letters. In most cases little explanation is offered, suggesting that such activities were taken for granted as a normal part of soldiering on both sides of the wire. Private Bertie Sporton (7th Royal Scots Fusiliers) noted during an action on the Somme: 'The Argyles take a trench and now everybody is souvenir hunting. Some very good helmets have been found' (Sporton, 21 August 1916) (Figure 1:2). An officer, Cecil Sommers, credits a narrow escape from a party of Germans in mist-shrouded no-man's-land to the fact that: 'They had not seen me, but were apparently intent on a search for souvenirs while they had the chance' (Sommers 1917: 170). Dr Dunn, who served with the Royal Welch Fusiliers even characterizes a dead man by reference to his souvenir hunting habits: 'Napper was found dead, bayoneted in several places; he was a great souvenir hunter' (Dunn 1987: 527). Only Charles Carrington, writing some years after the event, goes so far as to analyse the sociological basis of such behaviour:

> To be a soldier on active service means to reject the sanctity of life and property. Your end in battle is to compel your enemy to submit and if you succeed his body and his possessions are at your disposal . . . The captors may

Figure 1:2 Men of 10th Battalion Nottinghamshire and Derbyshire Regiment pose with trophies captured on the Somme. German pistols, bayonets and fighting knives can be seen, although most prominent are the much sought-after spiked helmets. (© and courtesy of the Trustees of the Imperial War Museum, IWM Q 130)

live on enemy rations, make free with their comforts, and seize badges, crests, helmets as trophies.

(Carrington 1965: 183)

Men serving behind the front lines were not presented with the same kind of opportunity to take trophies. This circumstance in no way lessened their appetite for such items, however; indeed some accounts suggest that their scarcity increased their attraction. David Doe, a signaller, recorded the aftermath of an aircraft crash:

It was a terrible heap of rubbish. It had caught fire and the petrol exploded. One airman was mangled almost and the other only just alive. I managed to get a piece of the wing with part of an iron cross in black paint on the canvas and a piece of wood. Some chaps got some of the MG cartridges, one had a belt of it. 1 got the compass. 2 shared the bloodstained goggles. 1 found the dead German's watch. 1 of our operators got a stay and plenty got strips and pieces of canvas. Some were stained with blood. *No doubt about it being the finest sight in the war, so far that many of us had seen* {my italics}.

(Doe, 30 September 1915)

Leonard Horner, a Quaker serving with the Friend's Ambulance, wrote to his schoolboy cousin:

Had about 1/2 doz helmets on board last trip, but the fellows won't part with them, of course no German ever has one by the time they get to us – he wouldn't have it long! I can probably get you a forage cap all right if you want one.

(Horner, 16 July 1916)

Not surprisingly, trophies redolent of the battlefield were at an even greater premium when soldiers took them home. Robert Burns of the Cameron Highlanders recalled the eagerness of both the headmaster and children of his old primary school to acquire German helmets and other souvenirs from him (Burns 2000: 95, 139, 167). Frank Richards, a regular soldier, recorded, in typically laconic style, how he and his comrades used German helmets as latrine buckets (Richards 1964: 43) and the incredulous reaction to this by people whom he later met while on leave (ibid: 105).

The relative scarcity of trophies away from the front inevitably invested them with a monetary value. Front-line soldiers were guaranteed a ready market for any such items they might wish to sell. Frank Richards recalled losing heavily at cards on Armistice Day but: 'The following day I sold some German field-glasses and automatic pistols and tried my luck once more at Pontoon' (Richards 1964: 314). L.J. Ounsworth, a signaller with the Royal Garrison Artillery, recalled an incident on a train in Birmingham in 1916, while travelling to hospital with a friend:

he had a German helmet – I had one but not being able to get back to my Battery, I'd lost mine and everything you see. But he was showing his and they started to bid him for it, and eventually the bids got up to £4 10s, which was an awful lot of money in 1916 – and then the train suddenly begun to move, and we were off, and I remember several times after, when we were in hospital, Bill used to say (we were broke) 'I wish I'd sold that bloody helmet when I had a chance.'

(Ounsworth: IWM)

Enlisted men might also consider selling their trophies to officers. Graham Greenwell wrote to his mother regarding a helmet that he had been offered:

My Platoon made a successful sortie from the trenches at 4 o'clock yesterday morning behind a convenient mist to an old disused trench some ten yards away in front which they found pretty full of dead Germans; they collected considerable booty, including some smart picklehaubes, three or four German rifles, lots of ammunition and twelve pretty little silver drinking cups. So they didn't do badly. They gave me some ammunition and a rifle and revolver, and I could have bought one of the helmets for 10s., but wasn't sure whether you would appreciate it.

(Greenwell 1972: 25)

Sergeant J.P.O. Reid of the 6th Gordon Highlanders recalled refusing an offer of 200 Francs for two hard-won (see below) German helmets by an artillery officer (Reid: Reel 3). Conversely, Frederic Manning's account (fictionalized but firmly based on actual events) of the Somme battle has one of the characters righteously outraged at the loss of two sets of German binoculars to his commanding officer without compensation (Manning 1977: 37).

As can be seen from many of these accounts, German helmets – particularly the spiked *pickelhaube* were the most sought after of all trophies. Charles Carrington recalled that

No trophy was so highly valued as a pickelhaube, and proud I was when I captured one on the Somme; sorry, too, when I gave it to my girlfriend of the moment, who didn't seem to care for it. About that time the Germans were moving into steel helmets, the coal-scuttle kind that fitted down over your ears, and there were no more spiky-tops to be seen in the trenches.

(Carrington 1965: 154)

(See also Chapter 12, Figure 12:2, where both types of German helmet can be seen hanging from the webbing of men coming out of the line on the Somme.) *Pickelhauben* were, of course, highly decorative, with their shiny leather and elaborate badges (which served no protective purpose). Their attractiveness may also have been enhanced by their popular perception as the embodiment of 'Prussian' militarism, making them peculiarly representative of the enemy from whom they were captured. As the quotes from Ounsworth and Greenwell above make clear, they could command a good price.

The pre-eminence of *Pickelhauben* among potential trophies evidently encouraged men to take considerable risks to acquire them. Sergeant J.P.O. Reid of the 6th Gordon Highlanders recalled finding them in a captured dugout. They hampered his escape when the position was retaken by a German counter-attack, as he had to negotiate a narrow exit: 'I had to drop down again into the dugout and take off my pack and then put my head through and I pulled up the helmets after me. I said "Well I'm not going to lose them now."' (Reid: Reel 3).

The gathering of souvenirs in general was seldom undertaken without some element of risk. As Doctor Dunn pointed out, 'Most men in their early days were interested in souvenirs; some were easily satisfied, not a few lost their lives souvenir-hunting (Dunn 1987: 179). He tells the story of a German officer's corpse that was stripped of personal effects despite being in a position exposed to incessant fire (ibid.: 87).

George Coppard recalled, 'I was canny about touching anything in case of booby traps. Some choice souvenir could well tempt me to a sticky end' (Coppard 1969: 124). Often it did not require anything as subtle as a booby trap to endanger the lives of trophy seekers. V.E. Upton, serving on a Hospital ship at Gallipoli wrote:

> the Chief Steward had a big shell given to him and I was holding it for him while he tried to get the top off with a hammer and chisel after about 10 mins hammering we managed to get it to unscrew and then we got a shock for we found it was fully loaded, with high explosives there was enough to sink the ship.
>
> (Upton: 31 August 1915)

Rowland Fielding admitted to a similar moment of madness with a German grenade:

> It had been lying about so long that I did not think it could possibly have any sting left. However, I pulled the safety cord to make sure, and immediately there followed a hissing sound. I called to the two doctors to take cover and threw the bomb, which a second or two later went off with a loud explosion.
>
> (Fielding 1929: 367)

The National Archive preserves a Home Office file relating to munitions brought home as trophies from the Great War. Evidently they continued to present problems for many years after the cessation of hostilities (NA HO 45/18998 Dangerous War Trophies file.).

Graham Greenwell recorded one further risk involved in trophy taking, that of being found in possession of recognizable personal effects if captured:

> I was told by a friend this morning that two German officers were captured, one with the watch and the other with the revolver of my poor friend Fream.

I don't think either of them lived very long: feelings run a bit too high to make the unwounded prisoner's lot a happy one.

(Greenwell 1972: 119)

Several of the sources quoted above hint at another interesting aspect of the hunt for personal trophies, that officers tended to stand somewhat aloof from the activity. There were of course exceptions: Fielding sent home numerous small items to his wife, and Dr Dunn candidly reveals a trick played on him by a brother officer in 1914:

I dug myself a hole in a haystack where I kept quite dry. To me Williams remarked casually that he had seen a dead German grasping a lance on which was a pennon with the skull and cross-bones device. I dashed out to get this interesting souvenir, only to realize before I had gone ten yards that I had been sold, and Williams was sitting snugly in my hole.

(Dunn 1987: 61)

However, the general type of behaviour expected of officers is indicated by the fact that John Glubb could note that the sight of a Colonel laden with battlefield trophies 'caused some amusement' (Glubb 1978: 145).

Actual weapons seized from the enemy were evidently more acceptable as officer's trophies than other items. Graham Greenwell's men gave him the weapons they found (quoted above) and Carrington recalled a brother officer who habitually seized and used German rifles, while he himself 'long coveted and at last won a German officer's pistol' (Carrington 1965: 183). The Imperial War Museum possesses a rifle won by an officer in hand-to-hand combat on the Somme (IWM FIR 7100). The habit was not limited to British officers: Dunn records that 'A revolver was taken off one of their dead officers . . . it was a French weapon dated 1875' (Dunn 1987: 87).

One aspect of trophy gathering in which officers enjoyed a distinct advantage over their men was in their ability to retain them and get them home. They generally had billets or (while in the line) dugouts capacious enough to store their treasures. Furthermore, they could send packages home – often labelled as 'officer's surplus kit' (see Sommers 1917: 47). Dunn recalled seeing a brother officer in possession of 'a complete German light mortar he was taking home *sub rosa* for the Brigadier' (Dunn 1987: 580). Fielding managed to get his batman to carry home a German rifle for him (Fielding 1929: 99). It was certainly more difficult for enlisted men to manage such matters. The poet and composer Ivor Gurney, who served with the 2/5th Gloucestershire Regiment, was particularly aggrieved by this issue, and wrote to his friend Marion Scott :

O the souvenirs I might have had! But only officers have any real chance of souvenirs, since only they can get them off. The men find things, and people who live in dugouts will hang them up and brag of great deeds in that old time. But the men, who could not carry very well, and had no place to store things and hardly a leave, will be empty handed. You see, if one finds something interesting, it may be in a hot corner, and how is one to carry it, for the haversack is full. Suppose one gets it out of the line, then one must wait for leave, or a friend's leave. And if a wound comes all your stuff is lost. A man found a quartermaster's stores at Omiecourt, near Chartres, with hundreds of brand new helmets, but all that could be done was a little traffic with officers. I had two books and some papers for you, all lost at Vermand. Men hang on to revolvers and badges, watches and compasses etc., all that can be easily carried.

(Thornton 1983: 210)

Possibly Gurney was over-influenced by his own lack of success in trophying, as Sgt Reid of the Gordon Highlanders recalled his success in sending home the two German helmets which he had risked so much to obtain (see above), wrapped in straw in a sandbag (Reid: Reel 3). However, the difficulty of achieving such a thing undoubtedly encouraged those capturing trophies to sell them as soon as possible, rather than risk losing them entirely.

There would appear to be no evidence for the taking of ghoulish souvenirs such as human body parts, although such practices were attributed to Indian and African troops (see Gore 25, IWN; Bellow IWM), but it was certainly deemed acceptable to take more conventional trophies from enemy corpses. George Coppard admitted that 'Goulish [sic] curiosity drove me to turn over Jerry corpses for souvenirs, and I got a couple of watches and a Luger pistol' (Coppard 1969: 89). Opinions varied with regard to the validity of taking watches. Carrington expressed disdain at this activity, claiming that it was not the sort of thing done by front-line soldiers (Carrington 1965: 183), but it seems to have been widespread. Writing in 1917, Fielding recorded that 'A large number of the men of the battalion are now the proud possessors of wrist watches – trophies of war' (Fielding 1929: 193). A battalion of Royal Welch Fusiliers, upon being reprimanded when a prisoner complained that his watch had been taken, reputedly sent two dozen of them to Brigade Headquarters for him to choose from (Holmes 2004: 546). Frank Richards (of the same regiment) was amused when a comrade responded to the presentation of a wristwatch, while on leave, with the words: 'Well, Mr Chairman and gentlemen, I thank you very much for this magnificent present, but I can honestly assure you that I have pinched dozens of better watches than this from the dead Jerries laying out between the lines' (Richards 1964: 140).

A hint of a troubled conscience is perhaps noticeable in an interview given by former Royal Fusilier Donald Price. He recalled taking the watch of a 16-year-old German whom he discovered cowering in a shell hole in 1918: 'He was a nice little chap and I just took it and, you know, it was the normal thing – they'd take ours so we used to rob them you see – rob their helmet, take their helmets, knives.' He goes on to say,

and inside the watch was this photograph of his girlfriend. And I often thought I made a mistake in not sending the photograph back to Germany, you know, as soon as the war had finished, y'see, to see if he was still alive and see what happened to his family or something.

(IWM SA 10168)

The watch, complete with photograph, now resides in the collections of the Imperial War Museum (IWM EPH 4500) (Figure 1:3).

It is evident, however, that, despite his concerns about the watch, Price was convinced of his right, as a soldier, to take trophies from captured enemies. Other sources make clear however that, in the eyes of many, this right had to be earned. Private 'Tanky' Taylor, of the Worcestershire Regiment, witnessed a comrade, yet to go into the Line, being put in his place by an NCO:

Rogers had spotted the German's Iron Cross ribbon in his tunic buttonhole, and thought he'd like it as a souvenir, but as he stretched his hand to grab it, the sergeant knocked it down and said 'What the hell do you think you're doing?'

(Taylor 1978: 76)

Figure 1:3
German pocket watch, incorporating a picture of its former owner and his girlfriend. Taken by Fusilier Donald Price in 1918; now in the collections of the Imperial War Museum. (© and courtesy of the Trustees of the Imperial War Museum, EPH 4500)

Robert Burns recalled his diffidence when making his first attempt to take a trophy:

> Somehow I managed to convey to one of the German Officers that I would like his button-like cap badge as a souvenir, but in view of his surprisingly polite retort 'please wait until the war is over', I saw no reason for persuasion, as there were sure to be others.
>
> (Burns 2000: 113)

Ivor Gurney, whose own haul of trophies was limited to a 'noisome fragment of a German NCOs note-book' (Thornton 1983: 196), had strong views on such matters:

> There is too much sniping for the fighters to get souvenirs, the salvage and burial parties get them . . . People unfitted for the line, lunatics, funks, bosseyed idiots and such like, from whom an officer with 50 francs may make himself rich with booty – and reputation, the ASC do well, for they have room to store. R.T. [Rail Transport] officers with Real Homes. Brass Hats can get what they would. Only the poor fool who goes over the top – and under the bottom – seems to be without anything at all.
>
> (Thornton 1983: 210)

The final word on eligibility to take trophies should perhaps be given to Rowland Fielding, a tireless recorder of the material aspects of life at the front. His words to his wife, after taking an American Medical Officer around the old Loos battlefield, make abundantly clear the position that trophies occupied in the psyche of the front-line soldier:

> I began to feel sorry that I had undertaken to bear-lead the American sightseer. He is a good enough fellow, but was too entirely absorbed in the collection of souvenirs. I remember one of my officers – Barron, during the battle at Croisilles – telling a private whom he found relieving a German prisoner in a dug-out of his watch – if he wanted souvenirs – to go out and get them in the firing line. How much less right has a mere sightseer to souvenirs? It is horrifying to see this sacred ground desecrated in this way, and still more to think of what will happen when the cheap tripper is let loose. With his spit he will saturate the ground that has been soaked with the blood of our soldiers.
>
> (Fielding 1929: 367)

Souvenirs are unusual objects, whose value emerges from the circumstances of their acquisition rather than simply their shape or substance (see Belk 2001). War souvenirs in particular resonate with memories of life and death situations, suffering or glory. Trophies carry with them additional layers of complexity. Their acquisition during the First World War can be considered to have gained the proportions of a 'mania'.

Once acquired, whether public or private, they became symbols of victory and triumph.

In common with other elements of material culture, the 'social life' of Great War trophies has been a varied one. They were bought, sold and fought over by rival claimants while still 'hot property', but in later years many were neglected (e.g. Vance 1995: 53–5). By contrast, some were carefully preserved within families, in commemoration of a family member's war service. Others have survived in museum collections (see Cornish 2004) to provide a tangible link to the motivations and aspirations of the generation who fought in the war that, more than any other event, established the political and social contours of the modern world.

Acknowledgements

My thanks to Nick Saunders for inspiration and to Annemarie Bruseker, Bob Courtenay, Paul Gough, Alan Jeffreys, Chris McCarthy, Fergus Read and Tony Richards for material assistance.

References

Archives

UK National Archive

NA HO 45/18998 Dangerous War Trophies
NA NATS 1/258 Irish Recruiting Council Request for Captured War Trophies
NA T1/12438
NA AIR 1/1084/204/5/1714 Misc. Air Ministry correspondence on war trophies

Australian War Memorial Archive

AWM Archive Series 16, File 4386/1/48

Imperial War Museum Department of Documents

Bellow, Hugh, IWM Docs 91/23/1
Doe, David H., IWM Docs P326
Floyd, William M., IWM Docs 87/33/1
Gore, Harry, IWM Docs 01/36/1
Haines, O. C. M., IWM Docs 95/16/1
Horner, Leonard W., IWM Docs GB62
Sporton, Bertie V., IWM Docs 01/52/1
Upton, V. E., IWM Docs 81/35/1

Imperial War Museum Sound Archive

Ounsworth, L. J., IWM S/A 332
Price, Donald, IWM S/A 10168
Reid, J. P. O., IWM S/A 322

Published Sources

Anon (1919) *The Golden Horseshoe*. London: Cassel & Co Ltd.

Belk, R.W. (2001) *Collecting in a Consumer Society*. London: Routledge.

Blaser, B. (1926) *Kilts Across the Jordan*. London: Witherby.

Burns, R. (2000) *Once a Cameron Highlander*. Bognor Regis: Woodfield Publishing.

Carrington, C. (1965) *Soldier From the Wars Returning*. London: Hutchinson.

CDVA (2000) Commonwealth Department of Veterans' Affairs (Australia): http://www.dva. gov.au/media/publicat/memories/page_04.htm

Coppard, G. (1969) *With a Machine Gun to Cambrai*. London: HMSO.

Cornish, P. (2004) '"Sacred relics": objects in the Imperial War Museum'. In N.J. Saunders (ed.), *Matters of Conflict: Material Culture, Memory and the First World War*, pp. 35–50. Abingdon: Routledge.

Dunn, J.C. (1987) *The War the Infantry Knew*. London: Janes.

Fielding, R. (1929) *War Letters to a Wife*. London: The Medici Society Ltd.

Glubb, J. (1978) *Into Battle*. London: Book Club Associates.

Greenwell, G.H. (1972) *An Infant in Arms*. London: Allen Lane.

Holmes, R. (2004) *Tommy*. London: HarperCollins.

Kimball, J.A. (2004) *Trench Art: An Illustrated History*. Davis, CA: Silverpenny Press.

Manning, F. (1977) *The Middle Parts of Fortune*. London: Peter Davies.

Richards, F. (1964) *Old Soldiers Never Die*. London: Faber.

Saunders, N.J. (2003) *Trench Art: Materialities and Memories of War*. Oxford: Berg.

—— (ed.) (2004) *Matters of Conflict: Material Culture, Memory and the First World War*. Abingdon: Routledge.

Skennerton, I. (1989) *Australian Service Machineguns*. Margate, Queensland: Skennerton.

Slater, G. (ed.) (1973) *My Warrior Sons*. London: Military Book Society.

Sommers, C. (1917) *Temporary Heroes*. London: John Lane the Bodley Head.

Taylor, F.A.J. (1978) *The Bottom of the Barrel*. London: Regency Press.

Thompson, D (2005) 'The Great War record of the 15th Service Battalion Durham Light Infantry'. *Stand To! Journal of the Western Front Association*, 72: 11.

Thornton, R.K.R (ed.) (1983) *Ivor Gurney War Letters*. Ashington: Mid Northumberland Arts Group.

Vance, J.F. (1997) *Death So Noble*. Vancouver: University of British Columbia Press.

—— (1995) 'Tangible demonstrations of a great victory: war trophies in Canada'. *Material History Review*, 42: 47–56.

Whitmore, M. (1989) *Mephisto A7V Sturmpanzerwagen 506*. Brisbane: Queensland Museum.

2

SHAPING MATTER, MEMORIES AND MENTALITIES

The German steel helmet from artefact to afterlife

Fabio Gygi

The First World War triggered a series of technological innovations in the field of weaponry that changed the face of battle dramatically. The use of poison gas and the deadly effectiveness of modern artillery-fire[1] created demand for better protection for soldiers and eventually resulted in development of gas masks and steel helmets. Introduced in France in 1915, and in Germany and England in 1916, the steel helmet became one of the most widely distributed, mass-produced artefacts during and after the war. Far reaching, beyond its original purpose of protection and national distinction, the German steel helmet developed into a modern icon that embodied heavily contested war experiences and carried them through the interwar years. The paramilitary *Freikorps* appropriated the helmet as early as 1918, and it subsequently became a part of the Nazi regalia together with the swastika and the black SS uniforms. After 1945, the iconic shape of the German helmet resurfaced as a symbol of evil and destruction, and up to today authentic German steel helmets are much-desired objects for collectors and 'living history' re-enactors.

The literature on the steel helmet – though vast and detailed to the point of obsession – can be broadly divided into two categories. One encompasses the historical–iconographic narratives where the steel helmet is seen as a symbol of the dramatic changes in the perception of the war in the political arena of the Weimar Republic (Hüppauf 1990; Hillringhaus forthcoming). The other genre is concerned with materiality rather than history, and is mainly aimed at collectors, who, among other things, are interested in whether pigskin or cow-skin straps were originally employed, so as to determine the authenticity of their items (Baer 1985; Tubbs and Clawson 2000). Both historians and collectors abruptly end their quest in 1945, when both the symbolic saliency and the range of 'authentic Second World War helmets' is assumed to have ended.

But how is one to understand the lingering power of the steel helmet, its persistence and its disappearance, and its resurfacing in different contexts? If it is taken to be a symbol, then its materiality is reduced to a mere arbitrary signifier leaving open the question of continuity, and failing to account for its lasting fascination. Alternatively, if it is understood as an artefact, its material endurance is accounted for, but its contextual shifts of meaning and its power to act upon the world are neglected. I would suggest that what is often laconically described as the 'affective component' of the symbol is, in the case of the steel helmet, its very agency, its concrete ability to induce fear in others by evoking the circumstances of its conception – the violence and mass deaths of industrialized war. These circumstances gave the iconic steel helmet an intensely powerful 'energy charge' which it retained independent of its status as a material artefact, and thus reached an even wider audience in its 'disembodied' form.

It is my contention that the steel helmet is best seen as an artefact–icon system whose effectiveness lay in the sheer number of similar artefacts and their wide distribution and circulation. As a modern mass-produced object, it left its imprint on popular consciousness as well as on the cultural memory of the two world wars, a memory which persisted even after most of the helmets had been destroyed. In the artefact of the helmet, we are not dealing with a single piece of material culture, but with a totality of tokens of one type, which form the remnants of a system of power-through-fear.

To account for this methodologically, I will focus on the emergence, destruction and afterlife of this system. Rather than choosing a clearly defined historical setting, and then declaring the steel helmet to be a 'symbol' of it, I will take the opposite approach and follow the steel helmet on its trajectory through history and society. In so doing, the classical boundaries of disciplines are easily crossed, and what emerges is a genealogy of objects that is neither archaeology, nor history, nor anthropology, although it depends heavily on the sources of these disciplines.

The remnants of the distribution of the steel helmet, both in its embodied (as artefact) and symbolic form (as icon), constitute a rhizome (Deleuze and Guattari 1977). The rhizome is a network of decentred underground connections that can emerge irregularly to form overground plateaux. The power that is mediated through the steel helmet cannot merely be erased by destruction; it can be redirected, appropriated or suppressed, while its effects keep on appearing as the plateaux of subterranean growth. The appearance and disappearance of an artefact are traces of social agency we cannot reconstruct directly, but only by means of the study and analysis of material culture.

Forged in the crucible of war

Following the establishment of trench warfare conditions on the Western Front, the medical authorities in France, Britain and Germany reported that the main cause of death was infectious wound rather than direct fire. The shrapnel shells fired by field guns, and the fragments and splinters created by the explosion of high-explosive munitions, created little projectiles that easily penetrated the traditional leather and brass headgear and caused severe brain damage. It was as a defence against these unpredictable fragments and splinters that the steel helmet was commissioned and designed – metal thick enough to withstand direct small arms fire would have made it impossibly heavy. Emphasis was laid on a functional yet beautiful design, which distinguished it from the steel helmets of other nations.

The French *Casque Adrian*, named after its designer, August-Louis Adrian, was the first to be officially introduced, and resembled the fire helmet of the *Sapeurs-Pompiers* (fire fighters) (Kraus 1984: 31). The British version, the Brodie helmet – also named after its designer, John L. Brodie, but known to the troops as 'tin hat' – resembled a medieval *chapeau de fer* (Dean 1920: 128–31). The streamlined German model M16, with the characteristic low-neck protection and ventilation bolts, was perceived to be in accordance with a German tradition of military aesthetics. Professor Friedrich Schwerd, the designer, had to find a compromise between a heavy version which would give some protection against direct fire, but would be too heavy to wear for marching, as desired by General von Scheuch, the Prussian War Minister (Baer 1985: 17), and a version light enough for general wear, that would only protect against shell fragments.

The ability to protect was the subject of a prolonged debate between military advisers, military doctors and technicians. One of the main concerns was whether a light helmet would not wreak more havoc than it would prevent by enlarging the target area and by aggravating the injury through metal scraps of the helmet, as well as by making the soldiers overconfident if they were allowed to think they were sufficiently protected (see expert opinion issued by the medical section within the war ministry dated 23 November 1915, quoted in Baer 1985: 21–2).

Schwerd eventually convinced the authorities of the benefits of his design, and the first 30,000 of the resulting M16 steel helmets were issued to assault units at Verdun in January 1916. They were pressed out of steel 8 mm plates in six sizes, 50–62 cm in diameter, and consisted of a steel dome, a leather strap and a liner system that separated the dome and the scalp by two fingers' width. To prevent it from being an easy target for snipers, it was painted a dull grey. The reactions of the soldiers were generally favourable, in spite of complaints about the weight, and demand rocketed until the end of the war, by which time approximately 7.5 million helmets were in circulation (Baer 1985: 66).

Interestingly, the helmet only began to be perceived as an icon of modernity during the interwar years, when the myth of the new, cold, armoured man associated with Verdun started to supplant the myth of the heroic, light-hearted youth formed in the battle of Langemarck, in the cultural memory of the war (Hüppauf 1990). Popular soldier myth linked the helmet to the gothic *Schaller* (Sallet) helmet of the 15th century, and thus to chivalry and its ideals of sacrifice and heroism (Kraus 1984: 83), although Schwerd, who had never seen one of the alleged medieval predecessors, had designed the helmet strictly according to 'pure, simple purposefulness of form' (quoted in Baer 1985: 73). The myth of the 'revival' of medieval headgear created historical continuity, and alleviated the newness of the rules of engagement in a war of attrition fought mainly by and through machines.

The existential conditions in the 'storms of steel' that were First World War battles made the allocation of sense and meaning essential to understand the new nature of the war. Through its function as an instrument of protection in this life-threatening context, the helmet also became an instrument to think with (Lévi-Strauss 1966: 21). The master metaphor of steel with its connotations of protection, resistance, resilience, endurance and armour made sense of a world in which classical martial values such as bravery and heroism amounted to little. As a bodily extension, the steel helmet became a tool with which to rethink the soldier's body in the language of steel. As metal is shaped and hardened to resist shrapnel and bullets, this 'homeopathy' of steel was extended to the body and the mind of the soldier. To endure the onslaught of steel, the soldier himself had to become steel-like, an iron vessel of indomitable willpower with 'nerves of steel', a mentally armoured individual against the atrocities of war – as 'cool as steel' throughout confrontation (Jünger 1934).

The shaping of the helmet through the war, its necessity in a battlefield dominated by artillery, and the fact that it was literally pressed from steel and hand-hammered into the final shape, was a salient metaphor for the process of formation which the soldier underwent in the crucible of modern war. The power of the steel helmet did not reside in the artefact, but in the transformation it could cause in the one wearing it, mediated through the materiality of steel. It was not a mere symbol, but the main agent of the 'metallization of the discursive space of imagination' which the historian Aribert Reimann describes as one of the main features of Weimar Republic semantics (Reimann 2000: 49).

As a life-saving device, the steel helmet paradoxically evoked the danger and violence of the battlefield against which it was conceived. Its association with death was strengthened by its physical and symbolic ability to substitute for the head of a soldier. Indeed, many makeshift soldiers' graves were adorned with simple wooden crosses and a steel helmet on top to mark them as German for later disinterment and reburial. Furthermore, the ability to represent the head of the foe also made the helmet a desired trophy (see Chapter 1).

Although in the first years following its introduction the helmet was rarely seen by civilians because of its short supply, it soon became the main recognizable attribute of the German soldier through its distribution as a popular icon in illustrated newspapers, magazines, post cards and posters (Hillringhaus forthcoming: 108). Recruitment and war-loan campaigns thrived on the imagery of 'the German soldier' who, armoured in mind and body, and singled-out from the chaotic masses, could withstand the onslaught of the enemy forces (Figure 2:1).

Aesthetics of protection: the case of the Swiss steel helmet

The complex overlap of archaic and modern elements, of practical and psychological protection, of national identification and power embodied in the steel helmet is not easily disentangled. One way to see these psychic and symbolic factors at work is to investigate the steel helmet's introduction in neutral countries that were spared by war. We can draw on source material from the Swiss military department, now found at the Swiss Federal Archive in Berne, to illustrate some of these aspects.

The Swiss federation, albeit neutral, faced general mobilization on 3 August 1914, when three divisions were dispatched to guard the borders in case the combat

Figure 2:1
German war loans poster by Fritz Erler. The face of the soldier is dominated by the steel helmet and the shadow of the helmet merges with the person depicted in this archetypal example of steel man iconography.

engagement spilled over onto Swiss territory. The introduction of steel helmets by the French and the Germans pressured the Swiss military department to devise their own model. Surprisingly, they commissioned a patriotic sculptor, Charles L'Eplattenier, to develop a suitable helmet (Figure 2:2). Since, in 1916, Swiss involvement in actual combat was considered highly unlikely – though not impossible – the modelling of a suitable helmet became a matter of taste and psychology rather than of actual protection. It seems that L'Eplattenier drew upon romantic paintings of historic Swiss battles and French sources in his design. In a report dated 6 September 1916, divisional commander Brügger informed the military department:

> Of course the helmet obviously does not protect against everything, especially not against direct rifle shots. But if the other armies have the steel helmet and with it some protection of the head, we must offer the same protection to our soldiers, if only not to let them feel inferior. This is an imponderable in the field of psychology which must be appreciated as well.
> (BAR E 27 19206, my translation)

Thus, a possible feeling of inferiority is identified as one of the main dangers of not having the steel helmet. But just imitating an existing helmet seemed insufficient: 'The different armies have different types, none of them is beautiful,' wrote Brügger. In opposition to this, the model 'L'Eplattenier' was introduced as 'the best, the nicest and the most agreeable in form and aspect . . . practical and tasteful, a good solution' (ibid.).

The man responsible for the model L'Eplattenier, divisional commander Tretoyens de Loys, could not resist its fashionable pull and posed with it in a photo shoot (as Göring did later, in 1923) for the *Schweizer Illustrierte* of 15 September 1917. This premature presentation was not favoured by the military department. Although the helmet was described as 'beautiful, original and historically Swiss' (Brügger, 11 October 1917), it was found impossible to press out of steel, and a simpler form was devised. This course of action led to two lawsuits, one from L'Eplattenier, who complained in a letter to the army headquarters that his helmet, which resembled 'those of our ancestors', was renounced for a model 'mimicking the German steel helmet' (Pellaton 1984: 48). The Swiss federation eventually paid him 30,000 Swiss francs as compensation. The second was a copyright lawsuit by the *Torfwerke* in Bremen in 1930, who claimed the patent they had bought from Schwerd was illegitimately copied by the Swiss. The federal court dismissed this in a rather hair-splitting manner, whereupon the Germans proceeded to sue for violation of cultural

Figure 2:2
One of the first sketches for the Swiss steel helmet by Charles L'Eplattenier. Note the distinct shape and the adorned Swiss cross. (© and courtesy Swiss Federal Archive)

properties. Subsequently, the Swiss government paid a fine of 5,000 Marks (Pellaton 1984: 49). This last example beautifully elucidates the extent to which the steel helmet was thought of as a cultural as well as a martial asset.

The preoccupation with a distinct Swiss helmet reflected not only the struggle to keep up with the modernization of warfare and war material, but also a concern with Swiss identity. While the neighbouring countries forged their national identity out of the collective experience of war, Switzerland had only the doctrine of neutrality to draw upon. This inferiority complex, while saving thousands of lives, was arguably alleviated by imitation. The Swiss army was mobilized, a steel helmet was designed, the borders were guarded, food was rationed and trade was restricted. For the Swiss, surrounded by warfare, it was *as if* they were actually *in* a war. This mentality is reflected in the war memorials of the First World War that imitated the commemorative gestures of the combatant nations. The First World War memorial in Solothurn embodies this idea most prominently: it consists of a mounted statue of a naked figure wearing only a steel helmet with a cross and holding a dagger (Figure 2:3). The inscription simply reads 'To the protectors of the homeland 1914–1918'. The names of approximately 2000 fallen soldiers are inscribed into two square stone plaques laying flat on the ground. The fact that two-thirds of these men died from an influenza virus, and the other third from accidents, is conveniently omitted (Kreis 1994: 130).

Figure 2:3 The Swiss First World War Memorial in Solothurn. The steel helmet strongly resembles the German version except for the cross. Ironically, the real Swiss helmet did not bear the cross originally envisioned by L'Eplattenier. (© author)

The Swiss army didn't see action until the war was over. Ironically, the real deployment of troops was not directed against an enemy threatening to attack the nation, but against an enemy from within, taking the form of revolutionary forces that called for a general strike on the day of the armistice in 1918. In this context, the new helmet gained a new symbolic saliency in unexpected ways. The socialist revolutionaries would appear in uniforms to demonstrate their membership of the Swiss army as proper Swiss citizens, directed against the attempts to demonize them as unpatriotic elements or subversives. This was seen by the army as camouflage, and harbouring the possibility of misleading other troops that were dispatched to keep them in check. In a secret document dated 30 December 1918, the commander of the 4th division, Sonderegger, asked the army headquarters to immediately issue steel helmets to the military police in Zürich. His argument was as follows:

Who will be recognized as belonging to the military police? Only those who wear the helmet . . . if the military police don't look uniform, there is insecurity. [on Kepi and armbands:] those can be obtained or imitated from similar textiles by the revolutionary groups, a danger that doesn't exist for the steel helmet.

(BAR E 27 19206)

The troops ended up wearing the steel helmet when encountering the revolutionary masses to present a unified front. But, contrary to Ernst Jünger, who rejoiced at the sight of a three-man machine gun team that dispersed revolutionary masses on the Bülow-Platz in Berlin 'as if by magic' with the threat of opening fire (Jünger 1934:174), the helmet regained its paradoxical ability to protect, not only the wearer, but also the potential attacker:

The fact that the helmet guards the head from the throwing of stones popular at insurrections should not be underestimated. I . . . would also like to direct your attention to the fact that soldiers who have stones thrown at them will be prone to open fire, when better protected comrades remain calm and resort to other means.

(BAR E 27 19206)

Representation and resistance: the interwar years

The end of a war and the cultural demobilization of a society hardly ever occur at the same time. The essential abolishing of the 'culture of war', consisting of alleviating propaganda-induced hatred and reinstalling the enemy as a human being, could only be achieved if the meaning of the sacrifice of millions of men and women could somehow be settled (Horne 2002: 49). As the only purpose in war is victory, and Imperial Germany had lost the war, to give meaning to the war experience in a nationally unifying way proved extremely difficult. The reactions ranged from simple denial to a projection of the meaning of sacrifice into the future, as an obligation that would be redeemed by coming generations. This temporality of sacrifice could thus be exploited by both pacifism and revanchism.

Coming to terms with a traumatic loss of men, purpose and identity, the political discourse of the Weimar Republic relied heavily on symbolic politics rather than on political discourse (Korff 1986: 88). The steel helmet became one of the most effective and compelling of symbols, precisely because it was not arbitrarily, but rather metonymically linked to the war, and formed an essential part of what Nicholas Saunders calls the 'memory bridge':

> The memory bridge is one way of conceptualising the effects of the materiality of the First World War on those who lived during the interwar years. Objects, ideas and attitudes linked the two world wars during a period of dramatic social, economic and cultural change, forming a bridge composed of materiality, emotion and memory
>
> (Saunders 2001: 477–8)

As a medium of memory, the steel helmet carried the war into Weimar society and became a means of propaganda for right-wing politics. First, large numbers of helmets were appropriated by the paramilitary *Freikorps*, whose violent suppression of left-wing revolution (as well as military action against the Poles and Bolsheviks) was such a prominent feature of the period 1918–19.

The Versailles treaty ordered the destruction of a large quantity of military material including helmets, but the German military decided to sell surplus helmets for 19.75 Marks apiece (Baer 1985: 92). These helmets were then used by the paramilitary wings of German political parties, notably those of the Right. Foremost among these was 'The Steel Helmet: League of Front Soldiers' (*Stahlhelm*), founded in December 1918 by Franz Seldte, and composed of war veterans with a conservative, nationalist outlook. The martial virtues that the *Stahlhelm* claimed for its members were represented by public displays of uniforms, steel helmets and the rigid military ritual of marching. This was intended as a deliberate contrast with the less regimented rival organizations sponsored by the parties of the Left.[2] By occupying public space and monopolizing the war experience of the soldiers, it legitimized its power to disrupt the feeble democratic system. The helmet induced fear and the impression of might, which could only be dispelled by wearing it oneself. The embodied function of protection was thus transposed into a logic of political persuasion. By 1930, the *Stahlhelm* had 500,000 members. After Hitler's accession to power in 1933, Seldte was made Minister of Labour and the *Stahlhelm* was subsumed into the Nazi SA.

The Weimar pacifists were very aware that the appropriation of the steel helmet would not only empower right-wing paramilitaries to represent authentic war sacrifice, but also lend them an air of legitimate power. They devised their own strategy of 'aesthetic detoxification' to attack the artefact–icon power system that was formed by the right-wing groups. At the level of the artefact, Ernst Friedrich's 1925 anti-war museum in Berlin exhibited steel helmets that were transformed into flowerpots by turning them on their heads (an image that would be taken up by the peace movement after the war). At the level of the icon, John Heartfield's photo-montages are exemplary of these attempts to recontextualize the steel helmet as a symbol of oppression and militarism, as when he used a cut-out of a steel helmet to eclipse the sun ('Sonnenfinsternis am "befreiten" Rhein' 1930; see Figure 2:4) or when he 'cooked' the German people in a steel helmet used as a pot ('Gefährliches Eintopfgericht' 1934).

Figure 2:4 'Solar Eclipse on the "freed" Rhine', 1930. John Heartfield produced this photomontage after the inter-allied Rhine commission pulled out its forces from the occupied Rhine land. This led to a convergence of the President of the Weimar Republic, Paul von Hindenburg, and Prime Minister of Prussia, Otto Braun, depicted in the corner. (© and courtesy Deutsches Historisches Museum)

The symbolic battle over the contested helmet shows that making sense of an object is not a simple act of assigning meaning by popular consent. The right-wing paramilitaries and the Weimar pacifists had to deal with an object that was already charged with 'energy'. This 'effect of presence before hermeneutics', as Gumbrecht calls it (2004), must be semantically domesticated and diverted into particular ideological needs. The 'aesthetic detoxification' ultimately failed, because the anti-war museum had only a few original helmets while the *Stalhelm* and their ilk had thousands. Furthermore, the association with violence and war was too strong to be ironically subverted.

In 1935, an updated version of the helmet was introduced, but very few changes were made to the original design. At the same time, German officers were issued a lighter helmet made from fibre-plastic that was also worn on parades (Baer 1985: 120). A desire for display led to a dichotomy between the 'manoeuvre helmet' made from steel and a 'parade helmet' that was no longer camouflaged, a development that culminated in the black-satin finish of the SS helmet. The parade helmet transformed the protective properties into aesthetic qualities that added to the elite image of the infamous SS.

Gender and modernity: the steel helmet and fashion

The First World War generation carried the war into the Weimar Republic, both *in* and *on* their heads. The message encoded in hats and helmets became one of the main means of political communication centred on the appropriation of war experience (Hillringshaus forthcoming). The impression the steel helmet left on the public was so deep that the memory of its shape in turn shaped the memory of the war as a conflict of steel, matériel and machine-like soldiers. I maintain that the shape of the masculine steel helmet essentially spilled over into female hat fashion in the interwar years. Conspicuously, the pre-war hat was ideally large and sweeping, while what came to be associated with the Charleston dance and the 'Roaring Twenties' is the tightly fitting, bell-shaped toque, a reinterpretation of the steel helmet in a different material, usually felt. This can be understood not only in terms of the heightened symbolism of hats in the Weimar Republic, but also in the context of the masculinization of female fashion and the emerging aesthetics of Art Deco.

During the war, millions of German women not only cared for children, worked in hospitals and kept house, they were also employed in war factories, engineering and public transport, all traditionally male domains. Their performance was an essential part of the war effort, and the government falsely assumed that most women would vacate their positions for returning soldiers once the war was over (Bessel 1993: 18–21). But, with the newly granted right to vote (1918), and the economic independence their work allowed them, few female employees wanted to go back to the domestic sphere. In 1925, 11–12 million women were employed in Germany, a percentage significantly higher than in any other European country (Guenther 2004: 62).

The economic and political liberation of women led to the emergence of new patterns of female consumption that created the image of the 'new woman' as predominantly single, employed and independent. This idealized vision eclipsed the fact that many young women were actually widows who had to care for children, and whose jobs were monotonous and unrewarding, but who were nevertheless inspired by their new freedom to spend money on clothes and amusements, such as dancing and outdoor sports. Indeed, despite the economic turmoil after the war, the German fashion industry was very quick to recover, largely due to this new, expanding class of consumers, the ready-to-wear collections of the department stores, and the dissemination of knowledge through fashion magazines (ibid.: 56).

But the fashion that was created was perceived as 'masculinized' and did not find the approval of the critics of modern life. The gender confusion created through the ambiguous forms and cuts that hid female shapes was not only seen as a means of empowerment, but also as a consequence of war. In fact the 'women surplus', as it was commonly called, was precisely the opposite: a euphemism for the huge loss of men, which created a gender imbalance that left many women widowed or single. Military idioms were used to describe modern female attire as 'camouflage', hiding female forms, or even as a weapon to win a husband in a world where eligible men were rare (quoted in Guenther 2004: 62).

The appropriation of the helmet as the symbol of dominant masculinity remains ambiguous. It could be interpreted as the uptake of a popular form in order to exploit its aesthetic properties, namely the streamlined shape so desired by art deco, and the attempt to strip the iconic streamline of the helmet from its war context by reinstalling it as a design of functional and modern beauty.

Alternatively, the design of the fashionable hat did not perhaps refer to the steel helmet at all, but to the same forces that shaped it, namely aerodynamics and the wish for protection, both of which might have been an issue while riding open cars or bicycles. However, while the sight of German officers wearing steel helmets at official functions became commonplace in spite of its awkwardness (Hüppauf 1996: 87–8), claiming a war experience that had shaped them, the stylish toque might equally be understood as an appropriation of a hegemonic symbol to claim women's own war experience.

Disappearance and resurfacing: the post-war years

When Theodor W. Adorno returned to his native Germany in 1949, he wrote a series of essays on education after Auschwitz. He was very aware of the virulent nature of Nazism when he spoke of ghosts:

> The Third Reich lives on, and up to the present we do not know whether only as a spectre of what was so monstrous that it didn't perish with its own death, or whether it did not die at all; whether the willingness to do the unspeakable lives on in humans and the conditions that embrace them.
>
> (Adorno 1997 [1966]: 63)

The material culture of the Third Reich was subjected to a similarly ghostly existence. A large part of it was confiscated by the Allied Forces and destroyed in the process of denazification. A small contingent of helmets was reused by the police forces under allied control with the stencil 'Polizei' in big letters on the front. Material culture can also effectively reveal contradictions in the make-up of the 'reborn' nations: the second republic of Austria, for example, imported American helmets after the war for military manoeuvres, but retained the German helmet shape for marching and parades until at least 1957 (Mötz 1999: 97). A few steel helmets were appropriated as colanders, as manure ladles or as chamber pots. Although these objects were presented as the result of the creativity of necessity at a post-war exhibition in Berlin, a subversive element resonates with the interwar collages of the Weimar pacifists.

But the power of the artefact–icon system persisted, and resurfaced in a seemingly completely different context. Some of the notorious 'Hells Angels' motorbike gang members wore original Second World War German steel helmets, complete with Nazi decals, when they acted as bouncers at the infamous concert by the Rolling Stones at Altamont in California in 1969. A series of incidents involving the gang, including the murder of a member of the audience, aroused the media's attention. This event subsequently made the steel helmet a much-reproduced attribute of the Hells Angels.

Upon closer scrutiny, there are indeed some striking resemblances between the *Freikorps* of the Weimar Republic and the Hells Angels: both were/are hierarchical organizations with paramilitary traits, both maintained they were law-abiding while conducting underground criminal activities, and both resulted from war experience. As popular lore has it, the Hells Angels were founded in 1948 by returning American soldiers who could not assimilate to civilized society, and kept an adventurous lifestyle dominated by violence.[3] The name is said to derive from a B-17 bomber of the 303rd Bombardment Group, which in turn was named after the 1927 fictional film *Hell's Angels* by Howard Hughes, which featured a fighter-plane squadron of the First World War.

The Hells Angels used the aura of violence and fear embodied in the helmet, as a wartime trophy, to reinforce their own violent reputation. Significantly, in a move that resembled the use of the black-satin finished helmet by the SS, they often polished the helmet until the shiny steel surface was revealed under the camouflage paint. Its function was no longer to protect the inside from the outside, but to radiate its meaning from the inside to the outside, overpowering any resistance in advance.

Another ghostly appearance in this context was the very short glimpse of a steel helmet the audience was given in the 1975 cult film *The Rocky Horror Picture Show*. Eddie, a former lover of Frank N. Furter, and subsequently murdered by him, re-emerges accidentally from deep freeze as a revenant on a motorbike wearing a steel helmet, the visual equivalent of Adorno's idea of something that does not die at his own death, and stubbornly returns to haunt the present. The 'terrible' appears in surreal costume, and thus terror is transformed into harmless fright as Eddie performs the song 'Hot Patootie', and is then killed a second time with an ice pick. Frank N. Furter laconically refers to him as: 'One from the vaults'. But even after the second death Eddie returns in the form of the cannibalistic meal Frank N. Furter forces upon his guests.

While the steel helmet is used as a power object that is transformed into an ironic quote in *The Rocky Horror Picture Show*, the iconic shape of the helmet returns to the screen in George Lucas's monumental 1977 *Star Wars* saga. As one of the most impressive villains in cinematic history, Darth Vader, half man, half machine, wears a black full-body suit and an exaggerated black helmet-shaped headgear covering his entire face. Although the film espouses all the necessary criteria of science fiction, it is actually set in the distant past, as the opening credits reveal. The film music, composed by John Williams, is rich in Wagnerian allusions, especially the opening tune, which is clearly modelled on 'The Ride of the Valkyries', and the brooding 'Imperial March', theme tune of Darth Vader. Wagner is, in this context, used to signify Germanic monumentalism for which the Nazis admired him.

Other resemblances to the political life of the Weimar Republic become obvious if one looks beyond the sci-fi decor to the crux of the story, which features a Jedi knight seduced by the dark side of 'the force' and, almost slain in battle, returns as a cyborg to wage war against a dwindling democracy. The metaphor of the cyborg as a prosthetic being reflects the idea of the 'new man' expounded by Jünger in the interwar period as an entity in which man and machine are unified to form a powerful agent of the collective will. The helmet becomes a vital part of Darth Vader's body, one that cannot be dissociated from it without threatening his life, which again alludes to the protective element of the helmet. In the figure of Darth Vader, the phobic energy contained in the steel helmet is conjured up to signify an absolute evil that nonetheless has seductive and persuasive powers.[4] The political history of the Weimar Republic is thus transposed into the scheme of an epic battle between the good and the dark sides of the same force, while the iconography of the Third Reich is successfully employed to give the sci-fi fantasy a tangible element of threat.

A curious postscript to this is the helmet issued to members of the Iraqi paramilitary *Fedayeen Saddam* (Saddam's 'men of sacrifice'). This organization, founded in 1994, and prominent in the Iraq war of 2003, was equipped with a black moulded-resin helmet whose exaggerated neck protection and the arched 'eyebrows' mark it as the heir to both the Nazi parade helmet and Darth Vader's face mask (Figure 2:5). The plastic from which it was made offered little or no ballistic protection, and one can only presume that it was chiefly intended to confer an air of menace upon its black-uniformed wearers.

Value and authenticity: the present

Ninety years after its first prototypes were drafted, the steel helmet is still far from being a neutral object in any conceivable way. Most of the effects of its presence are still beyond the control of institutions such as military museums which attempt to domesticate and transform it into a historical artefact. A large number of German helmets continue to circulate as coveted objects in the well-informed circles of militaria collectors, many of them in the United States of America.

A survey of the London Military Market at the Angel Arcade[5] confirmed the 'energy charge' thesis in two ways: first, I found that the German helmet is a much more desired object for collecting than the American, French or British helmet, and fetched

Figure 2:5 Helmet of the Fedayeen Saddam ('Saddam's Men of Sacrifice'). It is made out of ordinary plastic and serves no other purpose than to top off their black uniform in a menacing fashion. The main task of this counter-insurgency brigade was to spread terror and fear among the civilians. (© and courtesy Paul Cornish)

significantly higher prices (for the 10 German helmets on offer prices started at around £600); second, the prices of the German helmets mirror not only their scarcity but also their symbolic charge – a First World War helmet in good condition, for example, although older and harder to find, fetches a lower price on the market than a Second World War helmet in similar shape. The peak of the value of a helmet therefore corresponds to the peak of its symbolic charge; helmets with Nazi insignia such as swastikas and Third Reich decals top the price range. The transformation of the ability to evoke fear into a symbolic charge, and its subsequent conversion into capital can be interpreted as different levels of the domestication of a powerful artefact into a collector's item.

The question of authenticity is crucial to determine the actual value of a given steel helmet, and is discussed by collectors with a plethora of expert knowledge on rivets, liner leather, and dome stamps. Adding swastikas or SS decals to original helmets is one of the more common forms of forgery that is seen as an ever-present danger, as prices of authentic helmets rise. Another ongoing debate among collectors is the question of restoration. To what extent can one repair a steel helmet and still maintain its authenticity? There are several workshops in the United States that specialize in the restoration of original helmets not only for collectors, but also for living history re-enactment, the second large market for authentic steel helmets.

Re-enactment societies are widespread in the United States and the United Kingdom, and span all historical periods, but tend to concentrate on mock warfare as a means of education and recreation. Among the First and Second World War re-enactment groups, German troops are popular, especially the notorious Waffen-SS, and some go as far as to devise German names and fantasy biographies for their members, like the 'Grenadier Regiment 980' in the north-eastern USA.[6] Meticulous attention to the details of the material culture of war, from uniform decals to heavy tanks, is vital to this enterprise whose authenticity lies not in time and space, but entirely in the original artefacts used to create the illusion of participation in an actual historical combat. Thus, re-enactment works only through the special position of the artefact in mediating time and space, through the actual factual nature of things as opposed to the narrative and memory of history. Or, as Jules David Prown put it in the aptly named essay 'The Truth of Material Culture', 'Artefacts constitute the only class of historical events that occurred in the past but survive in the present' (Prown 1993: 3). We may be cut off from accessing the landscape of history, but the artefact is not. It is precisely its ability to be coeval with other times, to create effects of presence at different points in time that allow the sort of time travel the re-enactors envision.

Taking into account the ongoing fascination with authentic war material such as the steel helmet, as well as its lasting effects, there can be no definite conclusion to its history. As long as we are dealing with something that appears and disappears, that retains its virulent energy, we are practising 'hauntology' rather than history, as Derrida has succinctly called it (Derrida 1994: 4). Hauntology draws our attention to the seamless nature of history, to the fact that it has no beginning and no ending, and to the idea that nothing that comes into existence just disappears. One of the most potent traces of war experience in the twentieth century is the steel helmet. As a symbol of war it evokes the ghosts of memory and the memory of ghosts, as if the dead really do persist, even in an artefact of steel.

Postscript

The post-war fate of the German steel helmet in a military context is suffused with irony. Before reunification, West Germany adopted the American helmet shape, while the armed forces of the Communist DDR were equipped with a helmet originally designed in wartime Germany, as an updated version of the M35, a design apparently vetoed by Hitler specifically because of the symbolic resonance of the existing helmet (Baer 1985: 383–402).

Later, in 1982, the American military adopted a shape reminiscent of the German steel helmet. It is still part of the Personal Armor System for Ground Troops (PASGT), and is made of Kevlar fibres. Its nickname is 'Fritz helmet', after Frederick the Great of Prussia, or 'Old Fritz', a term widely popularized during the First World War to refer to German soldiers in general. There being no end to History's sense of irony, the Iraq War of 2003 saw the desert-camouflaged Fritz helmet encounter its monstrous *other* – the black helmet of the *Fedayeen Saddam*.

Acknowledgements

I would like to thank Paul Cornish, Diana Espirito Santo, Claudia Schlager, Nicholas Saunders and the Swiss Federal Archive, all of whom have made this article possible.

Notes

1   The latter being the war's major cause of casualties. See Terraine 1980.
2   Who were in fact also characterized to a certain extent by their headgear: namely the *Blucher* cap of the Social Democratic *Reichsbanner – Schwartz – Rot – Gold*, the *Leninmütze* of the Communist 'Red Front Fighters'.
3   Objective information on the Hells Angels is hard to come by. I derive my short account from the official HAMC homepage and the 1967 book *Hells Angels* by counterculture journalist Hunter S. Thompson.
4   In a June 2005 interview with the magazine *Rolling Stone*, George Lucas stated that the helmet of Darth Vader was supposed to look like a Japanese Samurai helmet, because he was fascinated with all things Japanese at the time. Early sketches by the designer Ralph McQuarrie do indeed bear some resemblances to a Samurai helmet, notably the drawn-out nose protection and the rotund shape. (These sketches and the original helmet are on display at the Science Fiction Museum, Seattle, USA.) However, the designer clearly deviated from these first drafts as a Samurai helmet would not have suited the modernist decors of the film. The final version is much closer to the German steel helmet in its design, befitting the image of the military cyborg (Gavin 2005).
5   I conducted fieldwork at the London Military Market in January 2005 and interviewed three sellers and collectors.
6   See http://www.geocities.com/Pentagon/Bunker/3879/ (accessed 29 April 2009) for samples.

References

Archives

Swiss Federal Archive, Berne: BAR E 27 19206

Published sources

Adorno, T.W. [1966] (1997) 'Erziehung nach Auschwitz'. In R. Tiedemann (ed.), *Theodor W. Adorno 'Ob sich nach Auschwitz noch Leben lasse'*, pp. 48–63. Frankfurt: Suhrkamp Verlag.
Baer, L. (1985) *The History of the German Steel Helmet 1916–1945*. San Jose, CA: James Bender Publishing.
Bessel, R. (1993) *Germany after the First World War*. Oxford: Clarendon Press.
Dean, B. (1920) *Helmets and Body Armour in Modern Warfare*. New Haven, CT: Yale University Press.
Deleuze, G. and F. Guattari (1977) *Rhizom*. Berlin: Merve.
Derrida, J. (1994) *Spectres of Marx: The State of the Debt, the Work of Mourning and the New International*. London and New York: Routledge.
Gavin, E. (2005) 'The Cult of Darth Vader'. *Rolling Stone* 975 (2 June): 42–8.
Guenther, I. (2004) *Nazi Chic? Fashioning Women in the Third Reich*. Oxford and New York: Berg Publishers.

Gumbrecht, H. U. (2004) *Diesseits der Hermeneutik: über die Produktion von Präsenz*. Frankfurt: Suhrkamp Verlag.

Hillringhaus, A. (forthcoming) 'Stahlhelm, Blücher, Leninmütze: Politische Uniformen als Medien gesellschaftlicher Sinnstiftung in der Zwischenkriegszeit'. In G. Korff (ed.), *Kriegsfolklore*, pp. 97–124. Tübingen: TVV.

Horne, J. (2002) 'Introduction'. In S. Audoin-Rouzeau, A. Becker, J. Becker, G. Krumeich, C. Prochasson and J. Winter (eds), *Démobilisations culturelles après la Grande Guerre*, pp. 45–53. Péronne: Editions Noêsis.

Hüppauf, B. (1990) 'The birth of fascist man from the spirit of the front: from Langemarck to Verdun'. In J. Milfull (ed.), *The Attractions of Fascism: Social Psychology and Aesthetic of the Triumph of the Right*, pp. 45–76. Oxford: Berg Publishers.

—— (1996) 'Schlachtenmythen und die Konstruktion des "Neuen Menschen"'. In G. Hirschfeld and G. Krumeich (eds), *'Keiner fühlt sich mehr als Mensch . . .' Erlebnis und Wirkung des Ersten Weltkriegs*, pp. 53–103. Frankfurt: Fischer.

Jünger, E. (1934) 'über den Schmerz'. In E. Jünger (ed.), *Werke Band 5: Essays*, pp. 149–198. Stuttgart: Ernst Klett.

Korff, G. (1986) 'Rote Fahne und geballte Faust: Zur Symbolik der Arbeiterbewegung in der Weimarer Republik'. In P. Assion (ed.), *Transformationen der Arbeiterkultur*, pp. 86–109. Marburg: Jonas.

Kraus, J. (1984) *Stahlhelme vom Ersten Weltkrieg bis zur Gegenwart: Friedrich Schwerd, dem Konstrukteur des Stahlhelms zum Gedächtnis*. Ingolstadt: Veröffentlichungen des Bayrischen Armeemuseums.

Kreis, G. (1994) 'Gefallenendenkmäler in kriegsverschontem Land: Zum politischen Totenkult in der Schweiz'. In R. Koselleck and M. Jeismann (eds), *Der politische Totenkult: Kriegsdenkmäler in der Moderne*, pp. 129–39. München: Wilhelm Fink Verlag.

Lévi-Strauss, C. (1966): *The Savage Mind*. London: Weidenfeld and Nicolson.

Mötz, J. (1999) 'Vom Stahlhelm zum Kampfhelm'. *Truppendienst: Zeitschrift für Führung und Ausbildung im österreichischen Bundesheer* 239 (2): 96–9.

Pellaton, F. (1984) 'Suisse'. In J. Dagnas (ed.), *Les casques de combat du monde entier de 1915 à nos jours*, Tome 1, pp. 43–59. Paris, Limoges: Charles-Lavauzelle.

Prown, J. D. (1993) 'The truth of material culture'. In S. Lubar and W. D. Kingery (eds), *History from Things: Essays in Material Culture*, pp. 1–19. Washington and London: Smithsonian Institution Press.

Reimann, A. (2000) *Der Grosse Krieg der Sprachen: Untersuchungen zur historischen Semantik in Deutschland und England zur Zeit des Ersten Weltkriegs*. Essen: Klartext Verlag.

Saunders, N. J. (2001) 'Apprehending memory: material culture and war, 1919–39'. In P. Liddle, J. Bourne and I. Whitehead (eds), *The Great World War, 1914–45: 2. The Peoples' Experience*, pp. 476–88. London: HarperCollins.

Terraine, J. (1980) *The Smoke and the Fire*. London: Book Club Associates.

Thompson, H.J. (1967) *Hell's Angels*. Harmondsworth: Penguin.

Tubbs, F. R. and R. W. Clawson (2000) *A History of the German Steel Helmet*. Kent: Kent State University Press.

3

THE GREAT WAR
'TRENCH CLUB'

Typology, use and cultural meaning

Daniel Phillips

The 'trench club' is a hand held weapon resembling a medieval mace that was used for close-quarter fighting during the Great War. Despite its widespread use (particularly by British soldiers in 'trench raids'), its ironically primitive design in a war of industrialized technology, and its anachronistic but brutal effectiveness, little attention has been paid to this object, either as a weapon of choice, or as a distinctive expression of the material culture of war. In this chapter, I will develop a preliminary typology of these weapons – an initial classification that will document the variety in size, shape and materials used, and enable an exploration of the relationships between function and meaning for the soldiers who used them. The sample is 63 trench clubs that were selected from six London museums.[1]

Trench clubs appear in a variety of forms, though an initial division can be made into two general types – those that have been manufactured industrially (and perhaps mass-produced), and those that have been improvised on the battlefield, using whatever material was available, and are thus hand-made individual items (see Madoc and IFFM 1998: 15).

The Great War has been investigated for over 85 years from a variety of perspectives, with military history, cultural history and art history having produced the largest amount of scholarship. Archaeology and anthropology have only recently begun to engage with the many overlapping subjects and themes represented by the world's first global industrialized conflict, despite the iconic status of the war in cultural memory. Uniting these two closely related disciplines has been their mutual interest in the material culture of the Great War (N. Saunders 2002, 2004). Although trench clubs represent only a small element of the material culture of conflict, their study – long overdue – highlights many important interdisciplinary issues that are of central importance to these new ways of looking at the First World War.

The trench club was chosen for study for two main reasons: first, despite the large number and variety of extant examples, little systematic attention had hitherto been given to them, and so there was an opportunity to bring some kind of classificatory order to an amorphous mass of objects; second, although the Great War is commonly acknowledged as a war of industrialized technology, the trench club is essentially a medieval weapon, and so, in a sense, an anachronism. Where the common view of the First World War is one of senseless rushes across no-man's-land in the teeth of withering machine-gun fire, the trench club was a devastatingly personal weapon, which required face-to-face confrontations. The trench club therefore stands out as an age-old, single-combat weapon in a war of industrialized mass killing.

Trench clubs have hitherto received little scholarly attention, and historical references – while illuminating – are rare and fleeting. One example, from the early days of trench warfare, appears in a letter dated 11 August 1916 describing a night raid on enemy lines by Canadian soldiers. 'Patrols roamed no-man's-land by night where the bowie knife was the favourite German weapon. The cosh, a weighted stick was often used by the British' (Rutledge 1918: 22).

During the Great War, trench clubs were often referred to as knobkerries or coshes, a fact that adds to the difficulties of research because of the lack both of an agreed term and a definition. While there are numerous references to trench raiding and fighting in such books as *The War The Infantry Knew* (Dunn 1994), specific mention of trench clubs is much rarer (see below) (Figure 3:1).

Figure 3:1 A soldier of 1/8th King's Liverpool Regiment (bottom left), after returning from a trench raid on 18 April 1916. (© and courtesy of the Trustees of the Imperial War Museum, Q510)

It is appropriate to begin with a review of the different kinds of trench clubs that have survived and are available for study, and to gain some appreciation of function and context of use which might also shed light on their cultural meanings. This process aims to build an initial typology – a meaningful classification within which different kinds of trench club can be located and subsequently analysed.

The typology

This typology has been developed from a sample of 63 trench clubs, most of which are in the collections of the Imperial War Museum, London. To date, nine types have been identified, reflecting a wide range of styles, shapes and sizes. While the majority of types are of British or German origin, trench clubs were used by other nations. As with all typologies, the aim is not to force-fit all examples into a rigid classification, but rather to lay a meaningful framework over the material and thereby make some sense of diversity, suggest connections and guide the identification of trench clubs from museum collections and archaeological excavations.

Type 1: improvised clubs

(1A) Improvised clubs appear in many forms, and each is unique, made as individual 'one off' weapons. It is therefore difficult to provide meaningful statistical data, as size, weight and raw materials vary greatly. However, there are some shared characteristics. Generally, they have a home-made quality, are often irregularly shaped and the level of workmanship is poor when compared with other types. As the name implies, improvised clubs are usually adapted from existing materials, with the handles made of wood coming from a variety of sources. Because of their ad hoc nature, it is difficult to identify whether they are of British, French or German origin, although both sides used such objects.

(1B) This type is essentially the same as 1A, but shows evidence of more sophisticated craftsmanship in its production. Examples have separate heads which are made entirely of metal and which appear in a wide variety of styles. Some parts may be commercially made. Again, there is no obvious identification of national origin with this type.

Type 2: Goedendag clubs

This type represents the largest proportion of the sample, with 22 out of the 63 examples. All appear to be of German origin. The term Goedendag (roughly translated as 'good day') is adopted because this type is similar to the Goedendag medieval mace used by the Flemish at the Battle of Courtrai in 1302 (otherwise known as the Battle of the Golden Spurs).

The battle itself is significant in Belgian history because the defeat of the French on the morning of 11 July 1302 resulted in Flemish independence from France and continuation of the use of Dutch (Sutter 2002: 1). The Goedendag club may well have been chosen in order to combat the mounted French knight. The weapon was used in conjunction with the spear, so that, when the Flemish foot soldiers lined up for battle, each man alternately had either a spear or a Goedendag. Once the spear had disabled the horse, the Goedendag was employed on the armoured knight. The use of these weapons in this manner proved sufficient to hold the Flemish line and break up the French charge. The Goedendag proved to be a major factor in the defeat of the French, and has become one of the defining kinds of material culture associated with the battle.

(2A) This type has two diagnostic features: a smooth handle and a moulded head which slots over its end. The handle, which is made with a lathe, also has a flat pommel base. The head has a mace-like form, with six evenly spaced rounded notches around its outside. There is also a large rounded spike on top of the head. The head is slotted on top of the handle and fastened with a single screw.

(2B) This is generally of a similar design to Type 2A. The handle does not have a pommel base, but instead has a 'wine bottle' appearance. The head is also similar to Type 2A, but without the notches along the outside. The head has a conical shape, widening at the top.

Type 3: nail clubs

(3A/B) This type represents a manufactured wooden club, with handles reminiscent of a 'rounders' bat, a grooved grip and a lead-weighted head from which protrude an assortment of metal objects. Although the two examples discussed here have metal rivets and hobnails as protrusions, other clubs outside the sample had nails, studs and wire inserted into them (Figure 3:2). Sub-divisions A and B are based on the kinds of

Figure 3:2 Trench club whose head has metal studs and a protruding metal spike, from the site of Boesinghe, Ypres, Belgium. (© and courtesy Aurel Sercu)

material protruding from the head: 3A has metal rivets; 3B, hobnails. Where evidence of origin was found, this type of club was stated to be German.

Type 4: spring clubs

The spring club is technologically advanced compared with most other types, both in design and manufacture. This German club can be divided into three distinct parts: handle, shaft and head. The wooden handle has a grooved grip, and a leather strap is fitted into a square groove at the base of the handle. The shaft is a tightly coiled metal spring, hollow and extremely flexible. Spring clubs appear with a variety of heads, of which two have been recorded in this typology. The first is a solid square iron block, the second has a so-called 'morning star' design – a small, oval iron ball with five points.

Type 5: metal wire clubs

While the metal wire club has similarities to the spring club, there are sufficient differences to categorize it separately. The club is made entirely of metal, and is extremely short and heavy. The handle is cast iron, the shaft made from a tight, thick coil of wire in a spiral form – flexible but not to the degree of Type 4. The head is a roughly cast iron ball, around which are nine small round studs arranged in a symmetrical pattern.

Type 6: Royal Engineers' clubs

Royal Engineers clubs are the first industrially manufactured British examples in the typology, and were the main kind of trench clubs used by British forces during the Great War. Manufactured in the Second Army workshops at Hazebrouck, France, the Royal Engineers produced at least two official clubs, the MKI and MKII, although only the MKI is represented here.

(MKI) The Royal Engineers MKI trench club employs a simple but effective design (Figure 3:3). The handle is the same as that used for the British entrenching tool; the head is a flanged-iron ring, which slots onto the handle, in the same way as the blade of the entrenching tool. The head contains 8 vertical flanges.

(MKII) The MKII is of a similar design to the MKI, but uses the casing from a Mills grenade for the head.

Figure 3:3 A schematic drawing of a Royal Engineers MKI Club. (© and courtesy of the Trustees of the Royal Engineers Museum)

Type 7: swagger stick clubs

Swagger sticks are long, thin canes with metal-banded tips (sometimes decorated) and are part of the military paraphernalia of an officer. With no obvious practical function, swagger sticks may simply reflect the military rank distinction between an officer and the ordinary soldier, though it carries obvious referents to social class as well. The British swagger stick clubs are swagger sticks that have been adapted to make trench clubs, either by individuals altering existing swagger sticks or perhaps as items manufactured for this dual function.

(7A) Handles are extremely long and thin, utilizing hollow bamboo or a thin tree sapling. The head appears in two general forms – either a continuation of the handle with a bulbous head filled with lead or 'cosh'-like, with a sewn leather pouch weighted with lead.

(7B) This is a modified swagger-stick type made into a more general trench club form. The handle is shorter and thicker than in 7A, although it is still usually made of hollow cane.

Type 8: metal collar clubs

This type is of unknown origin. The handle is thick and heavy, and, interestingly, is made of soft wood rather than the hardwood handles of most trench clubs. The head is a steel collar, which is slotted over the end of the handle and fastened with a rivet.

Type 9: 'trench spear'

Although this is a spear, not a club, it has been included in this typology because it represents a trench weapon that may have been used in a similar way to the trench clubs. It is a unique and interesting object, and as such deserves study in its own right. The handle is a carved tree branch, and the head is a steel spear that fixes into the end of the handle. It is over one metre in length. One example, currently in the Imperial War Museum, is said to have seen use in British hands at Delville Wood on the Somme (IWM WEA 2166).

This brief description of types can be further developed by identifying two overarching categories into which this range of trench clubs can be divided: non-stylistic and stylistic. This in turn will facilitate discussion and analysis of issues concerning why, how and in what contexts such objects were used.

Non-stylistic clubs

Non-stylistic clubs are those designed for a solely practical function. Certain features of a trench club are important in assessing its effectiveness as a weapon used in enclosed spaces. Length is a critical factor, as a club needs to be long enough to be swung, but short enough to be used in the narrow confines of a trench. Weight is also important, since if it were too light it would be ineffective, but if too heavy it would be impractical. The type of wood used for the handle is also an index of the club's effectiveness: soft or thin wood (e.g. bamboo) might break easily, unlike a harder wood. However, the handle needs to be thin enough to be gripped effectively. The head can also indicate a club's function. A head with large sharp spikes would appear an intimidating and dangerous weapon, but contemporary accounts suggest that such examples were not very effective as trench clubs, because they would 'get stuck' (A. Saunders 2000: 144, but see Richards [1933] 2001: 195). A more effective head shape would be rounded and blunt, delivering powerful glancing blows.

Many examples in the sample show evidence of the above characteristics, including Types 1–6. Type 1, in particular, displays practical features, since this category was improvised by individual soldiers in the battle area, using whatever materials were to hand. It is clear that these clubs were first and foremost practical weapons, with few if any significant stylistic features, and any symbolic aspects being of secondary importance. The attributes associated with these practical clubs are:

- average length: 40cm
- average width: 2–3cm
- average weight: 600–700g
- wood type: hard/tree branches

The function of these clubs was simply to kill and maim at close-quarters, in hand-to-hand fighting, though knocking an enemy unconscious in order to capture them and bring them back as prisoners for interrogation was probably also an aim. However, unless they were used to disable a soldier by hitting a limb, the weight of the clubs and their viciously shaped heads would more likely prove lethal.

Stylistic clubs

These clubs differ from the previous category in that they incorporate an element of style in their design and appearance. The term 'stylistic' refers to any club that bears decorative elements, produced either by an individual personalizing the item, or as part of an industrial manufacturing process. Many stylistic clubs do not possess the functional characteristics that make for an effective weapon. Regardless of whether they were intended as practical weapons, therefore, they take on a symbolic role, of authority, fear, empowerment and of identity. Types 7 and 9 in the typology give a clear indication of this symbolic role.

Context and use

Trench clubs represent but one kind of a large variety of trench weapons used during the First World War. Specifically, trench clubs were used in trench raiding, as was the case with Siegfried Sassoon, the soldier poet, who talked of picking up his 'nail-studded knobkerrie' ready for a raid (quoted in A. Saunders 2000: 144). Raiding was undertaken by both sides, and involved small groups of about thirty soldiers, who raided sections of enemy trenches usually at night in order to harass and confuse the enemy, and to gain intelligence. The trench club proved an effective weapon in this situation, and the memoirs of the soldiers who served in the 2nd Royal Welch Fusiliers suggest it was the tool of preference for such activities (A. Saunders 2000: 144) – not least because of its silence. Documented accounts of trench clubs being used in such circumstances are nevertheless rare.

One of these scarce documentary sources is the account by Sergeant Mothersole of an unsuccessful raid on enemy trenches at Beaumont-Hamel on the Somme during the summer of 1916 by the Second Battalion, Royal Suffolk Regiment. 'Meanwhile, we were preparing, and everybody was arming to the teeth. Amongst other weapons we carried knobkerries. Some took bayonets to use as a sword, and we were all ordered to blacken our faces' (Hammerton 1938: 716). Charles Carrington provides another, relating to a night-time trench raid at Gommecourt Wood also on the Somme:

> [I] pick up my trench stick, a longish cudgel with which I can feel my way in the dark but which I've decorated at the business end with a binding of barbed wire to make a more formidable weapon of it.
>
> (Carrington [1965] 2006: 94)

In his classic *Storm of Steel*, the German storm trooper Ernst Jünger relates being attacked by Indian troops at dawn, 'headed by an enormous figure with an outstretched revolver, and swinging a white club' (Jünger [1920] 2004: 149, 152).

As trench raiding was a form of guerrilla warfare, the element of surprise was paramount. The trench club is a silent weapon, and therefore preferable to a gun, which would inevitably attract attention. Another possible reason for the use of trench clubs may relate to medieval technology. Edged weapons, such as knives or bayonets would simply glance off a steel helmet, whereas trench clubs could break through the metal (A. Saunders 2000: 145), and, in any event, the force of the blow would be sufficient to stun the victim. The same requirement to defeat metallic armour was the motivating force behind the evolution of the medieval mace.

Finally, in order to fight effectively in the narrow confines of a First World War trench, a compact weapon was necessary, as Robert Graves recalled: 'Some of the officers were going to carry clubs with spikes on, which were very handy weapons at close quarters in a trench' (quoted in A. Saunders 2000: 144). In 1917, the veteran soldier Frank Richards made an almost identical observation when he encountered a new officer 'twirling a club with spikes on. He said, "These are very handy weapons in a trench." I replied that they were, at close quarters . . .' (Richards [1933] 2001: 195).

An opportunity to test the sparse historical record of trench club use against physical reality occurred in September 2003, when, as part of the 'Serre Archaeological Project' on the Somme, it was possible to study the size and space of original Great War trenches (see Chapter 18). The excavation of two sections of a German front-line trench at Serre included recording their dimensions. Despite the fact these two sections no longer stood to their original height, it was possible to assess their average width as 1.5 m. This might have been even narrower if their sides had been supported by sheet metal or timbers, as was sometimes the case. Close-quarter fighting in such a confined space would have been extremely difficult using the British infantryman's standard issue Lee Enfield rifle that had a total length (i.e. rifle and bayonet) of just over 1.5 m (156 cm) (Wilkinson 1978: 99, 103). That this difficulty affected all sides during the war is illustrated by the fact that German and French rifles were even longer. The trench club would clearly have been a compact weapon of choice in these circumstances.

Cultural meanings

Combining the typology with the available historical evidence, it is possible to make initial suggestions as to the cultural meanings of trench clubs for the soldiers who used them and, perhaps to a lesser extent, the motivations of museum curators in the display of such objects after the war. This, in turn, allows trench clubs to be situated within wider spheres of interest to archaeologists, anthropologists, and museum professionals, and provides new evidence to be incorporated into the interdisciplinary study of the Great War's material culture. Five distinct but inevitably overlapping themes can be identified: recycling, regression, trench art, the representation of trench clubs in British museums, and the British class system.

Recycling

Recycling is the process of transformation of one or more objects into a different form (Coote *et al.* 2000). Although most examples of this genre of objects that have been studied to date are concerned with the interaction between traditional societies and modernity, recycling was an important aspect also of the Great War, officially and unofficially. This is particularly noticeable in the corpus of objects known as trench art, much of which incorporated the recycled waste from industrialized conflict (N. Saunders 2000; 2003: 183–5). In fact, the Great War represents the first large-scale recycling of industrialized scrap during the twentieth century (N. Saunders 2000: 66) (Figure 3:4).

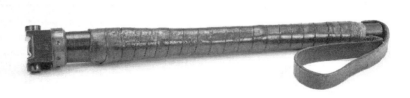

Figure 3:4 A photo of club no. 63. Leather-bound length of MGO8 barrel. (© and courtesy of the Trustees of the Imperial War Museum, WEA 2156)

The typology offered above reveals evidence of recycling in the manufacture of some trench clubs. Not surprisingly, the improvised clubs (Type 1) reveal the greatest level of recycling, since these would have been made using whatever material was available. There are many examples that reveal evidence for the reuse of objects that once performed a different function: two clubs in the typology are of particular interest in this respect. The first is club no. 59, which has been made from a pickaxe handle and studded with short spikes. Whether the head of the pickaxe has purposely been removed or not, this is an example of the recycling of a tool designed and used primarily for digging into a weapon used for killing and maiming. While many examples of trench art that incorporate recycled elements to produce 'something harmless from something designed to kill' (N. Saunders 2000: 66), club no. 59 represents the polar opposite.

However, the process of recycling does not necessarily imply that the end product must perform a different function to the original object. Club no. 61, a well-made trench club, has been crafted from the barrel of a German MG08 machine-gun. Both of these are killing weapons, but, and ironically, here the machine-gun, a modern automatic firearm, and one of the defining and iconic weapons of the Great War, has been transformed into a primitive concussive weapon reminiscent of medieval warfare. The element of recycling in trench club production brings their study within the wider anthropological investigation of recycled objects, or 'recyclia', and opens up a new kind of theoretical perspective for their analysis (Coote *et al.* 2000; Cerny and Seriff 1996).

Regression

The impression that trench clubs are virtual medieval maces is fairly accurate. There is clear medieval influence in the Goedendag clubs (Type 2) – 4 ft (1.2 m) long, tipped with an iron band and spike, and described as a 'weapon of medieval Flanders' (Connolly *et al.* 1998: 129). However, many of the characteristics seen in maces are common to all trench clubs. A comparison with three medieval maces from the Wallace Collection[2] identifies these shared features.

Mace A978 is of Gothic style, and incorporates a head containing six small flanges, each being angled so that they are wider at the base (Mann 1962: 458). Flanged heads containing between six and eight flanges were common in maces, and can be seen in the heads of the Royal Engineers' clubs (Type 6). Mace A983 includes a flat pommel base on the end of the handle (Mann 1962: 459), a feature observed in both Type 2A and Type 3. Mace A986 is described as being of the 'morning star' type, which has a spherical head containing 22 spikes (Mann 1962: 460). The spring club (Type 4B) has incorporated the morning star design for its head.

When medieval maces were introduced, they represented cutting-edge technology in combating plate armour, and continued in use until plate armour itself became obsolete (Foulkes 1945: 19). In a conflict dominated by the industrialized technologies of war, the introduction of the trench club appears as a regression to the medieval mace – a startling anachronism created by the needs of silence, portability and manoeuvrability in confined space. The very conditions of modern trench conflict that the Great War ushered in provided the impetus for this regression to a weapon of the pre-industrial age.

Trench art

A working definition of the term 'trench art' is 'any object made by soldiers, prisoners of war and civilians, from war material or any other material, as long as the object and the maker are associated in time and space with armed conflict or its consequences' (Saunders 2001: 20).

Trench art is a multi-vocal and multi-dimensional kind of material culture: examples can embody an individual's thoughts, feelings and experiences of war (ibid.: 23) and also serve as items for barter and commercial transactions – particularly in the sale of these objects as souvenirs and collectables both during and after the war (ibid.: 22). During the Great War, many objects (and fragments of objects) were converted into trench art. The most common and widespread type saw the recycling of metal – an abundant raw material – and these have survived mainly as decorated artillery-shell cases, usually with art nouveau-style flower decoration. However, other materials were also used including bone, textiles and wood (ibid.: 97).

By virtue of the diagnostic elements of recycling materials and decorating/ personalizing objects, some trench clubs can be considered as trench art – particularly those that are associated with (usually highly decorated) walking sticks (Figure 3:5).

Figure 3:5
A decoratively carved wooden walking stick topped with a carved head, as an item of walking stick trench art. (© and courtesy of Nicholas J. Saunders)

This particular style of trench art sees the transformation of plain and functional walking sticks – a common and fashionable item in early twentieth-century European society (ibid.: 19) – into highly decorative and elaborately carved items capped by carved heads of famous individuals (ibid.: 99). There is evidence of this walking stick style in two examples of trench clubs, though neither are included in the sample used in this typology. The first example is of French origin, and has a carved French soldier at the head of the club (Willmott 2003: 38). The second is a Zouave club, a hand-carved trench club with the head of a Zouave, a French colonial soldier in the North African infantry (Willmott 2003: 39). In these two documented examples, the trench club as a primitive and savage weapon has become beautified.

Representation of trench clubs in British museums

All of the trench clubs in this typology are from the collections of six London museums. Of the total of 63 clubs, 36 are German, 10 British, and 15 of unknown origin. There are more than three times as many German clubs as there are British examples – a fact that might simply reflect a bias in survival, the original collecting/ acquisitions policy of the museum concerned, or perhaps something more culturally interesting.

It is probable that British soldiers brought back German trench clubs as souvenirs of the war, and later donated them to the museums. Alternatively, it could be argued that the bias towards German clubs in some way conveys an overt message about the war. By their sinister appearance and clearly brutal nature, trench clubs are self-evidently weapons used to personally bludgeon people to death. The bias in favour of displaying German clubs could have been intended to indicate the types of 'barbaric' weapon used 'solely' by an equally barbaric enemy – the appositely termed Huns. This possibility opens up a potentially fascinating area for future research, one which explores the creation and manipulation of images of the enemy for propaganda purposes but which – unlike understandable activities during the war itself – seeks to perpetuate these attitudes and justify the conflict through the representation and display of such items during the post-war years.

British class system

The Great War embodied and represented the strengths and weaknesses of the British class system – particularly in the enhanced form in which it occurred in the military, where officers were usually gentleman of a higher social class than the regular soldier. One of the items which characterized an officer, but which served no particular function, was the swagger stick. This long and thin cane, tipped with a metal head, was used, as Colonel Blackie Cahill suggests, 'to keep hands out of pockets' (Cahill 2004: 6). Its other use was to administer on-the-spot punishment (ibid.: 6). However, as a weapon against a machine gun or bayonet it was useless. There is evidence, however, that these objects were adapted for trench fighting.

The swagger stick club (Type 7) shows an attempt to alter the swagger stick into a weapon, either intentionally in the manufacturing process, for a dual function, or by individual officers on the battlefield. By so doing, officers could have a weapon for trench fighting and still retain a symbol of class and authority. The principal addition was the weighted head, usually made of lead. However, the characteristics of a swagger stick are still retained, such as the long and thin cane-like handle, often made of hollow bamboo. Despite these modifications, their size and weight would still make them ineffective as trench fighting weapons. It could be argued that the swagger stick club took on a symbolic role instead, one of class and authority over the men in the raiding party, and above all a continuation of the image of the officer and gentleman, and the British class system.

This theme, which sees social class and military rank mediated by swagger sticks and their trench-club adaptations, once again opens up a new area for interdisciplinary research. It might fruitfully be combined with an investigation of why British officers went 'over the top' armed with a pistol as well as a swagger stick. If the swagger stick was a symbol of authority, the pistol had a very limited potential as a weapon compared with the rifles and machine-guns carried by the ordinary soldiers. Was the British class system perhaps working itself out in the superior bravery of the officer who fought the enemy with clearly inadequate weapons and who could clearly inflict less damage on his opponent than the ordinary soldier? Were both the swagger stick and pistol intended as symbolic weapons, and the dirty business of killing left to the rifle- and grenade-carrying rank and file soldier?

Conclusion

The preliminary typology attempted here aims to provide a basis for understanding trench clubs as a distinctively anachronistic (but nevertheless effective) kind of Great War material culture. Previously unstudied, such objects clearly allow for a number of cross-cutting interpretations concerning their origins, practical use and symbolic propensities. In other words, trench clubs can be brought within the interpretive theoretical framework of material culture studies rather than simply stand alone as fascinating but isolated objects of war.

Even a basic classification permits an assessment of cultural meaning, as it anchors typological variation to the social factors that produce differences in use and symbolism. This process can also identify future (and perhaps hitherto unsuspected) directions for more detailed problem-oriented research.

In some respects, the trench club has been the 'forgotten weapon' of a war usually defined by its iconic industrialized nature. That it was ambiguous even during the war is suggested by the comparative dearth of documentary, photographic and audio evidence, which in most cases give only fleeting mentions of this elusive weapon. The prospects for further research – archival, archaeological and collections based – are significant. The 63 examples of this sample represent but a small proportion of the total number observed during this research, but which were for various reasons not included here. These, in turn, are almost certainly but a fraction of the total number of Great War trench clubs that still survive in museums and private collections across the world. With a larger sample, a more detailed classification should be possible.

Equally significant is the opportunity for an international comparative study, in which trench clubs in German and Austrian museums are analysed to ascertain whether the British bias in favour of German trench clubs is confirmed or perhaps reversed. This in turn could throw light on the symbolic valuation of such objects as 'barbaric weapons' representative of a 'savage uncivilized' enemy, and perhaps also on their nature as battlefield souvenirs (see Chapter 1). It is possible that further investigation might reveal a correlation between trench clubs and specific regiments, perhaps even with particular individuals.

It is worth mentioning at this point that there is evidence that such objects were also used by the British during the Second World War, as make-do weapons by the Home Guard, and as batons by the military police. This represents an interesting migration of a vicious front-line weapon in 1914–18 to a domestic quasi-civilian context in 1939–45.

Trench clubs represent but a single category of the material culture of the First World War, but clearly deserve more specialist attention. The preliminary typology and study offered here is a first step towards a more comprehensive and contextually sensitized understanding of these unique objects.

Acknowledgements

The idea for this investigation arose from conversations with, and suggestions made by, Professors Peter Doyle and Lawrence Babits (East Carolina University). To them I would like to express my gratitude. I would like to acknowledge all of the museums that made this typology possible. I would particularly like to give my wholehearted thanks to Paul Cornish of the Imperial War Museum (IWM), the institution that provided the majority of the trench clubs analysed here. I am grateful also to the staff of the IWM's Weapons and Firearms Department, the Photographic Archive and the reading room. I am indebted to everyone within the 'No Man's Land' group for allowing me the opportunity to take part in the archaeological excavation at Serre. Particularly, I am grateful of the contributions given to me by Andrew Robertshaw (National Army Museum), Luke Barber and Justin Russell (Archaeology South-East), Jon Price (University of Northumbria), Martin Brown (MOD), David Kenyon (Cotswold Archaeology) and Peter Chasseaud. Further, I would like to take this opportunity to convey my appreciation to Dr Nicholas Saunders (UCL Anthropology) for his contributions to the anthropological debate contained within this piece of work. Finally I wish to express my appreciation to Mark Hassall (UCL Institute of Archaeology) for a critical reading of this manuscript. Those that have been acknowledged are not responsible for the opinions expressed within.

Notes

1   The Imperial War Museum, The Royal Engineers Museum, The Guards Museum, The London Scottish Regimental Museum, The Royal Fusiliers Museum and The Imperial War Museum (North).
2   The Wallace Collection is both a national museum and one of the finest private collections of art ever assembled. Located in the London's West End, it also houses a superb medieval armoury.

References

Cahill, B. (2004) *Pace Sticks and Swagger Sticks*. http://www.diggerhistory.info/pages-equip/pace-stick.htm (accessed 29 April 2009).

Carrington, C. [1965] (2006) *Soldier from the Wars Returning*. Barnsley: Pen & Sword Books Ltd.

Cerny, C. and Seriff, S. (1996) *Recycled Re-Seen: Folk Art from the Global Scrap Heap*. New York: Abrams.

Connolly, P., Gillingham, J. and Lazenby, J. (eds) (1998) *The Hutchinson Dictionary of Ancient and Medieval Warfare*. Oxford: Helicon.

Coote, J., Morton, C. and Nicholson, J. (eds) (2000) *Transformations: The Art of Recycling*. Oxford: Pitt Rivers Museum.

Dunn, J. C. (1994) *The War The Infantry Knew 1914–1919*. London: Abacus.

Foulkes, F. (1945) *Arms and Armament: An Historical Survey of the Weapons of the British Army*. London: George G. Harrap and Co.

Hammerton, J. (ed.) (1938) 'Humours and terrors of trench raids'. In *I Was There: The Human Story of the Great War of 1914–1918*, pp. 761–3. London: The Fleetway House.

Jünger, E. [1920] (2004) *Storm of Steel*. London: Penguin.

Madoc and IFFM (eds) (1998). *In Flanders Fields Museum Guide*. Ieper: In Flanders Fields Museum.

Mann, J. (1962) *Wallace Collection: European Arms and Armour, vol. II Arms*. London: The Trustees of the Wallace Collection.

Richards, F. [1933] (2001) *Old Soldiers Never Die*. Uckfield: Naval and Military Press.

Rutledge, S. (1918) *Pen Pictures from the Trenches*. Toronto: William Briggs.

Saunders, A. (2000) *Dominating the Enemy: War in the Trenches, 1914–1918*. Stroud: Sutton.

Saunders, N.J. (2000). 'Trench art: the recycla of war'. In J. Coote, C. Morton and J. Nicholson (eds), *Transformations: The Art of Recycling*, pp. 64–7. Oxford: Pitt Rivers Museum.

—— (2001) *Trench Art: A Brief History and Guide, 1914–1939*. Barnsley: Pen & Sword Books Ltd.

—— (2002) 'Excavating memories: archaeology and the Great War'. *Antiquity* 76 (291): 101–8.

—— (2003) *Trench Art: Materialities and Memories of War*. Oxford: Berg.

—— (ed.) (2004) *Matters of Conflict: Material Culture, Memory, and the First World War*. Abingdon: Routledge.

Sutter, J. (2002) *The Battle of the Golden Spurs*. www.liebaart.org/oxtaf4_e.htm (accessed 29 April 2009).

Wilkinson, F. (1978) *A Source Book of World War 1 Weapons and Uniforms*. London: Ward Lock.

Willmott, H.P. (2003) *First World War*. London: Dorling Kindersley.

4

THE JOURNEY BACK

On the nature of donations to the
'In Flanders Fields Museum'

Dominiek Dendooven

The phenomenon I describe and analyse here presented itself to me unexpectedly, when, in 1997, I began working as a historian for the In Flanders Fields Museum. This museum on the First World War is located in the rebuilt Cloth Hall in the equally reconstructed medieval city of Ypres (or Ieper in Dutch). The In Flanders Fields Museum focuses largely on the human experience of warfare.[1] It is the immediate successor of the quite different Ypres Salient War or Remembrance Museums that have existed in Ypres since the 1920s.

The remarkable phenomenon to which I refer here is that which sees hundreds of donations flowing into our museum – an average of one donation every one and a half days. However, what is exceptional is not so much the quantity of these donations, but rather the nature of the objects and documents that are donated and the motivations of the donors. More than half of the objects we receive are in fact 'returning home' after decades serving abroad as war souvenirs.

Ypres

To understand the phenomenon of the 'returning war souvenirs', it is important to bear in mind the fate of the city of Ypres and its inhabitants during the First World War. The war arrived in Ypres mid-October 1914, when the so-called 'war of movement' of August and September 1914 came to an end, and the German advance was halted. Ypres itself was the last gap in the line to be filled after the Belgian Army had taken positions behind the river Yser that lies between Ypres and the Belgian coast. From that moment, Ypres became one of the deadliest and most hotly contested areas on the Western Front, as the failure of German attempts to capture it left the Allied defences in a salient projecting eastwards from the city.

The Ypres Salient would last for nearly four years, and the battles that raged around Ypres itself reduced the ancient city centre to little more than a pile of rubble. The first German bombardments convinced the local population to seek refuge elsewhere: behind the front lines or abroad. Gradually, Ypres lost its civilian population, the last inhabitants being forced to leave at the beginning of May 1915. From this time, until the early months of 1919, not a single original inhabitant remained in the city. Ypres was dead, and the centre was occupied by allied troops who were billeted in its basements and cellars. Most soldiers came from different parts of the British Empire, but at various times Ypres was occupied also by French troops and, at the very end of the war, by the Belgian Army.

In their limited free time, it was inevitable that soldiers would go souvenir hunting in the ruins of the city. On Tuesday, 9 February 1915, Sir Morgan Crofton, a captain with the 2nd Life Guards, described Ypres cathedral in his diary.

> Not a window remained unbroken and the East Window and many of the other stained-glass ones were scattered in broken bits over the floor of the Cathedral. These pieces were very popular as souvenirs, and the entire church was by now filled with soldiers clambering over heaps, or digging about for mementoes. I secured several. It is surprising that efforts have not been made by the Belgian authorities to try and save some of the flotsam and jetsam, such as the chairs, the font, the pulpit, the brass fittings, the pictures and the organ, which is mostly composed of wooden pipes. If some effort is not made to safeguard the remains, the British soldier, as souvenir hunter, will complete the utter destruction of the Cathedral which was begun by the Germans.
>
> (Roynon 2004: 150)

Only the previous day, Sir Morgan Crofton had himself taken some pieces of glass from the east window which were lying about the floor (ibid.: 144). Along with the key of the west door, these glass fragments were formally returned to the Dean of Ypres Cathedral by Major Edward Crofton, son of the diarist, on 24 May 2003, after an absence of almost 90 years (Figure 4:1).

There is little doubt that the most sought-after souvenirs were woodcarvings, statues, parts of paintings and stained glass from the cathedral or the thirteenth-century Cloth Hall – the two most important ancient monuments in the city centre. However, private homes also provided souvenirs. Hence a photograph of an unidentified Ypres family which has finally returned to the city, 84 years after it was found in the ruins of a house in April 1916 by R. Campbell of the 2nd Battalion of the Scots Guards. In her accompanying letter, Campbell's daughter wrote: 'I am happy to think that after all these years the photograph goes back to Belgium' (quoted in Dendooven 2001: entry no. 18: 12). Another example is the brass slot of a letter box, allegedly 'taken off Church House – Ypres 2.11.1916' (IFFM, Registers of Donations) (Figure 4:2).

Figure 4:1 On 14 May 2003, 88 years after his father took some objects as souvenirs from the Ypres Cathedral, Major Edward Crofton hands over a piece of glass from the east window and a key to Jaak Houwen, Dean of the Ypres Cathedral. Insert: an excerpt from Sir Morgan Crofton's diary entry of 8 February 1915. (© and courtesy Edward Crofton/Gavin Roynon)

However, not all souvenirs from Ypres were actually found in the rubble during the war. Many of them – original or not – were traded after the war. Lode Opdebeek, a writer and publisher from Antwerp, gives the following description of Ypres in 1920.

> The hawkers are like madmen lusting after carrion. The streets are full of them. Everything is for sale. 'Un souvenir d'Ypres'. Wood and stone pieces of trash, souvenirs in iron, steel, bone, linen, cardboard, paper, earth. All souvenirs of a doomed city. If one could catch the sun, the stars, the air above Ypres, one would sell them as souvenirs. Oh Ypres, dear Ypres, 'beautiful crown of Flanders' democracy', they are fighting for your body and scattering your bones to all corners of the earth.
>
> (Opdebeek n.d.: 20)

This quotation makes clear that the post-war souvenirs traded in Ypres were made out of the same material as the souvenirs picked up or traded amongst soldiers during

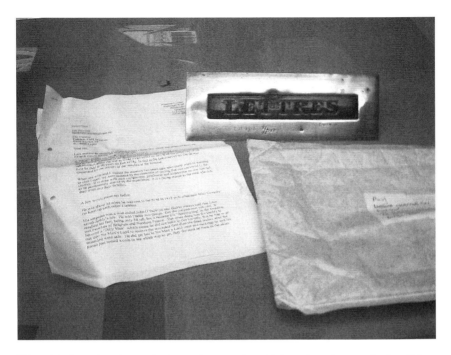

Figure 4:2 Some donations arrive in envelopes, such as this brass letter box, received on 3 June 2002. Allegedly, it was taken from a presbytery in Ypres in 1916 by the father of the donor. (© and courtesy In Flanders Fields Museum)

the war. However, as Saunders (2004: 14) and Saunders and Dendooven (2004: 10–14) have pointed out in relationship to trench art, the meanings and significance attributed to the souvenirs were very different, as they were no longer sold in circumstances of death and destruction. The shift from war to peace had not changed the 'raw material' of the souvenir, but had altered its intrinsic nature. Nevertheless, all were *bricolage*, new objects made from the broken remains of older pieces.

The importance of war souvenirs

We all know how unreliable memory can be, how transient reminiscences are, and how inaccessible the past will always remain. Experiences can never be duplicated or revived, and the visceral life-and-death conditions of war are forever beyond reclaim by those who took no part in the struggles. Herein lies the beauty and the power of conflict-related objects, some of which withstand the ravages of time in ways that memories do not. The past may be gone, but sometimes objects retain the power to evoke aspects of that past which gave birth to them, and thereby connect us to our own private and collective histories. Such objects provide us with something to hold on to – they provide emotional and intellectual purchase, turning back the clock of memory.

This explains the importance of material things to the ambiguously vague and almost indefinable process we call 'remembrance'. Little wonder that we often refer to such objects as 'mementoes' or 'souvenirs'. Souvenirs are objects that are valuable not just because of themselves, but because of their associations, because of their ability to evoke the memory of people, places and things which were important to us at the time, and which retain that importance today. Other objects, which are unable to define our relationship with our past in this way, are those we regard as being mere 'things'. They do not have the same power to move us (Meire 2001: 3–5; Hitchcock and Teague 2000), though who is to say that they might not acquire that power for others in the future.

Memories in material form quite literally offer us a grip on the past. This is particularly important with regard to the memories of war, where the balance of our relationship with others and with the world runs the greatest risk of being disturbed or distorted. It is precisely for this reason that in the years following the Great War, objects – 'things' – played such an important role in enabling individuals to come to terms with destruction and loss: of homes, possessions, loved ones and even personal histories. We can easily imagine the emotional value that a fragment of stained glass window from Ypres cathedral had for the veteran who once wandered through the devastated shell of the city, unsure even if he would survive the coming hours and days. For this man, in later years, the object-souvenir may have reminded him of a terrible period in his life, of the death of friends and comrades, and perhaps his own loss of innocence as well.

As mementoes and souvenirs, such objects carried (sometimes painfully) personal reminiscences, which were given an enduring identity when symbolically appropriated by having the individual's name (and/or service number and regiment) inscribed on them (see Chapter 1). During the 1920s and 1930s, such battlefield souvenirs or war trophies formed an important part of the 'Memory Bridge' that connected the two world wars (Saunders 2001: 477–8).

Within this corpus of 'material memory objects', there exists a unique category – items from the Great War in Belgian Flanders which are returned to the In Flanders Fields Museum.

These objects offer the opportunity to open up – to figuratively 'unpack' – what happens to a war souvenir when the original owner has died, and the meanings that he created for the object have disappeared. In one sense, the original significance of the object is lost forever, because no one else can understand or share the meaning which that object had for the individual who, in the act of acquiring it, changed its status from a piece of meaningless scrap to a poignant memory-laden souvenir of war. In many cases, once the original owner has died, a new meaning is attributed. The object might now become 'daddy's war souvenir', or 'granddad's war souvenir', and instead of being the icon of an old soldier's personal recollections of the war, it becomes instead an object that serves as a reminder both of a particular person, dear to the new owner, and of the role which the Great War played in this person's life. The attitude which the new owner (usually a relative) has towards this object is comparable to the phenomenon of supposed recognition of loved ones in First World War film and photographs (see Chapter 12).

Indeed, souvenirs and memories of the First World War in general, have a curious and phoenix-like regenerative power: they may sometimes fade but they never die. At least part of the explanation for this lies in the close association of these memories not only with the history of a very limited geographical area – the old front line – but also with the histories of so many individual families. Interest in the Great War was not stimulated by large-scale national ceremonies of remembrance, and perhaps not even by academic works detailing the military and political developments of the war years. The gradual reawakening of interest – which began in the 1970s, and has grown dramatically during the past fifteen years – owes almost everything to the desire of ordinary men and women to understand what happened to their own relatives (Meire 2003: 229–48).

Perhaps they stumbled across some old documents or a grandfather's diary, as was the case of Rudolf Zehmisch from Weischlitz, Germany. In the late 1990s, Zehmisch discovered in his attic a box containing the diaries, letters, photographs and other First World War memorabilia of his late father Kurt Zehmisch. His mother had hidden the case in 1945, with the arrival of Soviet troops, and as her husband never returned from a Soviet POW camp, and Weischlitz had become part of communist East Germany, she presumably decided it was better forgotten altogether – a conscious choice to forget one war mediated by the political consequences of a second conflict, and indicative of the largely unacknowledged relationships between the two world wars, in terms of memory and identity (see Forty 1999).

Rudolf Zehmisch's discovery is of considerable importance for those who study the First World War in Belgian Flanders. During the war, Kurt Zehmisch had been Ortskommandant (Town-Major) of Warneton/Waasten, twelve kilometres south of Ypres. He witnessed, and extensively documented, all the major battles in the Ypres Salient. Since the discovery of the box, Rudolf Zehmisch has donated hundreds of photographs and documents to the In Flanders Fields Museum in Ypres and the Documentation Centre in Warneton. In April 2002, he personally handed over to Mr Francis Desimpel of Warneton, the genealogy of the Desimpel family, handwritten by the latter's grandfather in whose house the Ortskommandantur was established, and from which Zehmisch senior had taken home the genealogy as a souvenir (Dendooven 2000; Parent 2002).

Some people become curious – and then fascinated – by the names inscribed on local war monuments. In this manner, the history of a four-year-long and half-forgotten war become entwined with their own personal history: they discover it was their grandfather who lived through the conflict; that these men and women were just like themselves, with the same hopes and fears, the same passions and desires. This is a modest, almost humble approach to world conflagration, but in the final analysis it is perhaps the most appropriate one. All wars are wars of the common man (Meire 2003: 292–3).

Let us return to our war souvenirs, whose original owners, the veterans, have passed away. In many cases, the new owners are afraid that, with the passing of time, the meaning of these objects will fade away, and that perhaps one day the object will no longer be recognized as a meaningful war souvenir and will be discarded or sold. They fear that, if the object loses its status as a war souvenir, the beloved person who once brought it home from a terrible war will be completely forgotten. This fear seems to be the impulse behind the solution of donating the object to a museum. If the museum accepts the gift, the donor can be sure that the object will be preserved – in theory for eternity, and in good condition. Moreover, if the object is properly catalogued, not only will the object survive, but also the 'proper' interpretation of that object, and the memory of that dearly loved person who had turned it into a war souvenir.

Indeed, it often transpires that a donor rationalizes his or her donation by telling the museum that there are no children – or that the children do not care about the object – and that he or she wants to be sure that the object is preserved because it ought to be: 'When I die, the family will die out, so it's nice to think these mementos will be in a safe place' wrote Mrs Marjorie Bilbow in a letter to the museum, dated 11 November (IFFM, Personal files: V. and H. Reis; Meire 2003: 294–6). It is only because they have been preserved with such love and such care for so long that the object can still appear relevant to us today. It is only because the owners of these objects have been so obsessed with their preservation that their value has become apparent, both to them and to us. In other words, perhaps, the objects have acquired an invisible patina of emotion, significant and self-evident for their owners, but requiring documentation to this effect by the receiving museum. Relinquishing the duty of care for such items is sometimes difficult for the donors – despite its voluntary nature. In this sense, the wartime and interwar stories told by the objects have been joined also by stories of their current owners. The power of such objects to embody and reconfigure personal and family memories, emotions and crosscutting ideas of identity and genealogy are as astonishing as they are currently undocumented.

The object and its stories

It is vital not only that the object be preserved, but also that the proper documentation and interpretation of that object – the stories attached to it – are also safeguarded. In many cases, the story that accompanies the object bestows its historical value. Very often, this is the only value an object has. For example, consider a small – 5 cm × 4 cm – fragment of stained glass. The commercial value is nil, even if you know that it came from a medieval window in Ypres Cathedral. It also loses the very relative value of uniqueness – of being the only surviving piece of a famous Gothic work of art – due to the fact that hundreds if not thousands of similar pieces have survived. The only claim to uniqueness therefore resides in the story behind the object, for example the Crofton case mentioned above, or the following one. At Easter 1916, Canadian Lieutenant James Rutherford was wounded when a stained glass window from Ypres Cathedral was blasted by enemy fire and blown onto him. He put one small piece in his pocket as a souvenir. Later, he had it mounted in the form in which his son presented it to the museum in August 2002 (Saunders and Dendooven 2004: 8) (Figure 4:3).

Figure 4:3
The pair of stained glass 'Christ's Hands' which James Rutherford put in his pocket when he was wounded in Easter 1916 when a cathedral window was blown on top of him. It was returned to Ypres in August 2002. (© and courtesy In Flanders Fields Museum)

For reasons such as this, it is vital that while cataloguing items, the personal stories attached to them are recorded in as much detail as possible. Only in this way can the material object and the immaterial memory-story which it carries be preserved together. For, without these stories, the biographies of the objects are incomplete. The objects are valuable precisely because they are linked to a particular memory or a particular story. The traditional respect that museum professionals have for objects, should be equalled by their respect for the stories behind them.[2]

The journey back

However, this does not explain why later generations decide that the time has come for these objects – cherished possessions of a lifetime – to make 'the journey back'. Why do people send or bring them back to the old frontline – in our case Ypres – instead of donating them to a local museum, a regimental museum, or a national war museum, such as the Imperial War Museum in London?

In many cases, it seems to me, that donors do not come to the In Flanders Fields Museum because it has a particular ethos or approach toward representing the Great War, but rather because it is physically in Ypres, and run by the City authorities. The same phenomenon occurs in other places in Belgium, for example the University Library of Leuven/Louvain, where people bring fragments, carvings or even burnt books that had been acquired as souvenirs from the old university library after its destruction by German troops in August 1914 (Derez 1996: 622).[3] In other words, there is some visceral connection in the minds of donors between object, person and place, which demonstrates how individuals recreate themselves through their perceptions of war-zone landscapes.

The reasons for 'the journey back' are less clear, and surely more ambiguous than simple preservation. Most of the time, a donor cannot explain why he entrusts the objects to a museum far away from his home town: a vague 'I feel it belongs here' is often heard, as is 'Well, it came from here!' Occasionally, donors refer to the fact that wartime souvenir hunting was rather close to looting, and that they feel a moral duty to return the souvenir to the place from whence it came. Indeed, certainly during the war, the distinction between looting and souvenir hunting was anything but clear, as proven by a long lasting court of enquiry into alleged looting by some British naval officers in 1915–16. Among other charges, they were accused of organizing a looting trip from Dunkirk to Ypres Cathedral, although they were finally acquitted (NA, ADM 156/78, ADM 156/79). From the proceedings of the enquiry, it becomes evident that the terms souvenir, loot, and trophy were open to interpretation (see also Chapter 1).

Sometimes, it was the explicit will of the veteran that the souvenir object should be returned to the city of Ypres, and the donors are simply respecting those wishes: 'Dad always told us that this should go back to Ypres after his death' is a typical comment in such circumstances. A remarkable example of this occurred in the summer of 2004: a family from Brittany returned a small bell from a chapel in Ypres, taken away by their grandfather and great-grandfather who was an officer in the French army, and who fought in the Second Battle of Ypres (April–May 1915). He removed it with the intention of returning it after the war. Unfortunately, he died in 1919. His wife and daughter knew about his intention, which they considered as one of his last wishes, and they tried in vain several times to contact the local authorities. Their letters were never answered or went astray. In the summer of 2004, almost 90 years after its removal, the bell was brought back to Ypres by the granddaughter and her two sons. On that occasion many photographs were taken to show her old mother that her father's wish had finally been fulfilled (Figure 4:4).

Another reason why people bring objects back to Ypres, is that they are convinced that the intrinsic value of the souvenir is greater for the people of Ypres than it is for themselves. This is the case with (parts of) works of art. Typical remarks are: 'Well, we know that this whole town was completely destroyed and that it lost all its works of art', or 'This is more part of your history than it is of ours.' And indeed, in some way, this helps us to understand the fabric of Ypres as it existed before 1914.

In 2001, Edward Baskerville presented the museum with an interesting and beautiful piece of art – a copper plate (30 cm × 50 cm) representing the Stations of the Cross, and dated and signed 'I.R. Gambier 1730'. Tradition suggests that it originates from the Cloth Hall but in fact it might have come from the pre-war

Franse vrouw schenkt klok je uit 1915 aan museum

IEPER – Een klok die tijdens de Eerste Wereldoorlog verdween, is eindelijk terug van weggeweest. De Française Marylise François uit Saint-Brieuc (Bretagne) overhandigde gisteren het Ieperse klokje aan schepen Piet Vandenberghe in het «In Flanders Fields Museum».

De klok werd in 1915 door haar grootvader uit een Ieperse kapel als souvenir aan zijn tijd aan het front meegenomen. Het was de expliciete wens van haar grootvader dat deze klok naar Ieper zou terugkomen. De schenking is interessant omdat luitenant Le Bonhomme deel uitmaakte van de Bretoense eenheden die de eerste slachtoffers werden van de gasaanval bij Boezinge op 22 april 1915. Hij overleefde de aanval en liet daarover ook een manuscript na. Le Bonhomme stierf uiteindelijk vrij snel na de oorlog in 1919. Met jaarlijkse regelmaat krijgt Ieper opnieuw voorwerpen uit de oorlogstijd in zijn bezit. Vele soldaten namen bij hun vertrek iets mee als herinnering aan de verwoeste stad.

(DDW. Foto Anckaert)

Figure 4:4 The official handing-over of objects 'returning home' is often covered by the local press and, occasionally, by the national media. On 3 August 2004, Mrs Marylise François from Saint-Brieuc, Brittany, presented a small bell to the Deputy-Mayor of Ypres. Her grandfather, Lt Le Bonhomme, removed it from an Ypres chapel shortly after the first gas attack on 22 April 1915. From *Het Laatste Nieuws*, 4 August 2004. (© and courtesy In Flanders Fields Museum)

Municipal Museum, just opposite the Cloth Hall. The donor's grandfather, James Baldwin, of the South Wales Borderers, smuggled his 'find' to England by folding the plate together and hiding it in his puttees, hence the marks still visible on the plate today (Figure 4:5) (see Chapter 1 for the difficulty of transporting souvenirs home).

The large number of objects which are returning to Ypres are fulfilling a wide range of roles that are in need of documentation and analysis. Such items reveal a hitherto uninvestigated arena within which objects, people and places circulate in unexpected ways. These objects also highlight the changing role of the In Flanders Fields Museum in relation to its valuation, documentation and display of donated exhibits.

Perhaps surprisingly, these items can also add to the knowledge of pre-war Ypres. The city was destroyed by the conflict, and then reconstructed as a virtual replica during the inter-war years in a fascinating but contested example of mimesis. Nevertheless, the loss of the pre-war city's original medieval works of art and associated objects was considerable. It is ironic indeed that by making the journey back to Ypres, these war souvenirs – already heavy with emotion and personal meanings – are also symbolically completing the reconstruction of the city, and lifting the burden of memory from the shoulders of those who donate them.

Acknowledgements

I am grateful to Gavin Roynon and Edward Crofton for the photographs from the Crofton diary and the handing over of the 'returning' key and stained glass

Figure 4:5 A copper plate showing Christ's Stations of the Cross, signed and dated 'I.R. Gambier 1730'. A remarkable piece of art, which, as tradition would have it, originates from the Cloth Hall, but might in fact have come from the pre-war Municipal Museum in Ypres. It was returned to Ypres on 8 May 2001. (© and courtesy In Flanders Fields Museum)

from Ypres Cathedral; Mark Derez, librarian at the University Library of the Katholieke Universiteit Leuven for information, and my colleagues Bert Heyvaert for proofreading and Frederik Vandewiere, who, as registrar of the In Flanders Fields Museum, is responsible for the proper registration of all the donations entering the museum's collection. Finally I would like to thank Nicholas Saunders for his stimulating perception of 'First World War stuff'.

Notes

1   See www.inflandersfields.be (accessed 25 March 2009).
2   Although occasionally in need of revival, this concept is not new. See Cornish (2004: 38–40).
3   Communicated on 7 September 2004 by Mark Derez of the University Library in Leuven.

References

Primary Sources

IFFM: In Flanders Fields Museum, Ypres, Register of donations, 1998–2004.
IFFM: In Flanders Fields Museum, Ypres, Personal files.
NA: UK National Archive, ADM 156/78
—— ADM 156/79

Secondary Sources

Dendooven, D. (2001) *The Journey Back: Donations to the In Flanders Fields Museum 1998–2001: Temporary Exhibition, Cloth Hall, Ieper, 1 April–1 October 2001*, Ieper: In Flanders Fields Museum.

Published Sources

Cornish, P. (2004) '"Sacred relics": objects in the Imperial War Museum 1917–39'. In N.J. Saunders (ed.) *Matters of Conflict: Material Culture, Memory and the First World War*, pp. 5–25. Abingdon: Routledge.
Dendooven, D. (2000) 'Kurt Zehmisch and the Great War in Waasten'. *In Flanders Fields Magazine* (4 July): 10–11.
Dendooven, D. and F. Vandewiere (1998–2004). 'Donations to the In Flanders Fields Museum'. *In Flanders Fields Magazine*, 1–13.
Derez, M. (1996) 'The flames of Louvain: The war experience of an academic community'. In H. Cecil and P. Liddle (eds) *Facing Armageddon: The First World War Experience*, pp. 617–29. London: Leo Cooper.
Forty, A. (1999) 'Introduction'. In A. Forty and S. Küchler (eds) *The Art of Forgetting*, pp. 1–18. Oxford: Berg.
Hitchcock, M. and K. Teague (eds) (2000) *Souvenirs: Material Culture of Tourism*. London: Ashgate.
Meire, J. (2001) 'Een tastbare herinnering'. In *De herinnering van de vergetelheid*, pp. 3–5. Ieper: In Flanders Fields Museum.

—— (2003). *De stilte van de Salient: De herinnering aan de Eerste Wereldoorlog rond Ieper*. Tielt: Lannoo.

Opdebeek, L. (n.d.) *Op Reis in Vlaanderen*, Antwerpen: Uitgeverij Opdebeek.

Parent, P. (2002) 'Des documents inédits sur la Première Guerre Mondiale: Grâce au fils d'un commandant allemand en place à Warneton en 14–18'. *Nord-Eclair*, 8 April: VIII.

Roynon, G. (2004) *Massacre of the Innocents: The Crofton Diaries Ypres 1914–1915*. Stroud: Sutton Publishing.

Saunders, N.J. (2001). 'Apprehending memory: material culture and war, 1919–1939'. In J. Bourne, P.H. Liddle and H. Whitehead (eds) *The Great World War, 1914–1945*, vol. 2, pp. 476–88. London: HarperCollins.

—— (2004) 'Material culture and conflict: the Great War 1914–2003'. In N.J. Saunders (ed.) *Matters of Conflict: Material Culture, Memory and the First World War*, pp. 5–25. Abingdon: Routledge.

Saunders, N.J. and D. Dendooven (2004) *Trench Art, Lost Worlds of the Great War: The Trench Art Collection of the In Flanders Fields Museum*, Brugge: Marc Van de Wiele.

5

'BROTHERS IN ARMS'

Masonic artefacts of the First World War and its aftermath

Mark J.R. Dennis

The existence of Masonic material culture associated with the Great War and its aftermath may surprise many. It becomes more understandable when the nature of English freemasonry is considered, namely that it is a male-only order, and is traditionally strong in members from the public services and the military. Here, I will draw mainly from the resources at my immediate disposal – those of the United Grand Lodge of England, whose headquarters, museum and library are situated in the heart of London's Covent Garden (Hamill 1994: 64–5). It should be stressed that freemasonry is an international movement, with most of the participant nations of the First World War having one or several Masonic Grand Lodges.

The stimulus for this investigation was research carried out during 2002–3 for an exhibition and publication focusing on one kind of war-related material culture known as trench art from a Masonic perspective. In the course of this research, a substantial body of material was identified which had relevance to the First World War, and which was either unpublished or published only within the limited context of Masonic periodicals and journals intended for internal consumption. The publication *Craft and Conflict* (Dennis and Saunders 2003) identified for the first time a corpus of Masonic trench art, but also situated it within a wider tradition of conflict-related objects of Masonic manufacture and iconographic development.

This chapter considers three specific aspects of the relationship between freemasonry and the material culture of the First World War and its aftermath: Masonic lodges whose identity and iconography is associated with the war; Masonic trench art, and the creation of the present Freemasons' Hall as the Masonic Peace Memorial.

An outline of freemasonry

Organised freemasonry developed in the 1700s, with the first Grand Lodge being formed in London in 1717 (Hamill 1994:19). These early lodges used the tools of the stonemason as allegorical symbols, termed the 'working tools', and developed a series of ritual 'initiation plays' based around the construction of Solomon's Temple and the role of the craftsmen who built it. For this reason freemasonry is often referred to as 'the Craft'.

Members wore symbolic versions of the stonemason's apron and badges – termed 'jewels' – suspended from collars to identify individual rank (Figure 5:1). As time progressed, lodge members began to wear decorations to identify Founders and those who had led the lodge as Master, though sometimes these were worn by all members. From 1813 onwards, after the creation of the United Grand Lodge of England, the 'lodge room' developed into a formal environment for ritual, with furniture and fittings that supported this role. In parallel with this development, and an expansion of membership, commercial items began to be created for sale to Freemasons.

Figure 5:1 Jewels of Progress, Silent Cities and Maguncor. (© and courtesy Library and Museum of Freemasonry)

The material culture of freemasonry consists of a restricted set of large and small objects: regalia and jewels to identify the mason and his place in the organization; lodge fittings including ornamental furniture; working tools (props for use in the ceremonies including stonemasons' tools, real or symbolic), and items made as collectables for Masons themselves, whether for wear, use in the home or as presentation items. In the wider sphere, Masonic halls with specially designed lodge rooms were created. The relationship between these individually designed large-scale environments for ritual and the small mobile objects that operated within them is highlighted by the development of a tradition of donating and presenting items for use in these environments. These were frequently of fine craftsmanship or made from symbolic materials that linked directly to the imagery of freemasonry or the individual lodges themselves.

In considering the role of freemasonry it is important to note that not all Masonic bodies have the same status or nature. Lodges recognized by the United Grand Lodge of England are termed 'regular'. This signifies that they behave according to a number of fixed rules that include male membership only and the mandatory belief in a supreme being, and that forbid any discussion of politics or religion. In many nations, other Grand Lodges exist (termed 'irregular') that do not obey these rules and, while to the outsider they appear very similar, members of the 'regular' Grand Lodges are forbidden to visit their meetings. All the Masonic lodge bodies referred to in this paper are regular. There may have been additional activities and material culture generated by other Masonic bodies and also by members of non-Masonic friendly and fraternal orders, but these are outside the scope of this chapter. One notable example of an irregular body of relevance to the participant nations of the First World War is the Grand Orient of France. This does not require a belief in a supreme being but remains the largest Masonic body in France.

Masonic lodges connected with the Great War

English Freemasons have been in proximity to war since the earliest days of the Craft, and it is partly a consequence of the masculine nature of the order, and of the military lodges of the eighteenth and nineteenth centuries, that significant Masonic communities were created in most regiments of cavalry and line infantry (Lane, 1895: 512–13). These 'travelling lodges' were so named because, unlike a normal fixed lodge, they were permitted to hold meetings wherever the military unit went. They carried freemasonry across the expanding empire. The basic lodge unit was created by like-minded Masons, grouped by shared interests, location or background.

The members' jewels were, from the 1880s onwards, very diverse in design. In the case of lodges connected with the armed forces, the jewels' iconography reflected changes in outlook caused by war and its effects. Prior to the First World War, the military lodges normally had a regimental or imperial outlook, sometimes pointedly so. A good example is 'Progress Lodge No 3727' founded in 1914 with its motif of 'savage to soldier' – the 'noble savage' turned into the private soldier of the King's African Rifles (Dennis and Saunders 2003: 60). The imperial symbolism could be subtle – 'Lodge Engineer No. 6964' was named to commemorate a Royal Engineer Victoria Cross winner of the Indian Mutiny rather than an item of architecture, and 'Ashanti Lodge' No 3717 refers to the Ashanti War Stool, by then an imperial trophy (Dennis and Saunders 2003: 17). There were exceptions to this imperial attitude, such as the 'Lodge of the Artists Rifles Number 2851', which was named 'Rosemary' to symbolize 'remembrance' after the Boer War. In antiquity, this aromatic herb was believed to strengthen memory and was burnt as an incense offering to the gods in Greece and Egypt, and on this account became an emblem of fidelity and a symbol of remembrance.

Lodges for victory and peace were created in the aftermath of the First World War, and wartime lodges such as 'Maguncor Lodge Number 3806' – the lodge of the Machine Gun Corps – addressed reality directly with their jewel depicting a machine-gun team wearing the early form of gas mask. Several members of the then newly formed Imperial War Graves Commission formed a lodge – 'Builders of the Silent Cities' – in France; one of its more famous members was Rudyard Kipling, a committed freemason.

The material culture of freemasonry associated with the Great War is still very much in evidence within the order. It includes the surviving lodges created by members of the military services, and the use of war relics such as the trench-art gavel of the 'Navy Lodge No. 2612' made from debris from the ruined cathedral at Ypres and presented to them by the Prince of Wales, later the Duke of Windsor (Dennis 2003: 37) (Figure 5:2) (and see Chapter 4). The fact that the London headquarters – Freemasons' Hall in Great Queen Street – is rich in resonances of this period has subtly influenced the whole culture of freemasonry. A recent debate over the introduction of a colourful tie for wear at Masonic meetings included the assertion that Masons wear black ties in memory of the war dead (Bell 2002: 52). This retro-fitting of meaning to formal dress that was quite unremarkable at the time is typical of the embedded meanings created in lodges.

The immediate effect of the Great War on freemasonry was to render a substantial number of its members liable to active service. This was particularly so in 'Apollo University Lodge' at Oxford University, where initiation was permitted from the age of 18 rather than the normal 21, and the overall age of members was younger than average. The order was not then large (around 3,700 lodges); ironically it was the aftermath of the Great War, with returning servicemen seeking comradeship, which led to a dramatic increase in Masonic membership. By the start of the Second World War there were over 5,800 lodges, most of which had a fully active membership. In other words, the great increase in numbers of Masonic lodges during the inter-war years – and the buildings, objects and social relationships that accompanied it – was a legacy of the Great War, a material aftermath which saw human relationships embodied in and represented by a distinctive kind of material culture rigidly controlled and ordered by the rules and regulations of freemasonry.

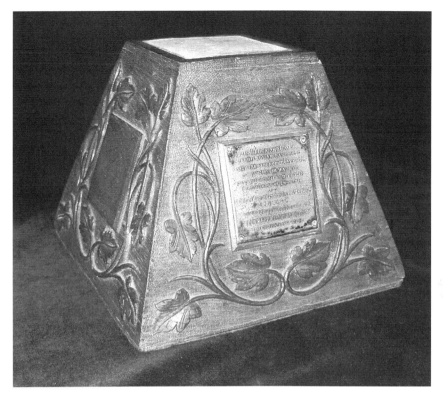

Figure 5:2 Gavel block made of materials from the ruins of Ypres cathedral. (© and courtesy
Library and Museum of Freemasonry)

Masonic lodges in war zones

In conditions of combat or duress, Masons practised freemasonry to boost morale and
develop team spirit. The majority of impromptu war lodges could not be 'warranted'
by Grand Lodge bodies, i.e. for lodges to meet and initiate members they must be
formally approved by a recognized Grand Lodge and in the English constitution the
approval document or 'warrant' must be present at every meeting. Consequently, these
unwarranted lodges existed as 'lodges of instruction' that created a social environment
and practised ritual but could not initiate new members.

Many servicemen in wartime found that forming a lodge of instruction was a
convenient device that enabled them to practise freemasonry in circumstances where
it would have been impracticable to obtain a dispensation to form a normal lodge. A
few lodges were legitimately formed where soldiers were in one place for an extended
period, such as 'Lodge Gastvrijheid', which was created by Masons interned in the
Netherlands after being transferred from German prisoner of war camps and remained
there until the Armistice of 11 November 1918. This lodge was properly authorised

77

by the 'Grand East of the Netherlands' – the Dutch Grand Lodge body – and, after the war, was transferred to England to became 'Lodge 3970' of the English constitution, under which it still meets.

Masonic meetings in war zones generated specific kinds of ephemera, which in some cases are the only record of the meetings themselves, so information about this activity is patchy and anecdotal. In this sense, by their physical existence, some Masonic objects served in the same way as did other kinds of Great War ephemera – configuring and fixing personal experiences whose otherwise transient nature would have left no permanent record. Such was the non-Masonic case of aluminium finger-rings made by French soldiers and traded with British soldiers in exchange for being taught popular songs (Saunders 2003: 5–6).

The lodge-making activities of Mason soldiers required that the same ornamental fittings as lodges outside the war zone be made, and these were frequently improvised using – i.e. reusing – local materials, and thus fulfilling the recycling element which brings many of these objects within the classification of trench art. Notable amongst these objects are items of furniture belonging to the 'Aegean Lodge of Instruction' (Figure 5:3). This lodge was formed at Mudros on the Greek island of Lemnos by Freemasons of the army and navy who were stationed at or were passing through the port. It was conceived by two members of 'Phoenix Lodge No.257' who found themselves serving there.

The 'Working Tools' (i.e. the symbolic copies of stonemasons' implements used allegorically in Masonic ceremonies) and the lodge fittings were mainly designed by W. Bro Joliffe (the dockyard foreman) and were all made by voluntary effort under his superintendence onboard the repair ship HMS *Reliance* and in the onshore aircraft repair shops. The lodge of instruction met in a signal hut and all the fittings had to be removed between meetings. The Master's pedestal cover illustrates how all the furniture was made from canvas, and could be thrown over a conveniently shaped table to form a complete set of lodge furniture that was easy to store between meetings. Masons of all regular constitutions met in this lodge. Today, the lodge fittings normally reside in the Masonic Hall in Old Portsmouth, and in accordance with the wishes of the original members they are used annually at the November meeting of Phoenix Lodge Number 257 in memory of the Armistice of 1918.

Lodges related to war service

Behind the lines and at home, Masonic lodges existed or were created that had a direct link to war work and were properly constituted and warranted. The commander of the Air Inspection Directorate (AID), Lt-Colonel (later Brigadier) Bagnall-Wild, realizing that many of his new directorate were Masons, and seeing an opportunity for team bonding, created 'Ad Astra' lodge. The lodge took as its emblems a biplane, the rotary engine of a fighter plane, and the initials AID made from Masonic tools. At the time of foundation this caused some debate as these items of aviation technology were all by then obsolete; eventually the lodge agreed to commemorate past achievements from its Great War days in France rather than reflect the future of military aviation.

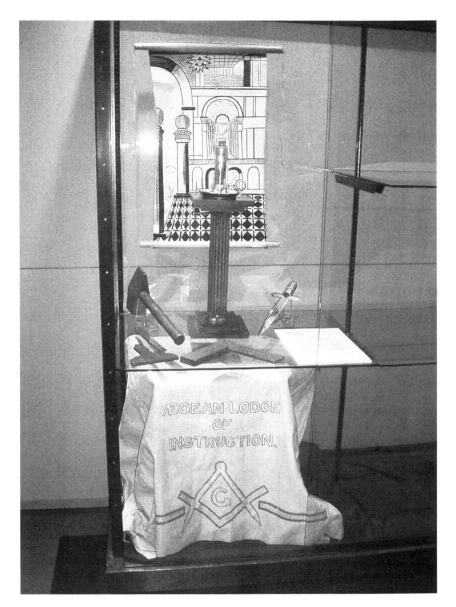

Figure 5:3 Aegean Lodge furniture. (© and courtesy Library and Museum of Freemasonry)

The air war of 1914–18 features in several of the items from Ad Astra Lodge (Figure 5:4). The gavel has an aluminium head marked 'Zeppelin L21 Cuffley 1916'. This simple inscription has deeper resonance: the views of the British public on Zeppelin attacks were at best ambiguous, with a writer as eminent as H.G. Wells describing how the shooting down of Zeppelins was becoming a much-enjoyed spectacle – while at the same time the crews were vilified as baby killers (Wells 1917). The recycling of material from wrecked Zeppelins as patriotic badges or other souvenirs was commonplace (Saunders 2003: 93, 96).

Masonic trench art is atypical of trench art in general particularly by virtue of the fact that a large proportion of Masonic examples possess a provenance (see below). Some lodges, notably the 'Royal Naval Anti-aircraft Lodge No. 3790', had small lodge museums that survived until after the Second World War. This lodge was formed by members of the Royal Naval Volunteer Reserve who had volunteered to man the anti-aircraft batteries around London (it still meets today). The snuffbox and neck jewels for its lodge officers were made from scrap aluminium retrieved from Zeppelin crash sites, and the consecration programme for the lodge, dated April 1917, was wrapped in aeroplane canvas (Dennis 2003: 31).

The most striking item in the lodge's possession is the lodge collecting tin, made from the case of an anti-aircraft shell and bearing the locations of the batteries of the unit after April 1918, when they relocated from London to Kent. Aeroplane models

Figure 5:4
Items from the Ad Astra Lodge.
(© and courtesy Library and
Museum of Freemasonry)

used in recognition training by the unit were later sold to raise funds for charity. Several of the models were purchased and presented to the lodge as table decorations, in one case mounted on stone from Solomon's quarry in Jerusalem – thus giving a Masonic identity to a wholly un-Masonic item. The Lodge retains a piece of Zeppelin Duralumin to allow for the making of further items if required, in the same way that an ingot of bronze from Russian cannon captured by the British at Sebastopol during the Crimean War is kept for the casting of future Victoria Crosses (Saunders 2003: 23). In both cases, the recycling element involved includes such items in the definition of trench art.

The use of war material to make lodge fittings (even when the procuring of the items was technically theft) was particularly prevalent in lodges that had a direct link to the war. These fittings created a bond with their lodge identity that, in some cases, has endured long after the actual link has ceased. The collecting box, gavels and stands of 'Armament Lodge No. 3898' are good examples of this. This lodge was formed just after the First World War in the Woolwich Arsenal. Its officers' jewels were made from silver extracted from the lead ore used to make shrapnel shells, and its collecting box and gavels were converted from the caps of artillery shells. The deep ambiguity that characterizes so much trench art in general is also present here in the tools of war being used fraternally as a reminder of the professional roles of the members.

Moving beyond the Great War momentarily in order to illustrate a wider point, a gavel that was used at the first Masonic meeting in Singapore after the Second World War was subsequently presented to the Grand Lodge in London as a sacred relic. It was believed to have been used on the Burma railway, although there is no evidence for lodges meeting there. Belief is the critical factor here. It is significant that only after the turn of the twentieth century do these votive offerings emerge and pass into the collections as exemplars of Masonic and imperial masculine behaviours.

In addition to objects intended for use in private lodges, a strong tradition was emerging of creating and collecting objects for display in the headquarters of the organisation at Freemasons' Hall in London. These material reminders from the aftermath of war are much in evidence within the library and museum located in this building. The preservation of items used in war zones and their display within the hall starts with Napoleonic items showing Masonic imagery, becomes more prominent with improvised items used in ceremonies during the second Boer War, and reaches its peak with items such as the gavel block made from the timber of the ruined Ypres Cathedral, presented to the United Grand Lodge of England by Major General Sir David Watson, commanding the 4th Canadian Division, on 11 November 1918.

The symbolism of this gift is clear and poignant: the desecration of the cathedral of Ypres stood for the loss of much that was physically and spiritually beautiful (see Chapter 4). Moreover, Ypres Cathedral was a monument to the medieval stonemason's art and skill. The presentation of the gavel block to United Grand Lodge of England for permanent display on Armistice Day was a powerful gesture by a senior imperial citizen on behalf of his men. 'Navy Lodge Number 2612' has a maul (a type of builder's mallet used to set stones in place) made, once again, from timber taken from Ypres cathedral. It was presented by HRH The Prince of Wales (later HRH The Duke of Windsor). This was a high-profile gift, carefully thought out and made, reflecting the circumstances of both giver and recipient. For a royal donor to choose such a gift is striking, particularly when its existence would be known to only a few people. The widely felt sense of remembrance and commemoration culminated in a proposal by the then Grand Master, HRH Arthur, Duke of Connaught and Strathearn, for a new hall to be created as a memorial to the war dead. This became a focal point for remembrance within freemasonry, and the largest single piece of material culture relating to the war.

Masonic trench art

Within this distinctive, albeit hitherto uninvestigated, corpus of Great War-related Masonic material culture are situated small-scale objects that can be identified as belonging also to the genre of trench art. Trench art has been defined as 'any item made by soldiers, prisoners of war and civilians, from war matériel directly, or any other material, as long as it and they are associated temporally and/or spatially with armed conflict or its consequences' (Saunders 2003: 11). This definition is particularly useful when applied to such items made by Freemasons.

There exists in individual lodges a body of trench art that has been little studied because access has hitherto been restricted or impossible. It is significant that Masonic trench art from the English constitution (i.e. those lodges originating from England and Wales or from overseas but governed by the United Grand Lodge of England) appears to have been made exclusively for use within lodges. The freemasonry of the inter-war years was discreet and reserved, and the making of items for display in the home was increasingly frowned upon. This stands in direct contrast to non-Masonic trench art, much of which was made specifically as memory objects (souvenirs, mementoes) for domestic display.

The creation of Masonic trench art was thus unselfish, and personal only in the context of a gift to a group rather than being overtly self-referential. In most cases, the name of the maker exists only in lodge minutes rather than on the piece; thus, although provenance is more fully attested than with the normal range of trench art, the maker's identity is subordinated to the intended use of the item.

In this important respect, Masonic trench art differs from non-Masonic mainstream examples in that the intention is one of enduring usage that transcends the identity of the maker and foresees an ongoing moral and historical role for the object. The range of Masonic trench-art items is limited, but the variety of materials used is diverse, both physically and in their intended symbolism.

The creation of these trench art objects was rooted firmly in the Masonic tradition, but reoriented and transferred to a new 'opportunity of production' created by the male comradeship of the services, and influenced by the life-and-death experiences of Mason soldiers in war zones. The limited range of forms created, and the often strongly provenanced nature of the items, stand in marked contrast to the extraordinary diversity and anonymity of the bulk of non-Masonic trench art objects associated with the Great War (Saunders 2001; Saunders 2003: 35–125). Masonic trench art items were generally created for reasons other than commercial sale, and have an apparent scarcity value for that reason. They are less visible, less overt and less frequently encountered than non-Masonic examples in the normal outlets of militaria fairs, car-boot sales, antique shops and the Internet. This is not because they are scarce per se, but rather that they were usually passed direct from the maker to his Masonic lodge where they were retained to be seen by successive lodge members, sometimes numbering no more than a few dozen individuals.

This fact separates Masonic trench art from all other kinds of the genre; it offers a new perspective on this distinctive type of conflict-related materiality by virtue of the fact that its trajectory through geographical and social space was limited, and the 'social life' or biography of the object truncated. Traditional kinds of trench art passed through many hands – variously from maker to consumer, soldier to loved one or relative, father to son, grandson to militaria dealer. Masonic examples, however, intersected the lives and memories not only of far fewer people, but these were only males, were only Masons, and probably only members of a specific lodge as well. In other words, the consumption of Masonic trench art was gendered in ways that non-Masonic examples were not, and restricted in the numbers and kinds of people who would have interacted with it.

In shape, form and iconography, Great War Masonic trench-art items differ from the mainstream varieties. Masonic examples do not reflect the free-for-all shapes and forms of non-Masonic trench art, nor the latter's usual art nouveau style of decoration. The whole purpose of Masonic trench art was not to make trench art for sale, barter or memory objects for the individual or his family, but to produce serviceable instruments for the rituals of freemasonry from available materials, and that just happen to be trench art from this perspective. A corollary of this is that, unlike ordinary trench art, there was no premium on producing large numbers of the same item.

There are relatively few examples of Masonic trench art that can be said with confidence to have been made and used under fire; the gavel of 'St Catherine's Park Lodge' (No. 2899) is the most potent example. The head of the gavel was carved from the wooden parts of a German Mauser rifle found in a captured trench by the New Zealand expeditionary force, and the gavel itself was used in meetings held within the combat area. It passed to the St Catherine's Park Lodge in the 1920s in recognition of that lodge's hospitality to overseas military Masons during the war (Dennis and Saunders 2003: 63). The use of the wooden parts of weapons for artistic purposes was well known; artists such as Henri Gaudier-Brzeska had created such sculptures for display (Ede 1931: 268).

The Masonic Peace Memorial: Freemasons' Hall

The single largest, most impressive and enduring of the many Masonic artefacts which can be judged material legacies of the Great War is the Freemasons' Hall, funded entirely from members' subscriptions, in exchange for which – in typically Masonic fashion – a medal or jewel was produced according to a strict hierarchy of value. Over

53,000 of these jewels were issued, and they became a strong visual indicator of the fundraising appeal for the lifetime of their owners. Members donating 10 guineas were entitled to wear it as a breast decoration in silver, those donating 100 guineas, in gold, and for lodges collecting an average of 10 guineas per member the master was granted a version in silver gilt to wear in perpetuity. The jewel – entitled the Hallstone Jewel – continues to be worn. Two of the three provincial/district jewels survive, one in use by the 'Province of Buckinghamshire' lodge, and the other on display in the museum gallery of Freemasons' Hall.

The design of the medal, the outcome of a competition won by Bro. Cyril Saunders Spackman, R.B.A., R.M.S., was described by him at the time:

> The jewel is in the form of a cross, symbolising Sacrifice, with a perfect square at the four ends, on the left and right, squares being the dates 1914–1918, the years in which the supreme sacrifice was made. Between these is a winged figure of Peace presenting the representation of a Temple with special Masonic allusion in the Pillars, Porch and Steps. The medal is suspended by the Square and Compasses, attached to a riband, the whole thus symbolising the Craft's gift of a Temple in memory of those brethren who gave all for King and Country, Peace and Victory, Liberty and Brotherhood.
>
> (Tudor-Craig 1938: 108)

The almost obsessive fundraising for the building defined the interwar years for the organization. At the outbreak of a second war in 1939, the term Peace Memorial was quietly dropped, and the building resumed the name Freemasons' Hall. Two of the three provinces whose Grand Master was entitled to the Hallstone Jewel were in war zones – Japan and Burma. All the jewels and representations of the 'Hallstone Angel' (i.e. the emblem of the appeal to fund the building) in other media depict a generic temple; only on the stained glass window above the shrine is the angel depicted holding the façade and tower of the actual peace memorial (Figure 5:5). The symbolic importance of the peace memorial at the time may be judged by the fact that King George V, although not himself a freemason, kept a model of the tower on his writing desk until his death.

Elements of war and remembrance are incorporated into key parts of the building's fabric. The architectural space of the main ceremonial rooms begins with an area termed 'the shrine', whose focal point is the casket for the scroll of remembrance. This takes the form of a biblical reed boat which incorporates Masonic and nationalistic imagery: at each upper corner kneels a figure representing one of the forces, defined here as Royal Navy, the Army, the Royal Marines and the Flying Services. Around the edge are three-dimensional figures of Moses with the tablets of the law, Joshua the warrior priest, King Solomon and St George; at each corner are the seraphim. In the centre, the Spirit of Man is held in the hand of God. The panels are filled with foliage of plants that grow in Flanders – a reference perhaps to the landscape of this particularly bloody battle-zone of the Great War. The main stained glass window of the shrine area shows pilgrims ascending to their rest, including soldiers from the war

Figure 5:5 Freemasons' Hall shrine. (© and courtesy Library and Museum of Freemasonry)

(Dennis and Saunders 2003: 64). The bronze cast doors of the main temple also feature two soldiers as emblems of the virtue of sacrifice among the otherwise classical iconography derived from biblical and legendary sources.

Conclusions

The relationship between the Craft and war, especially the First World War, is on-going, but the study of freemasonry in wartime is in its infancy. In particular, it would be valuable and insightful to compare the United Kingdom material described here with analogous Masonic materials from other participant countries of the war, where Masonic culture may be more open (as in the USA) or more closed (as in some Catholic European countries).

Masonic objects exist from the American and German forces of the war, but these are different in character. In the USA, for example, the Masons had not withdrawn from a visible presence in society and consequently objects such as table lamps could be made for home use. The German grand lodges created patriotic lodges, often incorporating genuine examples of the Iron Cross in their jewels. But the experience of freemasonry during the Second World War was to be very different. The German lodges were suppressed by the Nazis within months of Hitler taking power and their Masonic items destroyed or seized, an event which has distorted the surviving record of the material culture of European freemasonry.

As for Masonic trench art, it is unique in its limited range of forms, diversity of materials, and unity of purpose. The objects continue to function as they were designed to, and they represent a moral lesson for succeeding generations. Concerning the interface of these objects with masonry's 'peculiar system of morality – veiled in allegory and illustrated with symbols' – much remains to be written.

To date, little has been published on the subject of Masonic material culture related to war. *Craft and Conflict* (Dennis and Saunders 2003) is currently the main source, though *Serendipity* (Mendoza 1995) and *Behind the Wire* (Flynn 1998) also contain important information. Lodge histories, produced for a private circulation, are a further source, but available for reading only in a limited number of Masonic libraries.

We might ask what are the motivations behind this culture of perpetuating the memory and the material culture of war and its consequences. We can see an ambiguity in the perpetuation of the memory of warfare in a fraternal body committed to promoting peace and brotherhood. Did the Armament lodge, for example, take ongoing pride in the destruction that its wares had wrought?

In the first years of the twenty-first century, many of these lodges continue to function, often with a membership far removed in outlook and professional origin from that of the Founders. Units long disbanded live on as names and lodge property only. The increasingly elderly Masonic population finds itself in a generational time warp where the significance of these items, handed down over the years, has become fixed and immutable.

The material culture of freemasonry during the Great War and inter-war years embodies a period that was itself a turning point for the movement. The First World War, far from destroying the 'Indian summer' of Edwardian England for the Masons, actually stimulated it in the short term by creating a need for fraternity within masculine society. The complex emotions and resonances of the war thus became securely embedded, and, partly as a consequence, it is even harder for freemasonry to move on than for the population as a whole. The records of the organisation preserve facts rather than opinions, and it is therefore difficult to study the impact of this period anthropologically. But, in the mass of material culture that has survived, the underlying strength of feeling can still be seen and felt. Illustrated by symbols but evidenced by objects, Great War freemasonry tries to communicate its message.

References

Angell, G. (2003) *Freemasons Band of Brothers*. Privately published.

Bell, A.J. (2002) 'Letter to the editor'. *Freemasonry Today: The Independent Voice of Freemasonry.* 21 (Summer): 52. Bury St Edmunds: David Wilkinson.

Dennis, M.J.R. (2003) *Art of the Apocalypse: Exhibition Text and Review*. Privately published.

Dennis, M.J.R. and N.J. Saunders (2003) *Craft and Conflict: Masonic Trench Art and Military Memorabilia*. London: Savannah.

Ede, H. (1931) *Savage Messiah*. New York: The Literary Guild.

Flynn, K. (1998) *Behind the Wire: An Account of Masonic Activity by Masonic Prisoners of War*. Cardiff: Privately published.

Hamill, J. (1994) *The History of English Freemasonry*. Surrey: Lewis.

Lane, J. (1895) *Masonic Records 1717–1894*. London: Freemasons' Hall. Privately published.

Latchem, W.E. (1986) *The Phoenix Lodge No. 257 Bicentenary 1786–1986*. Privately published.

Mendoza, H. (1995) *Serendipity: Musings on the Precedence of Numbers and Names used by Lodges and Chapters*. Surrey: Lewis.

Saunders, N.J. (2001) *Trench Art: A Brief History and Guide, 1914–1939*. Barnsley: Pen & Sword

—— (2003) *Trench Art: Materialities and Memories of War*. Oxford: Berg.

—— (2004) 'Material culture and conflict: the Great War, 1914–2003'. In N.J. Saunders (ed.), *Matters of Conflict: Material Culture, Memory and the First World War*, pp. 5–25. Abingdon: Routledge.

Smyth, F.S. (1990) *The Master Mason at Arms: A Short Study of Freemasonry in the Forces*. Privately published.

Thorpe, J.T. (1900) *French Prisoners' Lodges*. Leicester: Privately published.

Tudor-Craig, Major Sir A. (1938) *A Catalogue of the Contents of the Museum at Freemasons' Hall in the Possession of the United Grand Lodge of England*. London: United Grand Lodge of England.

Wells, H.G. (1917) *War and the Future* (available at http://www.gutenberg.org/ebooks/1804; accessed 25 March 2009) London: Cassell.

6

SUBVERSIVE MATERIAL

African embodiments of modern war

Richard Waller

In the heart of Nairobi is a memorial to the African dead of the First World War (Figure 6:1). Three figures – a carrier (porter) and two *askaris* (soldiers) – stand on a plinth with an inscription that reads, in part, 'If you fight for your country, even if you die, your sons will remember your name'. The names of the dead are unrecorded, however, and their graves are unmarked. Similar memorials, with varying designs, but the same inscription, were erected in Mombasa and Dar-es-Salaam (Imperial War Graves Commission 1930–31). Together, these memorials express the conventional gratitude of the colonizers for the sacrifices of the colonized, and convey much the same sentiments about the war that were to be found in the metropole, albeit in a manner appropriate to the racial context (Winter 1995; King 1998).[1]

On the other side of East Africa, on the western shore of Lake Tanganyika, small clay images began to appear early in 1916, immediately after British ships had arrived and sunk their German opponents on the lake. The figures wore sun helmets and loincloths, and gripped binoculars in their tiny hands. Incisions on the chest and forearms imitated tattoos. Local people left offerings in front of the figures. The images represented *Bwana Chifunga Tumbo* (Mr Loincloth) or, more prosaically, Lieutenant-Commander Spicer-Simpson, the fearsomely tattooed and markedly eccentric commander of the British naval flotilla on Lake Tanganyika (Shankland 1968: 206–8). Evidently, the war resonated differently in these lakeshore communities than in European Nairobi, and it is with such local expressions of the meaning of military power and the memory of modern war that this chapter is concerned.

In comparison with the carnage of the Western Front, the African campaigns of the First World War were sideshows, for the Germans had not intended to make more than a token defence of their African colonies. One such show – the allied invasion of Togoland – was over in three weeks, and the conquests of German South-West Africa (Namibia) and Kamerun were completed by July 1915 and February 1916 respectively. Only in German East Africa (Tanganyika), as a result largely of the skill

Figure 6:1 War Memorial, Nairobi. From left to right: an African porter, a Kings African Rifles Askari, and an Arab rifleman. (Copyright G. Hodges)

and determination of the German commander, von Lettow-Vorbeck, and his troops, did a colonial campaign become a continuing drain on Allied resources. Here, hostilities were not concluded until some days after the Armistice of 11 November 1918: the German surrender came as a distant consequence of the collapse in Europe, not because the army had been beaten in East Africa. If anything, the Germans – considerably outnumbered, cut off from supply and reinforcements, and eventually forced to evacuate the colony and carry the war into neighbouring territories – had bested their enemies (Lucas 1924).

The numbers of combatants and casualties were consequently much higher here than elsewhere in Africa. By the end of the war, the Allies had been forced to put somewhere between 210,000 and 240,000 troops into the field against a German force which never exceeded 15,000 (Iliffe 1979: 243, 246). While the Germans relied throughout on the local *Schutztruppe* composed of Africans led by white NCOs and officers, regular British, Indian and Southern African units initially served in East

Africa together with locally recruited black and white troops. However, as whites succumbed to climate and disease, and the military value of Africans was recognized, the latter came to bear the brunt of the fighting. Some 13,000 troops and porters were brought in from Nigeria, the Gold Coast and Sierra Leone after the conclusion of the Kamerun campaign, and the local King's African Rifles (KAR) was rapidly expanded to reach a maximum strength of 22 battalions (30,000 men) in 1918 (Lucas 1924; Moyes-Bartlett 1956: 701). Both sides relied on human transport, which greatly added to the size of the military establishments. Official statistics are unreliable but suggest a total British recruitment of over 800,000 carriers. With the addition of front-line gun porters, medical personnel and casual labour, over a million non-combatants were drawn into the campaign. German needs were smaller, but they were employing 45,000 carriers in 1916 (Hodges 1986; Iliffe 1979: 249).

Exact casualties cannot be calculated from the records available, but they included at least 16,000 troops on both sides, about half of whom were African, and probably at least six times as many porters and other non-combatants, most of whom died of disease, malnutrition and exhaustion rather than from enemy fire: a total of over 100,000 dead or missing. Death rates varied. The KAR and the *Schutztruppe* lost 12–13 per cent, but the Carrier Corps rates were sometimes twice as high. Nearly one in four of those recruited in Kenya failed to return.[2] While these figures are in no way comparable to the vast mobilizations and losses in Europe, for the small-scale East African communities involved they were catastrophic enough to shape and sear the collective imagination. When the influenza pandemic swept through the region in 1918, some thought it was the wrath of God, angry because young men had allowed themselves to be taken away to fight and die in a foreign war; others believed that 'the blood of dead soldiers is killing us' (Huxley 1999: 277; Sachs 1957: 31–2; Page 2000: 171–2 and n. 51).

The campaigns in Africa were African wars fought largely by Africans. They were also the culmination of a much longer experience of modern warfare that had begun in the 1880s. In Africa, August 1914 did not put an end to a long Indian summer of civilization as it perhaps had in Europe; nor was the intensity of the subsequent fighting quite so unprecedented. Africans had seen and felt it before. Indeed, major rebellions in German East and South-West Africa had been put down quite recently; and with terrible severity. The Maji Maji Rebellion in southern Tanganyika (1905–7) cost the lives of a quarter of a million people, about one-third of the estimated population. The Herero War in South-West Africa (1904–7) was avowedly a war of extermination: perhaps 70 per cent of the Herero and 50 per cent of the Nama peoples failed to survive the rising and its aftermath (Iliffe 1979: 193–202; Drechsler 1980: 211–14).

We cannot know how many perished or had their lives disrupted in the decades of conquest, but we can have some sense of the military impact on particular small communities. In October 1894, the Hehe lost 250 men in one morning from the concentrated fire of 600 German *askaris* (Iliffe 1979: 112–13). Eleven years later, a British attack on the Gusii of western Kenya left 120 Gusii dead or wounded and, when the British-led columns returned in 1908, a further 240 became casualties in a community that numbered its households in hundreds not thousands. The more populous Nandi lost at least 1,700 people and 20,000 head of cattle in five confrontations with the British between 1895 and 1906 (Lonsdale 1989: 20). In French West Africa, the Songhay and Zerma areas of Southern Niger were devastated by an expeditionary column in 1899 and 'pacified' again between 1902 and 1906 (Fugelstad 1983: 55–71). Elsewhere, colonial forces had shelled forts and destroyed towns, hanged chiefs and exiled leaders, treated men like women and made the free work like slaves. Communities unlucky enough to be in the path of a military column saw their houses and granaries burnt and their livestock slaughtered or driven off. Although African auxiliaries had made up the bulk of government troops in many of these 'punitive expeditions', it was firepower and military discipline that made the greatest impact and that were appropriated as symbols of a strange and powerful modernity.

If the war in Africa did not draw the same imaginary line between past and present that it did in the West, it did nonetheless have a significant impact, adding to the repertoire of existing images, extending and sometimes changing their range of meaning, and adding new memories and points of reference. The war was different from what had gone before in two important respects: it demonstrated colonial power and presence to a wider audience, and it brought new experiences to those it engulfed and to some degree schooled in modernity. Colonial rule had to extend its reach and dig deeper, conscripting its subjects and their property into the war effort and often sending them 'to meet death far away' (Lunn 1999: ch. 5). A man taken from his family by the banks of the Niger might find his grave by the Rufigi or, for that matter, on the Marne or the Euphrates (Downes 1919: 44).[3] Between 1914 and 1918, many African communities confronted the totality of colonial rule for the first time. In French West Africa, though not elsewhere, conscription, *'la chasse a l'homme'*, evoked memories of the slave trade, and met with widespread resistance (Lunn 1999: 34, 39–50).[4]

For the civilian population, the dominant wartime experience was probably one of loss and privation. In Senegal, 'in every district you heard people crying' and in Bunyala, western Kenya, the immediate post-war famine was simply called *'Keya'* (KAR) (Lunn 1999: 41; Hodges 1986: 63). Combatants' memories were sharper but also more varied and ambivalent. Some, like Huxley's fictional character Reri, refused to speak of what they had done and seen. For them, service had been a horror made up in equal parts of fear, suffering and strangeness (Huxley 1999: 279–86). 'Once your companion died, you were gripped with fear for the rest of your time there', said one porter (Hodges 1986: 182). The living worried about leaving the dead in a strange land, and perhaps about their unquiet spirits. 'Somewhere in German East Africa', Bishop Willis came upon some porters reciting the Lord's Prayer, which they had learned from a convert back home.

> We are dying like flies [they said, in Willis's words] and none of us knows whether we shall ever again see our homes. On every side the door is closed and the only door open to us is the door of prayer to God.
>
> (Hodges 1986: 184)

In the war zone far from home, it was not difficult to imagine that other troops might be cannibals or that there were trees whose scent caused madness (Hodges 1986: 149–51).[5] Others, however, remembered the war differently: the taste of cigarettes and bully beef, the care of white nurses, encounters with new people and new things. For them, wartime service was a rite of passage, an entry into a different manhood, rather than a martyrdom. They were proud of what they had done and the respect they had earned. 'Our soldiers are exceedingly brave', sang the German *askaris* on parade before dispersing in 1918, in a song that made it clear that the African lion was stronger than its British counterpart (Ranger 1975: 53–4).

This self-confidence was reflected in European accounts. A British medical officer, whose opinions are otherwise unpleasantly racist, paid tribute to the discipline and endurance of African troops in East Africa and Kamerun and contrasted it with the poor performance of white troops in South-West Africa. Similar views appear in many other wartime memoirs. In some cases, appreciation arose out of shared battlefield experience, a particularly bounded and insulated field of relations where the norms of racial hierarchy could sometimes be temporarily transcended or even reversed (Dolbey 1918: xxiii–iv; von Lettow-Vorbeck 1957: 68, 178).[6]

Because of the nature of the campaigns, the terrain they were fought over and the identity of those who did most of the fighting, much of the familiar material context of the First World War is absent in Africa. These were not campaigns of permanent trench systems and massive bombardments. They involved minor engagements, often fought from ambush in dense bush, between small columns moving relatively fast over vast distances. The detritus of war was quickly swallowed up by the landscape as the armies moved on, and very little remains. Battlefields are not marked, and even gravesites are few: 38 registered by the Imperial War Graves Commission for the Tanganyika campaign and 23 for South-West Africa. They are almost exclusively European. Most of the dead were buried – or left – where they fell (Imperial War Graves Commission 1930–31; Fendall 1921: 185). If conventional 'sites of memory' are in short supply, so too are objects. Although some *askaris* and carriers did bring home souvenirs of their service, the obsession with Western Front memorabilia had no parallel here (Saunders 2004a: 13–18).

To find evidence of the impact of the war on material culture in Africa, we must look for its local expressions, and see it as part of a larger and longer interaction between colonizers and colonized in which appropriated military items, as symbols of both power and modernity, played an important mediating role, and acted as vehicles of emerging identities. We also need to see military images and objects as embedded in meditations about power and its manifestations that are part of the *longue durée* of African thought and memory. Indeed, the deeper context in which military symbolism had meaning predates the conquest period. African communities had used dance as a form of discourse long before they incorporated western drill movements, and items of clothing and weaponry had always been markers of identity and status.

Even though the horror and desolation of the Western Front had no parallel in Africa – French African troops who were sent there found it beyond anything they had experienced before (Lunn 1999: 28–35) – local images of European power, generated out of the brutalities of the conquest period, were equally surreal and graphic. When the Hauka spirits arrived in southern Niger in 1925, they came on the desert wind as the children of the thunder deity, Dongo, who, like the French colonial army, had the power to kill and burn without remorse. When the spirits manifest themselves by fusing with humans they take on the form of Europeans. Whatever their position as spirits in the complex Songhay otherworld, in the human world *Zeneral Malia*, the 'General of the Red Sea', and his entourage, have an authority and power derived in part from the fact that they are not merely 'like' Europeans but *are* Europeans in a different incarnation, and thus carry the same 'force' that animated colonial rule. As Stoller argues, Songhay spirit possession, emerging out of a 'fusion of the worlds', embodies collective historical memories of conquest and colonialism. The uniforms, military commands and ceremonial, whips and wooden guns of the Hauka are as much a part of the tangible memory of modern war as the monuments and cemeteries of Flanders (Stoller 1995, 1989; Fugelstad 1983: 113–14).

The infusion of apparently familiar symbols with new and different meanings, and their transfer into an alien cultural context, can be explored through Baule *'colon'* figures in Cote d'Ivoire (Ivory Coast). These small wooden figures were thought by Europeans to be whimsical representations of themselves, but the real point of reference was to the Baule otherworld, for the images were those of 'spirit spouses' who lived in a parallel world but married and interacted with their human partners (Ravenhill 1996). Although they may appear to mimic Europeans, their aesthetics are Baule and they represent the physical perfection and attributes of success that Baule desire in their spouses, and which can sometimes be conveyed by images of European-ness, as locally translated, much as the Hauka use of a 'European' idiom epitomises the kind of 'hardness' that Songhay respect (Stoller 1995: 101, 170–3).

The figures thus offer images of alternative Baule, not European, worlds. Many of them are military figures, and those produced in the years after the final conquest of the area by the French in 1911 offer a choice between different images of ideal Baule manhood, figured either as a traditional warrior or as his opponent, the *Tirailleur Senegalais* (or his white officer) (Weiskel 1990). This local understanding contrasts sharply with the European view – framed by different ideas of power relations – that the figures represent the colonizer as seen by the colonized, a cultural misreading similar to the assumption that the small clay figures by Lake Tanganyika were simply naive and worshipful representations of the colonial conqueror.

Hauka spirits and Baule figures, as examples of the appropriation of symbols of western modernity, raise two interesting questions: why was the symbolism so often military; and what particular aspects of the military were emphasized? Colonial states were conquest states first, and they retained the imprint of their origins. Niger, the home of the Hauka, was not transferred to civil rule until 1922. In German colonies, the military had precedence. Clifford, who shared the conventional Allied antipathy towards 'the Hun', saw German *askaris* as a cohesive and privileged military caste, above the law, and apart from the civilian population that they 'terrorized' (Lonsdale 1989; Fugelstad 1983: 80; Stoecker 1986: 203–6; Clifford 1920: 75–6).

Although there were alternatives on offer – missions, for example – Western modernity came to large parts of Africa with the tramp of marching feet and the shout of barked commands. Once established, colonial rule impressed itself on the landscape in an unmistakably military way. Camps were laid out with an alien precision, and, in German colonies especially, the most imposing public buildings outside the capital were military posts (Figure 6:2). The district administration in Moshi, below Mt Kilimanjaro, for example, was housed in a fort with an imposing double gateway, guarded by uniformed sentries, and with the Imperial Eagle embossed above it (Spear 1997: 78–9).

Yet, the omnipresence of the military in the early colonial period – accentuated during the First World War when conscription and requisitioning spread the impact of war over areas far beyond the actual theatres of operations – is only part of the answer. Although African images of modern warfare were often terrifying, they were far from universally negative. They were, in fact, accurate reflections of the Janus-faced nature of power in Africa: arbitrary and devastating, yet also protective (if not necessarily benevolent) and lucrative. The ambivalence of meaning in representations of power is evident in the Hauka spirits, who come to visit their mediums and to settle local disputes. It is also expressed in contrasting images of the *askari* on the East African war memorials that we began with. In Nairobi and Mombasa, the figures stand stiffly to attention as though on parade, martial but disciplined and obedient; in Dar-es-Salaam there is a single figure caught in the act of charging with bayonet thrust forward to kill (Figure 6:3).

Figure 6:2 Administrative Post, Tabora, German East Africa. (Copyright A. Calvert)

Figure 6:3
War Memorial ('Askari Monument'), Dar-es-Salaam. (Courtesy and copyright Utalii Travel and Safaris Ltd)

There was much that was positive about the military in African eyes. For East Africans who joined up, military service – *kazi ya bunduki* (the 'work of the gun') – was considerably more prestigious and better paid (with the addition of a uniform, housing and rations) than what was on offer elsewhere. In 1910, *askaris* in the KAR were getting 38 East African shillings a month, four or five times more than an unskilled labourer and, although military wages dropped during the war, the differential remained (Parsons 1999: 62, 64).[7] Their fellows in the *Schutztruppe* fared equally well, and, in addition, they acquired considerable local authority, since, unlike their British counterparts, German *askaris* often operated on detachment carrying out police duties (Mann 2002: 229–41; Clifford 1920: 75–6).

A senior African NCO like *Effendi* Plantan was a very powerful figure, and an attractive role model to many (Buruku 1973: 96–9). The prestige accruing to military service and its importance as a career open to ordinary Africans helps to explain two otherwise apparently contradictory aspects of the war in East Africa. Even though the *Schutztruppe* was in continuous retreat from early 1916, desertions were relatively few. Over 4000 Africans were still present at the final surrender in 1918 (von Lettow-Vorbeck 1957: 295–6).[8] Yet, captured *askaris* re-enlisted with their enemies – one new KAR battalion was initially formed from ex-POWs – for they were following the trade not the flag (Moyes-Bartlett 1956: 354; Page 2000: 32–3).[9]

The military was also associated with three aspects of authority and identity that were the focus of negotiation and debate: modernity, masculinity and age. By virtue of their membership of a modern army, *askaris* were closer than most to the strange repositories of European domination and difference: they were sometimes transported by rail or ship; they learned to be familiar with modern weapons; they wore a distinctive uniform from puttees to pillbox hats; and they marched to the sound of a band.

Clothing and music/dance in particular had powerful resonances. Band music and uniforms had already appeared in pre-war African parades in Mombasa. The KAR used its bands and their smart uniforms as recruiting tools in Nyasaland. 'The beauty of the parading band would blind us to the real issues of war', recalled Corporal Lipemba (Ranger 1975: 14, 34; Page 2000: 33–5). Carriers wanted uniforms, and the frontline gun porters were delighted to get them (Hodges 1986: 152).[10] Even the way *askaris* lived was conspicuously different: in 'lines' and under time-discipline, and governed by what must have seemed to onlookers as a mysterious set of rituals and observances associated with European power.

The wars of conquest and resistance were young men's wars, even if they were directed by elders, and the same was true of the First World War. War was an arena in which the young could assert their own responsibility and independent masculinity, and escape from the control of their seniors at home. They would return – if they returned at all – with status and material rewards that would enable them to speak back to age, and to outbid their coevals who had stayed at home. Kamba *askaris* sang a song mocking the elders who had sent them to die: 'That I will not do, but I will go back home to enjoy the company of beautiful women' (ibid.: 150).

Above all, perhaps, the assumption of military discipline and the acquisition of an arcane body of knowledge contradicted elders' complaints that the young were ignorant of the world, had no sense of propriety and social purpose, and must, therefore, remain subordinate. Moreover, at a time when familiar notions of masculinity were in flux, with the roles of elder, father and warrior being undermined or marginalized, the military offered an alternative model of manhood: powerful, disciplined and distinctive (Lindsay and Miescher 2003: Introduction; Parsons 1999: 149–50).

For those like the members of *beni* dance troupes, who wished to assert an aggressive modernity and were searching for new models of masculinity and for a way of negotiating the transitions and constraints of youth, the military offered both an organizational model and a rich field of symbols. *Beni* with its quasi-military structure provided young men with a social network under patrons of their own choosing, many of whom were in fact ex-soldiers, and with the trappings of a particularly potent form of modernity, inaccessible to their elders and attractive to potential spouses.

Beni probably had its origins in the competitive dance troupes of the towns of the East African coast (Ranger 1975: chs 1–2; Iliffe 1979: 248–9). In the 1900s, it spread, and took on its characteristic military gloss and divisions – *Marini* and *Arinoti* in Tanganyika – each with an elaborate hierarchy of office-holders with assumed military rank.[11] The spread of *beni* was stimulated first by the war, and then by labour migration. Recruits learned the dance in military depots and practised it in the field, both for entertainment and as an expression of solidarity. After the war, demobilized *askaris* took the dance home with them, and it spread further down the migration routes into central Africa (Ranger 1975; Mitchell 1956). Rival *beni* societies organized elaborate parades with flags and brass bands, and sometimes also with scale models of warships, a particularly potent symbol of military power on the coast.[12] They also held manoeuvres, apparently based on the pre-war German war games in which some of their members had participated. Their displays emphasized discipline, drill, precision dancing and immaculate military uniforms and comportment.

Beni might seem a mere pantomime of colonialism, a possibly satirical imitation of the dominant structures of power, yet, as Ranger points out, although both parody and play were present, the performances had a deeper and very different significance for those who participated. Dance had long been a means of incorporating the new, of fashioning identities and asserting or challenging status hierarchies, and of dramatizing conflict (Hartwig 1969; Glassman 1995). In apparently mimicking the military, *beni* dancers were drawing on a new range of expressive acts and symbols and making them their own.

The emphasis in *beni* on the detail of dress and drill brings us to our second question. Africans were often less interested in appropriating the modern technologies of death than in other aspects of the military world. Baule made wooden replicas of French guns and ammunition pouches, but they also carved Marine caps and bugles (Weiskel 1990). The act of appropriation involves elements of critique, dialogue and even confrontation. Uniforms, which speak a language of their own and had a particular social and military significance in Europe, were particularly good vehicles for making claims and statements (Joseph, 1986).[13]

A striking example comes from the Kingdom of Bamum in western Kamerun, appropriately expressed through the new medium of photography (Geary 1988). Bamum had come under German suzerainty in 1902, and its ruler, Njoya, became an ally of the Kaiser. The German government presented him with a picture of the Kaiser in military uniform and a set of cuirassier uniforms with brass breastplates and helmets for his royal guard. The king had himself photographed accepting the portrait accompanied by his guard in their new uniforms. In 1908, he went further and commissioned a photograph of himself and companions wearing locally made versions of German hussar uniforms (Figure 6:4). The pose adopted in front of the camera recalls that of the German Crown Prince, himself Colonel-in-Chief of a Hussar regiment, in prints and postcards (Geary 1988: 60).[14]

The photographs reveal the dialogue clearly. If uniforms and military poses were the idiom of royal exchanges in this new world, then Njoya was the equal of Wilhelm. Njoya may also have been aware of the disruptive power of images of black bodies in 'white' uniforms. After 1909, however, Njoya no longer appeared in German uniform. He had been warned to stop 'playing soldiers', and his territorial ambitions had been dashed. The king now adopted the Hausa dress of the Islamic states to the north-east, thus signalling photographically his shift in political orientation.

Figure 6:4 King Njoya (left) with his bodyguard in locally made German Hussar uniforms. (Photography by Rudolf Oldenburg, *c.*1980, courtesy and copyright Museum fur Volkerkunde, Hamburg)

The connection between identity, military symbolism and memory can be pursued by looking at the *ortruppe* movement among the Herero in Namibia (Werner 1990; Kruger and Henrichsen 1998). Like *beni* dancers, *ortruppe* units, sometimes condescendingly referred to as 'Truppenspieler', wore uniforms, adopted German military ranks and marched in formation. Unlike *beni*, however, the movement was not competitive. It was internally divided into three units or 'flags' – red, green and white – reflecting differing historical identities among the Herero.[15] Each had an active women's 'wing' whose members wore 'traditional' Herero dress – itself a newly elaborated version of the 'mission' dress of the late nineteenth century – in the colours of the 'flag', thus embodying both communal memory and identity (Hendrickson 1996). Unit members gathered for annual rituals of commemoration, the first of which was for the burial of the former Paramount Chief in 1923 at Okahandja, a site of particular significance for Herero (Hartmann *et al.* 1998: 125–31). Moreover, the *ortruppen* had both a millenarian and irredentist tinge absent from *beni*, and a far more explicit connection with the historical memory of defeat and dispossession, although some ex-German *askaris* may have joined *beni* in order symbolically to reverse their loss of status after 1918 (Ranger 1975: 56–8).[16]

While *beni* dancers used appropriated colonial military symbols to negotiate modernity and build social networks, *ortruppen* used the military structures of the former enemy both to regain a Herero identity that had been partly dissolved by the loss of land and the destruction of the community in the 1900s, and to assert a degree of autonomy from colonial rule. Units issued identification documents and travel passes to their members, not in 'imitation' of colonial practice but as a way of creating a parallel or alternative world; and, like King Njoya's Hussars, their use of uniforms recognized the reality of colonial power yet subtly challenged its meaning (Gewald 1999: 265–6).

The *ortruppe* were above all engaged in recovering, creating and enacting a collective historical memory, both through uniforms and performances that recalled the experience of war with the Germans and through the organization of rituals of commemoration that had a deeper significance for the community (Connerton 1989). The attendance of men in 'German' uniforms at the gravesites of pre-colonial Herero chiefs suggests something of the complex relationship between the different levels of memory and meaning involved. The experience of war can shape historical consciousness and provide a powerful means to express and enact it collectively through the use of sites, practices and artefacts. In this respect, *ortruppe* is perhaps closer in spirit to the mourners of the Western Front and to the Hauka than to *beni*.

Colonial authorities were deeply suspicious of *ortruppe* and *beni* and remained so long after the war, but they found it difficult to explain why they found them subversive. A partial explanation lies in their military connotations, in the capability for wide organization and cohesion amongst subject peoples that the movements revealed, and in a fear that Europeans were being mocked by imitation.

Immediately after the war, there might have been some grounds for unease. The British were aware of Herero land grievances and that their replacement of German rule in Tanganyika was resented in some quarters. Yet *beni* dancers did not carry arms, and troupes in Tanganyika willingly substituted British flags and music for German to suit the new regime. The *ortruppe* units may have seen themselves as the reincarnation of a Herero national army, but it did not confront the British openly. The 'occupation' of Okahandja in 1923 was intentionally symbolic (Ranger 1975: 56; Kruger and Henrichsen 1998: 158). In fact, Europeans were not the main 'target', despite the outward display of apparent European-ness, for these movements were intensely self-referential. Colonialism was part of their context, but never the whole.

Yet, African representations of war *were* subversive, in three contexts. Colonial rule rested on its creation and control of disciplined force, as exemplified by the *askari* and his officer. Indeed, the staged passage from 'savage' to 'soldier', in which African men were refashioned and subordinated through uniforms and drill, sometimes stood as a metonym for the colonial project.[17] African appropriation of European symbols denied the colonizer's sole ability to control access to and determine the meaning of socially significant items. Members of *beni* dance troupes or *ortruppe* units used military dress and ritual to fashion themselves as autonomous actors, not as colonial subordinates. As Cooper has put it, the edifice of colonialism could be 'taken apart brick by brick and parts of it used to shape quite different cultural visions' (Cooper 1994: 1527).

On a different plane altogether, *Zeneral Malia*, *Bwana Chifunga Tumbo* and perhaps '*colon*' figures and Njoya's Hussars were disturbing because they confronted Europeans with a reflection of themselves that was simultaneously familiar and alien.[18] Images and symbols had been emptied of their conventional meanings and infused with new ones; familiar 'texts' were being 'read' by different audiences in alien contexts (Bhabha 1986). It was a matter of power. The signs of modern warfare, which Europeans had confidently believed was 'theirs', now pointed to the world of the Other. If native spirits could 'become' Europeans and Europeans 'become' spirits, and if African 'admirals' could direct parades in which the symbols of colonial power were reduced to models dragged through the streets, where lay the assurance of white superiority and difference?

The third context brings us back to memory and materiality, for public performances embodied and enacted communal memories of war and violence and derived power from them. So too did the Remembrance parades that marched past the Cenotaph. Yet these were part of an officially sanctioned memorialization in which African enactments had no place. Indeed, they challenged that memorialization, both in their performance of alternative public memories that called into question the meaning, significance and 'ownership' of war, and in their creation of another materiality through a double process of displacement and sedimentation centred on the bodies and objects involved. As they are transferred, appropriated or copied, objects carry with them the imprint of previous ownership, use and significance. Over time, the memories that inhere in them become layered, interactive and ambiguous; the original memories are displaced, but not entirely erased, and their traces enhance the expository power of what is superimposed on them (Appadurai 1986; Saunders 2004b). In the African context, this raises the troubling question of whose memories were being embodied and for what purposes – indeed, whose war and what war?

African embodiments offer two perspectives from the periphery on the Great War. The first points up, but from a different angle, the slipperiness, ambiguity and contestation of material memories (Saunders 2004b). The second addresses the totalizing and Eurocentric bias inherent in the notion of 'world war'. Public discourse in Europe had little to say about the war in the colonies, except as an adjunct or a celebration of empire (Lucas 1924). Colonial discourse followed a similar line, approving memorials but worrying whether Africans might have learnt the 'wrong' lessons from the experience of being simultaneously exploited and shown the vulnerability of their exploiters (Page 2000; Hodges 1986). Since then, the frame of reference has hardly changed. Yet African responses do not appear to lie within the same experiential field. Their war had been longer and only tangentially connected to Europe, and its meanings were configured differently. There were perhaps many 'world wars', just as there were many memories, voices and materialities. If we are to look for commonalities, we must view them through the lens of difference, and seek them across a very broad range of historical and cultural specificities.

Acknowledgements

I wish to thank the editors for their invitations first to the initial conference and then to contribute to this volume; Paul Stoller who started me thinking; and my student assistant, Richard Swanson.

Notes

1 White casualties were buried and commemorated separately. Memorials in West Africa to the Gold Coast and Nigeria Regiments did record African names.

2 Figures from Iliffe 1979: 246; Hodges 1986: 110–11 and Appendix I; Moyes-Bartlett 1956: 701. German post-war estimates are considerably higher, at 350,000 carriers on both sides and an additional 300,000 civilians dead from hunger and disease (Stoecker 1986: 279).

3 170,000 French West African troops were recruited for the Western Front and 30,000 (18 per cent) were killed in action (Echenberg 1991: 46). A small British contingent from West Africa served with river transport in Mesopotamia late in the war, and there were plans to send more to Palestine (Lucas 1924: 17–18, 42).

4 There was alarm among the watchers when the transports taking the Gold Coast Regiment to East Africa steered out into the Atlantic instead of hugging the coast (Clifford 1920: 5).

5 Such beliefs may have functioned similarly to the 'rumours' of the Western Front in making the meaningless comprehensible (Fussell 1977: 115–25).

6 Sometimes, both the intimacies of the battlefield and the perception of racial hierarchy persisted after death. Local Tabwa resent the fact that the grave of a white officer lies separate from those of his *askaris*, the iron chains surrounding it preventing his spirit from joining those of the men he had once led (Roberts 1987: 210).

7 High wage levels also reflected difficulties in securing sufficient recruits.

8 Their numbers included 1200 *askaris*, 1500 carriers and 1700 other followers (Iliffe 1979: 245).

9 Traffic was two-way. When the Nyasaland battalion of the KAR was disbanded in 1911, some of its *askaris* crossed the border to join the *Schutztruppe* (Moyes-Bartlett 1956: 153, 265).

10 Uniform was crucial to status in the ranks. Carriers had to be specifically forbidden to wear (high status) 'KAR' cap badges.

11 *Marini* assumed a higher status, associated with the urbanity of the coast, in opposition to *Arinoti* who were associated with 'inland'. Askaris joined *Marini* and carriers *Arinoti*. In Tanganyika, ranks were taken from the German hierarchy, from 'Kaiser', 'Bismarck' and 'Hindenburg' downwards.

12 Warships, together with other Western military images, also appear as symbols of power and competitiveness on the flags of rival Fante town militias in Ghana (Adler and Barnard 1992).

13 For clothing, identity and conflict in colonial Africa, see e.g. Prein 1994; Allman 2004, esp. chapters by Fair and Hay.

14 Thanks to Paul Cornish for confirming this identification.

15 Flags, as signs of identity and allegiance, had been first adopted by Herero groups in the 1860s (Hendrickson 1994: 228–36; see also Adler and Barnard 1992). Photographs of the 1929 'Herero Day' in Omaruru show 'White Flag' members with a flag in the German Imperial colours black/white/red (Hartmann *et al.* 1998: 49).

16 Ironically, similar rituals of commemoration and identity were performed by the German-speaking community after the War (Hartmann *et al.* 1998: 123).

17 See e.g. the description of the Tattoo at the 1937 Coronation celebrations in Kampala (Bates 1972: 102–3). Thanks to John Lonsdale for the reference.

18 For a similar confrontation with images of 'Self' as 'Other', see Taussig 1993: 3–8, 236–9.

References

Adler, P. and N. Barnard (1992) *Asafo*. London: Thames & Hudson.

Allman, J. (ed.) (2004) *Fashioning Africa: Power and the Politics of Dress*. Bloomington: Indiana University Press.

Appadurai, A. (ed.) (1986) *The Social Life of Things*. Cambridge: Cambridge University Press.

Bates, D. (1972) *A Gust of Plumes*. London: Hodder & Stoughton.

Bhabha, H. (1986) '"Signs taken for wonders": questions of ambivalence and authority under a tree outside Delhi, 1817'. In H.L. Gates (ed.) *'Race', Writing and Difference*, pp. 163–84. Chicago: Chicago University Press.

Buruku, D.S. (1973) 'The townsman: Kleist Sykes'. In J. Iliffe (ed.) *Modern Tanzanians*, pp. 95–114. Nairobi: East Africa Publishing House.

Clifford, H. (1920) *The Gold Coast Regiment in the East African Campaign*. London: John Murray.

Connerton, P. (1989) *How Societies Remember*. Cambridge: Cambridge University Press.

Cooper, F. (1994) 'Conflict and connection: rethinking African colonial history'. *American Historical Review* 99 (5): 1516–45.

Dolbey, R.V. (1918) *Sketches of the East African Campaign*. London: John Murray.

Downes, W.D. (1919) *With the Nigerians in German East Africa*. London: Methuen.

Drechsler, H. (1980) *Let Us Die Fighting*. London: Zed Press.

Echenberg, M. (1991) *Colonial Conscripts*. Portsmouth NH: Heinemann.

Fendall, C.P. (1921) *The East African Force*. London: Witherby.

Fugelstad, F. (1983) *A History of Niger, 1850–1960*. Cambridge: Cambridge University Press.

Fussell, P. (1977) *The Great War and Modern Memory*. New York: Oxford University Press.

Geary, C.M. (1988) *Images From Bamum*. Washington DC: Smithsonian Institution Press.

Gewald, J.-B. (1999) *Herero Heroes*. Oxford: James Currey.

Glassman, J. (1995) *Feasts and Riot*. Portsmouth NH: Heinemann.

Hartmann, W., J. Silvester and P. Hayes (eds) (1998) *The Colonizing Camera*. Cape Town: University of Cape Town Press.

Hartwig, G.W. (1969) 'The historical and social role of Kerebe music'. *Tanganyika Notes & Records* 70: 41–56.

Hendrickson, H. (1996) 'Bodies and flags: the representations of Herero identity in colonial Namibia'. In H. Hendrickson (ed.) *Clothing and Difference*, pp. 213–44. Durham: Duke University Press.

Hodges, G. (1986) *The Carrier Corps: Military Labour in the East African Campaign, 1914–1918*. Westport CT: Greenwood Press.

Huxley, E. (1999) *Red Strangers* (new edn). London: Penguin.

Iliffe, J. (1979) *A Modern History of Tanganyika*. Cambridge: Cambridge University Press.

Imperial War Graves Commission (1930–31) *The War Memorials of the British Empire*, vol.42, London.

Joseph, N. (1986) *Uniforms and Nonuniforms: Communication Through Clothing*. Westport CT: Greenwood Press.

King, A. (1998) *Memorials of the Great War in Britain*. Oxford: Berg.

Kruger, D. and D. Henrichsen (1998) 'We have been captive long enough. We want to be free'. In P. Hayes, J. Silvester, M. Wallace and W. Hartmann (eds) *Namibia Under South African Rule*, pp. 149–74. Oxford: James Currey.

Lettow-Vorbeck, P. von (1957) *East African Campaigns* (new edn). New York: Robert Speller.

Lindsay, L. and S. Miescher (eds) (2003) *Men and Masculinities in Modern Africa*. Portsmouth NH: Heinemann.

Lonsdale, J. (1989) 'The conquest state, 1895–1904'. In W. Ochieng (ed.) *A Modern History of Kenya, 1895–1980*, pp. 6–34. Nairobi: Evans Bros.

Lucas, C. (ed.) (1924) *The Empire at War*, vol. 4. Oxford: Oxford University Press.

Lunn, J. (1999) *Memoirs of the Maelstrom*. Portsmouth NH: Heinemann.

Mann, E.J. (2002) *Mikono ya Damu: 'Hands of Blood'*. Frankfurt: Peter Lang.

Mitchell, J.C. (1956) *The Kalela Dance*. Rhodes-Livingstone Papers, 27. Manchester: Manchester University Press.

Moyes-Bartlett, H. (1956) *The King's African Rifles*. Aldershot: Gale & Polden.

Page, M. (2000) *The Chiwaya War: Malawians and the First World War*. Boulder CO: Westview.

Prein, P. (1994) 'Guns and top hats: African resistance in German South West Africa, 1907–1915'. *Journal of Southern African Studies*, 20 (1): 99–121.

Ranger, T.O. (1975) *Dance and Society in Eastern Africa*. London: Heinemann.

Ravenhill, P. (1996) *Dreams and Reverie*. Washington DC: Smithsonian Institution Press.

Roberts, A. (1987) 'Insidious conquests: wartime politics along the southwestern shore of Lake Tanganyika'. In M. Page (ed.) *Africa and the First World War*, pp. 186–213. London: Macmillan.

Sachs, W. (1957) *Black Anger*. New York: Grove Press.

Saunders, N.J. (2004a) 'Material culture and conflict: the Great War 1914–2003'. In N.J. Saunders (ed.) *Matters of Conflict: Material Culture, Memory and the First World War*, pp. 5–25. Abingdon: Routledge.

—— (ed.) (2004b) *Matters of Conflict: Material Culture, Memory and the First World War*. Abingdon: Routledge.

Shankland, P. (1968) *The Phantom Flotilla*. London: Collins.

Spear, T. (1997) *Mountain Farmers*. Oxford: James Currey.

Stoecker, H. (ed.) (1986) *German Imperialism in Africa*. London: Hurst.

Stoller, P. (1989) *Fusion of the Worlds*. Chicago: University of Chicago Press.

—— (1995) *Embodying Colonial Memories*. New York: Routledge.

Taussig, M. (1993) *Mimesis and Alterity*. New York: Routledge.

Weiskel, T. (1990) 'Would that wood could talk: facts and artefacts in African art history'. Paper presented at 'The European as Other' workshop, Boston University.

Werner, W. (1990) '"Playing soldiers": the *Truppenspieler* movement among the Herero of Namibia, 1915 to c.1945'. *Journal of Southern African Studies*, 16 (3): 476–502.

Winter, J. (1995) *Sites of Memory, Sites of Mourning: The Great War in European Cultural History*. Cambridge: Cambridge University Press.

7

MEDALS, MEMORY AND MEANING

Symbolism and cultural significance of Great War medals

Matthew Richardson

It can be argued that British campaign medals of the First World War represent one of the clearest examples of what the anthropologist Michael Thompson (1979) has called 'rubbish theory'. This states that an everyday, commonplace item may well acquire cultural status via the rarity accorded to it by the passage of time. Thompson distinguished between three categories of objects: transients, rubbish and durables, and argues that some transients pass through the status of rubbish before becoming durables.

The study of the material culture of the First World War in this way is a new endeavour, but Thompson's model has been applied in the past to the relics of battle (Liddle and Richardson 1997). Here, I will examine how the theory can be applied to First World War campaign medals, in order to show that these objects, albeit struck for a functional purpose, have eventually acquired social and symbolic meaning, and to chart the way in which their changing status has mirrored shifting public perceptions of the war (see Miller 1994).

A world of medals

I begin by examining the differences between gallantry medals and campaign medals, and by documenting attitudes towards the latter prior to the First World War. Gallantry medals are awarded, as their name suggests, for acts of bravery on the battlefield. Chief among these is the Victoria Cross, followed by the Distinguished Conduct Medal and the Military Medal. Gallantry awards have probably always had a following among collectors and, in the late Victorian period and early 1900s, a collector might have paid £100 for a Victoria Cross. In contrast, campaign medals were awarded simply for 'being there', and do not seem to have exhibited any interest for collectors at this time. The First World War was to mark a sea change in what campaign medals stood for. In other words, the relationship between physical and mental worlds (Miller 1987: 99), as mediated by medals, was transformed by the world's first global industrialized conflict.

Campaign medals were issued for most of the colonial actions of the Victorian period, up to and including the Second Boer War (1899–1902). These wars were small, and the numbers of British soldiers involved relatively few. The campaign medals issued tended to be ornate, with a high silver content, and with the name of the recipient often hand-engraved on the rim. The British Government's War Office could afford the time and expense involved because so few medals were required.

However, when the First World War ended, several previously unencountered practical problems arose. First, how were the authorities to assess who was entitled to which medal? It took well into the early 1920s to establish this. In addition, how were recipients' details to be established and recorded upon some six million sets of medals? The Army Medal Office opted for a simplified system of naming, which, for a private soldier, included number, name and regiment, and, for an officer, simply rank and name. Nevertheless, even this was an admirable effort when compared with those who issued a similar number of medals a generation later during the Second World War, who simply balked at the task and issued the medals unnamed, thereby alienating the object from the individual and his participation in and experience of the life-changing events of that second global conflict.

Nevertheless, even at an early stage, the sheer number of medals that were liable to be issued for the Great War threatened to devalue them, particularly in the eyes of the old Regular army. A fascinating exchange of letters took place in 1917 between the War Office, the Admiralty and King George V over the award of the '1914 Star' (widely known as the 'Mons Star'). This campaign medal was intended to recognize the part played by those who had held the Germans at bay in the critical months of autumn 1914. The King it seems was keen for the award to be open to all British army, Indian army and Royal Naval personnel who served on land in Europe throughout 1914. However, there were those – not least in the Royal Navy – who wanted the award confined to members of the army who had served in France and Belgium in the autumn of that year. They felt that any extension to members of the Navy – for the actions at Antwerp – would devalue the award. Writing to Sir Reginald Brade at the War Office on 23 September 1917, Admiral Everett asked for clarification of the proposed entitlement:

> For instance, is it intended that the Royal Naval Division sent as a forlorn hope to relieve the situation at Antwerp are to share the same medal distinction as those of the old army; also is it intended that those who took part in no fighting, but remained say at a French sea-base during those critical times are to be similarly honoured? I know that the problem is full of difficulties, of which the greatest is to know where to draw the line, and because it is not possible to define the limits, it may be better, in order to prevent discontent and jealousy, to be safely inclusive rather than critically

exclusive. On the other hand, I presume that it is for the honour of the old Army which bore England's sacrifice of those early days that this medal is struck, and the inclusion of those amateurs who, disguised as sailors, did their best during a few days to retrieve an impossible situation, may easily detract from the dignity of the decoration in the eyes of the old Army's posterity.

(Fevyer and Wilson 1993: 227)

In a similar vein, the Australian army pressed for an exclusive 'Gallipoli Star' to commemorate the service of the Australian and New Zealand forces (ANZACs) on the Gallipoli peninsula. King George V was apparently favourably disposed to this award, and a member of the Australian Department of Defence, Mr R.K. Peacock of Melbourne, drew up a design for an eight-pointed bronze star. Each point of the star represented a state or territory of the Commonwealth of Australia, plus New Zealand. On the face of the star was a silver circle, with a crown at the centre, surrounded by the words 'GALLIPOLI 1914–15' (Figure 7:1). Several thousand yards of ribbon were also produced, featuring the gold of the Australian wattle and the silver of the New Zealand fern, alongside red and blue stripes. However, objections were raised in West-minster and in the British press, as the award was not open to British and other imperial troops who had served there, and the scheme was dropped. Yet, for well over seventy years, the British Government's decision that the '1914–15 Star' served to commemorate *all* campaigns of that year has been felt in the anti-podes to be unfair. One commentator wrote:

> There is nothing about the '1914–15 Star' that especially appeals to Australians, neither is there anything on the British War Medal to indicate an 'Anzac' who served on the Peninsula, as no battle clasps were ever sanctioned.
>
> ('Aussie' 1972: 10)

Figure 7:1
'The Gallipoli Star'. This award, which was intended to denote service with Australian and New Zealand forces at Gallipoli, fell foul of the Westminster Parliament and was never issued.
(© and courtesy of Bryn Dolan)

By its widespread applicability, the '1914–15 Star' was also seen as devalued, and several unofficial 'Gallipoli Stars' were produced and sold in Australia in response to this feeling.[1]

With so many medals to be issued, further concessions became necessary. Traditionally, British campaign medals were issued with bars denoting the actions in which the wearer had participated. The Second Boer War, lasting four years and covering four states of South Africa, is an illustrative example. It was marked by the issue of the Queen's South Africa Medal, one of the most complex campaign medals ever instituted (Joslin *et al.* 1988: 187–203). The various actions of the war had produced an unprecedented twenty-six bars, with nine being the maximum awarded to any individual. However, the bars served closely to delineate exactly who had done what in the war. They would show if the wearer of the medal had been one of the gallant defenders of Ladysmith (3 November 1899 to 28 February 1900), or if he had been in the Relief Force battling to reach the town. More importantly, it would show if the soldier had simply arrived just as the war was ending! The battle bars, awarded for various actions in the war, earned the recipient most respect, with the so-called 'state bars' and 'date bars' simply denoting service in one of the states or during a particular year. Frank Richards, a Regular soldier at the time, and a noted authority on the views and attitudes of the British Tommy, has the following humorous aside concerning his own regiment, the Royal Welsh Fusiliers.

> Two [reinforcement] drafts had been sent; the first arrived in Capetown about two months before peace was proclaimed. As they had travelled through three different colonies to reach the battalion, which was now in blockhouses . . . they were awarded a medal and three colony bars. The second and last draft to Africa were always known as the cease-fire draft; they were still a week's sail from Capetown when peace was proclaimed. If they had arrived at Capetown only twenty-four hours before peace was proclaimed, they would have been entitled to a medal and perhaps one colony-bar. Some men of this draft used to complain that they had been cheated out of their medals; they seemed to think that they had been largely responsible for bringing the war to a close. No doubt the Boer leaders had the wind up as soon as they knew this draft was on its way and quickly made up their minds to sue for peace.
>
> (Richards 1936: 80)

Sorting out the entitlement of 178,000 recipients was an administrative nightmare in the two years that followed the cease-fire in 1902. One would perhaps have thought that the British military establishment should have learned its lesson. Nevertheless, at the close of the Great War, committees were formed with the purpose of assessing which bars should be issued to accompany the British War Medal for 1914–19. The only list produced was that covering naval actions, and the sheer complexity of this alone led to the whole idea being abandoned on the grounds of cost, and medals were eventually issued without bars (Figure 7:2). This meant that it was now impossible

Figure 7:2 The badges and medals of this Royal Navy Petty Officer tell the observer a great deal about him. His rank and length of service are indicated by the crossed anchors and stripes on the left sleeve, whilst his trade or branch of service are on the right. However, although a list was drawn up, the British War Medal (second from left) was issued without bars, thus giving no clue as to the actions in which he had served. (© author)

(or at least extremely difficult) to distinguish at first glance between those who had seen action and those who had not. This in turn led to much discontent among ex-servicemen, as Richards again describes:

It is Armistice Day to-day and the ex-Service men are on parade wearing their War medals. The men who served at the Bases and a hundred miles behind the front line are wearing their medals more proudly than the men who served in the firing line. There is no distinction between the War medals. In former wars, for each engagement a man took part in he was awarded a bar, and a pukka old soldier would be very nearly ashamed to wear a war medal that did not have a bar attached. They were known as bare-arsed medals. The thought has often struck me during these parades how vain we all are, and how much preferable the old Red Indians were. In their belts they wore the scalps of their enemies that they had slain in action, as proof of their soldiering: but we just wear medals, and there are some on parade to-day wearing war-medals on their breasts as if to say that they have been in action – but the only action they were ever in was with some of the charming damsels in the Red Lamps behind the Front and down at the Bases where they served. The Red Indians were vain but they were honest.

(Richards 1933: 323)

The 'social life' of Great War medals

In the years that followed the First World War, campaign medals often acted as a barometer for the feelings and attitudes of the men to whom they had been awarded. These small metal objects embodied and represented the social worlds of their wearers. In the case of medals issued to men who had been killed, their families sometimes went to enormous lengths to have them mounted in ornate frames, often hung in pride of place in the front room, a tangible symbol of pride in the sacrifice of one who did not return (Figure 7:3). As for the medals of survivors, in some cases they were polished and worn proudly, but in a good many others they languished forgotten in a drawer, still in the boxes and registered envelopes in which they had arrived. They were put to the back of the mind along with the memories of a war that many ex-servicemen wished to forget.

The evidence indicates that the purpose of medals was closely defined by the ex-servicemen themselves. One former soldier, after a period of unemployment during the 1920s, wore his medals in order to gain sympathy while hawking goods on a market. After just one day he returned home ashamed at having, as he put it, debased himself, and vowed never to use his medals for this purpose again (Richardson 2000: 272). For others, the wearing of medals was an important part of being accepted by their peer group – even to the extent of wearing medals to which they had no entitlement, thereby using the object to enter a social world from which they otherwise would have been excluded (Figure 7:4). Many regimental associations have stories of men who turn up wearing all the correct medals, but no one knows them and no one served in action with them. It is tacitly and rather sadly acknowledged that these men were fantasists or Walter Mitty characters.[2]

Other reasons are more complex. Several years ago an old Australian soldier at the Menin Gate Memorial at Ypres in Belgium was seen wearing a '1914–15 Star' trio (i.e. Star, British War Medal and Victory Medal – 'Pip, Squeak and Wilfred' in old soldier's parlance). An acquaintance of mine asked him about Gallipoli, and in which unit he had served. It emerged that the man's battalion had served only in France, and

Figure 7:3 'A tangible symbol of pride in the sacrifice of one who did not return.' Campaign medals were often mounted in ornate frames such as this, hung in the front room. By the 1960s, however, such frames were frequently turning up in domestic rubbish. (© and courtesy of Manx National Heritage)

Telephone :—Rodney 3768-9.

All further communications on this
subject should be addressed to :—
The Under-Secretary of State,
The War Office,
Records Section,
Arnside Street,
Walworth, S.E.17,
and the following number quoted :- ·

THE WAR OFFICE,

ARNSIDE STREET,

WALWORTH,

S.E. 17.

Houns/15766/3833.(R.Records)

29 June, 1938.

By Registered Post.

Sir,

       With reference to your letter of 13th June, I am directed
to inform you, for the purposes of an application to the Old
Contemptibles' Association, that according to the records of the
Department No.15766, Private Alfred George David Adams, Royal
Fusiliers, was awarded the 1914 Star and Clasp and the British War
and Victory Medals in respect of his services during the Great War.

       It has been ascertained from the General Secretary that
this letter will meet the requirements of the Association.

       The enclosures to your letter (Army Forms B.2067, and
B.2079) are returned herewith.

              I am,

                  Sir,

                    Your obedient Servant,

                    S.P.Hampshire

Mr. A.G.D. Adams,
   92, Fairlawn Park,
     Lower Sydenham,
       S.E. 26.

Figure 7:4 Medals allowed the wearer acceptance into social groups. Here a former soldier has
obtained verification of his entitlement in order to be formally accepted by his peer
group. (© author)

that he had 'acquired' the medal for 1915 some years after the war. For what reason he had done this, only the old ANZAC could really answer, but it seems probable that given the reverence attached to Gallipoli in modern Australia, wearing the medal made the soldier feel as if he was held in greater esteem.[3]

A similar situation can be found within the Leeds 'Pals', the 15th Battalion West Yorkshire Regiment. Part of the battalion had gone ashore in Egypt in December 1915, thus earning the '1914/15 Star', while the rest had not. However, over the next 30 or 40 years, a number of the survivors, who felt it an injustice that some 'Pals' had the medal and they did not, took it upon themselves to acquire and rename an example from local jewellers, thereby using the medal to create a fallacious social identity.

For many old soldiers, the 1920s and 1930s were times of hardship. The British War Medal, having a fairly high silver content, was often sold for scrap in households where money was tight. Sometimes medals are found with pawnbrokers marks on them; occasionally the name of the recipient has been obliterated to avoid any embarrassment in small towns where the family were unable to reclaim the medals and the pawnbroker passed them to a jeweller for scrap. Here was another complex example of where a kind of self-imposed alienation from the medal separated object, person and society.

After the Second World War, while there remained a market for decorations like the Victoria Cross, as there always had been, campaign medals remained unloved and unwanted ugly sisters. Two anecdotal examples illustrate this point. The first comes from a man who grew up in London just after the last war. He relates that a bric-a-brac dealer with a stall on the local market had a pint glass full of medals each priced at one shilling (5 pence), which was then about a week's pocket money. They were almost all five- or six-bar Queen's South Africa medals, today among the most highly prized of these awards among collectors. The second story also concerns Queen's South Africa medals. In the 1970s, the parents of a Second World War fighter pilot, who had been killed in action, themselves died, and their house and contents were auctioned. An old trunk was found in one of the greenhouses. As a boy during the 1930s, the pilot had collected medals, and bundle after bundle of Queen's South Africa medals emerged from the trunk. They were offered in lots of twenty at the auction, one of the largest collections of Boer War medals ever to go on sale at one time. The point was, of course, that in the early 1930s the boy had been able to amass this superb collection because it was very much a buyer's market, quite the reverse of the situation today.[4]

However, of the entire British campaign series, First World War medals languished at the bottom of the value system right through the 1960s and into the 1970s. A medal dealer in Nottingham recounts how in the 1960s he regularly sold carrier bags full of Victory Medals to a customer for about £1. At the time, this customer was the only person in the area interested in such items, and other collectors laughed at his strange tastes. Today, this collection is worth several thousand pounds, though the owner has so far refused to sell.

What caused the medal-collecting fraternity, and the world at large, to disregard First World War medals? And more significantly, what led them to change their minds? The most likely reason for the former case of affairs is that, during the 1960s, the First World War was viewed largely as a tragic waste of lives and effort. Books such as Leon Wolff's (1959) *In Flanders Fields* characterized the war as unnecessary and mismanaged. Alan Clarke's (1961) *The Donkeys* portrayed the British High Command as incompetent grandees, their men as misguided and beguiled by xenophobic propaganda against the Hun.

This image of the Great War was further propagated by prominent historians of the day such as A.J.P. Taylor, whose monologues – delivered straight to camera and without cue cards or notes – attracted record television audiences during the 1960s. Taylor's views on the First World War were uncompromising. In his opinion, men had been slaughtered in stupid battles by stupid generals. In one lecture, he had paraphrased a wartime song, saying that the men 'fought because they fought because they fought'.[5] Overall, he thought that the war was not a great testament to human intelligence (Taylor 1966). Many among his audience would have been veterans and, whatever their own private experiences of the war, few would have liked to consider themselves out of step with prevailing liberal/academic thinking. It is little wonder that no one attached much value to medals commemorating such a national fiasco.

At the beginning of this paper, reference was made to 'rubbish theory' in relation to First World War medals. This holds true, literally and figuratively, as during the 1960s First World War medals were being thrown out with the trash, in acts that further situate them within the developing anthropological study of discarded, recycled and revalued objects (see Gregson and Crewe 2003; Küchler n.d.). Several antique dealers who made their living from house clearances at this time confirm that, once they had purchased house contents, the first thing they did was look through the contents of the dustbin to see what the family had thrown away. The house contents were going nowhere for the time being, but the dustbins were likely to be emptied in the morning. Framed certificates, scrolls and even medals were frequently found in dustbins. A medal dealer in Nottingham testified that the finest First World War group he had ever found in a dustbin was a Military Medal and '1914/15 Star' group, which came from a house clearance at Nanpantan, near Loughborough.[6]

What led to the remarkable volte-face, to the situation today where the humble '1914 Star' trio sells in excess of £100? The answer is partly economic. With the rise in the value of scrap silver, and the relative scarcity of such items on the market, by the late 1970s it had become impossible to put together any sort of collection of Victorian medals without a major financial investment. Put simply, they were out of the reach of most ordinary people. This led to the realization that the First World War was the last major issue of medals that were individually named for the recipient. It was possible to put together quite cheaply a respectable collection of a particular regiment.

Soon after, in the early 1980s, came a revival of interest in the events of the Great War. As veterans of the conflict passed away, television producers turned their cameras not upon historians but upon the last of these men, and allowed them to tell their own stories for the first time. An early example of this genre was a minor documentary entitled 'Lions Led by Donkeys' screened in 1986. I well remember my own fascination watching this programme and hearing these men speak, when I was aged about fifteen.[7]

This revival in turn led to a huge upsurge in interest in the 'Pals' battalions, raised locally from the same streets and factories, and so often destroyed in a few moments, as on the Somme in 1916. Medals of the 'Pals' battalions are still among the most eagerly sought after of any of the British units of the First World War. For the first time since the 1930s, visiting the First World War battlefields in France (and Belgium) became a major industry (Walter 1993). Martin Middlebrook was among the first authors to remark that in the 1960s he had been virtually alone on his visits to the battlefields, but by the 1970s a whole industry was growing up around British visitors (Middlebrook 1971).

For a measure by which to chart the growth of interest in the First World War, you need look no further than the rise and rise of the Western Front Association. Founded in 1980 by the historian John Giles, it was the first major organization connected with the war that was not founded by veterans themselves, but served instead those with an historical interest in First World War battlefields. At the same time, rapid advances in information technology meant that information could be exchanged ever more rapidly. The recent growth in Internet auction sites such as eBay means that medals are now more likely to be auctioned rather than sold, again forcing up the price.

Ten years ago, few would have predicted that medals could be traded in this way, but more medals are probably now sold electronically than through traditional paper catalogues. Many confidently predict that, within a few years, hardly any First World War medals will be sold in traditional transactions. The Internet allows those with a commodity that is in short supply – such as ageing medal collectors in the UK – to quickly and easily communicate with, say, a US customer base which often has large amounts of disposable income. Today, you are frequently pressured by medal dealers to purchase items at over-inflated prices 'as it's going on eBay next week and I'll get twice that for it'.

What motivates the collector of First World War medals, and what do the medals mean to him or her? John Mussell, writing in *Medal News*, has this to say:

> Sometimes it is easy to see why people collect what they do – and whether those reasons are aesthetic or because of the intrinsic value of the collection, few eyebrows are raised . . . However there are some collections that cannot be so easily explained . . . After all, leaving aside the Orders of Chivalry there are few British medals that can be said to be truly beautiful and, whilst many of them might be silver, even a large collection isn't going to be worth that much in scrap terms, so why collect them? The simple answer of course is that *collectors of medals are really collectors of people* [my italics], be they individuals or regiments, and the medals themselves are just indicators of who these people were, what they did and where they went. It is for this reason that so many medal collectors are also medal researchers or military historians – they don't just want to hoard pieces of metal with coloured ribbons attached, but want to learn everything they can about the history of

the pieces they own. Who were they awarded to? Where was the campaign? Why was it being fought?

(Mussell 2001: 5)

Somewhat ironically, the growth in price of some groups of medals has out performed the stock market. In 2001, one medal dealer in Sydney, Australia (where interest in medals of the First World War is prodigious and probably exceeds that in the UK), remarked that you could have made worse provision for retirement than invest several thousand dollars in a few quality First World War medal groups. Over the past four years or so, the value of some has tripled.[8]

Certain groups of First World War medals have always attracted attention, even when the market was small in the 1970s. The regiments of southern Ireland were disbanded upon the creation of the Free State (Eire) in 1922. With small recruiting areas and comparatively few battalions raised during the war, medals associated with these regiments were always sought after in England. The growth in interest in collecting these medals in Eire during the 1980s came too late – the really impressive Irish groups were by then in the hands of collectors in England or the USA.

Similarly, medal groups to officers of the aviation services – RFC, RNAS or RAF – command premium prices, and probably have done so since the 1960s. The glamour of the air war as portrayed by writers such as Captain W.E. Johns and his 'Biggles' character played a significant role in this. The air war was never tainted with the same sense of futility that was attached to the ground war, and this to some extent accounts for the high level of interest.

Since the mid-1970s, medals to men who had been killed in action attracted more attention than those who had died of wounds or survived. The most infamous day in the history of the British army – 1 July 1916, when twenty thousand men were killed at the beginning of the Battle of the Somme – has probably attracted most interest, particularly as many of those involved were serving in 'Pals' battalions. But the inexorable rise in prices has forced collectors into ever narrower fields, as they husband their resources, now waiting several months between purchases until a group in their particular field of interest comes onto the market. So you may encounter collectors who specialize in particular regiments, for example the Leicestershire Regiment or the Border Regiment, or to men from certain localities. Certain campaigns or battles also attract a following, particularly the Gallipoli campaign, and one collector seeks out groups to men who fell in the 33rd Division's attack on High Wood on 20 July 1916 at the height of the Battle of the Somme.

What all this masks, however, is the fact that the real interest in early-twentieth-century British medals rests on the fact that, unlike their counterparts issued by France, Germany or the United States, they are named, and as a result information can be linked with them. This is the chief reason that many collectors from these other countries are drawn to British medals, rather than those of their own country. It was noticeable that the release to the Public Record Office of the medal index cards in the 1980s and the army service records in the 1990s greatly enhanced the value of some groups of medals, as collectors could now associate the recipients with places and events. Here we see plainly that commercial valuation and collecting habits are linked with the inscription of a name on metal that in turn either creates a 'social life' for the object or adds significantly to its biography (see Belk 2001).

The passion for information about the recipient as much as the medal itself has also led to new developments among forgers. Previously, they would attempt to fake the medals themselves, by crudely altering naming or adding bars where there should be none. In recent years, with the growth in access to information (such as official 'medal rolls') in the public domain, no dealer could now realistically hope to succeed in such deception. Thus, the latest development has been in the fabrication of 'evidence' about the recipient. Photographs, fake letters and fake diaries have all been added to otherwise ordinary groups of medals in recent years, thereby providing a false biography and making them more saleable.

Conclusion

The transformation in attitudes towards these inanimate pieces of bronze and silver has been truly remarkable. From worthless and discarded objects to venerated and prized possessions, the shift in attitudes mirrors those towards the participants in the Great War itself. From forgotten men, the soldiers of the First World War have become the focus of renewed interest, as a younger generation struggle to comprehend what their forefathers endured on the battlefields.

Frequently, one encounters examples of their pride in their town or district channelled into very productive areas, for example researching the contribution of a town or city through its 'Pals' battalion, and through biographies of the fallen from that district.[9] However, in terms of medal collecting, this growth of interest makes for a difficult field for younger and less-wealthy newcomers to participate in. It is only to be hoped that in future years this does not produce a reverse effect and cause a *decline* in the collecting and researching of First World War medals. Many people are only too aware that speculators wrecked the stamp market in the 1970s, and a similar fate could befall medals.

The wider benefits of this interest, in terms of museum representation of the First World War, preservation of First World War battlefield sites, and, most crucially, interest in the Commonwealth War Graves (CWGC) cemeteries, has been enormous. Many who own First World War medals feel that they must make a pilgrimage to see the battlefields and the graves of these men that they have come to know through researching their medals. A strong case can be made that, were it not for the revival of interest in the First World War led by medal collectors and researchers, the cemeteries might well have been closed down by hard-nosed bureaucrats, concerned about the costs of maintaining them.[10]

It would be a great shame now if all the social benefits which have been achieved, in the name of these little pieces of bronze and silver, should be lost, simply because they had priced themselves out of the market.

Acknowledgements

I am indebted to the many medal dealers and collectors with whom I have spoken over the years, and who have shared so many fascinating insights with me.

Notes

1 I am grateful to Bryn Dolan for this information.
2 An example of this would be Walter Biheler, who in the 1920s appears to have created for himself an entirely fanciful war record as a fighter pilot. His papers are held in the Liddle Archive in the Library of the University of Leeds.
3 I am grateful to Paul Reed for this account.
4 I am grateful to Mike Wood for this account.
5 A.J.P. Tayor, BBC TV lectures.
6 This anecdote, like others in this chapter, came to me from one of a number of medal dealers and collectors over the past fifteen years.
7 Since 1986 this documentary has been followed by a number of others in the same vein, 'Prisoners of the Kaiser' on Channel 4 being a more recent example.
8 I am grateful to Mr Richardson (no relation) a medal and militaria dealer of Sydney, New South Wales, for this information during a conversation in April 2001.
9 The 'Pals' series, published by Pen and Sword Books Ltd of Barnsley, South Yorkshire, UK, are excellent examples of this phenomenon, but there are many other books privately produced by desk-top publishing methods and without ISBNs in the same field.
10 The annual reports of the Commonwealth War Graves Commission (available from the Commission at its headquarters, 2 Marlowe Road, Maidenhead, Berkshire) give an insight into the methods by which the war cemeteries are maintained, visitor numbers and the annual cost of upkeep.

References

'Aussie' (anonymous author) (1972) 'Gallipoli Star'. *The Fighting Ninth*, December: 10.

Belk, R.W (2001) *Collecting in a Consumer Society*. London: Routledge.

Clarke, A (1961) *The Donkeys*. London: Hutchinson.

Fevyer, W.H. and J.W. Wilson (1993) *The 1914 Star to the Royal Navy and Royal Marines*. London: Naval and Military Press.

Gregson, N. and L. Crewe (2003) *Second-Hand Cultures*. Oxford: Berg.

Joslin, E.C., A.R. Litherland and B.T. Simpkin (1988) *British Battles and Medals*. London: Spink.

Joy, J. (2002) 'Biography of a medal: people and the things they value'. In J. Schofield, W.G. Johnson and C.M. Beck (eds) *Matériel Culture: The Archaeology of Twentieth Century Conflict*, pp. 132–42. London: Routledge.

Küchler, S. (n.d.) 'The anthropology of rubbish'. Unpublished mss.

Liddle, P.H. and M. Richardson (1997) 'Passchendaele and material culture: the relics of battle'. In P.H. Liddle (ed.) *Passchendaele in Perspective*, pp. 459–66. Barnsley: Pen and Sword Books.

Middlebrook, M. (1971) *The First Day on The Somme*. London: Allen Lane.

Miller, D. (1987) *Material Culture and Mass Consumption*. Oxford: Blackwell.

—— (1994) 'Artefacts and the meaning of things'. In T. Ingold (ed.) *Companion Encyclopedia of Anthropology: Humanity, Culture and Social Life*, pp. 366–95. London: Routledge.

Mussell, J. (2001) 'Out and about'. *Medal News* 39 (3): 5.

Richards, F. (1933) *Old Soldiers Never Die*. London: Faber and Faber.

—— (1936) *Old Soldier Sahib*. London: Faber and Faber.

Richardson, M. (2000) *The Tigers*. Barnsley: Pen and Sword Books.

Taylor, A.J.P. (1966) *From Sarajevo to Potsdam*. London: Thames and Hudson.

Thompson, M. (1979) *Rubbish Theory: The Creation and Destruction of Value*. Oxford: Oxford University Press.

Walter, T. (1993) 'War grave pilgrimage'. In I. Reader and T. Walter (eds) *Pilgrimage in Popular Culture*, pp. 63–91. Houndsmills: Macmillan.

Wolff, L. (1959) *In Flanders Fields*. London: Longmans.

8

DISTINGUISHING THE UNIFORM

Military heraldry and the British
Army during the First World War

Alan Jeffreys

Distinguishing marks or signs have been used throughout the history of warfare – a distinctive kind of conflict-related material culture that redefined personal identity by changing an individual's appearance through clothing and symbols. These changes were directly attributable to war, enabling soldiers quickly to recognize comrades and allies in the confusion of battle. These marks and signs were more than emblems of military prowess and parade ground display; they were visually arresting symbols designed for saving human lives (and achieving military ends). Viewed in this way, military heraldry is of great significance not only to military history (its traditional home), but also to the investigation of the ways that material culture can objectify the relationships between human beings and war.

One of the oldest surviving signs is the leek that was used by the Welsh as a 'field sign' as early as AD 640, and is still in use today in the form of the Welsh Guards' cap badge. Heraldic devices in Europe, carried on shield, helm and surcoat (i.e. the helmet and the mantle worn over armour), became common towards the end of the twelfth century. In 1385, Richard II ordered his soldiers to wear the cross of St George on their surcoats. Precursors to uniform began at the end of the sixteenth century, and, in the seventeenth century, individual regiments were often identified by coloured ribbons worn at the shoulder, at the knee or on the boot, and by sashes or scarves.

During the English Civil War, both sides wore similar clothes, and hat ribbons were one of the few marks of recognition – Cavaliers tended to use red, while Parliamentarians favoured orange. With the development of regular uniforms in the eighteenth and nineteenth centuries, distinguishing marks were systemized. In the British Army, this typically took the form of different coloured facings to lapels and cuffs. With the adoption of single-coloured uniforms at the beginning of the twentieth century, recognition marks were reintroduced. The 1909 Field Service Regulations provided for the use of 'armlets' or brassards by certain staff officers, and recommended the use of recognition marks in night operations.

This chapter will regard military heraldry as including metal regimental headdress badges as well as the cloth Divisional, Brigade and Battalion flashes and patches. Until near the end of the nineteenth century, regiments were differentiated by, among other things, the use of the regimental number inserted into the 'helmet plate' worn on the front of the dress helmet. Smaller badges, still bearing the regimental number, appeared in 1874 for wearing with the distinctive Scottish-style Glengarry cap that was introduced for infantry Other Ranks at that time.

However, regimental cap badges as we know them today came into existence as the result of a series of army reforms that culminated in 1881. The regular line infantry regiments lost their numbers and adopted county titles, becoming at the same time two-battalion units, one to serve overseas and one to serve at home as a depot, training and draft-finding unit. At the same time, the old volunteer and militia units became as a general rule affiliated to one or other of the regular county regiments. Both regulars and volunteers saw it as important to retain their individual identities, and from this sprang the design of the cap badge, each encapsulating important elements of the regiment's history.

The Cameronians (Scottish Rifles), for example, was a merger of the old 26th (Cameronians) Regiment and the 90th (Perthshire Volunteers) Light Infantry. The new badge included a mullet (five-pointed star) from the arms of the Douglas family, as James Douglas, the Earl of Angus, had formed the 26th regiment in 1689. The bugle denoted Light Infantry for the 90th. The regiment was initially called the Scotch Rifles in May 1881, and then changed in July to the Cameronians (Scotch Rifles) with the two battalions differentiating themselves as the 1st Cameronians and the 2nd Scottish Rifles until after the First World War. Until 1900, the two battalions even wore different headdress badges (see Haythornwaite 2002: 29–30, Gaylor 2003: 39 and B.T.H. 1943: 200).[1]

Cap badges came to embody the spirit of the regiment according to *Cap Badge*, the history of the Bedfordshire and Hertfordshire Regiment:

> The cap badge worn on the headgear of the soldier identifies him as belonging to a particular organization or a member of a Regimental group . . . It is understandable because of the tribal nature of the British Infantry Regiments why the cap badge has such meaning to those who wear it.
>
> (Medley 1995: xii)

Kaushik Roy, writing about the construction of regiments in the Indian army, deemed it necessary to establish regimental traditions to encourage primary group cohesion. He noted that: 'Primary group solidarity among the soldiers encouraged them to fight. Primary group cohesion increased among personnel of a unit if they were made to believe that they were distinct from the society and from other units of the army.' (Roy 2001: 139). This was established by the invention of regimental traditions such as regimental depots where troops trained together and which gave the soldiers some stability, and was backed up by the use of standards, different badges and uniforms to maintain the regimental ethos. Lastly, he mentions inter-unit games such as football tournaments and rifle competitions (ibid.: 139–44).

This invention of tradition in British and Indian army regiments stemmed from the invention of traditions within nations and nationalism at the end of the nineteenth century (see Hobsbawm and Ranger 1992; French 2005). Thus a regimental *esprit de corps* was created that David French has remarked upon:

> The 'regiment' was conceived as being based upon a shared comradeship that transcended the inequalities of power and rewards that existed within it. It was something so fundamentally pure that it could call upon its members to lay down their lives for it.
>
> (French 2005: 79)

By 1914, the fostering of regimental ethos was largely symbolized through badges, as uniforms had been standardized into khaki and a regiment's standards and colours were no longer carried into battle. As David French has pointed out, regimental badges 'were a visible symbol of the common identity that each member of the regiment shared, and they enhanced each regiment's sense of separateness' (French 2005: 85). For example, during the Mesopotamia Campaign, Field Marshal Slim related how one of his fellow officers in the Warwickshire Regiment rallied his men with the cry 'Heads up the Warwicks! Show the – yer cap-badges!' (Slim 1959: 50). Slim continued: 'They had no cap-badges for we wore Wolseley helmets but they heard the only appeal that could have reached them – to their regiment, the last hold of the British soldier when all else has gone.' (ibid.). Thus, regimental loyalty was paramount, particularly with regular soldiers, a point reinforced by another regular soldier interviewed by Richard Holmes, who stated that he fought for 'the Regiment and its traditions, also my comrades' (Holmes 2004: 114–15).

This could apply equally to Kitchener New Army battalions, who often adopted their own badges to keep their own identity as opposed to the regimental cap badge, such as the 17th to 20th Battalions of the King's (Liverpool) Regiment, otherwise known as the Liverpool Pals. These Battalions were raised by Lord Derby, and adopted his family crest of an eagle and child and the motto *Sans changer* on their cap badge (Slater 2004: 145). Lord Derby presented a silver cap badge to each man who joined before 16 October 1914 (see Richardson, this volume, for the attractiveness of regimental badges even to those who had no right to wear them).

These regimental traditions probably did not mean so much to later conscripts in the war. For example, in September 1916, the 12th (Reserve) Battalion, Welsh Regiment, became the 58th Training Reserve Battalion, then the 230th (Graduated) Battalion, and finally the 51st (Graduated) Battalion of the South Wales Borderers. As Peter Simkins has pointed out, in the later stages of the First World War the British Army had become a 'nationalised' force (Simkins 1994: 259). Private F.A.J. (Tanky) Taylor was conscripted into the 19th County of London Regiment (St Pancras). He remarked,

> 'Why couldn't I have been sent to the Manchesters, my brother's regiment, instead of this damn cockney battalion?' I thought. I never did develop any

feelings of loyalty or pride in this regiment. In any case no one took any trouble to tell us about this regiment or its traditions.

(Taylor 1978: 25)

He remained disenchanted when transferred to the Worcestershire Regiment in 1918:

We were regrouped and parted with our insignia identifying us with the 19th City of London Regiment or St Pancras Rifles for ever. Our cap badges, shoulder names, fancy buttons we all discarded to be replaced by insignia linking us now to the 2nd Battalion Worcestershire Regiment. As I had never developed any particular loyalty for the London Regiment, into which I had been unceremoniously thrust a few months previously, and no one had taken time or trouble to tell us anything about traditions or battle honours of the regiment, it was not difficult to transfer to a new regiment equally unknown. We got new cap badges, a star with the brief motto 'FIRM' below, brass shoulder regimental names, flashes to sew on our upper arms. The white double domino, with its six black dots, representing the 33rd Division. We knew no more about this division than we did about the 2nd Worcesters who, we gathered, were mainly a Birmingham or Brummagen mob.

(Taylor 1978: 47–8)

However, even Taylor became attached to the Regiment, and thanks the Regimental Association in the foreword to his book, *The Bottom of the Barrel* (see also French 2005: 283). George MacDonald Fraser reiterated this in his Second World War memoir, *Quartered Safe Out Here*:

Back in Blighty, or even out of the line, a soldier's first loyalty was to his regiment, and even the most cynical reluctant conscript was conscious of belonging to something special. If he came from the regimental area, the tie was all the stronger; he could call himself a Devon, an Argyll, a Gloucester, or a Middlesex, and take some pride in belonging to the Bloody Eleventh, the Thin Red Line, the Back-to-Backs, or the Diehards, as those regiments were nicknamed; he would probably know how they got them. And regimental pride would stay with him, as I'm sure it does still, even after amalgamation has played havoc with the old territorial system.

(Fraser 1995: 11)

Regimental cap and collar badges therefore symbolized the regimental ethos and as such were given away as prized souvenirs, particularly to young ladies – an interesting material link between a soldier's military identity and his romantic aspirations and sexual activities when out of the front line. Frank Richards wrote in his memoir *Old Soldiers Never Die*:

The majority of men in my battalion had given their cap and collar badges to the French ladies they had been walking out with, as souvenirs, and I expect in some cases had also left other souvenirs which would either be a blessing or curse to the ladies concerned.

(Richards 1994: 14; see also Dunn 1987: 15)

Robert Burns of the 7th Battalion, Queen's Own Cameron Highlanders commented that after a dance with the WAACs (Women's Army Auxiliary Corps), 'As a souvenir each of the girls was presented with a much sought after Cameron badge' (Burns 2000: 162). Soldiers also collected cap badges from other regiments and corps as souvenirs and often attached them to a belt, an army tradition that preceded the First World War. This habit frequently extended to captured enemy badges also called 'hate' belts (see Cornish, this volume).

It has been suggested that, during the First World War, a soldier's loyalty was transferred from the regiment to the division, and at least one contemporary commentator associates this with the arrival of the New Army Divisions (see Wheeler-Holohan 1920: xiv; Chapple 1998: 3–4; Robbins 2005: 10). However, there is little evidence to support this assertion, and indeed the divisional sign was rarely worn by other ranks (see Carman *et al.* 1971: 170). The relative strength of attachment to regiment or higher formation would be difficult to assess, but the balance of evidence suggests that the smaller the group the more powerful the attachment is likely to be (French 2005: 283–4). As Keith Simpson has clearly stated, 'The group loyalty of the British soldier on the Western Front usually did not extend beyond his own battalion, battery or squadron, and in practice, did not go much further than his "muckers" [comrades] in his section or platoon' (Simpson 1985: 147). George Macdonald Fraser reinforces this view:

On active service, in my experience, the loyalty, or perhaps I should call it dependence, narrowed down to the infantry section . . . it was the section that mattered to the private soldier. It was his military family, those seven or eight other men were his constant companions, waking, sleeping, standing guard, eating, digging, patrolling, marching, and fighting, and he got to know them better, perhaps, than anyone in his whole life except his wife, parents, and children. He counted on them, and they on him.

(Fraser 1995: 11–12)

Soldiers rarely developed an affinity with their formation (brigade and above). As Keith Simpson again points out: 'Higher formations were seen as impersonal authorities who were liable to threaten the regimental soldier's sleep, leave, comforts and ultimately his life' (Simpson 1985: 147).

Thus, divisional loyalty did not permeate throughout the army. The degree of loyalty a soldier was prepared to offer an organization greater than his regiment is arguable in general terms. It was nevertheless the case that certain divisions such as the Guards Division, 9th (Scottish) Division, 10th (Irish) Division, 38th (Welsh)

Division, 36th (Ulster) Division, 40th Division, 46th (North Midland) Division, 51st (Highland) Division and 56th (London) Division were recognized as having an *esprit de division* symbolized by their badges (Beckett 2001: 22; French 2005: 261; Lee 1997: 224–6).

Contrary to popular opinion, the 51st Highland Division was not as enthusiastic about volunteering for overseas service. In fact, it was six battalions short, and a Lancashire Brigade joined the division in Spring 1915, and the 11th (Reserve) Battalion the Black Watch went on a recruiting drive of Edinburgh, Glasgow and Manchester (Spiers 1996: 316; see also Bewsher 1921: 8). Major-General Harper took over command of the division in September 1915 and tried to instil a divisional identity, made slightly easier with its Scottish identification, fighting traditions and cultural differences. This he achieved through thorough training. The Divisional Historian commented that 'the Highlanders proved that they possessed qualities which enabled them to respond to training in a degree which few other troops could equal' (Bewsher 1921: 47). Thus, a distinctive divisional identity was instigated through training and the ensuing battle experience. This was enhanced when it was found out in 1917 that 'the Germans feared the Highland Division more than any other Division on the Western Front' (ibid.). This was summed up by Major Bewsher in his divisional history:

> One of the great factors on which the reputation of the 51st Division rested was its intense *esprit de division*, which continuously increased as success followed success. No matter what arm of service he might be, the Jock was proud of the 51st. As a result, the various arms were all animated by the common ideal of enhancing the reputation of their division.
>
> (Bewsher 1921: 410)

The letters 'HD' on the formation sign stood of course for Highland Division, but the irony of the British soldier invited the self-mocking nickname of 'Harper's Duds'. It could be argued that Harper was successful in this creation of a separate divisional loyalty as it was one of the very few formations to reuse the formation badge during the Second World War, when they were nicknamed 'Highway Decorators' for displaying HD wherever they went. The sign was only dropped from use in the British Army at the turn of the twenty-first century.

From the beginning of the war in August 1914 until mid-1915, figures and initials were in general use on vehicles and brassards for indicating the formation to which both machinery and individuals belonged. An order of July 1915 by the French GQG (Grand Quartier General) then drew attention to the fact that the enemy was gaining information of military value from the numbered and initialled signs used by the French Army, and discussion arose at British General Headquarters in consequence. On 2 August 1915, a circular was sent to the three armies, the Cavalry Corps and the Indian Corps, pointing out this observation. The consensus was that distinguishing marks should be used for vehicles, numbers should not be worn on armbands, and the numbers of officers wearing them should be reduced. As General Robertson pointed out:

The wearing of armbands by officers has been carried to such an extent as not only to defeat its own object, but to become a positive danger. The band was never intended to be a badge of office, but merely to facilitate finding Staff Officers.

(IWM EN1/60)

Flags were still to be used for Commanding Officer's motorcars and HQ Flags, but numbers and titles were not to be used on them as had previously been the case. As a result, General Routine Order 870 was amended on 24 August and these changes were made.

The convenience of 'recognition' marks was admitted by all especially for transport vehicles. It was also noted that brassards showed a tendency to develop into badges, a purpose quite different from that originally intended. Eventually, an order of 21 September 1915 from the Quartermaster General's Office (QMG) of GHQ forbade the use of easily interpreted inscriptions, but gave units permission to 'adopt for their convenience certain signs and figures', provided that they were not such as an enemy secret agent could easily interpret.

Purely symbolic formation signs would fulfil both the roles of a distinguishing mark and increase security against enemy identification, although, as Charles Carrington commented: 'Soldiers of all countries are much addicted to distinguishing badges which no system of security overcomes' (Carrington 1965: 157). Interestingly, Carrington remarked that these flashes and patches could also serve a social role, rather than a purely military purpose, by marking out front-line soldiers from those in less physical danger further down the line. This was a wartime language of symbols, involving the recognition of cap badge and formation sign in conjunction with chevrons denoting overseas service, and stripes signifying the wearer had been wounded.

Experts in the lore of the B.E.F. [British Expeditionary Force] could make an accurate judgement of a man's fighting record by considering all the factors. Look at a man you meet on the leave-train: his cap-badge tells you he belongs to a good fighting regiment, but since he has four blue chevrons and no wound stripe you may be confident he has a safe job down the line. His neighbour who has one chevron and two wound-stripes has had a very different war.

(Carrington 1965: 158)

The matter now being in the hands of the Headquarters of individual formations and units, something like a revival of heraldry arose, and signs of great ingenuity proliferated. Captain Wheeler-Holohan (1920: xiv–xv) identified five different kinds of sign, the first being First Army's simple white stripe or 6th Division's white circle on a black square. The second was an obvious 'territorial sign' such as 9th (Scottish) Division's thistle or 38th Division's Welsh Dragon. Arguably the most imaginative were the 'cipher type', where an apparently abstract design hid a clue to the identity of the formation. This was adopted by several divisions and examples include the three figure '7's conjoined at the base to form a circular fan, indicating $3 \times 7 = 21$ for 21st Division, and the 'ATN' of 18th Division, the letters pronounced quickly sounding like 'eighteen'. The fourth type was the rebus or 'canting' heraldic device, where the design was a visual pun on the name of the General Officer Commanding (GOC). Perhaps the most striking example is that of 18th Corps, the letter M above two crossed axes referring to the commander at the time of adoption, Sir Ivor Maxse. The fifth type was the 'battle honour', where the design incorporates a reference to an action where the division had excelled. A good example of this is the umbrella of 54th Division commemorating their raid on Umbrella Hill outside Gaza in the Middle East.

To this list might be added more directly heraldic signs, such as those where elements of a GOC's armorial bearings were adopted. For example, 4th Division was commanded by Major-General the Honourable Sir William Lambton who adopted his family crest, a ram's head, as a divisional sign. At least one division, the 59th (North Midland), consulted the York Herald at the Royal College of Arms. They adopted Offa's cross as the division was raised in the area of the old kingdom of Mercia.

The signs adopted could also be self-referential and could change over time. It is illustrative to look at the development of the formation sign of 35th Division, which started as a 'Bantam' division, i.e. it was partially composed of men shorter than the regulation height. The first divisional sign was a bantam cock, designed by Lieutenant Meadows, 204th Field Coy, RE and forwarded by his commanding officer to the GOC, Major-General Sir Reginald Pinney. Pinney approved the design, with the caveat that the cock's tail should display 'less droop'. However, the sign was to be superseded, most probably when the division ceased being a bantam division in 1917 (IWM EN1/60, see also Messenger: 135). Then a different and very ingenious sign of the 'cipher' type was adopted, being seven figure '5's linked top to tail to form what looked like a toothed circle, thus disguising the underlying motif of '$7 \times 5 = 35$'. 40th Division was the other original bantam division. They only adopted the bantam cock on the formation sign in 1917, when Major-General John Ponsonby took over the Division and discovered that the diamond sign currently in use was also used by 48th Division. The acorn and oak leaves were added in commemoration of the division's capture of Bourlon Wood, thereby incorporating the 'battle honour' element.

The use of distinguishing marks began to be used from 1915 on troop uniforms taking the shape of coloured or embroidered cloth patches on the individual's back or shoulders, with different signs devised for brigades, battalions, and companies. 41st Division used the Divisional sign of a white diagonal stripe against different coloured backgrounds to denote different brigades and divisional troops. Elsewhere, some brigades adopted their own signs. For example, 19th Brigade adopted a butterfly of which Captain Dunn comments 'one of the men defined as "an insec" that does as they does, it flies from one (obscene) flower to another.' (Dunn 1987: 381).

At battalion level, the 1/5th Leicesters adopted yellow patches which, according to the unit history, 'were rather bright at first, and earned us the name (amongst other ruder epithets) of the "Corn-plasters".' (ibid.: 244). In the plans for the Battle of the

Somme, a small number of battalion patches were even listed and described in Corps orders (NA WO 95/820). Perhaps the most consistent and thoroughgoing use of signs down to at least battalion level was the system used by the Canadian Army. Here a simple coloured rectangle denoting the division was topped by a different shaped and coloured geometric shape denoting the specific brigade and battalion.

Distinguishing marks were also used tactically, and by 1916 it was acknowledged that they were particularly useful in night assaults and raids (NA WO 92/852; Lewis 2004: 89). An early example of a tactical mark was the brassard issued to officers and Non Commissioned Officers (NCOs) of the first Gas Companies, Royal Engineers, for the Battle of Loos, 25 September 1915. The Companies were made up of men with qualifications as chemists, specially enlisted or transferred from other arms. They were instrumental in the first British gas attack made with chlorine. The brassard enabled them to enter the frontline unchallenged (IWM Accession number 18351). Not surprisingly, there was little commonality in the way these very low level signs were employed. For example, runners in 21st Division during the Battle of Somme wore a two-inch square yellow badge on each forearm, whereas runners in 8th Division in the October 1916 attack at Le Transloy wore bright green brassards (NA WO 95/1675 & 95/922).

By 1917, most units had adopted a battalion patch, and by 1919 the War Office compiled a list with colour diagrams of the signs adopted by the Armies, Corps, Divisions, Brigades and Battalions for sale (IWM EN1/60). Q (Logistics) Branch also made a complete list for General Donald, Director of War Trophies, but it does not seem to have survived (IWM EN1/60). Months, or even years after the divisions had been disbanded, the signs appeared on the back of books, menus, and Christmas cards produced by regimental and Divisional Associations. The only collection of these distinguishing marks to exist is held in the Imperial War Museum, as the then Director General Designate of the National War Museum, Sir Martin Conway, sent out a circular letter to all the units in the British Army in Autumn 1917. In particular he requested 'the special Battalion badges or marks of distinction worn by the Battalions on the sleeve or on the back of the Service Dress Jacket', as 'These badges were as you know, not made by the Army Clothing Department, and therefore unprocurable except from the Regiments themselves' (circulated letter from Sir Martin Conway to British Army units).

There was a huge response to the request, all the more commendable as a large number of the units were then involved in the Third Battle of Ypres in Belgium. Commanding Officers usually sent examples of the patches worn or sent a description or illustration. A questionnaire was also sent out to all the regiments in 1919–1920, but the information sent back depended on whether any surviving officers were still in the battalion, and a number of battalions had been disbanded by this time. The response was not as complete as the 1917 survey, but together these surveys provide a unique reference to all the cloth patches worn by the British Army except, unfortunately, for those of the Corps and Services. Correspondence conducted with these formations during the 1917 survey does not appear to have survived and questionnaires were not circulated to them in the second survey. The signs were all displayed in the Imperial

War Museum during the 1920s and 1930s, and there is correspondence from officers and soldiers of particular units and formations in the museum's central files concerning whether they were correctly displayed, and asking for badge details to use on menus for reunion dinners and booklets for regimental reunions (IWM EN1/60).

The post-1915 revival of military heraldry in the British Army was short-lived, and regular army formations and units discontinued the wearing of formation signs and battalion patches at the end of the Great War. They had all but disappeared by 1920. Some of the territorial divisions retained their signs, or variations of them, when the Territorial Army was reformed in 1921 – for example the 51st (Highland) Division and 52nd (Lowland) Division. The formation sign had to await the arrival of the Second World War to see a revival, when it enjoyed considerable elaboration in terms of both vehicle markings and uniform patches.

Acknowledgements

Thanks to Paul Cornish, Chris McCarthy and Mike Taylor for their help and advice.

Notes

1   The Scottish Rifles had 'SR' in the strings of the bugle-horn, and for pagri badges and the pipers of the 1st Battalion, there was a mullet upon a scroll saying, 'The Cameronians'. The cap badge evolved from the helmet plate centre of the full dress spiked infantry helmet that disappeared in 1914 for the service dress cap, although the Cameronians had already replaced the spiked helmet with a rifle-green shako in 1892.

References

Primary Sources

National Archive

VIII Corps War Diary July 1916 WO 95/820
X Corps War Diary July 1916 WO 95/851
XV Corps War Diary July 1916 WO 95/922
8th Division War Diary WO 95/1675

Imperial War Museum Central Archive

Part I – Distinguishing Marks of Formations, Armbands etc., July 1915 to September 1917 EN1/60

Part II – Distinguishing Marks of Formations, Armbands etc., September 1917 to February 1919 EN1/60

Correspondence in Badges Lorry and Divisional 3 EN1/60

Correspondence between Captain Meadows and the IWM Curator and Secretary Aug-Sept 1929 EN1/60

Published sources

B.T.H. (1943) 'Regimental badges and their meanings'. *The Journal of the United Service Institution of India* LXXIII, 311: 196–204.

Beckett, Ian (2001) *The Great War 1914–1918*. Harlow: Pearson.

Bewsher, Major F.W. (1921) *The History of the 51st (Highland) Division*. London: William Blackwood.

Burns, Robert (2000) *Once a Cameron Highlander*. Bognor Regis: Woodfield Publishing.

Carman, W., Y. May and J. Tanner (1974) *Badges and Insignia of the British Armed Forces*. London: Adam & Charles.

Carrington, Charles (1965) *Soldier from the Wars Returning*. London: Hutchinson.

Chapple, Mike (1998) *British Battle Insignia 1 1914–1918*. London: Osprey.

Dunn, J. C. (1987) *The War the Infantry Knew 1914–1919*. London: Jane's.

Fraser, George Macdonald (1995) *Quartered Safe Out Here*. London: HarperCollins.

French, David (2005) *Military Identities: The Regimental System, the British Army and the British People c.1870–2000*. Oxford: Oxford University Press.

Gaylor, John (2003) *Military Badge Collecting*. Barnsley: Pen & Sword.

Haythornwaite, Philip J. (2002) 'Badges of the Cameronians (Scottish Rifles)'. *Medal News*, November: 29–30.

Hill, Captain J. D. (1919) *The Fifth Leicestershire*. Loughborough: Echo Press.

Hobsbawm, E. and T. Ranger (eds) (1992) *The Invention of Tradition*. Cambridge: Cambridge University Press.

Holmes, Richard (2004) *Tommy: The British Soldier on the Western Front 1914–1918*. London: HarperCollins.

Lee, John (1997) 'The British Divisions at third Ypres'. In P.H. Liddle (ed.) *Passchendale in Perspective: The Third Battle of Ypres*, pp 215–26. London: Leo Cooper.

Lewis, Bernard (2004) *Swansea Pals: A History of 14th (Service) Battalion Welsh Regiment in the Great War*. Barnsley: Pen & Sword.

Medley, Major R.H. (1995) *Cap Badge: The Story of Four Battalions of the Bedfordshire and Hertfordshire Regiment (TA) 1939–1947*. London: Leo Cooper.

Messenger, Charles (2005) *Call to Arms: The British Army 1914–1918*. London: Weidenfeld & Nicolson.

Richards, Frank (1994) *Old Soldiers Never Die*. Sleaford, Lincolnshire: Phillip Austen Publishing.

Robbins, Simon (2005) *British Generalship on the Western Front 1914–1918: Defeat into Victory*. London: Frank Cass.

Roy, Kaushik (2001) 'The construction of regiments in the Indian army: 1859–1913'. *War in History* 8 (2): 127–48.

Simkins, Peter (1994) 'The four armies 1914–1918'. In D. Chandler and I. F. W. Beckett (eds) *Oxford Illustrated History of the British Army*, pp. 241–62. Oxford: Oxford University Press.

Simpson, Keith (1985) 'The British soldier on the Western Front'. In P.H. Liddle (ed.) *Home Fires and Foreign Fields: British Social and Military Experience in the First World War*, pp. 135–58. London: Brassey's.

Slater, Stephen (2004) *Living Heraldry*. London: Southwater.

Slim, Field Marshal Sir William (1959) *Unofficial History*. London: Cassell.

Spiers, Edward (1996) 'The Scottish soldier at war'. In Hugh Cecil and Peter Liddle (eds) *Facing Armageddon: The First World War Experienced*, pp. 314–35. London: Leo Cooper.

Taylor, F.A.J. (1978) *The Bottom of the Barrel*. London: Regency Press.

Wheeler-Holohan, V. (1920) *Divisional and Other Signs*. London: John Murray.

9

THE CONSUMER SPHINX

From French trench to Parisian market

Gulya Isyanova

The objects of war are visceral embodiments of the life and death experiences endured by all who are caught up in the fury of conflict. From shell fragments to ruined villages, from devastated landscapes to memorabilia, artefacts large and small are invested with variable meanings by different individuals and groups. These meanings are transformed by time and by generations, reconfiguring themselves as fields of memory, heritage attractions, memory objects, museum exhibits and collectables. The social life of portable objects in particular does not end with the closing of war, but extends beyond it to intersect the lives of future generations.

In this chapter, I consider one hitherto neglected aspect of the biography of First World War objects – their valuation and acquisition by private collectors at the beginning of the twenty-first century. We will see how, amongst a small group of Parisian collectors, the market in First World War objects is entwined with the social networks that envelop them, the modern consumer culture within which they circulate, and the nature of materiality itself.

Consumption

The study of consumption – of how and why we consume material culture – is a relatively recent interest for anthropology (e.g. Douglas and Isherwood 1978; Miller 1998a, 1998b; Slater 1997). What makes it distinctive and valuable is that, unlike macro assessments of our consuming behaviour, the anthropological study of consumption focuses on micro assessments through ethnographic inquiry. What inspired this interest was the recognition, generally postmodernist in orientation, that the principles and practices of a modern market economy permeate every aspect of Western society. This process of commodification has turned the West into a 'market society' (Bruckner 2002), where anything can be bought or sold, and where the act of purchasing is ubiquitous.

A permanent and insatiable desire for the new, and a permanent dissatisfaction with the old, appear to dominate this relentless consumption. Eventually everything becomes a victim of disposability and replacement. In fact, there is a feeling that consumption has become such an intrinsic part of Western life, that we have *ipso facto* become consumed by it ourselves.

This is a problematic notion. It is clear that 'consumption [has] been artificially abstracted out of the whole scheme' (Douglas and Isherwood 1978: 4) and demonized unfairly due to its synecdochic relationship to capitalism. Consumption, being only a part of the capitalist process, has been made to represent capitalism as a whole. As such, in blaming capitalism for social and economic inequality, environmental problems and a general disenchantment of humanity, this critique has focused specifically on consumption as the epitome of what has gone wrong with Western society.

Furthermore, there appears to be no consensus as to what consumption actually is. For a long time, as an object of research, consumption was 'pre-paradigmatic' (Kuhn quoted in Storey 1999: XIII), for it had 'no history, no community of scholars [and] no tradition of scholarship' (McCracken quoted in Storey 1999: XIII). It was considered peripheral. The past few decades, however, have seen consumption studies become an 'academic subculture' (Miller *et al.* 1998: 1), and one which now has an extensive interdisciplinary involvement. It has finally become identified as a social phenomenon in its own right, but appears to be understood differently by different disciplines. Various proposed conceptualizations of consumption can be differentiated by the perceived effects that consumption is believed to have on the individual and on society. What most views lack, however, is knowledge of the consumption process at the micro level. It is in fact the case that while living in a state of advanced capitalism and ubiquitous consumption, we are still unsure 'how people use and [are] affected by commodities' (Kellner quoted in Featherstone 1983: 73). It is our 'consumer sphinx' (de Certeau quoted in Featherstone 1983: 73).

Trench art

The sphinx-like quality of consumption is shared by the corpus of objects known as 'Trench Art' (Saunders 2001, 2003) (Figure 9:1). This misleading but now inescapable name is an umbrella term for 'any item made by soldiers, prisoners of war and civilians, from war matériel directly, or any other material, as long as it and they are associated temporarily and/or spatially with armed conflict or its consequences' (Saunders 2003: 11). Although by definition it relates to objects made during, or otherwise associated with, any conflict, it is best known from the vast quantity of such items produced during the First World War and its aftermath. A typical example of trench art, and one favoured by many French collectors, is the cigarette lighter (*briquet*), such as those made in 1916–18, and whose curiously metallic, cartoon-like qualities commemorate the appalling losses of the German army on French soil at Verdun (Saunders 2003: 88–9) (Figure 9:2).

Figure 9:1
Trench art
produced by
French soldiers,
showing a variety
of items including
artillery shell
vases. (© and
courtesy
N.J. Saunders)

Trench art objects can be deeply ambiguous artefacts that objectify many different feelings and experiences of the war that gave birth to them, depending in part on whether they were made by soldiers or civilians, and during or after the conflict. Their ambiguous and slippery nature is also evident in the variety of purposes for which they were made – one of which was as souvenirs, and saw them entering the (quite different war-time and post-war) networks of consumption as souvenirs for sale and exchange, and, ultimately, the post-war world of private collectors with its highly specialized patterns of consumption. Here, I focus on locating, describing and interpreting the afterlife of some of these objects, those identified by Saunders (2003: 38–44) as 'category 1' in his classification of trench art.

Category 1 refers only to objects made by First World War soldiers, and has three sub-categories: category 1a objects were made by soldiers in active service between 1914 and 1918, mainly behind the lines; category 1b items were made by Prisoners

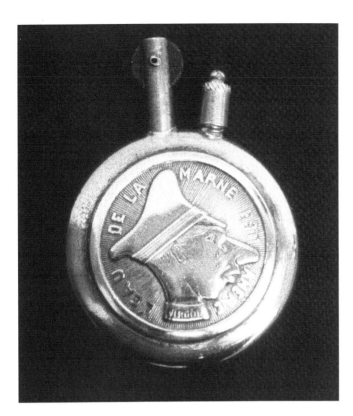

Figure 9:2
French cigarette
lighter (*briquet*),
showing a
caricature of the
German Crown
Prince Wilhelm.
(© and courtesy
N.J. Saunders)

of War between 1914 and 1919, and category 1c was produced by wounded soldiers
during their convalescence. Most category 1 objects tend to have a functional nature
– such as items related to smoking (e.g. lighters, ashtrays) or writing (e.g. bullet-pens,
bullet-pencils, and inkwells) – but some are purely decorative, for example miniature
aeroplanes and tanks, personal adornment (rings, bracelets), as well as elaborate
artillery shell cases fashioned into 'flower vases'.

The other two major categories have been excluded: category 2 covers everything
made by civilians between 1914 and 1939, and category 3 refers to trench art that was
commercially produced throughout the twentieth century. The reason for this
exclusivity lies with the location of my field research, which took place entirely among
trench art collectors in Paris. Despite the availability of an academic classification,
many collectors still adhere to their own criteria for defining trench art, based on
different understandings of what constitutes its authenticity.

The collectors involved in my research consider only category 1 to be true trench
art. These rare and unique objects are much sought after and are very valuable
commodities. Academically, however, very little is known about this market activity,
and this was the initial reason for choosing the collecting of trench art as an example
of commodity consumption. I subsequently realized that First World War trench art

was particularly appropriate for the exploration of patterns of consumption for three main reasons. First, in general terms 'collecting [can be considered as] consumption writ large' (Belk 1995: 1). A collection can be defined as 'a group of objects, brought together with intention and sharing a common identity of some kind, which is regarded by its owner as, in some sense, special or set apart' (Pearce 1995: 159) – a highly prolific and systematic form of consumption. Approximately one-third of Westerners collect something (ibid.).

Second, this specific area of collecting seemed especially appropriate due to its commercial aspect. In one sense, trench art has always been a commodity. Objects in category 1 were often made by soldiers as a supplement for meagre wages and for bartering purposes. It was 'almost the only way a soldier could increase his worldly wealth' (Saunders 2003: 130). Between the two world wars, battlefield pilgrimage ensured these objects remained souvenir favourites, and trench art was further commodified in the 1960s and 1970s with the explosion of commercial tourism to First World War battlefields. Currently, war memorabilia is an industry in itself. There is a huge albeit fragmented worldwide market of collectors and dealers, spread over a network of clubs and associations, markets and fairs, auctions and the Internet (see Fabiansson 2004). It is a 'world of extreme interest, humour, passion and even obsession' (Pearce 1995: 159).

Third, trench art itself is 'a powerful tool for investigating the relationships between people and objects' (Saunders 2003: 3), and hence the nature of the consumption process. For soldier-made trench art, this worked on two levels. Such items are examples of recyclia, i.e. 'a reworking of . . . matter . . . to make something new' (Saunders 2003: 184), and the making of these objects was symbolically ironic. Material made for the purposes of destruction was being used in a process of creation, and typified by the manufacture of so-called 'flower vases' made in a variety of decorated shapes from empty (i.e. spent) artillery shells (Figure 9:3).

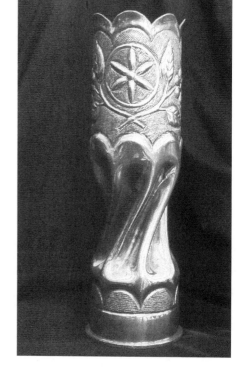

Figure 9:3
Artillery-shell 'flower vase'
with a fluted waist.
(© and courtesy N.J. Saunders)

134

Trench art also possesses another dimension of social relations. These objects are, after all, the embodiment of personal experiences and memories. Every item tells a story, insofar as trench-art objects are a 'three-dimensional biography of war experience' (Saunders 2003: 75). They can convey personal details, relationships, emotions, the situational context of their production and the soldier's reaction to war. If we consider the contemporary context, people coming face to face with these objects bring their own meaning to them. There is thus a strong, dialectical relationship between those who made the objects, the object itself and those who consume them (in the past as well as today).

The focus of my ethnographic research was Patrice Warin, an avid French collector of trench art, and an ethnographer of First World War soldiers' lives. Although his collection is large and diverse, his special interest lies with *briquets* (cigarette lighters), of which he has around 650, and with reconstructing the biographies of these objects. In fact, a First World War *briquet* is what first inspired his interest in trench art, which has subsequently become a passion in his life. In 2001, and unusually for a collector, Warin published a detailed and beautifully illustrated book on trench art – *Artisanat de tranchée et briquets de poilus de la guerre 14–18* (Warin 2001). It became apparent that the main aim of my research should be to explore how Warin engaged with these objects, and how his life was affected by his attitudes towards them and their consumption.

Through Patrice, I met two other collectors, Jean-Paul Noiret and Philippe Billot (Figure 9:4). They all seemed surprised and flattered that someone who was not

Figure 9:4 Jean-Paul Noiret, Patrice Warin and Philippe Billot at the *Puces aux Vanves* market in Paris. (© author)

involved in collecting was taking in interest in what they were so passionate about. They told me that there is an increasing number of people taking an interest in trench art, but that this is mainly due to its economic value. There is, after all, a finite quantity of such objects, and the rarer the commodity the higher its price. By comparison, there are very few people who are interested in the cultural value of these objects. In the photograph, Patrice is holding a guitar that he had just bought, which he believes to have been hand-made by a First World War POW. The cultural significance of such musical instruments is explored by Saunders (2003: 109).

Rather than simply presenting my research as a narrative account, it seemed more appropriate to engage with it in a framework that sought to explore the findings through the lens of two prominent issues in the interdisciplinary study of consumption. The first issue is that of materiality, and, more specifically, considerations of the effects that the ubiquity and the abundance of material matter have on social life. The second issue concerns the idea of stability, or rather the supposed lack of it – a view that stems from pessimistic postmodernist perspectives that argue that we live in a fragmented society of uncertainty, dislocation and transience.

Assailed by materiality

There are two principle ideas concerning the relationships between people and objects that are especially pertinent to the analysis of consumption from the perspective of collecting First World War trench art. First, there is the notion of mass reification of social relations (Slater 1997), where an excessive assimilation has taken place in modern society between humans and the material world. Humanity and matter have become fused to such an extent that social relations have become 'object relations' (ibid.). The objectification of sociality is compounded by the second notion of personal gratification, which appears to have a direct correlation with the accumulation of material possessions (Gabriel and Lang 1995).

From a theoretical perspective, these charges are questionable. They appear tainted by an essentialist 'fear of objects supplanting people' (Miller 1998b: 169), and, in effect, they construe material objects as somehow inauthentic and alien to humanity. This argument ignores the fact that our use of objects is essentially what makes us human. It is 'through the medium of things' that 'we come to be ourselves' (ibid.). Cziksentmihalyi and Rochberg (quoted in Desmond 2003: 265–9) have proposed, for example, that our socialization depends to a great extent on our physical surroundings – we invest ourselves in them, and this allows us to negotiate the processes of integration and differentiation in our quest for self-definition and self-realization. We extend ourselves into the material world and forge a metaphorical relationship where accumulated objects become the 'outward signs and symbols of particular ideas in the mind' (McCracken 1988: 58). This is what McCracken refers to as the Diderot Effect – 'a force that encourages the individual to maintain a cultural consistency in his/her complement of consumer goods' (ibid.: 123). They are thus an instance of 'distributed personhood' (Gell 1998: 20–21, 104) – a concept particularly appropriate to the analysis of objects, such as trench art, associated with war.

As for the issue of accumulation, I am not convinced that a quantitative increase automatically equates with a qualitative decrease. There is no logical correlation between a number of objects accumulated and the ability to consume them – a quality which is not measurable, because it is neither finite nor tangible.

As for the objectification of the self, it can be noted that Patrice Warin has greatly assimilated trench art into his private sphere by filling most of his home with it. In fact his home is a home *for* trench art. He collects it because, to him, the whole seems like more than the sum of its parts, and it is these objects that make him a collector and an ethnographer of First World War material culture. These objects are part of him, and make him who he is – it could even be seen as part of the Diderot Effect. While each and every trench-art object that Warin has collected is one part of the whole process of 'constructing' his identity, there are some objects that, for one reason or another, inspire a personal attachment or sentiment. A small wooden tobacco box made by two POWs is one of Patrice Warin's favourite objects (Figure 9:5). He finds it *touchant* (touching) – the embodiment of friendship in the strangest and most dangerous of circumstances, and an example of humanity's better qualities in the midst of one of its worst pursuits.

In addressing the issue of objects reifying social relations, several points must be made. First, trench art can be viewed as the materialization of soldiers' relationships and experiences. Second, reification of social relations in trench-art objects allows these relationships to live beyond the soldiers themselves. While the makers and early consumers of these objects passed away long ago, their voices are still being heard through the trench-art items they made and its many different interpreters. These objects physically carry the past into the present, allowing for collectors such as Warin to engage in a direct and tactile way with the lives of First World War soldiers. Social relations between collectors are also materialized in the objects they collect, bringing them together and bestowing an identity and status as trench art collectors.

Furthermore, it could be suggested that Warin and his two friends also 'make' trench art by virtue of recognizing it amongst the mass of war memorabilia and miscellaneous objects that they encounter at markets and auctions. If they were not

Figure 9:5 Patrice Warin's tobacco box. (© author)

engaging with this material as specialist and knowledgeable collectors, the trench-art status of specific objects would remain latent. As mere pieces of war memorabilia, many items would not be recognized as the objectification of personal war experiences, and the deep irony with which each item is inherently laden would go unrecognized and unacknowledged. Patrice Warin and other knowledgeable collectors add cultural saliency to what might otherwise appear as an amorphous mass of war-related objects.

Finally, there is the issue of my own presence and involvement as an observer of these collecting activities. Trench art is an unusual array of objects that I would never have encountered in everyday life had I not decided to investigate its patterns of consumption. I met Patrice Warin and his friends because of trench art, and this has led to my creating an instant and direct association between these individuals and objects. In this sense, trench-art items are the reified medium for relations between objects and their makers, between collectors brought together through a shared interest in the objects, and for my relations with them – relations that arguably heighten the sense of cultural worth in their collecting activities.

In assessing the issue of the accumulation of objects, it appears that accusations of diminished quality are inapplicable in this case. Warin's sense of understanding and perceptibility, and thus his ability to consume trench art, cannot be measured and evaluated solely (or even mainly) in economic terms. Warin's apartment, like the homes of many such collectors, is practically a trench-art museum, and, as such, it is not a case of random or meaningless hoarding, but of knowledgeable and focused collecting. It is also a case of rearranging domestic space – altering the patterns of habituated movement, and presenting his collection (and new additions to it) to friends and guests who are invited to his home.

There are numerous display cabinets, a glass-covered coffee table full of First World War *briquets* and boxes of miscellaneous items; he has around 650 trench-art *briquets*, displayed in special cabinets (Figure 9:6), 400 other miscellaneous objects and about 500 postcards. What distinguishes Warin from the majority of trench-art collectors – in France and internationally – is the presence in his home of cupboards full of information that he has collected concerning these items. Whereas most collectors acquire only the objects and some associated literature (composed essentially of militaria and auction house magazines offering the latest commercial valuations), Warin's data relates to the war itself, soldiers' experiences, and rare and scattered contemporary sources and images concerning soldiers' trench-art making activities. It is Warin's informal library that bestows enduring cultural value to the objects he searches out, purchases and displays.

At the time of my research (January–May 2004), Patrice was in the process of reconstructing a biography of an ordinary French soldier (*poilu*). The only initial information available was a postcard the soldier had written. Warin was also aiding the Musée de l'Armistice in its preparation of an exhibition of trench art. In Warin's case, it appears that quantity has a definite positive correlation with quality. The more objects he amasses, the more he contributes to a better understanding of the First World War experience, specifically vis-à-vis the day-to-day experiences of the *poilu*.

Figure 9:6
Patrice Warin's
display cabinet of
trench-art cigarette
lighters (*briquets*).
(© author)

An unstable society

There are many sources of social instability in the modern world, though two stand out in relation to the study of collecting trench art. The first concerns the seemingly contradictory status of the individual in the age of mass production. The onslaught of industrialization and rapid urbanization between the eighteenth and twentieth centuries resulted in a state of permanent social dislocation and of constant reorganization for huge, heterogeneous and densely concentrated urban populations. One might say that people are now 'living in a world that no longer provide[s] the cushion of community and the web of taken-for-granted beliefs that protect against the spectres of meaninglessness and spiritual void' (Hollander 2002).

It was at the time of the Industrial Revolution that the idea of the construction of the individual came into full force, rather ironically as 'the mass [is in fact] the modern individual's hell' (Bauman 2001: 103), whose encompassed individuals only begin to count 'when they no longer can be counted' (Canetti quoted in ibid.: 102). It has been suggested that the resultant individualism of our times, and its concomitant process of atomization can in a sense be blamed for the supposed feelings of isolation and alienation arguably experienced by the modern individual. This lack of a feeling of belonging is sometimes seen to be countered by the creation of 'phantom communities' (ibid.: 106), which are essentially nothing more than transient groups based on common preferences, and are a step short of complete inconsequential gregariousness. After all, 'similarity does not make community' (ibid.: 105). It would seem that individualism – the gift of the Enlightenment – has come at a high price.

The second source of instability is seen to be the pervasive aestheticization of our society (Featherstone 1983; Miles 1998), whereby images, whether actual or imagined, have become the master paradigms, replacing traditional 'meta-narratives' that have collapsed (Lyon quoted in Miles 1998: 24). Baudrillard suggests that not only is the sign-value of an object now superior to its use-value, but that these signs are entirely self-referential and have no bearing on reality (ibid.:). Thus, we live in a 'hyper-reality' of transient, fleeting signs and images, which results in a feeling of shallowness. This is compounded by the presence of a plethora of material objects, which have arguably arisen inorganically – the 'need' for them created and 'calculated in relation to profit' (Slater 1997: 63). There is a sense here that nothing is real or authentic anymore. This creates an arduous challenge to the individual who is required to constantly negotiate and renegotiate his identity.

Examining these two sources of instability, one is ultimately confronted with sweeping generalizations that include assumptions about personal life in the pre-industrial era, for which we only possess historical data. 'Anthropologists [however] more than most scholars recognise that history is bound to be partisan, imprecise and ephemeral' (Lowenthal 1992: 23). The past is a cultural construct and, in this sense, as much an artefact as a piece of trench art from Warin's extensive collection. We can acknowledge that pre-industrial life was more localized, less dynamic and less prone to disruptive change, but we cannot know how people perceived this existence.

Our understandably incomplete knowledge of the past is accompanied by an equally patchy knowledge of the present. Do people today genuinely feel isolated from and unconnected to each other? The charge that we have no more communities is surely false. Community is, after all, a group of people who have something in common. In the past, this was built on kinship, locality and religion. Today, this type of commonality still occurs, even in urban centres, but, for many, community also comes from professions, hobbies, political affiliations, schools, universities and lifestyles. Anthropological knowledge of these interlocking groups is far from complete, and so, despite the fact that such groupings are largely amorphous, they cannot be regarded as inconsequential.

The issue of authenticity – in relation to the suggestion that symbolic para-digms have replaced traditional 'meta-narratives' – remains problematical. Did such 'meta-narratives' ever exist? Perhaps, as with the notion of the 'isolated individual', this is a concept over-reliant on an essentialist view of the past (Storey 1999: 1–2). Conceptualizing 'use' only in materialist terms, and 'sign' as being inherently superfluous, is surely unhelpful, as for many objects their sign-value *is* their use-value. This does not make them inauthentic. The capacity for abstract thinking is, after all, an integral part of our humanity.

Patrice Warin, Jean-Paul Noiret and Philippe Billot go to the *Puces aux Vanves* market in Paris almost every weekend, and also meet at auctions and other markets as often as possible. The three of them know some of the stallholders, who put things aside for them that they think might be of interest. Their wives are friends too, and socialize with each other. All these people are linked by one commonality: the strange objects made by long-dead soldiers from a 90-year-old war – trench art. This is a group bound by a specific form of emotional 'glue' and not a postcode. It might be a small community, but a community nonetheless as there exists 'an organic sense of commitment between [these] individuals' (Maffésoli quoted in Storey 1999: 139).

Trench art is collected for its sign-value and not its use-value. It would be wrong, however, to argue that this is due to the collectors' insensitivity to the use-value of these commodities. Most of these objects are still functional, and can be used as cigarette lighters, letter-openers, tobacco boxes, flower vases, etc. Such use, however, would make trench art little more than a set of tools. By engaging with them in 'symbolic work' (Slater 1997), in a polysemic material world, these war-related functional objects become the cultural category of trench art, and an integral (if under-recognized and little-investigated) part of First World War history.

The consumption of First World War trench art has always been an intensely personal and active engagement with materiality, though the commercial transactions enveloping it had different impulses during that war, the inter-war years, after the Second World War and according to personal experiences. Wartime soldiers bought trench art as souvenirs of life-and-death experiences during the conflict, whereas bereaved widows purchased it as heart-rending mementoes of a battlefield pilgrimage in the post-war years. Each group was a distinct community, for whom the objects reified their very different engagements with the war and its aftermath (Saunders 2004: 145).

Today, the dialogue between the collector and the objects entails bringing order to the apparent incongruousness and chaos of this amorphous mass of material. Rather than being overwhelmed by the sheer quantity of objects, collectors are a good example of how a stable microcosm can be created through personal interaction with the many meanings that are latent in materiality. Collecting and classifying trench art in private collections can also bring hitherto ignored (or unacknowledged) narratives to the surface, releasing, as it were, stories long ago attached to the objects but since forgotten.

Trench-art objects allow us to encounter the past in its physicality, a past that is not one of the many official First World War histories, but rather belongs to the 'everyman' experience of the trenches. As such, in seeking out the manifestation of these latent meanings, the consumption of trench art does not resemble an example of an unstable existence. There is cohesiveness and purpose to this activity, and it stems from a preoccupation with reality and with what past experiences were really like. As Patrice Warin says, it is a question of preserving his country's heritage and of unearthing something that would otherwise be lost forever. In fact, he feels he is fulfilling his duty to his country by making an important contribution to its historical and social self-knowledge. Understandably this gives him a sense of personal satisfaction and of belonging.

Conclusion

I have attempted to show how Parisian collectors, and Patrice Warin particularly, view and use trench art, and how their consumption of it affects them. While this is only a preliminary study, I believe the results have demonstrated the social dimension of consumption in a positive and constructive way, and, more specifically, identified a rich but hitherto unrecognized field for anthropological research.

The consumption of trench art can be seen as an example of a distinctive – perhaps mutually beneficial – relationship between humans and objects, mediated by the passing of time, the construction of memory and identity, and of ever-changing cultural and commercial valuations. Collecting trench art is a social activity that engages and defines this small group of people, thereby creating a community, and perhaps a particular social microcosm within contemporary French society.

More widely, though no less significantly, the social nature of collecting such items highlights the cultural value placed on these objects through investigating the distinctive social origins of the objects themselves – a value which seems at variance with purely commercial imperatives. Also revealed is the complex, if usually invisible power of classification, inasmuch as Warin and his collector friends apply a prescriptive typology to the kinds of objects they recognize as 'true' trench art – i.e. objects made by soldiers during conflict. The claim to authenticity inherent in Warin's definition inevitably raises the issue of what is and what is not an authentic experience of war: is it only experiences endured by soldiers in 1914–18 or does it additionally include experiences of civilians who also suffered the consequences – internees, refugees, battlefield pilgrims – both during and after the conflict?

Patterns of consumption of trench art and associated war souvenirs from the First World War (and the twentieth century's many other conflicts) are only now beginning to be investigated. What is apparent from this brief study is that the relationships between objects and their collectors offer unique and significant insights into the ways in which war is experienced, remembered and reconfigured by the generations who came after. Trench-art collectors seem to be collecting objects; in fact, as Patrice Warin and others know well, they are also collecting and reclaiming the dead.

References

Bauman, Z. (2001) 'On mass, individuals, and peg communities'. In N. Lee and R. Munro (eds), *The Consumption of Mass*, pp. 102–13. Oxford: Blackwell.

Belk, R.W. (1995) *Collecting in a Consumer Society*. London: Routledge.

Bruckner, P. (2002) *Misère de la prospérité: la réligion marchande et ses ennemis*. Paris: Grasset & Fasquelle.

Desmond, J. (2003) *Consuming Behaviour*. Basingstoke: Palgrave.

Douglas, M. and B. Isherwood (1978) *The World of Goods: Towards An Anthropology of Consumption*. Harmondsworth: Penguin.

Fabiansson, N. (2004) 'The Internet and the Great War: the impact on the making and meaning of Great War history'. In N.J. Saunders (ed.) *Matters of Conflict: Material Culture, Memory and the First World War*, pp. 166–78. Abingdon: Routledge.

Featherstone, M. (1983) 'Consumer culture: an introduction'. In M. Featherstone (ed.) *Theory, Culture and Society: Exploration in Critical Social Science series*, 1 (3): 4–9 (Special Issue on Consumer Culture). Middlesborough: The University of Teesside.

Gabriel, Y. and T. Lang (1995) *The Unmanageable Consumer: Contemporary Consumption and Its Fragmentation*. London: Sage.

Gell, A. (1998) *Art and Agency: An Anthropological Theory*. Oxford: Clarendon Press.

Hollander, P. (2002) 'Politics of envy'. http://www.travelbrochuregraphics.com/extra/politics_of_envy.htm

Lee, N. and R. Munro (eds) (2001) *The Consumption of Mass*. Oxford: Blackwell.

Lowenthal, D. (1992) 'The death of the future'. In S. Wallman (ed.) *Contemporary Futures: Perspectives from Social Anthropology*, pp. 23–35. London: Routledge.

McCracken, G. (1988) *Culture and Consumption: New Approaches to the Symbolic Character of Consumer Goods and Activities*. Bloomington: Indiana University Press.

Miles, S. (1998) *Consumerism – As a Way of Life*. London: Sage.

Miller, D. (1998a) *A Theory of Shopping*. Cambridge: Polity Press.

—— (ed.) (1998b) *Material Cultures: Why Some Things Matter*. London: UCL Press.

Miller, D., P. Jackson, N. Thrift, B. Holbrook and M. Rowlands (eds) (1998) *Shopping, Place and Identity*. London: Routledge.

Pearce, S.M. (1995) *On Collecting: An Investigation into Collecting in the European Tradition*. London: Routledge.

Saunders, N.J. (2001) *Trench Art: A Brief History and Guide, 1914–1939*. Barnsley: Leo Cooper.

—— (2003) *Trench Art: Materialities and Memories of War*. Oxford: Berg.

Slater, D. (1997) *Consumer Culture and Modernity*. Cambridge: Polity Press.

Storey, J. (1999) *Cultural Consumption and Everyday Life*. London: J. Arnold.

Wallman, S. (ed.) (1992) *Contemporary Futures: Perspectives from Social Anthropology*. London: Routledge.

Warin, P. (2001) *Artisanat de tranchée et briquets de poilus de la guerre 14–18*. Louvier: Ysec Editions.

10

'THE RETURNED SOLDIERS' BUG'

Making the Shrine of Remembrance, Melbourne

Catherine Moriarty

War memorials are significant components of commemorative landscapes in urban, suburban and rural contexts. Though their prescriptive intent is usually evident, they achieve meaning in complex ways, sometimes intended and in other cases, not. Like many objects of material culture, war memorials possess biographies whose social networks and shifting cultural resonances are layered and multi-vocal (Kopytoff 1986). The appearance and location of memorials, the texts inscribed upon them (see Chapter 11), and the speeches conducted at the ceremonies that take place around them all contribute to their existence as distinctive sensory environments. Importantly, each spectator's engagement, at different times and in changing contexts, involves an experience that might be spatial, iconographic, literary, performative or a combination of all these. While commemorative intent might be clearly visual, for example by the use of particular kinds of materials from which memorials are constructed, other factors were less evident and were bound up in the very processes by which memorials were made – the designing, transforming and placing of matter in post-war landscapes.

Our knowledge of the construction of major projects commemorating the First World War is often based on the study of two kinds of document: the minutes and papers produced by the bodies charged with the commissioning of memorials; and reports published in the press. However, this essay incorporates a very different source. It refers to the experiences and views of Paul Raphael Montford (1868–1938), the English sculptor responsible for the external sculptural components of the National War Memorial of Victoria in Melbourne, also known as the Shrine of Remembrance: a monument to the 114,000 Victorians who served in 1914–18, of whom 19,000 did not return (Figure 10:1).

Many of the committees charged with overseeing war memorial projects from inception to unveiling often preferred to commission sculptors or architects with local

Figure 10:1 The north façade of the Shrine as the tympanum nears completion. (© and courtesy Montford Estate, Brighton)

associations, or those who had participated directly in the conflict commemorated. This chapter, focusing on Montford's experience, examines the identity of the designers and makers of memorials, and the importance that was placed on their credentials, for, although the criteria were not always consistent, an examination of this factor offers another route to understanding how value was invested in commemorative objects.

During the war, and in the immediate years after, Montford, based in his London studio, had been occupied with an ambitious and elaborate project: designing four large-scale figurative groups that were to be placed on the bridge over the River Kelvin in Glasgow.[1] They were described in the *Architects' Journal* in December 1922 as 'the highest level of his achievement'. During this time, in 1921, he also completed a war memorial at Croydon, an interesting and effective pairing of a wounded soldier and a grieving woman holding a child, cast in bronze, and placed either side of a stone cenotaph.[2] But this commission did not bring him further memorial projects, nor did Montford win others when he competed for them. Yet a world war, involving thousands of troops from around the Empire, left in its wake a need for memorials in these other countries too. The cost of their loyalty, amounting to comparably heavy death tolls, needed to be made equally visible.

Competitions for memorials overseas were advertised in the trade press or through professional associations such as the Royal Society of British Sculptors. In September 1922, an announcement appeared in *The Architect* inviting competitors to submit designs for the memorial to Anzac troops killed in Egypt, Syria and Palestine that was to be erected at Port Said on the Suez Canal. Australian and New Zealand architects

145

and sculptors living overseas were permitted to enter the competition as were British architects and sculptors resident in Australia or New Zealand. In order to be eligible, Montford decided to take a dramatic step and emigrate. Arriving in Melbourne in early 1923 he waited several months only to learn that the first prize had been awarded to the local sculptor Charles Web Gilbert (1867–1925).[3] Though unsuccessful on this occasion, Montford established himself in Melbourne and later that same year assisted the Australian architects Philip Hudson and James Wardrop with their winning entry for the Shrine competition. It was to be a huge structure based on the tomb of Mausolus at Halicarnassus (c. 350 BC) in Asia Minor (modern Turkey), and located 'on probably the finest site that Melbourne can offer' at the southern entrance to the city.[4]

An experienced architectural sculptor, Montford was well placed to undertake the sculptural embellishment of the memorial. At this time he was writing regularly to his brother in London, who was a stone carver employed on architectural projects, and it is these letters that provide a considerable amount of detail about his work on the Shrine. They are a fascinating unofficial record of the building of a major commemorative structure that took over a decade to complete. They tell us much about the issues that were debated, the decisions that were contested, and the practicalities of making commemorative material culture, in a British dominion, on a monumental scale (Figure 10:2).

Before turning to Montford's experience with the Melbourne Shrine, it is helpful to consider various broad characteristics of commemorative activity in Australia. As in Britain, commemoration took place at a variety of levels and at different locations; from the dominion-embracing, multimillion pound burial, construction and administrative projects of the Imperial War Graves Commission (Longworth 1985) to the countless private rituals in domestic space centred on photographs, letters, returned effects and, primarily, absence (Moriarty 1999, 2004).

For the bereaved in Australia, the battlefields of Europe were so far away that visiting a grave, even if there was one to see, seemed an impossibility. Yet the bereaved far nearer felt similarly: ultimately, death itself brought with it a permanent distancing.[5] Again, as in Britain, most energy and enthusiasm centred on local

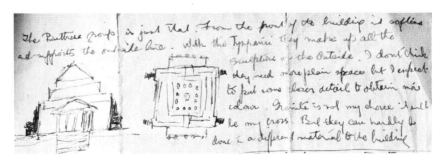

Figure 10:2 Montford to Louis, September 1929, a sketch in a letter describing the location of the sculptural elements of the Shrine. (© and courtesy Montford Estate, Brighton)

memorial schemes where communities could commemorate those who had served and those who had died from the surrounding area, whether a substantial town or smaller suburban or rural centres of population. These projects were the first to be completed. Fund-raising was largely enthusiastic and objectives realistic.

As Ken Inglis has observed in his important study of Australian war memorials, it was the 'national' memorials erected in each state capital that commemorated each state's war dead and the service of those who survived, but in a dominion-wide context, that took the longest to realise (Inglis 1999: 280–4). Heavily dependent on government subsidies as well as state-wide fund-raising campaigns, these projects were impressive civic projects that had an important role in promoting regional interests and aspirations. In many respects they were a political obligation and, as Inglis has pointed out, arrived too late to be of much comfort to the bereaved. The memorial obelisks in Tasmania and Western Australia were unveiled in 1925 and 1929 respectively, Queensland's circular colonnade, in 1930, South Australia's arch – rich in sculptural detail – the following year, and both the Victorian Shrine and the New South Wales Anzac memorial in Sydney, in 1934. The very last to be completed, in 1941, was what might be perceived by overseas audiences as a truly 'national' memorial – the Australian War Memorial in the federal capital of Canberra.

At the end of the war, there was some reason to suppose that, as the site of the federal government before its move to Canberra in 1927, Melbourne might be chosen as a location for a national memorial, and that Commonwealth government funds might be forthcoming. Though this idea failed to win support, Melbourne City Council and the Victorian government each committed £50,000 to the state's own memorial. By the summer of 1921, a monumental project, rather than a utilitarian one, had been decided upon, and the domain site was selected in March 1922, an area of high ground south of the Yarra River, at one end of Swanston Street, the main axial route through the city.

A competition was announced in November 1922, and, by July the following year, the judging committee had produced, from a field of 83, a shortlist of six entrants who were asked to submit scale models of their designs for exhibition at the Melbourne Town Hall. It was at this point that Hudson and Wardrop contacted Montford and asked him to model, in plasticine, the sculptural details of their design. For the winning architects, like many of their competitors, sculpture played an important part in their monumental scheme. Hudson, writing about the project soon after its unveiling, described how he wanted to create a landmark that was visible from afar, even from the sea, like the Acropolis at Athens, but one that was physically removed from the daily life of the city. Situated high on the Domain with its stepped pyramidal roof, the Shrine was to reference ancient monumental precedents.

Another important feature was the interior of the building. Rather than an empty tomb denoting absence in the tradition of a cenotaph, the memorial was to have a rich inner core, 'a soul', as Hudson described it (Hudson 1934: 1–3). While the Cenotaph in London worked well within a city already rich with accumulated memorials to the great deeds of great men, Hudson felt that an Australian city, with no comparable commemorative fabric, required a more elaborate solution. Certainly, early on, he envisaged some kind of Pantheon with the sarcophagi of national heroes incorporated in an ambulatory. His main aim was to convey 'the true birth of a Australian tradition' (Hudson 1934: 3). To this end, sculpture was incorporated at key points both outside and within the structure, acting as a vehicle to link the symbolism of the interior and the exterior.

Hudson and Wardrop's original design actually included several sculptural elements that were later abandoned, primarily in order to stem rising costs. These were four equestrians of Australian war leaders, to be placed on the lower terrace around the memorial, and eight figurative 'sentinels' that were to guard the inner shrine, representing Love, Peace, Courage, Integrity, Strength, Faith, Honour and Brotherhood. The sculpture considered indispensable, and that which visitors see to this day, comprised: the four exterior buttress groups representing Sacrifice, Patriotism, Justice, Freedom (later changed to Peace and Goodwill); the two tympanum friezes, The Call to Arms on the north façade, and The Homecoming on the south; and the twelve interior reliefs illustrating 'deeds of Australian valour'.

The placing and type of sculpture required, as well as what it should represent, was firstly Hudson's decision. He had indicated on the competition drawings the overall impression he intended to achieve. It was only when Montford was asked to create scale models for the final stage of the competition that the designs achieved a more detailed form (Sturgeon 1978: 86).

Montford's early involvement in the project and his developing friendship with Hudson gave him a high level of confidence that when the memorial came to be built he would be invited to undertake the sculptural components. The small number of sculptors with comparable experience and standing within Melbourne, indeed Australia, must have contributed to his confidence. Badly needing the work, and the kind of sums such a large project would bring him, Montford regularly reported to his brother on latest developments, or lack of them. As it turned out, an incoming Labor state government during 1924 questioned the appropriateness of a monumental war memorial, believing that a utilitarian project would be of more worth. In power for just four months, they raised doubts as to what kind of memorial would be most appropriate, doubts that were exacerbated by a further change in government. The new Country–National government preferred a victory arch to the Shrine, and the popularity of a temporary cenotaph outside the Parliament Building, which acted as a focus for Anzac Day parades, had brought about a new scheme for a permanent structure in its place; an option that was favoured by members of the Returned Services League (RSL). Montford wrote to his brother in May 1925: 'If only that dashed Memorial was starting but Hudson reckons on starting about the end of next year! Not so long when you consider the time the Monument is to be up, but a hell of a time to wait, for me.'[6]

It was at this juncture of renewed debate that Sir John Monash, the war-time general and chairman of the committee that had selected Hudson and Wardrop's design for the Shrine, decided to enter the fray. He was urged on by the influential right-wing Melbourne Legacy Club, a select association of ex-service businessmen, formed in 1923, whose aim was to keep the bonds of military service alive, supporting each other and their dependents. For Legatees, the Shrine represented the values of service and loyalty to the nation for which they had fought, and the perpetuation of these ideals was regarded as paramount, as their official ode concludes 'We'll not break faith with you who lie / On many a field'.[7] Their intentions were focused, and avoided, as Inglis describes it, 'the boozy egalitarianism of the RSL', they were mindful of the potential of the latter for fostering unrest, yet it was through their campaign to win RSL support that a groundswell in favour of the Shrine grew (Inglis 1999: 322).

On the eve of Anzac Day 1927, a day of increasing political significance in the Australian commemorative calendar at this time (Thomson 1994), Monash, the great hero and embodiment of Australian war-time prowess, urged in an emotive speech that Hudson and Wardrop's original scheme be revived and pursued with vigour. This plea was taken up by RSL members despite fierce opposition from some who felt that the material needs of ex-servicemen's families should come first, and that the memorial could only glorify war. Montford reported to his brother in May 1927, 'Hudson says that the Great Nat War Mem is coming along fast and his hopes are very high.' The foundation stone was laid on 11 November 1927, a ceremony attended by 5,000 people, including disabled soldiers in cots from the Caulfield Repatriation Hospital. Monash, as deputy chairman of both the General and the Executive committees, continued to play a major role in overseeing the construction of the Shrine and the search for further funds. In addition to his military standing, Monash was a successful civil engineer and a past president of the Victorian Institute of Engineers; he was fully qualified to comment on matters technical as well as emotional.

The Melbourne firm Vaughan and Lodge were appointed builders and construction commenced. By July 1928, Hudson was finally in a position to advise the executive sub-committee to take immediate action regarding the statuary; the sculptor needed to be appointed so that 'the requisite stone jointing might be determined'.[8] Yet, rather than simply approving Montford's involvement 'on the nod', it was decided that a special subcommittee should be formed, 'to consider the questions relating to the appointment of a sculptor' and 'to consider matters relating to statuary'.[9] There were two reasons for this, and Montford had cause to be anxious. First, cash-flow problems meant that the sculpture was to be 'rolled-out'. The cost of the entire memorial was estimated at over £247,000, with the sculptural components alone amounting to £33,500. The buttress groups, costed at £15,000, were considered indispensable features of the building (though they performed no structural function) and integral to the memorial's external appearance, and had to be carried out first, but the tympanum friezes and the inner relief panels were to come later when funds allowed. Thus the designation of discrete 'sculptural' tasks with their own budget meant that Montford's role was administered much like a subcontractor, working on components, rather than, as Hudson later acknowledged, an artist collaborating closely with the architect, contributing vision as well as experience to the scheme as a whole (Hudson 1934: 22) (Figure 10:3).

Yet, more critically, the issue of Montford's suitability for the work had been called into question, not in terms of skill, but rather in terms of his identity. Since the competition five years earlier, the difficulties of ex-servicemen, soon exacerbated by

Figure 10:3 The buttress on the groups on the east side of the Shrine soon after completion, with the city in the distance, *c*.1932. (© and courtesy Montford Estate, Brighton)

the depression, had become a major political issue. They should, it was felt by many, in all instances be given priority in employment – in terms of the Shrine, this was seen as especially pertinent. It was the Legacy Club, the key advocate of the scheme and driver behind Monash's decision to reinvigorate the project in 1927, which was most persistent in challenging assumptions as to Montford's entitlement to all the sculptural work. Since the competition, Hudson had travelled to Europe, including a visit to Scotland where he saw the Kelvingrove groups. Montford reported to Louis on 17 May 1927, 'After seeing my work at Glasgow he wouldn't have anybody else on that job.' Yet despite remaining Hudson's first choice, Montford was neither an ex-serviceman, nor Australian.

What is particularly interesting about the objections of the Legacy Club is that, though the entitlement to work was flagged as the main concern, between the lines it seems clear that the real issue was founded on a fear that the integrity of the ideals conveyed by the memorial would be diminished if one who had not known the intensity of wartime camaraderie was involved in its construction. Both Hudson and Wardrop were ex-AIF and Melbourne-based, and this had contributed to their popularity as project architects in 1923.

Despite these objections and in order not to delay building, the executive sub-committee instructed Montford to proceed with one-eighth scale models of the buttress groups. Each took the form of an allegorical female figure, with accoutrements indicative of the particular virtue she was intended to represent, standing upon a chariot led by a pair of lions and a young boy. Montford strove to create figures in sympathy with Hudson's classically derived structure but, in truth, they would not have looked out of place on a large-scale Edwardian building in any British city. Rather like the building itself, they are awkward amalgams of components that appear unresolved in both form and meaning. A scathing attack appeared in *Stead's Review* on 2 December 1929, 'the charge against this sculpture for the great monument is that it is foreign to its object, its country and its date. . . . What part or lot has any dweller in this corner of the newest of continents in a parade of lions, led by Cupids in undress uniform and peaked caps?'[10]

Montford had modelled the groups full scale and plaster casts were made for carvers to use as a guide as they created the granite replicas. The stone to be used was quarried locally, from Tynong, Victoria, and the marble for the interior columns came from another local source, the Buchan quarry. As the structure began to develop one *Argus* journalist was moved to write: 'Stone upon stone, out of a painful birth, for stone and marble have been torn from the earth to make this vision tangible, the Shrine is being raised towards the sky.'[11]

Although hoping that the Legacy Club would perhaps suspend their complaints, the Executive Committee was aware that in all likelihood action would be needed to pacify this vocal and influential lobby questioning Montford's suitability. Things came to a head in March 1929 when Montford reported to a new subcommittee, whose task it was to consider the sculpture of the inner frieze, that he would need help with the work on the Shrine if charged with undertaking the buttress groups, the tympanum and the inner reliefs. Apparently unaware at this stage of the challenge to his position from such powerful quarters, he suggested bringing a capable sculptor over from England. Hudson, it seems, chose this moment to reveal to Montford what the executive sub-committee had in fact decided upon months earlier: that the interior reliefs to be carved in freestone become the subject of a limited competition open only to Australian sculptors. Montford, Hudson suggested, would oversee this appointment and indeed, the work, when a suitably able candidate was engaged.

Shrewdly, Hudson and the executive sub-committee had devised a plan which meant they retained the skills and experience of a leading architectural sculptor in Montford but, by involving a token Australian, they would pacify the complainers. Committee member Alderman Stapely agreed to this idea, stating 'the public would want an Australian sculptor if possible'. He himself, he said, 'had been questioned on the grounds that Mr Montford was not an Australian or a soldier'.[12] Clearly, the Legatees were still at large.

Agreeing to proceed with this plan, two sculptors were suggested, the Sydney-based Australian-born Eva Benson (1891–1949) and Wallace Anderson (1888–1975), a Melbourne sculptor who had served with the AIF in France. Anderson had worked with the war records section and latterly for the Australian War Memorial creating dioramas of key battles that were to become one of its most popular attractions.[13] Visits were made to inspect their work. Montford wrote to Louis on 24 March 1929:

> The architect came to see me and was evidently somewhat embarrased [sic]. Finally he told me a subcommittee had been formed to push on with the

Sculpture and to that end it had been determined to consider the possibility of giving the inside frieze (12 panels of 6' × 7') of the Services to some one else and he discussed who? I am on this subcommittee and when we met and I laid down plans for the advancement of the work by getting help or another sculptor from England the Architect had to confess that the trouble was not so much 'Time is the essence of the Contract' as a matter of Patriotism! Members of the Committee rather are of [the] opinion [that] an Australian Sculptor – preferably [sic] a 'Digger' ought to be given a 'chance'. Whatever a 'chance' really means I don't know, but a competition is suggested – which I tell them wont make a sculptor. I fancy they think a Sculptor can spring up in a night, like a mushroom, if only given sufficient incentive. Tomorrow we the sub. go to see Wallace Anderson a man who was doing the war groups for the War Museum and who has lately been doing a frieze on a war Memorial for Ararat. I don't suppose he knows the first principles of relief – but I'll see tomorrow. Also there is a girl in Sydney who is quite an artist and who had done a frieze in a theatre there, and we are going to consider her work even if I have to go to Sydney. Anyway I do the Buttresses and Tympanii.[14]

As it turned out, neither was selected. Montford put forward his own proposal, the young, talented Sydney-based Lyndon Dadswell (1908–86). Dadswell was a pupil of British émigré sculptor Rayner Hoff (1894–1938), whose commemorative sculpture for the Anzac Memorial in Sydney, and for the National War Memorial, Adelaide, achieved a standing and appeal, as well as a notoriety, that Montford could envy. Hoff, who had arrived in Sydney to take up the post of head teacher of sculpture and modelling at East Sydney Technical College the same year that Montford arrived in Melbourne, was an ex-serviceman and ensured prospective clients were aware of this. Younger than Montford, he rejected conventional symbolism and offered a more vigorous commemorative language (Spate 1999). Hoff's preference for female studio assistants is suggested as one reason why he was happy to recommend Dadswell to Montford (Edwards 1992: 9):

> just when the Committee want an Aussie for the Shrine comes photos from a fellow of 21 at Sydney which seem to show him to be all I have been asking for! What use I shall make of him remains to be seen but he is very anxious to come to me to work! The reliefs of Wallace Anderson are too melancholy for words, quite impossible – that is the man we went to see last Thursday.[15]

Dadswell's appointment provided a convenient compromise, for the time being. He had great respect for Montford and Montford admired Dadswell's ability as a sculptor. Luckily for the executive sub-committee, they had approved a good match. Dadswell was appointed on a temporary basis, his first design for one of the friezes was approved in July, and his contract was extended (Edwards 1992: 9–13). Likewise, Montford's models for the buttress groups had been approved in May and work was underway on the full-scale models.

However, not everyone was happy. In July 1929, the executive sub-committee received a letter from A.N. Kemsley, who represented the Legacy Clubs of Victoria on the general committee. He objected to the powers of the executive sub-committee, and again protested at Montford's involvement on the grounds that, 'he is neither a Returned Soldier or an Australian'.[16] Kemsley stated how he represented the view that the memorial should be 'entirely' constructed by either returned soldiers or 'persons of Australian birth'.[17] To reinforce his point, Kemsley had gone to the trouble of compiling a list of fifteen sculptors who would meet one or, preferably, both these criteria. In fact, Wallace Anderson was top of the list for not only was he a returned soldier and Australian, but Victorian to boot. Kemsley had undertaken this exercise because, he wrote:

> I am aware that the reply to this point of view will be that we have no returned soldier sculptors capable of doing this work. Without posing as any way as a judge of such a matter, I respectfully submit that this is not the question at issue. It is a question of national sentiment and the acknowledgement of the principle which it is felt should be the deciding factor.[18]

As Inglis has described it, 'for this elite of digger nationalists the Shrine became a test case of the nation's gratitude' (Inglis, 1999: 322).

After lengthy discussion it was agreed, finally, that Montford would be given the north and south tympana, presumably because the executive committee was happy with the work he had produced thus far and was mindful of the additional work appointing new sculptors would involve. Hudson's views are not recorded but he must have experienced great frustration at these delays. It is tempting to wonder if he was aware that Montford's designs bore a close resemblance to one the sculptor had prepared for the pediment of the New Government Offices in Whitehall thirty years earlier. Inevitably, Kemsley recorded his vote 'against the motion for the execution of the Tympana by Mr Montford'. However, it was agreed that the figures to occupy the inner shrine – the eight 'values' included in the competition design six years earlier – would be allocated to sculptors on Kemsley's list. This proved to be such a fraught and protracted process, with designs of different types and standards proposed, sculptors dropping out, or dying, that in the end this component of the scheme was abandoned, primarily due to lack of funds and, thankfully perhaps, a mismatched assortment of attributes was avoided.

Finally, in January 1932, Hudson suggested that bronze urns might be placed in the niches, where the marble figures would have stood: 'I am convinced that if floral tributes were brought by those who visited the Shrine and if these offerings became a vogue, that much beautiful and added sentiment would result.' Perhaps, then, Hudson was somewhat relieved that the heavy burden of designing and commissioning sculpted symbolism had gone as far as it could, accepting that ultimately the success of the Shrine, and any significance vested in it, depended as much on visitors and what they brought to it as on the architectural and sculptural structure that was presented to the city's citizens on Armistice Day, November 1934.

A report published in the journal *Building* soon after the unveiling paid attention to every symbolic component of the structure. Whether this was achieved by iconography, text, labour or materials, to the writer it accumulated in such a density of implied meaning that it required anthropomorphic summation: 'The entire memorial, constructed of the most lasting materials – granite, bronze and freestone – just breathes out its commemorative soul.' A few paragraphs later he expanded this theme:

> Already it is full of sentiment, sad and fragrant memories which are as precious to people capable of deep and intense feeling as is the display of art to those of artistic leanings or as wealth is to the more mundane. They keep their feelings secretly locked in their breasts. The emotional side of life is comforted in such surroundings.[19]

Achieving such intensity of meaning involved, as we have seen, engaging architects and artists with credentials that imbued their work with added sentiment. This applied to craftspeople and builders too, and the carving of the exterior granite buttress groups had generated further controversy in this respect. Montford had intended to arrange carving in Britain, or to arrange for British carvers to come out to work in Australia. He felt that local masons did not have the necessary experience to work with such hard stone. He then considered employing Italian carvers and this caused something of a scandal when the local press found out. In the end, local carvers Joseph Hamilton and William Hutching were taken on.[20]

Stakeholders in the project were activated to bring 'added value' in other ways or, more precisely, as another means whereby the singularity of the Shrine and its sacred purpose would be asserted, distancing it further from the mundane and the commercial concerns of the city and its citizens (Kopytoff 1986). The buttress groups designed by Montford had been identified as the component of the Shrine to be financed with funds raised by school children throughout Victoria. The children were encouraged to become active participants in the project and school parties visited the Shrine to inspect the sculptures as they were completed. The young boy leading the lions in each buttress group was described as 'symbolical of the school children of Victoria who collected the funds required for the carving of the groups', although it is more likely that Montford had originally designed them to represent 'youth' or 'young Australia' more generally.[21] A photograph of visiting children shows them climbing a scaffold, appearing more interested in the bare-breasted figure of Patriotism than anything else (Figure 10:4).

Schoolteachers who had been active in orchestrating the appeal, together with the Director of the Board of Education, visited Montford's studio in 1929, not to vet his work but certainly to feel that their opinions mattered. Indeed, concessions to their views were made; at their request the title of one of the groups, 'Freedom', was altered, becoming 'Peace and Goodwill'. Montford commented to Louis on 4 March 1930,

> People who don't know, think what I mean to be is the thing and will have it that that is so much more important than what I have done. But what they think I ought to have meant is of more importance still.[22]

Y.A.L. BOYS AT THE WAR MEMORIAL.—About 75 boys of the Young Australia League were conducted over the Shrine of Remembrance yesterday by Brigadier-General J. P. McGlinn and one of the architects for the memorial (Mr. P. B. Hudson). A feature of interest was the sculptured group, "Patriotism," at the north-west corner of the Shrine, the first of four such groups to be completed as the result of the contribution of £16,000 from Victorian school children.

Figure 10:4 Schoolboys inspecting the figure of Patriotism. (© and courtesy National Library of Australia)

Perhaps because of the close observation of the Legacy Club and the furore over Montford's appointment, great care was taken to achieve consensus in the building of the Shrine wherever possible. Dadswell's reliefs were submitted to naval and military experts, 'who were most helpful in assuring the sculptors that action and dress were correct'[23] (Figure 10:5). Many of the calligraphers engaged to transcribe in books of remembrance the names of the 89,100 Victorians who enlisted and served overseas or died in training camps, were ex-servicemen. Work began on the compilation of the books in mid-1930 as the Melbourne *Argus* reported: 'it will be nearly a year before the names . . . are satisfactorily copied on to cream-tinted parchment with quill pens in lasting Indian ink'.[24] One book was sent to London to be signed by George V. Here, then, was another instance of the 'added value' achieved by the amalgamation of the activity of making, by those with direct association with the dead, and the use of 'meaningful' materials: long lasting, expensive, symbolic in origin.

As the Depression set in, even greater efforts were made to dilute the blatant extravagance of the monument. Premier, and member of the committee, the anti-Labor Sir Stanley Argyle arranged a scheme whereby ex-servicemen assisted with the landscaping of the site. A new labour-generating project was added in the final stages, the digging of a 'reflecting pool' in front of the memorial, the gift of the Melbourne businessman and philanthropist Sir Macpherson Robertson, though this was later filled in because it hindered processions and other ceremonial gatherings.

Figure 10:5 Montford and daughters on the scaffolding inside the Shrine, in front of Dadswell's reliefs. (© and courtesy Montford Estate, Brighton)

156

Despite the ill feeling Montford received from some over the Shrine commission, he had become, throughout its construction, something of a local celebrity. When interviewed for the Melbourne magazine *Table Talk* in 1930, one of the reasons Montford gave, perhaps with some irony, when asked about his decision to emigrate in 1923, was the apparent preference of British war memorial committees for soldier sculptors that had made it so difficult for him to win commissions.[25] Little did he suspect that he would suffer a similar fate in Australia pursued with even more vigour, or maybe he felt his skills and experience would outweigh this handicap? Certainly, 'The Returned Soldiers Bug', a phrase used by Montford in a letter to Louis of August 1927 to suggest why two suburban memorial commissions did not seem to be coming his way, indicates that he understood the situation very clearly indeed.

Despite his experience with the Shrine, he was responsible for two other important memorials in Victoria where his experience, ability and artistic kudos were valued. He designed a vigorous bronze Britannia proffering her sword to the Dominions for the wealthy Western District town of Camperdown, unveiled in December 1929. This symbolism was questioned by the commissioning committee: did it represent Australian subjugation to the crown? Rather, it was interpreted locally as defining British dependence on the Australian forces and her full recognition of the Australian nation. For the citizens of the Melbourne suburb of Malvern, Montford designed a marble version of the Croydon memorial but with the soldier wearing AIF uniform and holding a slouch hat; he asked a local girl and baby to pose as models for 'the young mother'. The design was unanimously approved by the Malvern RSL and unveiled in 1931.[26] Montford's identity, and even the use of Italian marble, were acceptable in this instance. The committee wanted only the best, though they did insist that in every other respect, 'the whole of the work in connection with the execution and construction of the said Memorial shall be carried out in Australia and as far as is possible by returned soldiers'.[27] Montford described himself as a 'peace man' and, while the sculpture on the Shrine was criticised as inappropriate European iconography representing little of Australian experience (Young 1924), this suburban memorial makes clear his recognition that the bereaved of Croydon and Malvern, though on different sides of the world, suffered loss that was much the same. At the unveiling ceremony of this memorial, the Premier, Stanley Argyle (who was to succeed Monash as deputy chairman on the National Memorial Committee), applauded the fact that the suffering of those on the home front had been referenced in the design.

Rather than the sculpture visible outside the Shrine, perhaps Montford's most powerful contribution to the Australian commemorative fabric is his portrait bust of Monash. While working on the Shrine, Montford requested sittings from its chairman, who was to die on 8 October 1931 and so never saw the Shrine completed. Montford wrote to his brother on 13 September 1927, 'Am starting a bust of Sir John Monash this week end – a love job.'[28] The plaster of this bust was acquired by the Australian War Memorial after Montford's own death in 1938. Charles Bean reported to the Memorial's director, John Treloar, 'the Monash bust is the best portrait I have ever seen of him – a speaking likeness in every way'.[29] The Memorial arranged for a bronze cast to be made using metal from a 15-inch enemy gun captured on the

Western Front at Chuignes, which Treloar described as 'to lend a sentimental touch'.[30] The appropriation of the material of conflict for commemorative purposes was a widespread phenomenon, bringing such recycled items into the corpus of objects known as 'trench art' (Saunders 2003; and see Kidd 2004: 161).

Thus, on the grand scale – for the Shrine has to be the most monumental structure ever built in Australia, perhaps only rivalled by the Australian War Memorial in Canberra – and on a more modest scale, the representation of Australian wartime experience and the activity of situating it within urban and rural space was an amalgamation of processes of making rituals and materials, each vested with as much significance as possible. In this way, the activity of creating commemorative objects employed strategies that served to define memorials as sacred and distinct – as objects with only one possible purpose. Yet herein lies the assumption that by creating a monument on the model of other monuments, and by making it conspicuous and didactic, it would in fact promote remembrance (Forty 1999).

In the case of the Melbourne Shrine, we are left wondering whether the process was perhaps more cathartic for those involved with its construction than either the bereaved, who had already been grieving for sixteen years or more by the time it was unveiled, or for the majority of ex-servicemen who were busy trying to make ends meet. Ultimately, the Shrine made visible, literally as a landmark, the restitution of the war dead by locating them in the official narrative of the nation's history. How the dead were remembered by Victorians as part of narratives personal, familial and communal was altogether more pervasive, yet more elusive, and less stable than the parameters defined by the guardians of the Victorian memorial project.

Transformed from a site of construction and with its various component parts finally in place, the Shrine became a focus around which a commemorative performance took place. Over 300,000 people were present to witness the dedication by the Duke of Gloucester on 11 November 1934. Legatees would have approved of his speech. The Shrine, he said, was built to

> perpetuate the memory of the men who fought to secure to the world the blessings of peace . . . It is for us to seek to repay their devotion by striving to preserve that peace and by caring for those left bereaved or afflicted by the War.

Yet, not all present endorsed the proceedings and the rhetoric uniting the dead with the living and the past with the future, for among the crowds were protesters who were in Melbourne attending a counter-event, the All-Australia Congress Against War (Inglis 1998: 316–17).

The Times reported the following day: 'The ceremony took place under heavy, dark clouds, with occasional bursts of sunshine. It was estimated that enough returned soldiers, many of them in uniform, and all with medals, were present to constitute an entire division.'

The ceremony incorporated various elements that temporarily animated the structure with movement and sound. At the eleventh hour, and as a result of careful astronomical calculations, a ray of light shone through an aperture in the roof of the Shrine, lighting a 'Rock of Remembrance' in the inner chamber and the inscription 'Greater love hath no man'. The sounding of a gun then indicated the commencement of the two-minute silence, the national anthem and other hymns followed, speeches were made, an ode especially written for the occasion by Rudyard Kipling was read aloud, drums rolled, the bands played Chopin's Funeral March, the Anglican archbishop pronounced the benediction and, as a finale, 20,000 pigeons were released to the skies, 'to fly to all parts of outback Victoria as an announcement of the dedication'. Now, the ceremony would be remembered as an historic civic event in itself, the dense symbolism of the building compounded by spectacle.

While Hudson was invited to sit with the dignitaries at the unveiling ceremony, Montford was not. He threatened to return his ticket, until his wife intervened. By this time Louis had died and so there is no account of the event, simply a brief note in a diary:

> Shrine opened. Saw it and shook hands with the Dook. To Warrendite in aft: with Marian, Adrian & Bobby.

Acknowledgements

This essay stems from researching Montford's papers, located with the Montford family in Brighton, and from study undertaken while based at the Australian Centre, University of Melbourne, January–April 2005, made possible thanks to an Australian Bicentennial Fellowship awarded by the Menzies Centre, King's College, London, and a British Academy research grant. The essay develops the paper '"Granite is not my choice; it will be my cross": building the Shrine of Remembrance, Melbourne' presented at the University College London/Imperial War Museum second conference on 'Materialities and cultural memory of twentieth-century conflict', entitled 'Conflict, memory and material culture: the Great War, 1914–2004', held at the Imperial War Museum on 11 September 2004.

I would like to thank Alan Krell and Eric Riddler, who supplied helpful research material on memorials in Australia for the paper I prepared in 1997 and which has also proved invaluable for this chapter. I am particularly indebted to the following for their assistance and support: Adrian, Selma and Piran Montford, Gail Braybon and Al Thomson in Brighton; Laura Back in Canberra; Kate Darian-Smith, Caroline Jordan and Jean McAuslan in Melbourne; and Di Foster at Malvern Archive.

Notes

1 See the detailed entry in McKenzie (2002) pp. 236–42.
2 Photographs and an elevation of this memorial were featured in the *Architects' Journal*, 2 November 1921. The architect was James Burford. The pairing is a contemporary rendering of the Kelvingrove group representing Peace and War.
3 The Desert Mounted Corps Memorial, as it was known, has a long and interesting history of its own. Montford ended up swallowing his pride and working as assistant to

C.W. Gilbert in his Fitzroy studio. When the latter died in October 1925, the commission was handed to Montford, only to be passed, to his dismay, to Sir Bertram Mackennal early the following year. This was the subject of a paper presented at the Imperial War Museum ANZAC conference 23/24 April 2005.

4   *Building*, 12 December 1934.

5   Moriarty, C. 'Home and away: distance as a theme in the commemoration of the First World War', paper presented at the Imperial War Museum/Australian War Memorial joint symposia, *Continuities, Challenges and Changes: Australia and Britain in War in the Twentieth Century*, London, July 1997, and Canberra, September 1997. Unpublished.

6   Paul Montford to Louis Montford, 27 May 1925. Montford Estate, Brighton.

7   Legacy continued to develop in every state and there are fifty clubs in Australia today with 7,000 members. Today the support of the dependents of military dead and promoting the ideals of military service remain its prime function; it retains the motto 'Carry the Torch'. See www.legacy.com.au.

8   Minutes of the Meeting of the Executive Committee, National War Memorial of Victoria, 17 July 1928, Melbourne City Council Archive. The Executive Committee was established in August 1927 as a subcommittee of the general committee; the latter was known until this time as, confusingly, the Executive Committee.

9   The subcommittee comprised Sir John Monash, Dr Stanley Argyle, Alderman Stapley and Philip Hudson. Minutes of the first meeting of the subcommittee appointed to consider the questions relating to the appointment of a sculptor to consider matters relating to statuary, 24 July 1924. Melbourne City Council Archive.

10   *Stead's Review*, 2 December 1929.

11   *The Argus*, 8 November 1930.

12   Minutes of the First Meeting of the Subcommittee appointed to consider the selection of a Sculptor to carry out the Inner Frieze, 28 March 1929. Melbourne City Council Archive.

13   Two sculptures by Benson are held by the Art Gallery of New South Wales. Wallace Anderson went on to win the competition for the sculpture 'The Man with the Donkey'. Located in the grounds of the Shrine, it is arguably the most popular sculpture in the city (see Scarlett 1988: 10–14). Laura Back is preparing the first detailed study of the instructive yet emotive and, indeed, commemorative dioramas at the Australian War Memorial (see Back 2004: 12).

14   Paul Montford to Louis Montford, 24 March 1929. Montford Estate, Brighton.

15   Paul Montford to Louis Montford, 9 April 1929. Montford Estate, Brighton.

16   Minutes of general (formerly executive) committee, National War Memorial Committee, 2 August 1929. Melbourne City Council Archive.

17   Ibid.

18   Kemsley to Chairman, National War Memorial Committee, 17 July 1929. Melbourne City Council Archive. The list of 'Australian sculptors' was arranged as follows (interestingly, Kemsley had no objection to women sculptors or Australians living abroad):
Victorian Returned Soldier
Anderson; W. Wallace

Other Returned Soldiers (in alphabetical order)
Bowles; W. Leslie, ARBS
Lambert; George W. ARA
Lynch; Frank

Other Australians (in alphabetical order)
Baskerville; Margaret
Cohn; Miss Ola
Cowan; Miss Theo (sic)
Doble; ?William or Gilbert [This is Kemsley's uncertainty, it was Gilbert]
Lyle; Miss Nancy

Mackennal; Sir Bertram, RA
Macintosh; William P
Mayo; Miss Daphne
Chilfsen; Dora
Parker; Harold; RBS
Richardson; Charles Douglas

19 *Building*, 12 December 1934: 25–6.
20 The front page of the Melbourne newspaper *The Sun* on 26 November 1930 featured a large photograph of one of the lions for the granite buttress groups being carved, entitled 'Statuary for War Memorial taking shape'. News cutting, Montford Estate, Brighton.
21 *Building*, 12 December 1934: 23. A bronze cast of the plaster maquette for the buttress group 'Patriotism' is located outside the Australian War Memorial, Canberra. ART41008.
22 Paul Montford to Louis Montford, 4 March 1930. Montford Estate, Brighton.
23 Hudson, 1934: 9.
24 *The Argus*, 6 September 1930.
25 *Table Talk*, 25 September 1930. News cutting, Montford Estate, Brighton; also referenced in Edwards, 1992: 9.
26 Folder of copies of assorted papers relating to the memorial, comprising contract with sculptor, assorted correspondence of committee and arrangements for the unveiling ceremony. Malvern Archive, Stonnington City Council History Collection, Victoria. For a detailed account of the Camperdown memorial see Willingham, 1995: 418–32.
27 Agreement between the Mayor, councillors and citizens of the City of Malvern and Paul Raphael Montford. 1928. Malvern Archive.
28 Paul Montford to Louis Montford, 13 September 1927. Montford Estate, Brighton.
29 Bean to Treloar, 17 February 1937. AWM93 13/1/71. Canberra: Australian War Memorial.
30 Treloar to Gregory, 8 March 1938. AWM93, 13/1/71. Canberra: Australian War Memorial.

References

Back, L. (2004) *Shaping Memory: Sculpture at the Australian War Memorial*. Canberra: Australian War Memorial.

Edwards, D. (1992) *Lyndon Dadswell, 1908–1986*. Woollahra, NSW: Dadswell & Edwards.

Forty, A. (1999) 'Introduction'. In A. Forty and S. Kuchler (eds) *The Art of Forgetting*, pp. 1–18. Oxford: Berg.

Hudson, P. B. (1934) *Thesis on the Shrine of Remembrance*, unpublished paper. Melbourne City Council Archive.

Inglis, K. S. (1999) *Sacred Places: War Memorials in the Australian Landscape*. Melbourne: Melbourne University Press.

Kidd, W. (2004) 'The lion, the angel and the war memorial: some French sites revisited'. In, N.J. Saunders (ed.) *Matters of Conflict: Material Culture, Memory and the First World War*, pp. 149–65. Abingdon: Routledge.

Kopytoff, I. (1986) 'The cultural biography of things: commoditization as process'. In A. Appadurai (ed.) *The Social Life of Things*, pp. 64–91. Cambridge: Cambridge University Press.

Longworth, P. (1985) *The Unending Vigil: A History of the Commonwealth War Graves Commission 1917–1984*. London: Leo Cooper (rev. edn, first published 1967).

McKenzie, R. (2002) *The Public Sculpture of Glasgow*. Liverpool: Liverpool University Press.

Melbourne City Council, Shrine of Remembrance Records, 1921–2001.

Montford, P., Mss letters 1922–38, Montford Estate, Brighton.

—— (1930) 'The application of sculpture to modern architecture'. *Journal of the Royal Victorian Institute of Architects*, January: 129–35.

Moriarty, C. (1999) 'The material culture of Great War remembrance'. *Journal of Contemporary History*, 34 (4): 653–62.

—— (2004) '"Though in a picture only": Portrait photography and the commemoration of the First World War'. In G. Braybon (ed.) *Evidence, History and the Great War: Historians and the Impact of 1914–18*, pp. 30–47. Oxford and New York: Berghahn.

Saunders, N.J. (2003) *Trench Art: Materialities and Memories of War*. Oxford: Berg.

Scarlett, K. (1980) *Australian Sculptors*. Melbourne: Nelson.

Spate, V. (1999) '"If these dead stones could speak": Rayner Hoff's sculptures and the Anzac Memorial'. In D. Edwards *'This Vital Flesh': The Sculpture of Rayner Hoff and his School*, pp. 53–67. Melbourne: Art Gallery of New South Wales.

Sturgeon, G. (1978) *The Development of Australian Sculpture 1788–1975*. London: Thames and Hudson Ltd.

Thomson, A. (1994) *Anzac Memories: Living with the Legend*. Oxford: Oxford University Press.

Willingham, A. (1995) *Camperdown: A Heritage Study. Study findings and final report to the Corangamite Shire*, Vol. 1. Camperdown, Victoria: Conrangamite Shire.

Young, B. (1924) 'The designs for the Victorian War Memorial'. *Art in Australia* 3 (7).

Zimmer, J. (1990) 'Paul Raphael Montford'. *Art in Australia,* 28 (1): 94–101.

11

EXPLORING A LANGUAGE OF GRIEF IN FIRST WORLD WAR HEADSTONE INSCRIPTIONS

Sonia Batten

Introduction

As an oral history event documenting the negotiated experiences of bereavement, grief and mourning, the First World War has all but disappeared. A few of the very young men who saw active service during the war survived, all centenarians, to see the ninetieth anniversary of the war's outbreak. Richard van Emden records the esteem, even awe, in which these veterans are often held (Van Emden 2003: 3). The stories these men tell are fascinating chunks of reminiscence, but, at a distance of over eighty years, they are inevitably complex, multilayered documents that tell us as much about the politics of remembering as the events they explicitly recount. They cannot, by definition, be representative, as their owners are ambassadors of a generation that has mostly slipped away. Soon, it will be possible to listen to such accounts only through the medium of sound archives.

It is too late to interview the very old about their reactions to the personal and traumatic loss of male relatives in the First World War. Even if this were not so, such a project would encounter significant methodological problems. Language is a conscious tool and in this context would replicate the problematic issues of remembering (Davies 1997: 1). Although it is too late to replicate the emotional and linguistic reaction to the experience of bereavement during the First World War, it is possible to identify some of its principal elements.

Material culture represents one means of reconstructing the experience of mourning during and after the First World War. The research on which this chapter is based considers three particularly rich linguistic sources: the personal correspondence of the bereaved, the *in memoriam* notices they placed in local newspapers, and the personal inscriptions they chose for their sons' headstones in the post-war cemeteries.[1] It is with personal inscriptions that I am concerned here, from which the hypothesis of a 'language of grief' emerges. My aim is to consider the purpose of such a language. I argue that a language of grief served not only to express the emotions of the bereaved, but also to assert issues of identity that were bound up between the deceased, the bereaved and ideas of nationhood, sacrifice and death.

Death and the First World War

Written media dominated the first two decades of the twentieth century. Although the number of radio licences had increased dramatically by 1929, the 1920s remained the age of the newspaper. A range of national and provincial titles catered for different reading markets, and newspapers were the primary medium for transmitting information and forming opinion. Casualty lists, giving the names of those killed, wounded and missing were a staple feature of wartime newspapers. Death in the First World War was primarily mediated through literary forms.

Once a death had occurred or was believed to have occurred, the army's postal service – one of the logistical triumphs of the war – prevented the delivery of any remaining letters home. Instead, a letter or, most notoriously, a telegram was despatched to the next-of-kin informing them of the death.[2] In the case of soldiers reported as 'missing', a period of agonizing uncertainty followed for family and friends, in which speculation and condolence featured in equal parts.[3] Where no ambiguity existed, the soldier's commanding officer or chaplain, and sometimes his comrades, wrote letters of condolence to the next-of-kin. Such letters ranged from isolated communications to full, reciprocated correspondence. As soon as circumstances permitted, the soldier's personal effects were also returned. Since the British government had prohibited the repatriation of bodies for burial, the return of such effects was arguably the closest approximation to the repatriation of the soldier's body.

The burial and commemoration of the dead during the South African War had been handled somewhat haphazardly, prompting public disquiet. Recalling this experience, the British government responded quickly to calls for a systematic approach to the burial of the dead. In 1914, Fabian Ware was too old to qualify for military service. Instead, he joined the Red Cross and was instrumental in locating, identifying and recording the graves of British servicemen in northern France. He quickly realized the scale of the task and lobbied Major-General Nevil Macready, then Adjutant-General of the British Expeditionary Force, to establish a Graves Registration Unit. Meanwhile, the British government issued an order prohibiting the repatriation of the dead for burial. A few months later, in the autumn of 1915, the Graves Registration Unit was formalized and its status recognized within the BEF. Its work remained the same. Two years later, in May 1917, the Unit was established under Royal Charter as the Imperial War Graves Commission, with the Prince of Wales as its president.

One of the Commission's founding principles was the equality of treatment for all British servicemen, regardless of rank or status. The 2 foot 6 inch tall Portland headstone was designed with this aim (Figure 11:1). To commemorate the tens of thousands of men whose bodies were never recovered, the Commission designed vast memorials to the missing on whose walls were engraved their names. Such individuals could have no personal inscription, but to compensate for its absence many families

Figure 11:1
Imperial War Graves
Commission (IWGC)
stonemason working on a
headstone. (© author)

placed *in memoriam* notices in their local newspapers. The notices fulfilled another important function: that of communication between the bereaved and their local community.

Public interest in the design and construction of the cemeteries was widespread (Figure 11:2). Families wrote to the Commission requesting the details of their sons' graves. Such was the level of interest that the Commission allocated extra resources to its photographic and horticultural departments. David Lloyd's fine study of pilgrimage on the Western Front illustrates how significantly these sites were viewed by the bereaved (Lloyd 1998: 101). Even before the war had ended, civilian interest in battlefield visits was widely anticipated, not least by Philip Johnstone in his poem 'High Wood':

Madame, please,
You are requested kindly not to touch
Or take away the Company's property
As souvenirs; you'll find we have on sale
A large variety, all guaranteed.

(Gardner 1989: 157)

Figure 11:2 View of Ypres Reservoir Cemetery in 2003. (© author)

Memorials sprang up in almost every British community. Although the iconography of memorials to the First World War was shaped by many centuries of powerful visual imagery, it was unusual for a memorial to rely solely on its architectural power. The Whitehall Cenotaph was inscribed to 'The Glorious Dead', and traditional memorials in the form of crosses or crucifixes evoked written accounts of Christ's Passion and the scriptural quotation 'Greater love hath no man than this, that a man lay down his life for his friends'. Catherine Moriarty has noted that 'memory' was specifically articulated on many memorials, but that its appearance was never negatively qualified: as she has pointed out, 'we never read of "regretful memory", "angry memory" or "broken-hearted memory"' (Moriarty 1997: 137). By looking only at monuments as evidence of public and private grief, historians limit their perspective. As King (1998: 100) has shown, war memorial committees tended to be dominated by influential males from the community in question, ranging from the local gentry, the Member of Parliament and civic officials, to local employers and businessmen. As such, the committees relied on men from the generation that had prosecuted, rather than fought, the war. Ex-servicemen, women and children struggled to find a voice within these communities. Ex-servicemen were able occasionally to force committees to listen. In 1921, Robert Lorimer, one of the Commission's architects, wrote despairingly to Major Durham[4] to explain that:

> One of the men belonging to the parish was shot as a deserter in 1916 and
> he had I understand an unfortunate record. It was proposed to omit his name

as being unsuitable for a Roll of Honour. The Ex-servicemen have created a disturbance and wish to insist on this man's name going on otherwise they say they will wreck the memorial. On the other hand a number of parents whose sons have been killed say that if this man's name goes on the memorial they will not permit their sons' names to go on – so there you are, a fine kettle of fish you will agree!

(CWGC Archives, Item WG1606)

The names of the ex-servicemen were eventually inscribed in an illuminated Roll of Honour, which is now on display in Newport Central Library.

The newly renamed National Council of Women complained that there was no female representative on the Commission.[5] Although it was not all that common for women to enjoy a significant public voice in the 1920s, their role was both practical and symbolic. Gender roles were closely defined when it came to unveiling community war memorials. Most monuments were unveiled by men who possessed the appropriate military, political or social connections.[6] Women unveiled a few community war memorials. Princess Henry of Battenberg unveiled Sandown's memorial on the Isle of Wight, and Princess Alice, Countess of Athlone, performed the ceremony at Roehampton. There were also some examples of bereaved women taking part in the opening ceremonies. In Manchester in 1924, a Mrs Dingle, who had lost three sons in the war, assisted the Earl of Derby in the ceremony. In 1926, a Miss Williams of Blaina was photographed sitting at the front of the memorial, dressed in black and wearing her brothers' medals. Although she was not part of the ceremony itself, she had been introduced to the unveiling party beforehand. As Gaffney notes, she was 'physically and mentally detached from those around her' (Gaffney 1998: 172).

On occasion, the gender lines were blurred, as when George V visited the newly created cemeteries in France in 1922. At Etaples, he took out of his pocket an envelope that contained a small bunch of forget-me-nots. The flowers had originally been sent to Queen Mary by a bereaved mother, with the request that the Queen place them at the grave. Royal itineraries conspired to have the King perform this simple act of remembrance instead (Longworth 1967: 80). When it came to their physical depiction on war memorials, women received cyclical representation, firstly as wives and mothers waving off their male relatives, then as nurses tending the wounded, before reverting to wives and mothers either receiving their wounded men folk or accepting the loss of bereavement. Examples may be found in Goscombe-John's 'The Response' at Newcastle-under-Lyme, in William Bloye's bas reliefs in Birmingham's Hall of Memory, or in William Dick Reid's figure of a mourning woman in the Bushey memorial. Women's other major function was fund-raising, particularly selling poppies on behalf of the British Legion after their adoption in 1921 (Gregory 1994: 101).

Whose language?

In 1917, the Commission appointed Sir Frederic Kenyon as their architectural adviser. Kenyon had built a reputation as a distinguished biblical and classical scholar, and at the time of his appointment he was director of the British Museum. His first task was to consider the construction of cemeteries abroad. In January 1918, he submitted his report, 'War Graves: How the Cemeteries Abroad will be Designed', to the commissioners. It was a comprehensive document, covering site selection and clearance as well as architectural and horticultural development. Kenyon recommended that the next-of-kin should be allowed to choose a personal inscription for their sons' headstones, but argued that it was 'clearly undesirable to allow free scope to the monumental mason, the sentimental versifier, or the crank' (Kenyon 1918: 7).

He considered that inscriptions should be 'of the nature of a text or prayer' and be limited to three lines; in the end the Commission allowed a maximum of 66 characters (including the spaces between words) (Figure 11:3). This amounted to an upper limit of around twelve words. Kenyon was also certain that the next-of-kin ('or other person or organisation . . . whose claim is approved by the Commission') should pay the cost of the inscription, fixed at 31/2d (threepence ha'penny) per character. The idea of payment was accepted by all the commissioners with the exception of Harry Gosling, president of the Transport and General Workers' Union. He was appalled by the idea, arguing that it violated the Commission's own principal of equality of treatment. 'Supposing they have got enough only for three letters, what will they put on?' he asked at the commissioners' meeting in October 1919 (CWGC Archives, Minutes of Meetings, 21 October 1919). Although Ware conceded that the Commission had received 'letters, pathetic letters' requesting financial assistance, he argued that in practice no family should be unable to pay, citing the working-class habit of saving for funerals. Since the Commission had paid the costs of burial and headstone, Ware felt that families should possess a small financial surplus. Other commissioners felt that to charge for inscriptions was entirely proper, and Rudyard Kipling pointed out that some families had specifically requested to pay for them. Kenyon argued that poor families should rely on local philanthropy rather than petition the Commission for assistance. After a lengthy discussion it was moved that families should be sent a statement detailing the cost of their chosen inscription. If that statement did not produce payment, then the inscription would be engraved regardless and the matter quietly dropped.

The Commission did not appear to offer formal advice to bereaved families on the choice of inscriptions. Starting at the end of the war, the next-of-kin were sent final verification forms asking them to check the veracity of the personal information held on the deceased and allowing the option of a personal inscription. The majority of final verification forms sent to British families were destroyed in the 1960s. One of these

Figure 11:3
A personal inscription
on a headstone in 2005.
(© and courtesy Douglas West)

surviving forms (date stamped 1937) shows that the next-of-kin originally selected the first four lines from the second verse of 'Eventide':

Swift to its close ebbs out life's little day;
Earth's joys grow dim, its glories pass away;
Change and decay in all around I see:
O thou that changest not, abide with me!

The form showed that the third and fourth lines had been struck through by a member of Commission staff and a note added, 'Agreed with NOK'. It is interesting to note that the first two lines actually exceeded the 66-character limit for inscriptions. Had this limit been applied rigidly, the text would have ended at the word 'dim' on the second line. The remainder of that line was presumably included to retain as much of the intended meaning as possible (as well as maintaining the flow and rhyme of the verse). It is also a useful reminder that censorship might not have been an impersonal and unyielding process.

In contrast to the British experience, the final verification form issued to Australian next-of-kin through the Anzac Agency included four sample inscriptions. All four endorsed certain ideas relating to men, women, children, war, sacrifice and nationhood:

HIS DUTY FEARLESSLY AND NOBLY DONE
EVER REMEMBERED
GREATER LOVE HATH NO MAN THAN THIS
THAT HE LAY DOWN HIS LIFE
DEARLY LOVED & SADLY MISSED
BY LOVING WIFE ANN & SON GILBERT
LOVING SON OF MR & MRS J. BLANK OF ADELAIDE
SOUTH AUST. R.I.P.

The first inscription upholds the idea of war service as a duty: a dual duty presumably owed to the nation (as Australia had only come into formal existence in 1901) and to the empire, represented by Britain. Many Australian casualties were first-generation immigrants whose parents continued to live in the United Kingdom. The qualities identified in the inscription (fearlessness and nobility) chimed with Victorian and Edwardian notions of war and chivalry, while blending with the emerging Australian myth of war service (a myth that took hold remarkably quickly and which was represented by the archetypal Australian soldier, the 'Digger'). The inscription also associated fearlessness and nobility with the serving male, suggesting implicitly that women and children should 'ever remember'.

The second inscription is a familiar text on many community war memorials built in Britain between 1920 and 1925. Although rarely employed in pre-war civilian cemeteries, it was widely evoked in the commemoration of losses such as Captain

Scott's polar expedition or the sinking of the Titanic in 1912. The fuller variation, 'for his friends' is also ambiguous.

The third sample inscription uses 'love' in a different context. Its repetition ('dearly loved' and 'loving wife') emphasizes not the love of duty or of nation, but of family. Its domestic overtones serve to emphasize personal grief and to recognize that the casualty was not only a chivalric warrior, but also a husband and father. This sense of grief is underlined by identifying by name (Ann and Gilbert) the bereaved wife and son. The text continued to depict women and children as passive sufferers of the war, in marked contrast to their wartime representation as instigators of male service and sacrifice (as represented on wartime propaganda posters).

The final sample inscription recognizes that, where the next-of-kin was listed, it was often the parent or parents. This formulation reminds the onlooker that it was this parental generation that was realistically the first to expect to predecease their children. The First World War shattered this expectation for many families. The text also acknowledges regional and national identity, and a link with Australia.

At a distance of several decades it is no longer possible to eavesdrop on the complex negotiations that must have taken place between different family members. Although most entries listed their parents or wives as next-of-kin, a significant proportion cited siblings, aunts, uncles, cousins, grandparents or step-parents. Another significant group listed no next-of-kin at all, demonstrating some of the administrative difficulties faced by the Commission.

It is important to read personal inscriptions in conjunction with the cemetery register. The latter can provide a wealth of information for which there was no room on the headstone: regional identity, school, civil employment, previous military service, date of enlistment and citations of gallantry from the *London Gazette*. Crucially, the register entry also states the name of the next-of-kin and his or her relationship with the casualty. This information makes a potentially vital connection with the structure and content of the personal inscription. It was unlikely – but not impossible – that an entry listing no next-of-kin would have a personal inscription. Hierarchical issues are implicitly present in inscription choices. Texts allowed individuals, families and, on occasion, whole communities space in which to wrestle with their own impressions of loss and to express them within a framework stipulated by the Commission.

Children are wholly absent from register entries, but appear in the inscriptions. Although they could not assume the legal or administrative responsibilities of the next-of-kin, their inclusion in inscription choices and other memorial texts provides a powerful reminder of the social and emotional impact of bereavement. Their absence from the registers reinforces the impression that the commemoration of the war was contested by the two older generations, namely their parents and grandparents. Children appear in the inscriptions in two different ways: as appendices to the primary mourner (usually the widow of the casualty) or as primary mourners themselves and the mouthpieces of the inscription. An inscription of the first type might read:

LEAVING A SORROWING WIFE
MOTHER, SISTER
AND 3 YOUNG CHILDREN

[Headstone of Gunner John Philip Morgan, 36th Group,
Australian Heavy Artillery, died of wounds
4 October 1917. Buried at Ypres Reservoir Cemetery]

In hierarchical terms, the children in this inscription are not secondary but tertiary mourners. The Morgan family hierarchy appears to be based broadly on age rather than relationship to the deceased. The onlooker is not given the names, ages and genders of the children. However, their inclusion at the end of the inscription (the last line to be read), and the fact that they have been given a line to themselves, is significant. Morgan's register entry shows that he died of wounds on 4 October 1917. He was 30, and was survived by his parents, John Philip and Eva Elizabeth. As a married man his next-of-kin was his widow, Dorothea. The entry also shows that by the time the Commission verified Morgan's family information, his widow's surname had changed to Gaddsen, but that her status as the next-of-kin was defended by the formulation '(formerly Morgan)'. The likely conclusion is that Dorothea remarried after her husband's death, with a less plausible possibility being that she reverted to her maiden name in widowhood.

Another type of inscription to feature children presented them as the primary mourner(s), of which the following is an example:

THY WILL BE DONE
OUR DARLING DADDY
GONE FROM HOME
BUT NEVER FORGOTTEN

[Headstone of Gunner P.H. Clarke, 113th Siege Battery,
Royal Garrison Artillery, date of death 28 September 1918.
Buried at Ypres Reservoir Cemetery]

Clarke was 32 at his death on 28 September 1918. The register entry listed his parents, Thomas and Elizabeth, and his widow, Charlotte. Although their voices appear to be excluded in the personal inscription by the use of the affectionate familiarity of 'our darling daddy', the inclusion of 'thy will be done' and 'home' could be interpreted as oblique references to the voice of the wider family and its concerns.

Lieutenant Alexander Miller was killed in action on 25 September 1917 at the age of 32. As was customary in cases where a casualty was survived by his parents and widow, the register entry listed Alexander and Marian Miller, followed by his widow Belle. The personal inscription, however, indicated a different balance of power within the family:

MY BELOVED HUSBAND
OUR DEAR SON

CHERISHED IN OUR HEARTS
FOR EVER

> [Headstone of Lieutenant Alexander Miller, 57th Battalion,
> Australian Infantry, killed in action 25 September 1917.
> Buried at Hooge Crater Cemetery]

The inscription suggests that Belle Miller assumed the role of primary mourner. As next-of-kin she would have been the recipient of any correspondence from the Commission. The voice of her parents-in-law takes second place, but the last two lines of the inscription are slightly ambiguous. Without further evidence to the contrary it seems probable that 'cherished in our hearts for ever' represented the shared voice of a family in grief.

Inscriptions sometimes distinguished between a casualty's parents. One parent's voice could be privileged over another's, for example when the father's position as head of the family was underlined:

GIVEN BY A LOVING FATHER
AND MOTHER
WITH PROUD BUT ACHING HEARTS

> [Headstone of Gunner Francis Joseph Gell,
> Australian Heavy Artillery, killed in action 4 October 1917.
> Buried at Ypres Reservoir Cemetery]

This formulation emphasized the father's position in visual terms. There was sufficient room on the headstone for the following order to be engraved:

GIVEN BY
A LOVING FATHER AND MOTHER
WITH PROUD BUT ACHING HEARTS

One way of avoiding these potential disparities was to employ a 'spokesman' text. This was a phrase that purported to speak for a wide group of people (related or not), without privileging one group over another. It was also more economical in practical and financial terms to use a spokesman text than it was to identify a long list of individuals. The inscription chosen by Thomas and Emma Allan for their son Private W.G. Allan is a good example of this practice:

FONDLY REMEMBERED
BY ALL AT HOME

> [Headstone of Private W.G. Allan, 11th Battalion,
> The King's (Liverpool Regiment), killed in action 13 December 1915.
> Buried at Ypres Reservoir Cemetery.]

Allan was recorded as having been killed in action on 13 December 1915 at the age of 31. His inscription was a spokesman text in more than one respect. The word 'all' included anyone who missed Allan: family, friends, neighbours and colleagues. The word 'home' was almost as ambiguous. It was an easily extendable concept, ranging from the Allans' family home at 45 Harrowby Street, to Princes Park, to Liverpool, the county of Lancashire and Furness, to England or indeed to the British Empire.

Hierarchical issues were not restricted to families. At their meeting on 20 April 1920, the commissioners discussed the disposal of the original wooden crosses that had been erected over battlefield graves. At the request of bereaved families the originals could be shipped back to Britain where many were endowed with sacred status. Representatives of ex-servicemen's associations had visited the battlefields and had reported positively on the Commission's work constructing cemeteries. The only point of issue was the treatment of the impromptu personal inscriptions that had been scratched onto the wooden crosses by military burial parties. The ex-servicemen wished to see these inscriptions transferred to the permanent headstones. Ware commented that the texts were 'often very pathetic and very appropriate' but reported that he had explained that the Commission 'could not let them take precedence of inscriptions selected by the next-of-kin' (CWGC Archives, Minutes of Meetings, 20 April 1920).

Textual re-inscription

The land on which the cemeteries had been built was given to the Commission 'in perpetuity' by the French and Belgian governments. This act lent a permanence to the cemeteries and to the memorials they enclosed. Once an inscription had been engraved, the Commission regarded it as a permanent feature of the headstone. Personal inscriptions could not be removed, although *bona fide* relatives of a casualty could choose an inscription for a headstone that had not already received one. Such was the case with Gunner J. Wolstenhulme. Although his register entry included no details of his next-of-kin, his headstone reads:

THE SEARCH HAS ENDED
I KNEW NOT WHERE YOU LAY
REST IN PEACE DEAR FATHER
EDITH 8TH OCTOBER 1993

> [Headstone of Gunner J. Wolstenhulme,
> 19th Battalion Machine Gun Corps (Motors),
> date of death 1 October 1916. Buried at Hooge Crater Cemetery.]

The metaphorical power of the cemeteries has changed over time. The emotions associated with 'grief' embrace such disparate impulses as anger, bitterness, confusion, resentment and loneliness. Personal inscriptions reflected all these emotions. They also maintained a connection between the deceased and the bereaved (and sometimes too with God and onlookers). What they could not do was reflect the ebb and flow of grief as experienced by a particular family, individual or group.

In this respect, *in memoriam* notices enjoyed an advantage: families could place as many notices as their finances allowed, and newspaper editors did not place any explicit maximum length on texts. Consequently, separate notices could be placed for parents, siblings, children, friends, colleagues and neighbours, and could be repeated or changed as desired over a period of time. On the other hand, personal inscriptions were just a small part of a framework defined not by the bereaved family but by the Commission. Their physical position underlined their incidental nature: right at the foot of the headstone. Ironically, this position could also be interpreted as the closest physical position to the bereaved and to the land in which he had died. The Commission published both the Kenyon report and Kipling's exposition of Commission policy, *The Graves of the Fallen*, and politely acknowledged any suggestions received from members of the public keen to suggest designs for the cemeteries. The Commission did not appear to adopt any of the suggestions.

One of the criteria against which the idea of cruciform grave-markers fell short in 1920 was their ability to resist the weather conditions. As time passed it became apparent that while the headstone design was sufficiently sturdy, the Portland stone from which it was fashioned was increasingly vulnerable. Weather damage prompted the Commission to replace badly worn markers with duplicates made from Bottocino marble. The physical re-inscription of the headstones reinforced the voice and sentiment of the original text. Visitors to the cemeteries found that the headstones' legibility relied on the stonecutter's incisions and the quality of sunlight. In 1999, *Stand To!*, the journal of the Western Front Association, printed a letter from a correspondent who recommended smearing mud over the inscriptions in order to obtain a good photograph. The letter prompted accusations of sacrilege and a concerned reply from the Commission deploring such practices (Dalley 1999). The debate illustrated how, in the intervening decades, the cemeteries had been commonly interpreted as sites of tourism as well as sites of sacred commemoration.

Any visitor to the military cemeteries in France and Belgium today will find a variety of objects laid at the foot of many headstones. These range from British Legion remembrance crosses (many of which are inscribed with the names of the deceased or of the donor), letters, photographs (of the deceased or his relatives), flowers, wreaths, pot plants and candles. Jewish headstones are sometimes marked with pebbles – literal 'stones of remembrance'. Many of the fragile items donated are securely wrapped in food bags or cling film. Such measures represent an attempt to protect the objects from the elements. Frequently they are original objects, such as sepia photographs. While donors may well have made copies of these objects before leaving them at the donation site, it says much of the donors' perception of the cemeteries, and of their trust that other visitors will respect the objects and leave them in their original place. Letters can usually be found propped up against headstones – sometimes brief notes, at others long and detailed missives. Beneath one headstone in Hooge Crater Cemetery, I found a plain bookmark on which had been printed a digital colour photograph of a woman. Underneath was printed: 'Margaret Joan Berger. "Marg". Born to this life 8 July 1941. Born to eternal life on 28 October 2002. To live in the hearts of those you leave behind – is to live forever.' On the reverse side was handwritten the following text:

Dear Uncle Ray, I am the eldest granddaughter of your brother, John Ray
Drew. He had three daughters & a son Michael Raymond – and 18
grandchildren. Uncle Eric was childless, but Auntie Anna had a daughter
and a son, Raymond. Pappa spoke of you always and my sister, Margaret, &
I loved listening to his stories. Margaret is buried next to Auntie Anna your
niece, in the [name illegible] Cemetery. She would be pleased to know this
bookmark is left at your headstone so far from home. Our brother is John
Raymond, also, so you will always be remembered.
Love,
Beverly

(Author's field notes)

The *ad hoc* decoration of Commission sites is not restricted to the cemeteries.
Occasionally, similar artefacts are left propped up against the walls of the Menin Gate
in Ieper (Ypres). This is an even greater act of faith than leaving artefacts in the
cemeteries, as the Menin Gate is a busy thoroughfare both for traffic and pedestrians
seven days a week (and when the road is closed at 8 pm each evening for the sounding
of the Last Post a considerable crowd gathers beneath the memorial).

In recent years, the practice has developed of pushing single, leafless British Legion
poppies between the stone panels of the memorial on which individual names are
engraved. The aim is presumably to distinguish one name from the next. In reality, a
mass of poppies collects within arms' length, thereby commemorating names that
may physically be reached, rather than those that are engraved several feet higher
up the wall. In this context, one name – which has no personal connection with the
visitor – comes to represent the deceased serviceman whose name the visitor came to
commemorate. It is regrettable that the Imperial War Graves Commission preserved
only the number of visitors to its sites during 1926–39, and not the visitors' books
that were stored alongside cemetery or memorial registers. These books 'would have
provided an invaluable source for the feelings of travellers' (Lloyd 1998: 101). Storage
space for this considerable task has been offered by the Historiale de la Grande Guerre
at Péronne, where visitors' books from 1992 onwards are now archived.

Conclusion

Did a 'language of grief' exist in the aftermath of the First World War? The answer
surely is 'yes', but because this chapter has not attempted to contextualize that
language by considering the pre-1914 period, it is not possible to judge the extent to
which it was influenced by its Victorian and Edwardian predecessors. A language of
grief had many different expressions and purposes. Its influence on contemporary
linguistic expression at Commission sites may be recognized in the memorial for
Margaret Berger at Hooge Crater Cemetery. The phrase 'to live in the hearts of those
you leave behind – is to live forever' is clearly derived from Thomas Campbell's lines
'to live in the hearts we leave behind is not to die', a popular choice for personal
inscriptions. Francis Palgrave chose to include some of Campbell's work in his *Golden*

Treasury, an anthology first published in 1861 and so popular it went through several impressions and is still in print.

It is difficult to summarize the purpose of a language of grief, though it involved a complex relationship between the deceased, the bereaved, God and visitors to the cemeteries that cannot be condensed into a single explanation. It would also be misleading to evaluate a language of grief from this single source: for one thing, the research from which this chapter is taken is necessarily based on a sample of data. For another, personal inscriptions were a closely regulated form of expression, and limited to an average of around a dozen words. It is far more profitable to compare a language of grief from the other two sources mentioned at the beginning of this chapter.

These reservations aside, some of the purposes of a language of grief include different needs: to say goodbye; to reclaim the casualty from his military burial setting for his family (this was sometimes achieved by engraving the deceased's name and dates on the family grave-marker at home); to communicate with other pilgrims; to justify the casualty's war service; to comment on the war; to display conflicting sentiments ('with proud but aching hearts'); and to emphasize the practical and/or emotional aspects of bereavement (such as distance, separation, widowhood). These lines of enquiry show how much more there is to be learned from exploring the language of grief from the First World War.

Acknowledgements

Extracts from the archives of the Commonwealth War Graves Commission are quoted with the Commission's kind permission. I should also like to thank Maria Choules at the Commission for her help on research visits.

Notes

1   In this context 'sons' is an inclusive term for any male relative.
2   One aspect of the Croydon memorial features a woman clasping a baby and in her outstretched hand is a crumpled slip of paper – presumably a telegram. See Boorman 1988: 128.
3   While civilians associated 'missing' with a faint hope that the man concerned might still be found alive, soldiers knew that 'missing' was more likely to denote a manner of death that left little trace of a man's body (see Booth 1996: 29–30).
4   Major Durham was an official in the Office of Works.
5   The organization had been founded in 1895 as the Union of Women Workers, but changed its name in 1918.
6   Hence Field Marshal Sir William Robertson unveiled the Twickenham and Richmond memorials, and the Marquis of Lincolnshire, in his role as Lord Lieutenant of Buckinghamshire, performed the honours at Flackwell Heath, near High Wycombe, in 1921. Members of the Royal Family were also popular choices to perform unveiling ceremonies.

References

Commonwealth War Graves Commission, Maidenhead

Minutes and proceedings of meetings, 1919–30
Item WG1606, Catalogue Number 899, Box 1097, 'Memorials UK: General File'

Secondary Sources

Boorman, D. (1988) *At the Going Down of the Sun: British First World War Memorials*. York: The Ebor Press.

Booth, A. (1996) *Postcards from the Trenches: Negotiating the Space Between Modernism and the First World War*. Oxford: Oxford University Press.

Dalley, R. (1999) 'Photographing headstones'. *Stand To!: the Journal of the Western Front Association* 54: 37.

Davies, D.J. (1997) *Death, Ritual and Belief: The Rhetoric of Funerary Rites*. London: Cassell.

Gaffney, A. (1998) *Aftermath: Remembering the Great War in Wales*. Cardiff: University of Wales Press.

Gardner, B. (1989) *Up the Line to Death: The War Poets 1914–1918*. London: Methuen.

Gregory, A. (1994) *The Silence of Memory: Armistice Day 1919–1946*. Oxford: Berg.

Kenyon, F. (1918) *War Graves: How the Cemeteries Abroad will be Designed*. London: HMSO.

King, A. (1998) *Memorials of the Great War in Britain: The Symbolism and Politics of Remembrance*. Oxford: Berg.

Lloyd, D.W. (1998) *Battlefield Tourism: Pilgrimage and the Commemoration of the Great War in Britain, Australia and Canada, 1919–1939*. Oxford: Berg.

Longworth, P. (1967) *The Unending Vigil: The History of the Commonwealth War Graves Commission*. London: Constable.

Moriarty, C. (1997) 'Private grief and public remembrance: British First World War memorials'. In M. Evans and K. Lunn (eds) *War and Memory in the Twentieth Century*, pp. 125–42. Oxford: Berg.

Van Emden (2003) *The Trench*. London: Corgi Adult.

12

'P'RAPS I SHALL SEE YOU . . .'

Recognition of loved ones in
non-fiction film of the First World War

Roger Smither

In early 2005, the British Film Institute held a national exposition of the extraordinary recent find of Mitchell and Kenyon films from the early years of the twentieth century, which was accompanied by a three-part television series. These two events can have left few people in Britain unaware of the extent to which early cinemagoers were willing to pay in order to catch a glimpse of themselves and their friends on the silver screen.[1]

It has long been recognized that the strips of celluloid which an operator cranked through a camera in one place, and which he or a colleague later cranked through a projector in another, were the means by which the first audiences for moving pictures saw the faithful representation of real events, from the arrival of a train to a classic horse race, or were transported into a fantasy world – a gardener comically fooled into watering himself, or a trip to the moon. The newly discovered films emphasize that celluloid strips were also agents that brought audiences face to face with themselves and their neighbours.

A travelling moving picture show could guarantee to draw an audience in each new town it visited if it offered them material filmed locally – especially if filled with local faces offered up for recognition. Mitchell and Kenyon were of course far from being the only entrepreneurs to realize the commercial potential of this phenomenon. The text of an advertisement by film producer Cecil Hepworth in the June 1901 issue of *The Showman* clearly stated the attractions of such programming from the exhibitor's and the audience's point of view (the attraction for the producer could of course remain unstated):

> The most popular Cinematograph Film in a Travelling Show is ALWAYS
> A LOCAL PICTURE containing Portraits which can be recognised. A Film
> showing Workers leaving a Factory will gain far greater popularity in the

town where it was taken than the most exciting picture ever produced. The workers come in hundreds, with all their friends and relations, and the Film more than pays for itself the first night. In other words this is THE GREATEST DRAW you can have, and it is OUR BUSINESS to provide it for you in Advance for Each Town you visit.

(Toulmin 2001: 122)

As moving pictures and the film-going habit became more established, audiences demanded more. Travelling picture shows were superseded by purpose-built cinemas, and the ad-hoc programme gave way to more structured presentations. The possibilities of recognition remained an attraction, however, and were lodged firmly enough in popular consciousness to become a staple theme in pre-war magazines, with almost every conceivable variation of on-screen discovery explored in news stories or urban legends of identification which reached across time and even across continents (see Smither 2002).

Told as comedy in short stories and cartoons, the most usual variant of the recognition story concentrated on the distinctly local possibilities for the embarrassing disclosure of marital infidelity – a topic which also made its way into popular song. A verse of one song describes the discomfiture of the hero, Jeremiah Jones, who takes his mother-in-law to see a moving picture show only to conclude that they should leave, rapidly – 'For on that picture was Jeremiah / With a pretty girl upon his knee'. As 'Ma' demands an explanation, the rest of the audience launch into the chorus (which is also the title of the song): 'Hello! Hello! Who's your lady friend?'[2]

Given this history, it should come as no surprise that the possibility of recognition carried forward into the experience of film-making and cinema-going during the First World War. Static and lingering shots of columns of men marching cheerfully through their home towns to enlist, or through military encampments, or, later, tramping along the roads of France or Belgium to reach the front, were a frequent device. They should be seen as continuations of an established tradition, placing the largest possible number of potentially familiar faces on the screen in front of an audience of family and friends, rather than as examples of unimaginative camerawork or efforts to fill the screen with anything when frontline filming was difficult if not impossible.

Not only imagination is required to see the films in this light – they were, on occasion, advertised to the public for exactly this purpose. A newsreel advertisement in the British cinema trade journal *Pictures & Picturegoer* in the autumn of 1916 showed Tommy and his mother agreeing that a trip to the pictures is the best way of spending an evening out, especially as a major part of the attraction is the possibility that mother will recognize Tommy in the *Pathé Gazette* (Figure 12:1). A similar suggestion is included on the film itself in an item from *Scottish Moving Picture News* with the title 'Return of the Interned'. This 1918 production showed the arrival at Leith in Scotland of a ship of internees returning from Europe, and one of its captions invited the audience to 'Watch the picture carefully, and see if you can identify anyone.'[3]

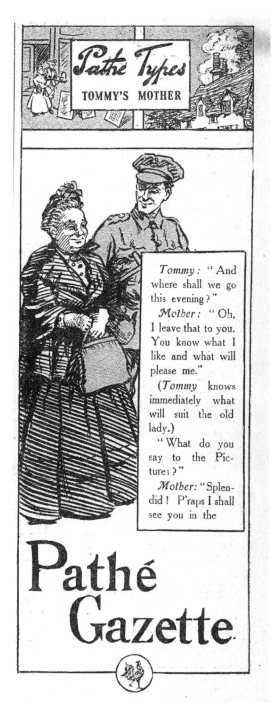

Audiences three years earlier had been doing exactly that – and demanding material evidence of what they had seen. On 29 May 1915, *Cassell's Saturday Journal* published an anonymous article with the title 'Running the topical films'. In the course of an extended study of recent achievements and current practice in the emergent news film sector of the cinema trade, this article took note of the French Government's having 'appointed Pathé's official photographers to the French Army', so that they could counteract the propaganda impact of enemy film. It then relates the following anecdote:

> Recently, one of their [i.e. Pathé's] men paid a professional visit to the internment camps at Groningen, Holland, and photographed the British prisoners there. The film thus secured was exhibited in various parts of the country, and the Editor of *The Animated Gazette* was promptly inundated with letters from relatives of the interned men, begging for pieces of the film. The firm actually printed thousands of feet of this film simply to give away to anxious people who had, as it were, discovered their husbands and brothers and sons and lovers on picture-palace screens.
>
> (Anon. 1915: 44)

In this way, segments of film – fragments of celluloid material culture – para-doxically gained an enhanced value to their new owners at the very moment that their usefulness for their original purpose was, literally, cut short. These segments thus became biographical objects in their own right, embodying images of absent loved ones, and testifying to the service of these men in defence of their homeland and empire. At the same time, these objects belonged to individual families, yet remained part of a larger cinematic narrative of the war.

While cinema audiences were encouraged to keep an eye open for people they knew, soldiers being filmed were fully aware of the possibility of being seen by friends and family. Even the 'enemy' was not excluded from the charm of this idea. While the single film *The Battle of the Somme* (IWM Film Archive, IWM 191) contains many examples of British soldiers reacting in classic 'Hello, Mum' style, waving or otherwise putting on a show for the camera, it is also remarkable for the number of occasions when Tommies point out the camera to German prisoners of war. On at least one occasion in the film, a German prisoner doubles back to make sure of his moment in front of the lens.

Logic would suggest that recognition of loved ones would be a common expectation and a far from rare experience in film of the First World War. It was certainly a possibility to which the press at the time was alert: the *Bath and Wilts. Chronicle*, reporting on the 11 September 1916 local screening of *The Battle of the Somme*, wrote:

> the pictures are so clear that thousands will be recognized by friends and relatives who see the film at home. They march away to the front battle line singing, waving their hats and always, in the words of the song, they 'Smile, smile, smile'.[4]

In spite of this logic, however, it is surprisingly difficult to find documented case histories of the phenomenon, particularly at the individual level (as distinct from generic evidence, of the kind offered by the *Cassell's* story quoted earlier). The Imperial War Museum has a large range of first-person narratives of First World War experiences, but in all this material I have yet to discover a single example of a correspondent at home writing to tell someone at the front that he had been spotted in the pictures.

There are, however, examples of letters in the opposite direction, which describe encounters with cameramen, and go on to discuss the possibility that the writer will be seen at home in a future picture show, or to wonder how the resulting pictures will be used.

One such encounter is described in a letter dated 19 November 1916 sent to his brother by Sub-Lieutenant Trevor Jacobs, who was serving with the Hood Battalion of the Royal Naval Division. Jacobs describes the fighting and heavy casualties suffered by his unit in the capture of Beaucort, and then includes the following passage. 'When we got back to Englebelmer we were cinematographed. I am marching alone as the second in command of my Coy. [Company] but I suppose my steel helmet & unshaven appearance will make me hard to recognise' (Brown 1996: 247). It is likely that the film shot to which Jacobs was referring (Figure 12:2) was used in a sequence

Figure 12:2 The scene described by Sub-Lieutenant Trevor Jacobs as it ended up in the 1917 film *The Battle of the Ancre and the Advance of the Tanks*. Jacobs is thought to be the figure in the centre of the picture, looking at the camera. (© and courtesy Imperial War Museum Photograph Archive, IWM FLM 2369)

introduced by the caption ' Troops going back to rest, loaded with mud, trophies and glory' at the end of reel 4 of the film *The Battle of the Ancre and the Advance of the Tanks*, released on 15 January 1917 (IWM Film Archive, IWM 116).

Descriptions of individuals being filmed also appear in diaries, and another match between surviving film and a diary entry comes from no less a diarist than Field Marshal Sir Douglas Haig himself. His entry for the day the fighting stopped – 11 November 1918 – includes the following.

> At 11 a.m. I had a meeting in Cambrai with the five Army Commanders and General Kavanagh . . . After the Conference, we were all taken on the [sic] Cinema. General Plumer, whom I told to 'go off and be cinemaed' went off most obediently and stood before the camera trying to look his best, while Byng and others near him were chaffing the old man and trying to make him laugh.
>
> (Blake 1952: 340)

The surviving film shows the scene exactly as Haig described it (Figure 12:3) (IWM Film Archive, IWM 132).

Figure 12:3 General Plumer is 'cinema-ed' on the orders of Field Marshal Sir Douglas Haig on 11 November 1918. (© and courtesy Imperial War Museum Photograph Archive, IWM FLM 3498)

The possibility that film could also be the agent for a much more awful form of recognition – that people might recognize loved ones among the wounded and the dead, or see someone fit and healthy on the screen whom they knew to have been killed subsequently – exercised many at the time.[5] Several days of debate in the correspondence columns of *The Times* were initiated when Hensley Henson, Dean of Durham, responded to the film *The Battle of the Somme* on 1 September 1916 by writing, 'I beg leave respectfully to enter a protest against an entertainment which wounds the heart and violates the very sanctities of bereavement.' The majority of those who responded to the Dean's letter took the opposite view – that the film helped the bereaved by giving them some idea of what their loved ones had experienced, and would help strengthen the bond of identification between the front in Flanders and the home front. Nonetheless, it is notable that the relative frankness on the subject of death of *The Battle of the Somme*, which had included both genuine and 'staged' film of British dead, was not repeated in later films. They showed only enemy dead and relatively lightly wounded British casualties.[6]

Recognition of all kinds remained (and still remains) possible after the war ended, when the reels of film passed from the domain of current affairs to become artefacts providing a basis for memory and commemoration. An intriguing, if second-hand, story comes from a post-war memoir (Taylor 1978), which includes the following story:

> After the war, in the early nineteen twenties, a friend of mine, Ted Grainger, who had served with a Manchester Battalion, along with his father . . . went into the Deansgate news cinema in Manchester to see a documentary film on the battle of the Somme. As Ted sat in the darkened cinema watching this film he became aware that the scenes and men were familiar to him and he began to recognise some of them and the location of the drama unfolding in front of him on the screen. When, with great excitement he saw himself, he jumped to his feet and yelled, 'That's me, and that's my dad, and he's going to get wounded in a minute.' Then he actually witnessed on the cinema screen his dad getting wounded and being carried away. This caused a minor furore in the cinema and in the local press and Ted and his family were invited by the manager to free seats for the rest of the week.
>
> (Taylor 1978: 10)

Although *The Battle of the Somme* does not contain any scenes of recognizable soldiers at the moment when they are wounded, it includes footage of several Manchester and Lancashire battalions, and extensive coverage of the treatment of wounded at dressing stations. It appears that Ted Grainger actually recognized such a scene, and the story was enhanced in later retelling. In any case, we can applaud the cinema manager's recognition of a first-rate marketing opportunity.

Remembrances of being filmed, or instances of the recognition of one's own or another's familiar face in a piece of 'old' film, provide some of the more interesting items of correspondence in the in-tray of a film archive specializing in non-fiction film.

In some cases, the Imperial War Museum has been able to bring about a kind of delayed reunion. One such occasion was published in the *Southend-on-Sea Pictorial* of 23 December 1964, under the headline 'That Grimy, Weary Soldier Was Himself!' This story told how 70-year-old Walter Lydamore had recognized himself in a First World War scene used in the Winston Churchill documentary *The Finest Hours* which had recently been screened in the town. The Museum confirmed that the footage came from *The Battle of the Somme*, and gave the newspaper a still photograph to illustrate the story. It is even more pleasing to read, as another echo of the *Cassell's* story quoted earlier, that the Museum gave Mr Lydamore an 8 mm copy of the sequence concerned as a personal keepsake.

On other occasions, the correspondence is doomed to disappointment. For the Imperial War Museum, the single greatest disappointment surrounds one of the most famous images in its collections – that of a man seen carrying a wounded colleague through the trenches, and which also originates in the film *The Battle of the Somme*. Whether as a moving sequence or a still photograph (Figure 12:4), this scene has become one of the iconic images of the First World War, widely used in books and newspapers and on television to evoke the experience of trench warfare and the heroism and suffering of the ordinary soldier. The identity of the soldier carrying the wounded man, however, remains unknown.

The fact that he cannot be identified from contemporary records of the filming is not surprising – the individual soldiers seen on film are rarely named in the official

Figure 12:4 The iconic 'trench rescue' scene from the 1916 film, *The Battle of the Somme*. (© and courtesy Imperial War Museum Photograph Archive, Q 79501)

records. One might initially have harboured higher hopes of a near-contemporary unofficial source. Geoffrey Malins, one of the two official 'kinematographers' who filmed on the Somme vividly described taking this shot in his post-war memoir, *How I Filmed the War*:

> I noticed several of our wounded lying in shell-holes in 'No Man's Land.' They were calling for assistance. Every time a Red Cross man attempted to get near them, a hidden German machine-gun fired. Several were killed whilst trying to bring in the wounded. The cries of one poor fellow attracted the attention of a trench-mortar man. He asked for a volunteer to go with him, and bring the poor fellow in. A man stepped forward, and together they climbed the parapet, and threaded their way through the barbed wire very slowly. Nearer and nearer they crept. We stood watching with baited breath. Would they reach him? Yes. At last! Then hastily binding up the injured man's wounds they picked him up between them, and with a run made for our parapet. The swine of a German blazed away at them with his machine-gun.
>
> But marvellous to relate neither of them were touched. I filmed the rescue from the start to the finish, until they passed me in the trench, a mass of perspiration. Upon the back of one was the unconscious man he had rescued, but twenty minutes after these two had gone through hell to rescue him, the poor fellow died.
>
> (Malins 1920: 167–8)

Malin's account gives us no name, but it does provide some additional clues. The cameraman's movements for the first part of 1 July 1916 are well authenticated, and the rescue scene conforms to what is known. This would suggest that he shot the film opposite Beaumont Hamel, where the line was occupied by 29th Division. In fact, the casualty can be seen to be wearing a 29th Division shoulder flash (see Chapter 8 for details on these insignia). Where the rescuer is concerned, however, it remains a fact that Malins's description actually offers little real help on the question of identification. He identifies only one man, and does so by means of his specialization rather than his unit. Even then, he does not say whether it was the 'trench-mortar man' or his volunteer colleague who actually carried the casualty through the trench, and the second man is not identified at all.

As in many other cases where this kind of gap remains in the official and semi-official record, the central figure in this scene has been named in correspondence received by the Museum from the general public. However, in astonishing contrast to the straightforward identifications offered in almost all those other cases, the 'Battle of the Somme rescuer' has been given many different names. My files contain almost fifty suggested identifications, including members of some 20 British infantry regiments and one Australian infantry battalion, two cavalry regiments (in one case for a chaplain), two different branches of the Artillery, the Veterinary Corps, the Royal Engineers and the Royal Army Medical Corps. It is clear that this specific case history has transcended the issue of simple recognition, and become a phenomenon of a different kind, even if it is hard to say exactly what kind that is (see Chapter 15 for a similar phenomenon of 'recognition' with regard to picture postcards).

The overwhelming majority of these identifications are based simply on a strong sense that the person seen on the screen bears an extremely strong resemblance to a father, grandfather or other deceased relative – the claim commonly being supported in correspondence by a copy of a photograph of the relative concerned. In a minority of cases, however, the claim has more depth than a simple (if belated) recognition. At least three correspondents have offered detailed memories or descriptions of family tradition about how the film came to be taken, or how it was first seen on the big screen. Unfortunately for the historian, these three correspondents name three different individuals.

These, and other more standard 'recognition'-based identifications offer a number of common sub-strands in the general perception of the 'truth' behind this image. The notion that the action was so brave that it deserved a medal occurs quite frequently, though often linked to the story that no such recognition was given. On the other hand, the suggestion that the whole episode was faked or staged for the camera is also found more than once.[7]

Confronted with so many names – backed up in numerous cases with passionate conviction, and in a few with apparently detailed circumstantial evidence – the Museum's policy has to be one of cautious impartiality. We neither endorse nor automatically discount any claim, though we do what we can when asked to help with further research. We explain what we know and believe about the circumstances of the filming, we record the names and other details of the suggested individuals, and we wait to see whether any of them can be confirmed by strong third-party evidence.

We also reflect on what it means, that so many people believe that they recognize this one individual. My own conclusion – which requires no great depth of psychological insight – is that there is obvious appeal in an image of warfare suggesting an act of strength, courage and initiative which is nonetheless unambiguously devoted to an attempt to save life, not to take it. If you must think of an ancestor exposed to the horrors of the First World War, how much better to recognize him in such a context than to picture what else he might have been going through. The 'rescuer' becomes an archetype, either genuinely heroic or, if the allegations of fakery are more to your taste, having a laugh at the thought of helping put one over on the gullible folks back home, by taking part in a 'stunt' for the camera.

By turning the person we recognize into an archetype, we return, some 90 years after the event, to a point originally articulated in 1916 by Arthur Conan Doyle in a letter to *The Times* published on 4 September in response to the Dean of Durham's letter, already quoted. It is a point which embodies and illustrates the multi-vocal nature of material culture: 'How can we learn to understand and sympathize with the glorious achievements and sacrifices of our soldiers so well as when we actually see them in action before our eyes? The film is a monument to their devotion.'

Notes

1 The British Film Institute's national cinema tour of the collection – *Mitchell and Kenyon: Edwardian Britain on Film* – was given its gala launch at King George's Hall, Blackburn, on 14 January 2005. The first of three episodes of *The Lost World of Mitchell and Kenyon* was broadcast on BBC2 at 9.00 pm the same day. An accompanying book had been published the previous October – see Toulmin, Popple and Russell 2004.
2 The song was written in 1913 by David Worton and Bert Lee, with music by Henry Fragson. Quoted in Arthur 2001, 24–5.
3 The film is held in the Imperial War Museum Film and Video Archive (IWMFVA) under catalogue number IWM 545.
4 Thanks to Nicholas Reeves for this citation.
5 Similar concerns were expressed about a different medium in the early months of the Second World War, when the BBC for the first time entertained the possibility of radio reports from the battlefield: the *News of the World* thought that 'A more ghastly idea was never conceived' (Nicholas 2005, p. 142).
6 See also Smither 1993.
7 Because the correspondence which forms the basis for these paragraphs is frequently bound up with strong personal emotion, and is largely private (only one of the correspondents has voluntarily made a public claim on behalf of his nominee) I consider it would be unethical to give details of the claimed identities or of the claimants who have nominated them in this publication. The correspondence relating to this issue is kept in the Imperial War Museum Film and Video Archive, and will be made available to researchers subject to the provisions of relevant data protection legislation.

References

Anon. (1915) 'Running the topical films'. *Cassell's Saturday Journal*, 29 May 1915. Republished in L. McKernan (ed.) (2002) *Yesterday's News: The British Cinema Newsreel Reader*, pp 42–6. London: British Universities Film and Video Council.

Arthur, Max (2001) *When This Bloody War Is Over: Soldiers' Songs of the First World War*. London: Piatkus.

Blake, Robert (ed.) (1952) *The Private Papers of Douglas Haig 1914–1919*. London: Eyre and Spottiswoode.

Brown, Malcolm (1996) *The Imperial War Museum Book of the Somme*. London: Sidgwick and Jackson.

Connelly, Mark and David Welch (eds) (2005) *War and the Media: Reportage and Propaganda 1900–2003*. London: I.B. Tauris.

McKernan, Luke (ed.) (2002) *Yesterday's News: The British Cinema Newsreel Reader*. London: British Universities Film and Video Council.

Malins, Geoffrey. (1920) *How I Filmed the War*. London, Herbert Jenkins. Reprinted, with an introduction by Nicholas Hiley, 1993, London: Imperial War Museum with the Battery Press.

Nicholas, Siân (2005) '*War Report* (BBC 1944–5) and the birth of the BBC war correspondent'. In M. Connelly and D. Welch (eds) (2005) *War and the Media: Reportage and Propaganda 1900–2003*, pp. 139–61. London: I.B. Tauris.

Reeves, Nicholas (1999) *The Power of Film Propaganda: Myth or Reality*. London: Cassell.

Smither, Roger (1993) 'A wonderful idea of the fighting': the question of fakes in *The Battle of the Somme*'. *Historical Journal of Film, Radio and Television* 13 (2): 149–68.

Taylor, F.A.J. (1978) *The Bottom of the Barrel*. London: Regency Press.

Toulmin, Vanessa (2001) '"Local films for local people": travelling showmen and the commissioning of local films in Great Britain, 1900–1902'. *Film History* 13: 118–37.

Toulmin, Vanessa, Simon Popple and Patrick Russell (eds) (2004) *The Lost World of Mitchell and Kenyon: Edwardian Britain on Film*. London: BFI Publishing.

13

'A FEW BROAD STRIPES'

Perception, deception and the 'Dazzle Ship' phenomenon of the First World War

Jonathan Black

In February 1915, Imperial Germany launched unrestricted submarine warfare against Great Britain – from henceforth any ship, allied or neutral, could be attacked in British territorial waters. This act led to a new chapter in the Great War, one that involved international boundaries, changing moralities, a potentially catastrophic economic threat to Great Britain, and a unique development and expression of the material culture of conflict. The war at sea was about to bring forth a monumental experiment in altering human perceptions of space and direction, thereby altering the actual or imagined balance of naval power between the British and the Germans.

Prior to 1915, U-Boats had usually surfaced in order to attack merchant shipping. They became increasingly cautious of employing this tactic, however, when the British Admiralty developed 'Q Ships' – warships cunningly disguised (in a sense camouflaged) as merchantmen by the addition of false sides, smokestacks and dummy piles of innocuous supplies on deck that concealed weapons. In response, U-Boats began more frequently to attack allied ships with torpedoes while submerged. The change in German strategy was successful, up to a point. Many thousands of tons of allied shipping were sunk. However, the sinking of the Cunard passenger liner *Lusitania*, in May 1915, was a public relations disaster for the Germans as 1,154 civilians were drowned. The sinking revealed that even the fastest, most recently constructed liner could be vulnerable to a single torpedo. Consequently, unrestricted submarine attacks around the British Isles were suspended at the beginning of September 1915 (Corrigan 2003: 186–7).

Germany reintroduced unrestricted submarine warfare in January 1917, and Britain quickly began to suffer catastrophic losses of merchant shipping carrying food and essential war matériel. By the end of February 1917, the British had lost 105 merchant ships to torpedo attacks (an average of 26 ships a week) totalling 310,868 tons. The end of April brought even more calamitous figures, as 169 ships were lost to torpedoes and mines (a staggering 42 ships a week or 6 a day), totalling 526,447 tons. (Liddle 1997: xxiv–xxv).

The British shipbuilding industry simply could not replace these lost ships fast enough and the situation was still serious even if one added the US merchant marine – the US had declared war on Germany on 6 April. By the middle of April 1917, the First Lord of the Admiralty, Sir John Jellicoe, warned the War Cabinet that if a solution to marauding U-Boats was not discovered very soon, Britain would be knocked out of the war as its population starved. On 27 April 1917, the British Cabinet compelled a reluctant Admiralty to adopt the convoy system in a desperate effort to reduce the losses (Bourne 1989: 70).

As the convoy system was being introduced, the Ministry of Shipping was more than ready to consider any suggestions as to how the U-Boat menace could be neutralized. Cometh the hour cometh the man, and a most unlikely 'father' of the 'Dazzle Camouflage' programme: Norman Wilkinson. As a painter of marine scenes in a quasi-Impressionist manner that would have looked completely at home in any pre-war exhibition of the New English Art Club – an institution not known for promoting cutting edge artistic modernism – he was far from being an artistically avant-garde figure.

In his memoirs, Wilkinson recalled that one morning in April 1917, serving as a Lieutenant in the Royal Naval Volunteer Reserve at Plymouth Devonport (in charge of a minesweeping fast motor launch):

> I suddenly got the idea that since it was impossible to paint a ship so that she could not be seen by a submarine, the extreme opposite was the answer – to paint her, not for low visibility, but in such a way as to break up her form and thus confuse a submarine officer as to the course on which she was heading.
>
> (Wilkinson 1969: 83)

His task would be to devise a series of erratic patterns that could be painted on to the sides of ships to confuse or 'dazzle' a U-Boat commander peering through a periscope so he could not accurately determine the course, size, speed or distance of a potential target. The camouflage would mislead the U-Boat commander as to where he should position his craft to fire upon a ship (torpedoes were not fired directly at the ship but towards a position where the ship would be in the time it took the torpedo to travel a given distance).

Wilkinson was convinced that 'having once failed to obtain a good position [a submarine] has little or no likelihood of regaining that position, owing to insufficient underwater speed' (Wilkinson 1969: 83). In addition, he correctly appreciated that a U-Boat commander would have little time while peering through his periscope to determine the size, course and speed of his intended victim. The longer the periscope was visible, the greater the chance it would be spotted by vigilant escort vessels (ibid.: 89). He also highlighted another advantage of dazzle camouflage – it could be quickly applied as ships were loading or unloading. As he later wrote to *The Times* 'despite being under every other disadvantage, such as rain and coal dust, we were sometimes able to get a hose on to a part of a ship blackened with coal dust while painting' (Wilkinson 1919).

As far as can be ascertained, at this point Wilkinson was not familiar with pre-war avant-garde geometrical abstraction, though he was aware of the activities of the Army's camouflage department, under the Pre-Raphaelite influenced academic painter Joseph Simeon Solomon. He may also have been aware of the qualified Cubist schemes produced for the French Army by *camoufleurs* such as André Mare, Othon Friesz and André Dunoyer de Segonzac (Dellouche 1994; Kahn 1984). However, there was an obvious difference in scale between landscape and seascape camouflage (see Prévost-Bault 1997). While the former sought to hide the small or middle-sized stationary features of war – from men to ammunition dumps to artillery batteries – the latter endeavoured less to conceal than to confuse the human eye as to the direction of movement of what were, by comparison, huge objects: ships.

On the very day the convoy system was introduced, 27 April 1917, Wilkinson sent his initial proposal to the Admiralty. He took care to insist that his idea was not 'to render the ship in any degree invisible, as this is virtually impossible, but to largely distort the external shape by means of violent colour contrasts.' (Wilkinson 1969: 79–80). Eventually, towards the end of May, Wilkinson was instructed by the Admiralty to paint the sides of the supply ship HMS *Industry* with two different camouflage schemes along the lines he had previously indicated. During the trial period, 46 sightings of HMS *Industry* were reported by ships at sea, of which 27 (59 per cent) judged the new dazzle camouflage to be effective; 71 sightings were recorded from shore-based installations, of which 26 (36 per cent) described the camouflage scheme as successful. In his defence, Wilkinson pointed out that dazzle camouflage was intended to work best at sea. (ibid.: 86).

Despite the ambiguous results, the trial was deemed a success, and in August 1917 the Ministry of Shipping ordered the creation of a new 'Transport Camouflage Section' (which within a matter of weeks was nicknamed the 'Dazzle Section' by those working within it) under Wilkinson, who was promoted to the rank of Lieutenant-Commander. The Ministry instructed him to promptly have 50 troopships dazzle camouflaged. (ibid.: 88).

The new section was situated in four studios of the Royal Academy at Burlington House, and had a staff of 17: five artists to design dazzle schemes; three model makers (two male, one female) and eleven female art students tasked with producing hand-coloured mechanical drawings to be used for painting actual full-sized ships (Figure 13:1) (by October 1917 the art students had increased to 25) (ibid.: 88.) In addition, dock officers were appointed for eight ports around the UK (Southampton, Newcastle, Hull, Glasgow, Liverpool, Bristol, Cardiff and Belfast) to supervise the painting of camouflage schemes devised in London and to supply their own on-the-spot modified schemes according to the size and configuration of the ships using their harbour.

The painter Edward Wadsworth, on medical leave in London after a period as a Lieutenant in the Royal Naval Volunteer Reserve on the eastern Mediterranean island

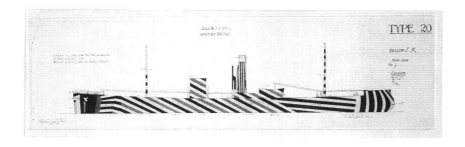

S.T.B.I..jpg

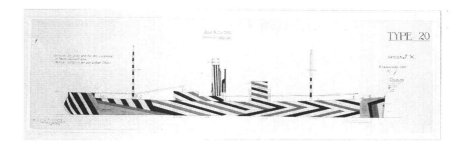

S.T B.I.jpg

Figure 13:1 Design JX for a Type 20 Merchant Ship, Norman Wilkinson and others, September 1917, pen and ink and pencil on paper. (© and courtesy Archive of Modern Conflict, London)

of Mudros interpreting aerial reconnaissance photographs, was appointed one of two supervising dock officers for Liverpool – along with an older academic traditionalist painter, Lawrence Campbell Taylor. It is possible that Wilkinson had sought out Wadsworth because the latter enjoyed a certain notoriety for his association with the turbulent pre-war Vorticist movement (founded by Wyndham Lewis in June 1914), and for the uncompromisingly geometrically abstract paintings and drawings he exhibited in London between 1914 and 1915 – many of which had maritime subject matter (Black 2006: 22–7) (Figure 13:2).

193

According to Wilkinson, the new Section quickly settled into a well-organized routine:

> In the initial stages a small wooden model of each ship was made to scale. On this a design was painted in wash colours for the purposes of rapid alteration. This model was then carefully studied on a prepared theatre through a submarine periscope, various sky backgrounds being placed behind her alternatively. [This involved an element of role-play with one of the artists taking the part of U-Boat commander attempting to see through the eyes of an enemy] A satisfactory design having been evolved giving the maximum distortion, the model was then handed to the trained plan-maker and copied on to a 1/16th-inch scale profile plan of the ship on white paper showing port and starboard side [see Figure 13:1]. The plan was then sent to the port officer at the port at which the particular ship was lying and transferred, under his supervision, to the ship (in question).
>
> (Wilkinson 1969: 96–7)

A unique design, with different schemes for port and starboard, had to be devised for each of the first group of 50 troopships. In other words, 100 separate designs were produced in Burlington House for distribution to ten ports. Once the 50 ships had been painted with the new camouflage, the Admiralty was keen to discover whether they had the desired affect. Initial reports greatly encouraged Wilkinson and his team: from the bridge of a destroyer for one ship a few hundred yards away as dusk fell 'it was almost impossible to say in what direction she was steering' (ibid.: 97).

Another ship, as the light on the water changed, seemed to be steaming one way and then, five minutes later, in 'the opposite direction' (ibid.). Between August and October 1917 the Ministry of Shipping received a series of reports from experienced Royal Navy captains confirming that they had found it almost impossible to determine the size and course of dazzle-camouflaged ships mainly because they could not work out the location of bow and stern and the precise direction in which the ship was steering (Behrens 2002: 90).

The Ministry of Shipping was so pleased with the results of the first 50 ships to be 'dazzled' that, in October 1917, it ordered that all merchant ships, armed and unarmed, should be painted with their own dazzle camouflage schemes, and that no one scheme should resemble another. This created a lot more work for the port officers such as Wadsworth, and they were encouraged to devise their own variations on the schemes originated in London to suit a distinctively shaped ship. By June 1918, some 2,300 British merchant ships had been dazzle-painted, and up to 100 ships were being similarly camouflaged in a British port such as Liverpool, Bristol, Southampton, and Newcastle, at any one time (ibid.: 91).

Wilkinson always maintained his system was the best because it was easily adapted to each individual vessel and took into account that the camouflage quickly wore off owing to the action of the sea and wind and had to be reapplied every 4–6 months. In 1919, for example, the war correspondent Hugh Hurst noted:

> It was necessary frequently for vessels to have their dazzle designs altered . . . Ships so treated would creep back in to port with a particularly odd-looking coat of many colours, the wear and tear of a winter journey across the Atlantic having played havoc with the fresh paint of her new design, causing the old one to appear in patches.
>
> (ibid.: 91)

Observers spoke of ships developing 'dazzle leprosy' after several months at sea. Still, that the ship had survived unscathed that long could be interpreted as proof that its various layers of dazzle camouflage were having the desired affect. The ships certainly attracted the attention of anyone who had been involved with the pre-war art world. The dealer René Gimpel recalled that a dazzle ship was akin to:

> an enormous Cubist painting with great sheets of ultramarine blue, black and green, sometimes parallel but more often with sharp corners cleaving

into one another, and, although you don't quite make it out, you can divine
a reason, a plan, a guiding principle.

(ibid.: 90)

He suspected that those devising dazzle camouflage were aware of pre-war
experimentation with geometric abstraction by avant-garde figures such as Kandinsky,
Balla and the Vorticists.

By the summer of 1918, the British ports of the Western Approaches would have
been choked with ships sporting dazzle camouflage: between April and November
1918 the Americans had 1,200 ships dazzle painted (ibid.: 91). In 1919, Hugh Hurst
asked the reader to imagine the arrival of two dazzle painted convoys at a port such as
Liverpool.

> the many miles of docks crowded with vessels of all sorts . . . each
> resplendent with a variety of bright-hued patterns . . . designs of stripes in
> black and white or pale blue and deep ultramarine, and earlier designs of
> curves, patches and semi-circles [which sounds rather akin to the 1913–14
> Orphism of Robert Delaunay]. Take all these, huddle them together in what
> appears to be hopeless confusion, but which in reality is perfect order, bow
> and stern pointing in all directions, mix in a little sunshine, add the varied
> and sparkling reflections, stir up the hotchpotch with smoke, life and
> incessant movement, and it can safely be said that the word 'dazzle' is not far
> from the mark.

(ibid.: 100)

Also, by the summer of 1918, Wadsworth was based in Liverpool, with Campbell
Taylor, in Room 229 of the Royal Liver Building, and thus enjoyed a grandstand view
for observing ships whose camouflage programmes they had supervised leaving
or arriving on the River Mersey (Figure 13:3). In charge of approximately 120
Liverpudlian painters, decorators, scaffolders and carpenters, Wadsworth took a series
of photographs of ships at anchor on the Mersey whose dazzle camouflaging he had
supervised.

The majority of the schemes would have been determined by Wilkinson in London.
However, he always gave his port officers latitude to extemporize, and some of the
applied designs Wadsworth photographed are reminiscent of the boldly contrasted
staccato black and white diagonal stripes and geometric shapes in prints exhibited by
Kandinsky and Franz Marc at the Twenty-One Gallery in London in March 1914, as
well as of the striped diagonal and chequerboard configurations evident in many of the
Vorticist woodcuts he produced between 1914 and 1915 (Greenwood 2002: 4–5).

Indeed, towards the end of 1914, Wadsworth produced one of his most challenging
geometrically abstract woodcut designs inspired by a passage from *Typhoon* – a short
story by that great writer about the sea Joseph Conrad (published in 1903) in which
the skilful seamanship of Captain McWhirr saves his tramp streamer the *Nan-Shan*
from foundering amidst a typhoon in the South China Sea. Intriguingly, the story also

"Mauretania" Landing Stage Liverpool October 1918

Figure 13:3 RMS Mauretania, Landing Stage, Liverpool, October 1918, Edward Wadsworth, photograph. (© and courtesy Alex Hollweg/The Estate of Edward Wadsworth)

includes passages which touch on the visual illusions created by the actions of the typhoon experienced by the Captain who – despite knowing full well they are illusions – finds them extremely hard to confidently discount.

In many of the photographs Wadsworth took in Liverpool, contrasts are obviously offered between ships sporting different dazzle camouflage schemes as though the artist revelled in the huge examples of moving Vorticist art works he had helped to bring into the world (Figure 13:4). He was probably more alive than most artists to the significance of calculation and precision in relation to technology because for a year (1906–7) he had trained in Munich as an engineering draughtsman (it was while in Munich he first encountered the increasingly abstract work of Kandinsky).

He was thus experienced in analysing and decoding blueprints and schematic drawings of the sort he would have received from Wilkinson in London. In addition, he was generally interested in technology and the latest contemporary motor-engineering, as he had learnt to drive a car as early as 1915 when only a small percentage of men of his age group had acquired such a skill. He was also familiar with all kinds of ships from the several visits he had paid to ports in France and the Netherlands between 1908 and 1914. He would probably also have had some experience of judging the size of ships at sea from a relatively low perspective, close to the surface of the water, from his experiences of sailing in a small skiff during 1916–17 in the eastern Aegean (Wadsworth 1989: 35). Meanwhile, his duties at Mudros – interpreting reconnaissance photographs taken by Royal Naval Air Service

S.S. "Zealandia" Liverpool August 1918

Figure 13:4 SS Zelandia and SS Alsatian, Liverpool, August 1918, Edward Wadsworth, photograph. (© and courtesy Alex Hollweg/The Estate of Edward Wadsworth)

seaplanes for naval intelligence – had involved the analysis of the silhouettes of warships and merchant ships in and around Turkish harbours, and deducing their identities, functions, tonnage, and capabilities.

During his time in Liverpool in 1918, Wadsworth produced a series of eight woodcuts of ships camouflaged in the 'dazzle' manner: *Ships Beside Warehouses*; *Dock Scene*; *S.S. Jerseymoor*; *Minesweepers in Port*; *Liverpool Shipping*; *Turret Ship in Dry Dock*; *Drydocked for Scaling and Painting* (Figure 13:5) and *Dazzled Ship in Dry Dock*. They do not depict dazzle-camouflaged ships at sea dodging the ever-lurking U-Boats, but in port, at the quayside or in dry dock. As noted previously, such was the corrosive action of the salt and the spray at sea, the camouflaged ships had to be repainted every 4–6 months. Doubtless the artist was alive to the irony that an art form established in the late fifteenth century involving an organic material (wood) should be utilized to so effectively depict the steel-clad products of the Industrial Revolution painted with the latest in abstract camouflage. In essence, a traditional, decidedly old-fashioned art form had been used to represent a most novel and twentieth century visual phenomenon.

Three of the woodcuts, *Turret Ship in Dry Dock*; *Drydocked for Scaling and Painting* and *Dazzled Ship in Dry Dock*, depict dazzle camouflage ships in dry dock. They may be in the process of being repainted or they may be under repair after a torpedo

198

Figure 13:5 Dry-docked for Painting and Scaling, Liverpool, Edward Wadsworth, 1918, monochrome woodcut. (© and courtesy Archive of Modern Conflict, London)

strike. If the ships had been hit by a torpedo, does this suggest their dazzle camouflage has been ineffective? This detail may constitute proof that the camouflage has achieved the desired objective in that, although the ship had been hit, it had not actually sunk and had managed to limp into port with its precious cargo. Then the ship was despatched to a dry dock for repair and would, shortly, be able to sail again.

The fact that ships that had been dazzle camouflaged were still being hit raises the questions of how effective it actually was as a diversionary measure. There is no doubt that, following the widespread introduction of dazzle during the autumn of 1917, the number of monthly sinkings did decrease – from 122 during June 1917 to 85 during December 1917. Thereafter, the monthly average dropped further to 55–60 ships lost (though this still represented just under a quarter of a million tons) (Liddle 1997: xxvi–xxix).

The press interpreted these figures as proof that dazzle had been a great success and the dazzle concept acquired a life of its own as it was commodified within society at large to produce dazzle-patterned pyjamas, pillowcases, curtains and bathing costumes. All manner of unlikely mass-manufactured objects such as delivery vans and motorized Women's Army Auxiliary mobile canteens were given the 'dazzle treatment'. Style, and the promise of modernity through visual novelty, quickly overtook any possible utilitarian benefit from the application of the dazzle look that anticipates the vogue for the streamlining of anything from the latest express steam locomotive to toasters in the 1920s and 1930s.

To some extent the very popularity of dazzle camouflage with the public made the Admiralty suspicious of its actual utility at sea. Senior eyebrows were raised with the appearance in the press of the following verse by one of Wilkinson's subordinates, G.A. Norton, which attempted to explain the aims of the dazzle section:

Captain Schmidt at his periscope
You need not fall and faint
For it's not the vision of drug or dope
But only the dazzle-paint
And you're done, you're done, my pretty Hun,
You're done in the big blue eye
By painter men with a sense of fun
And their work has just gone by
Cheero! A convoy safely by.

(Wilkinson 1969: 78)

Some influential Royal Navy officers argued that the marked reduction in ships lost monthly had much more to do with the introduction of the convoy system and the availability of additional escort ships provided by the US Navy. Eventually, the Admiralty's anti-submarine warfare department commissioned a study and, in September 1918, a 'Committee on Dazzle Painting' reported it could not provide conclusive evidence that a ship had survived because its dazzle camouflage had baffled a U-Boat commander and decisively put him off his aim. The number of unpainted ships that had never been attacked equalled that of dazzle ships. The Committee members did feel, however, that dazzle camouflage had prompted an 'undoubted increase' in the confidence and morale of the crews sailing on ships which had been dazzle-painted. They were convinced the odds were in their favour in a dazzle ship of never being attacked or of surviving a torpedo attack (Behrens 2002: 105).

When this report was publicised, 60 per cent of 50 captains sailing with the White Star Line declared they would have their ships in dazzle camouflage if presented with the opportunity. It was as if they found their very visibility in dock bestowed an almost magical invisibility amidst the ever-changing grey expanses of the North Atlantic (Wilkinson 1969: 93). The evidence strongly suggests that, in 1918, U-boats did not sink enough American troopships or merchant ships carrying oil, spare parts, food, ammunition, shells and machine tools to have a negative affect of the fighting ability of the Allies on the Western Front. On the other hand, the British Merchant Marine took a long time to recover from the U-Boat onslaught of 1917–18, and the losses left Britain owing the United States over 1 billion pounds Sterling in 1919. The British ship industry and the economy as a whole between the wars never really recovered from this Damoclean debt hanging over it (Ferguson 1999: 396).

Soon after the end of the war, Wilkinson wrote to *The Times* that he had never thought a ship could become invisible through camouflage: 'We know from some of the [sub] commanders themselves that they consistently located a vessel by her smoke . . . before the vessel could be seen at all.' (Wilkinson 1919). He did not believe that the camouflage schemes he had helped devise worked particularly well with larger ships. Dazzle had been originally designed 'for merchantmen singly, or in convoy, and war vessels working with them' (ibid.). On the other hand, he remained convinced that the form of a vessel could be broken up by 'strongly contrasting colours' so long as 'the perspective and balance of the design' had been carefully tested (ibid.).

The dazzle phenomenon continued to excite the interest of the press in 1919 as Wadsworth exhibited his series of woodcuts of dazzle-camouflaged ships, along with other prints, at the Adelphi Gallery in March 1919. The monochrome dazzle images fascinated many critics – the *Yorkshire Post* describing them as 'ciphers, or hieroglyphs to which the artist alone has the key' (7 March 1919). But then, as the artist wryly observed, such ships had been painted in a visual code that, thankfully, many U-Boat commanders had been unable to break on the high seas (ibid.).

Seven months later, an exhibition devoted to the output of artists who had worked on various aspects of camouflage for the nation's armed forces opened at the Royal Academy. Wadsworth's drawings and woodcuts of dazzle ships again attracted a disproportionate degree of favourable critical attention: on 11 October 1919, the *Evening Standard & St. James Gazette* declared 'the woodcuts of ships by Mr. Wadsworth are by far the best things, artistically, in the exhibition'.

The following month, *Colour* magazine also singled out Wadsworth's dazzle woodcuts for particular praise – though its critic, Herbert Furst, did wonder: 'It would be interesting to know if the "dazzle" designs by Mr. Wadsworth were more than ordinarily successful in practice' (November 1919). Furst comforted himself with the thought that, with the recent termination of the 'war to end all wars' and the destruction of the entire U-Boat fleet, circumstances would never arise in the future when artists would have to put at work again on a dazzle camouflage programme. He also noted: 'it was amusing to see that some of the amateur efforts at camouflage only succeeded in making objects glaringly visible that might have passed unnoticed if they had been left alone' (ibid.).

This was always the conundrum faced by those artists attempting to devise effective camouflage schemes, and which Wilkinson seems to have partially solved; to effectively mislead one has to divert the eye by making aspects of an object duplicitously visible. As Wadsworth later observed, in 1938, on the eve of another world war:

> The camouflage artist cannot make his vessel invisible, but with a few broad stripes on the bow and on the hull he can make the vessel appear to be steaming in a different direction. If the sub. commander is but two points out in his reckoning . . . he wastes his torpedoes on empty water.
>
> (Wilkinson 1938: 25)

Wilkinson's dazzle camouflage was not only, and paradoxically, a visually arresting experiment in large-scale art that altered perceptions of reality: it was also a unique expression of the contested materialities of industrialized war. For the price of a few cans of paint, the human eye could be misled, the most sophisticated weapons technology rendered ineffectual, and a ship and its crew saved.

References

Behrens, R.R. (2002) *False Colours: Art, Design and Modern Camouflage*. Dysart, Iowa: Bobolink Books.

Black, J. (2006) *Form, Feeling and Calculation: The Complete Paintings and Drawings of Edward Wadsworth*. London: Philip Wilson.

Bourne, J.M. (1989) *Britain and the Great War 1914–1918*. London: Hodder Arnold.

Corrigan, G. (2003) *Mud, Blood and Poppycock: Britain and the First World War*. London: Weidenfeld & Nicolson.

Dellouche, D. (1994) 'Cubisme et camouflage'. In J.-J. Becker, J. Winter, G. Krumeich, A. Becker and S. Audoin-Rouzeau (eds), *Guerre et cultures, 1914–1918*, pp. 239–50. Paris: Armand Colin éditeur.

Ferguson , N. (1999) *The Pity of War*. London: Basic Books.

Greenwood, J. (2002) *The Graphic Work of Edward Wadsworth*. Woodbridge: Wood Lea Press.

Kahn, E.L. (1984) *The Neglected Majority: 'Les Camoufleurs', Art History, and World War I*. Lanham: University Press of America.

Liddle, P. (ed.) (1997) *Passchendaele in Perspective: The Third Battle of Ypres*. London: Leo Cooper.

Prévost-Bault, M-P. (1997) 'La Grande Guerre camouflée'. In T. Compère-Morel (ed.), *Camouflage*, pp. 56–99. Péronne: Historial de la Grande Guerre.

Wadsworth, B. (1989) *Edward Wadsworth: A Painter's Life*. Salisbury: Michael Russell Publishing.

Wilkinson, N. (1919) *The Times*, 9 June 1919, p. 6.

—— (1938) *Cavalcade* 30 April.

—— (1969) *A Brush With Life*. London: Seeley Service.

14

MESSAGE AND MATERIALITY IN MESOPOTAMIA, 1916–1917

My grandfather's diary, social commemoration and the experience of war

John Schofield

Introduction

Having previously written about military archaeology, and its role in commemorating the fallen and documenting the experience of warfare in a detached and objective way (Schofield 2002), this chapter takes a different approach: more personal, more intimate. It takes as its starting point my grandfather's war diary and other related documents, and, as if by excavation, analyses their content and explores the layers of meaning contained within them. It takes the approach of the diary-as-object, in the homes and peoples' lives that it passed through, and it considers how visceral experiences become the written word – how the message is shaped by material culture.

The aims of this 'excavation' are: first, to assess the power of words and images, not so much for their historical content, but for what they reveal about the character and the feel of warfare: of being 'at war'. Second, to begin to unravel the personality of a grandfather I never knew. We know from official records that he showed 'courage and determination', and that he was a 'keen and energetic commanding officer'. But what was his experience of the war? How did it look through his eyes?

The process of researching and writing this chapter has itself constituted an exercise in social commemoration, excavation as a contribution to remembering past lives and events, and understanding aspects of my own. The study is in a sense archaeological in that it uncovers and offers an interpretation of the past and people within it – but it moves beyond conventional archaeology, by contextualizing my grandfather's words and images within the wider social framework of the Mesopotamian campaign in 1916–17. This view, taking the diary-as-object, is especially relevant in my case, where the object stands for a family member I never met and where my image of him is shaped only by the texts and photographs it contains.

This is the final paper in a trilogy on the social archaeology of warfare, and the personal experience of conflict and combat. The first part (Schofield 2005) discussed using personal stories to engage visitors to interpret monuments of conflict and discord. The second (Schofield 2004) was about the sense of place and social significance, and how some locations stir and store memories. This third part considers the experience of war. Increasingly intimate in outlook and scope, all three essays are primarily about people, and therefore also about humanity, and about what we can learn about war, ourselves and our approach to conflict from the experiences of others. The irony of the timing of this excavation, during the Second Gulf War, and while watching in real-time the actions of others in the same theatre, 85 years later, should not be underestimated.

Lieutenant Colonel H.J.H. Davson, DSO: a short biography

My grandfather, Harold John Hunter Davson (Figure 14:1), was born on 15 January 1880, the son of a doctor. During his career he had the distinction of serving in all three branches of the armed forces: Royal Marines (1898–1901), Indian Army

Figure 14:1
Lieutenant Colonel
H.J.H. Davson,
12 September 1918,
at Ranger's Corner.
(© author)

(1901–28), and Royal Air Force (1938–41). In addition, between 1941 and 1944, he served in the Home Guard, while, after the war, his fluent German led to his working as an interpreter at the Nuremberg trials. He was proud to have been one of 300 Gold Staff Officers at the 1937 Coronation, and excelled at sport, playing rugby for the Navy and the Army, and cricket for the Combined Services and the MCC.

With the Indian Army my grandfather served in France (fighting at the Battle of Neuve Chapelle in March 1915), Belgium and Egypt before being posted to Mesopotamia as a company commander with the 82nd Punjabis (5/1st Punjabi Regiment) (14th Indian Division) in March 1916. From June to November 1918, he served as officer commanding the 3/154th Infantry Regiment (53rd Division) in Palestine, before spending time at the 19th General Hospital in Alexandria. He returned to England in February 1919, after which he married Marjorie Garraway, the sister of a young officer in his company who died in a swimming accident (of which more later). Before his retirement from the Indian Army he also served in Burma (c.1925–8). Like so many, he would never speak about his campaign in Mesopotamia (or about his experiences at Nuremburg); he lost many friends and it went very deep with him.

My grandfather died in June 1961, eleven months before I was born. Yet, I recall, from a young age, the photograph of him in full uniform on a mantelpiece at home, side on to the camera, the perfect model of pride and elegant defiance, inspirational to others and courageous in the face of the enemy. It was my determination to dig deeper and attempt to uncover something of the personality beneath that rather austere, though inspiring image that was my motivation in writing this chapter. A personal journey into family history, military archives and ultimately of self-exploration: social commemoration at its most intimate.

The Mesopotamian campaign: a brief historiography

Troops were sent to Mesopotamia, remote from the war's main theatre on the Western Front, to protect the oil works and pipeline at Abadan, and to demonstrate to the Arabs in the region, and the sheiks in the Persian Gulf, that they would have British support against the Ottoman empire (Turkey). Yet this was an expedition of mismanagement and disaster (Woodward 1967; see also Buchanan 1938; Candler 1919; Moberley 1925; Townshend 1920. With the exception of Davis 1994, little historiography has appeared since Woodward's review). As the small force required for this expedition was to come from India, the War Office left its control to the Government of India and to the India Office, though they were clearly not suited to the control of such a geographically remote war. Furthermore, the British Army in India, and the Indian Army (with British officers), were primarily organized for the maintenance of internal Indian security, and had limited equipment as a result – the field army had no aeroplanes, no wireless and no motor transport (Woodward 1967: 99–100).

The first task of the expeditionary force in late 1913 was the occupation of Basra and this was easily achieved. The priority then should have been to ensure that Basra

– the only port – had adequate facilities, and to provide sufficient supplies through water transport and hospital ships before any move was made up river. Neither of these basic tasks was achieved. The issue of supplies is one regularly and critically referred to by my grandfather, and with good reason. A division needed a set amount of supplies daily; the quantity and types of supplies were known, as were the distances over which they had to be transported, and the information about river levels. Simply put, no operations north of Basra should have been undertaken before sufficient river-going craft had been assembled (ibid.: 102).

The next stage of the expedition was to occupy Qurna at the junction of the Tigris and the Euphrates rivers. This would ensure that the force would control all the navigable waters to the Persian Gulf and the fertile area between Qurna and the sea. Qurna was occupied without difficulty in early December 1914, while in June and July 1915 Amara (upstream on the Tigris) and Nasiriya (on the Euphrates) were captured. There were British and Indian casualties, mostly from sickness, and under these circumstances, and with the unlikelihood of getting reinforcements and river craft, an advance beyond Amara and Nasiriya should have been out of the question. The argument that an enemy force at Kut threatened both places had already been shown to be unfounded, while an advance on Kut would add 150 miles to the line of communication when the army was already short of men and transport (ibid.).

However, General Sir John Nixon – who was given command of the Mesopotamian Expeditionary Force in March 1915 – intended not only to hold Kut, but to advance to Baghdad. General Townshend was given command of the force sent to occupy Kut, which was captured, with heavy Turkish losses, in September 1915, though the Turks were able to make an orderly retreat to a prepared position at Ctesiphon. An attempt to pursue them was not possible as there was not enough land transport and the available steamers were too slow.

From this point on, the expedition, according to Woodward, 'fell into disaster' (ibid.: 105) for the simple reasons that, first, the significance of river boats was not taken seriously enough, and, second, the commanders in Mesopotamia were not in agreement over the decision to advance (Townshend being more cautious than Nixon). Townshend's attack on Ctesiphon, though made with great courage, was a disaster. The Turkish first lines were captured at a cost of 4,500 casualties out of the attacking force of 12,000. Without the resources to continue the assault, Townshend retired to Kut where his depleted army was surrounded (ibid.: 107), soon to run short of supplies. Fighting for the relief of Kut took place in January 1916, and again in March and April, after which Townshend surrendered.

After the fall of Kut, neither the British nor the Turks were capable of large-scale actions. The seasonal extremes of high floods and temperatures had arrived, and the troops suffered great hardship, not helped by the lack of transport. However, from the end of August 1916, conditions improved rapidly: there were more steamers, the port installations at Basra were much improved, and adequate arrangements were made for the sick and wounded. General Sir F.S. Maude took command in August. He was a much abler commander and, unlike his predecessors, wouldn't attempt any advance until he had sufficient troops, transport and supplies. At the end of December 1916,

Maude was ready to attack. By the end of February 1917, he had removed the enemy from their defences at Kut before chasing them to Baghdad, which he took on 11 March.

Following the transfer of the direction and management of the expedition to the War Office in February 1916, the government of India sent two commissioners to enquire into the medical arrangements in Mesopotamia. The terms of the enquiry were later widened, and a third commissioner added. As Woodward describes (1967: 112–13), the findings of the Commission were severe: first, 'the want of foresight and provision for the most fundamental needs of the expedition reflects discredit upon the organising aptitude of all the authorities concerned'. Second, shortcomings in the armament and equipment of the expedition

> were the natural result of the policy of indiscriminate retrenchment pursued for some years before the war by the Indian Government under instructions from the Home Government, by which the army was to be prepared and maintained for frontier and internal use.

The report of the Commission was published in June 1917, prompting demand in the popular press for the punishment of some of those concerned. The extent to which my grandfather's experience both reflects this official history of the expedition, and adds colour to it through accounts and personalities, forms the subject of the following section, though covering only the latter stages of the expedition from the relief of Kut in April 1916 to the capture of Baghdad in 1917.

Words and images

Bound in leather and tied neatly with string, the diary was delivered to my desk at the Imperial War Museum's Reading Room in London. I had recently seen a photocopy of the complete document, though this didn't prepare me in the least for the immediacy and clarity of the original: my grandfather's own handwritten comments, and the photographs, many of which had annotated notes identifying cultural landmarks and people. The cover simply conveyed the words

MY DIARY

Harold J. H. Davson

as though it were an account of a family holiday or a school term, without any trappings to betray what he felt might amount to historic or lasting interest. It seemed merely to be presenting a modest account – for his own interest and that of others at home – of what the campaign was like, and what he saw on his journey. And to a degree that is precisely what it was. But, as we dig deeper, the true significance of this document becomes apparent. A frontispiece bears the words

H. Davson's

DIARY IN MESOPOTAMIA

April 1916

to

April 1917

There is still no indication of his rank, or any explicit mention of the military campaign that the diary describes, or of its value as perhaps the only known record of some of its participants, and of the events that unfolded and held such significance in their young lives. The Preface however gets straight to the point.

Preface

Nothing has been altered in the type-written portion of the diary from what I originally wrote in my F.S. [Field service] note book. It is all there as it was written in moments of elation and depression, after victory and the loss of dear friends . . . the document is I think human

My mother and my aunts have confirmed that this was indeed a verbatim copy, but one compiled after the war from letters my grandfather wrote to his mother, themselves lifted from his Field Service note book which wasn't retained. Perhaps for this reason, he deliberately downplayed the suffering, placing greater emphasis on people and the cultural and physical landscape around him. So, not strictly speaking a diary, though it does contain first-hand accounts written at the time and – so far as anyone can recall – unaltered. And as my grandfather called it a diary I shall too.

The diary is essentially a personal history of the year April 1916 to April 1917, followed by a supplementary diary of the period May 1917 to February 1918 when he spent time in Palestine. It covers in some detail the conditions under which the Indian Army pursued their part of the Mesopotamian campaign, some of the people involved, and the extent to which the failure of the campaign is reflected in actions and reactions on the ground.

The diary's words and images reflect the conditions of the campaign, by which I mean the physical setting within which the conflict occurred, and the social contexts within which my grandfather lived and worked. The words tell us much about the author – they are 'not merely the residue of a lost world but eloquent historically contextualisable and contextualising artefacts' (Briggs 2000: 398). They are not neutral, but the products of human creativity, active in the production, negotiation and transformation of social relations (Moreland 2001: 31). Text is created as a projection of people's views about themselves and their place in the world; words serve to create meaning in and structure the routines of everyday life (ibid.: 80). Here, place, memory, reconstruction and diary-as-object all come into sharp focus; here all of these considerations are most clearly and obviously related.

In looking at the photographs, and especially those of my grandfather interacting with colleagues and friends (Figure 14:2), a similar point can be made about meaning and context, and about social relations. In examining these images, and the messages they convey, I can 'enjoy them as good historical scenes'; I can 'culturally participate in the figures, faces, gestures, settings, actions' (Barthes 2000: 26). Although photographs, like words, do not call up the past, they confirm that what I see once existed (ibid.: 82), and because I see and I feel, I also notice, observe and understand (ibid.: 21).

In terms of how these various sources convey aspects of the Mesopotamian campaign, there are of course legitimate arguments concerning historical accuracy and source criticism. Examining the Mesopotamian campaign isn't the point of this chapter, however. Here, my concern is for social commemoration at a personal level within the context of that campaign. Whatever he wrote and however historically accurate it may be, they are his words, projecting views about himself and his place in the world at that time. It is a text of trauma (Bourke 1999: 10), but one that through careful excavation can reveal much about the man behind the words . . . and behind the camera.

So, diaries and first-hand accounts are invaluable in documenting the character of such campaigns, and – significantly – in remembering the personalities involved, at least beneath the 'top brass' senior officers, whose personal and military histories tend to be well told in post-war biographies and official histories (several of which are listed in the references). And, where so few diaries are written, the significance and social

Figure 14:2 Breakfast after strafing an Arab fort. (© author)

commemorative value of each becomes immense. In fact, of the *c.*340,000 British and Indian Army soldiers involved in Mesopotamia, only 148 documents – diaries, Field Service note books and letters – are in the public domain, of which 53 relate directly and specifically to Kut.[1]

There is one further source relating to my grandfather's part in the campaign: a copy of Candler's *The Long Road to Baghdad* (1919), the account of a war correspondent, written 'on the scene of the actions described' (ibid.: vii) and annotated by my grandfather throughout, sometimes by simply underlining key words and sections, and sometimes amplifying or correcting the text with comments written in pencil at the margins (such as 'This is not how it was'). Although no attempt is made here to analyse this correspondent's accounts, or my grandfather's comments on them, it is nevertheless a relevant source, reflecting the thoughts and opinions of a correspondent, alongside those of an army officer active in the same campaign. As an example, the beginning of Candler's chapter IX ('The night of January 21st') has this comment added by my grandfather in pencil:

> Howell was killed on this night whilst out collecting wounded. Mrs H got in touch with a clairvoyant and for years refused to believe her husband was dead although the Turks reported burying a staff officer and he was the only one missing.[2]

My grandfather's diary

The diary begins with a series of comments on the conditions of the campaign, and specifically on the order and disorder in the army around the time of the fall of Kut (30 April 1916). Soon after his arrival on 30 April 1916, my grandfather notes how the

> heat is appalling, and only just begun. Flies bite hard – are in thousands. Cholera has started so things are very cheery. I was inoculated yesterday against it and then had to march in the heat of the day to relieve trenches. Great fun.
>
> We lie and gasp all day under a blanket, which we put up to keep the sun off which it does indifferently . . . in fact you may say that I am fairly fed up with Mesopotamia. Food now is disgusting. We are short of milk, jam, sugar, and exist on bully beef (fly blown) and stale bread. I am thankful to say so far I am very fit on it.

Resilience is implicit in these words. They communicate the ability to persevere and deal with the conditions, to work with them rather than against, and, of course, as was expected of a company commander, to help others to do so as well. From the official histories and reflective accounts of the campaign, mismanagement emerges as a significant theme, and this is borne out by the diary, which betrays an increasing sense of frustration, both with those managing the campaign from afar, and with those in charge on the ground. Several entries reflect this.

17 May 1916
It is an absolute scandal the way Basra mismanages things. There are stacks of provisions in Basra, which the authorities don't bother about sending up. One of the river captains told the authorities that he could bring up 80 to 100 tons of stores and he actually was not allowed to do so. They do not seem to care a bit about people at the front.

Also relevant are his descriptions of the conditions and circumstances of troop movements. Marching is a prominent theme, especially in the early months of my grandfather's time in Mesopotamia.

20–22 May 1916
The most awful march . . . We . . . marched at 4 am . . . and camped at a shrine called Immaen ali Mansur. The distance was only between 12 & 14 miles. There were however many delays and we arrived at 4 pm.

One water bottle per officer and man was the allowance and no more. En route men fell like flies. More than 1000 collapsed through heat and lack of water. This is an official figure.

When we got to our destination there was no water nearer than four miles. I was marching in rear of the Brigade, and men simply crumpled up. They looked just as if they had been shot. The last two or three miles I was carrying one man's rifle and pulling another along by the arm. I collected my strongest men, fell them in behind, and we kicked, cajoled, and pulled men along. Anything to get them in.

One felt an awful brute letting a man have it in the ribs as hard as one could, but it was a case of getting them in or leaving them out to have their throats cut by Arabs; to mutilation.

He clearly wrote what he felt, and no doubt spoke his mind too, to his own commanding officer, and to fellow officers, though less to the men under his command. It seems he was a man of great integrity, fully aware of his responsibilities, all of which he appears to have taken seriously. He felt the suffering of his men personally, and grieved at the deaths that occurred. Yet he remained strong, courageous and focused on the campaign, and on his own role within it, despite obvious moments of exasperation:

The 18th and 19th [of April 1916] struck me as a good example of a question I had set in my Military History paper on my exam for promotion. The question was – 'order, counter-order, disorder.' Comment on this as regards the French Infantry in August /70 – Enough said!

I may be quite wrong, I am only a regimental officer.

23 April 1916

We have lost since December from all causes 24,000 men trying to release 5,000 [after which a note is added: 'This estimate was wrong'.]. Is it worth it from the military point of view? Is it worth the enormous sacrifice from the sentimental point of view? I write in ignorance of course of the political.

15 August 1916

The redoubt having been finished has been abandoned before we have occupied it, another line having been decided upon. It is typical of things out here.

I and my scurvy-ridden crowd put our best work into something and the benefit eventually is nil. I am sufficiently educated to laugh; the sepoy isn't . . . Thank goodness we are a good, well-disciplined regiment. I refused to demolish, and gave the men two days leave.

The Commission, described by Woodward (1967: 112–13) and referred to earlier, is commented on in the diary, and the scepticism and doubt expressed by my grandfather on the scene appears to reflect a general mood back home and within the army at that time, that mismanagement had occurred, and that some degree of cover-up may be required if senior figures were not to face reprimand. The diary comments on the Commission as follows.

29 May 1916

A commission was sent out here to inquire into the medical arrangements etc. I imagine, as a matter of fact it was sent to whitewash things. Although next door to where the commission sat were three medical officers, who had been through the whole campaign, these were never called on to give evidence. It rather looks therefore as if the Commission had been sent as a blind to the people at home, and to obscure the real facts.

It is a myth that soldiers at war spend most of their time engaged in combat (Bourke 1999), but most war diaries talk of little else. While combat is mentioned by my grandfather, it is unusual that fighting isn't more prominent in his diary (but see Figure 14:4 below, and the related entry for 23 February 1917). The circumstances under which the diary was prepared may explain this. Even though the diary originates in entries in my grandfather's Field Service notebook, this was most likely written with letters to his mother in mind (ensuring that he sent her an authentic record of the campaign). If that was the case, it may understandably have been his intention to present as comparatively painless an account as possible, without compromising the fact that he was at war.

This may also explain the increasing attention paid to the cultural landscape (Figure 14:3) – the diary, and in particular the second part, in Palestine, refers in some detail to the architecture and cultural sights of Jerusalem. This includes numerous photographs, such as the Garden of Gethsemane and the Street of the Gentiles

Figure 14:3 Entrance to the Church of the Holy Sepulchre, Jerusalem. (© author)

(interestingly placed directly above three photographs of military training, the central of these appearing to show soldiers on bayonet practice). But there are references to fighting. An example follows, being the diary's final entry, describing the advance on Baghdad (Figure 14:4):

23 February 1917
The advance was the most magnificent thing I have ever seen. We advanced in quick time, no rushing over 3000 yards of flat ground with no cover. It took us 35 minutes and we had the enemy main position in our hands. We were troubled for a bit with enemy machine guns on our right, but got Artillery onto them and finished them off.

Baker poor old chap was killed half way across. Shell shock, not a wound anywhere.

Little Plowden was hit near the barracks. He's doing well. Anderson hit in the leg managed to get on. Later on I found he was in great pain, so I got him onto a stretcher and carried back. We had all our losses practically from machine gun fire on our right flank. We went through three belts of it. Whole platoons dropped, but the advance went on steadily. Half the regiment wiped out. Only two British Officers and three Indian Officers left, instead of 8 in 15.

For the third time in one year we have lost half the regiment in one swoop. I was awfully proud of my Company. They followed splendidly. Three or four times on the way over the men on each side of me fell. My great coat changed hands four times. My orderly was carrying it first. He was hit and threw it to another man, and so on. My Mohamedans made it a point of honour that my Great Coat must get in.

The thing that stands out is the magnificent conduct all through the regiment. I suppose the price paid is not too high, but Baker, Clerk, Stokes, Howell, Wignall (Wiggie), Stratton, Dickson and Garraway killed is a long list. A more charming crowd to serve with and a better lot of officers I shall not meet again. The regiment owes them a great debt. (Since writing this Milne has also joined Baker etc.)

FINIS.

For my family, one diary entry has more significance than any other, and that is the entry describing the death of Wilfrid Garraway (accompanied by a photograph; see Figure 14:5).

11 November 1916
We are all grieved to hear of the death of young Garraway of the regiment. He was our most promising officer. Scholar of Oxford, 1st into Sandhurst, Under Officer, Sword of Honour, Head of Bedford . . . he had hopes of a brilliant career . . . Briefly what happened was that he and a friend were training men in swimming, and swam the river. Two days later they swam

Figure 14:4 82nd Punjabis, Mirjana, April 1918. (© author)

it again on duty. His friend saw he looked a bit tired, 15 yds from the shore, practically in his own depth. He then saw he was in difficulties. He went back to help him. He plunged in three times, and actually the second time had lifted him up, I gather in their own depth, only to be swept away again. A third Tim Reeves, an old school friend of his, went after him, and got him by the pants. He was again sucked under, and only got ashore himself in a state of extreme exhaustion. No one but a man of extraordinary physique like Reeves could have done so much. I have had to write to his relations etc. The whole thing is so sad and I was so fond of the boy looking forward to the time when I might be C.O. with him as my Adjt.

Having written to Garraway's family, my grandfather received a letter back from 'Garraway's best girl' on 28 November 1916, and subsequently a small calendar notebook for Christmas 1918 from his mother. My grandfather went to Bedford in early 1919 to meet Wilfrid Garraway's mother. Her daughter Marjorie (most likely his 'best girl', though this isn't certain) met him off the train. They were married within the year, and my mother – Maureen – was the first child. Shelagh, Patricia and Wilfrid followed. Certainly in Patricia and Wilfrid, and in Peter and myself (two of my mother's three sons), the physical resemblance is strong. And Peter and I have also been influenced – indirectly perhaps – by my grandfather's military background and experiences. My own interest in military archaeology, my professional focus and development, and my brother Peter's service career and continued interest in the Royal Air Force, surely owe a debt to my grandfather, and to my father, though that's

215

Figure 14:5
W.F. Garraway. (© author)

another story. This episode is the central point of this chapter, clearly demonstrating the connection between the diary and my own experience: death and materiality producing love, marriage and children in the aftermath of the First World War.

Social commemoration and the experience of war

My motivations for researching and writing this paper were entirely selfish. I have always been aware of my grandfather – often spoken about, and whose photograph adorns the mantelpiece at home – as someone I didn't know, and didn't know very much about. I knew he had served with the Indian Army during the First World War and had served again in the Second, but I did not know in what capacity. Initially, all I wanted to know was what he had actually done, and what his role was. But, as my interest in military archaeology has evolved, and as I became more conscious of the relevance of this materiality of conflict to ourselves and our families, to the way we are (cf. Joy 2002), the questions became more sharply focused, and oriented more toward him as a person. What was he like? How did he deal with the conditions he encountered? To what extent was he a courageous and caring man, always attuned to the concerns and well-being of his men? In that respect at least, was he a good soldier? In other words, as time passed, the questions became less to do with the soldier, and more to do with the man, recognizing that the experiences of war are human experiences every bit as much as they are those of soldiers, sailors or airmen. Indeed, my grandfather's diary reflects that point perhaps more than any other.

While the content of his diary will be considered prosaic by some, it does reveal something of the character of the Mesopotamian campaign, while at a personal level it has value for reasons of remembrance and social commemoration. On reading my grandfather's diary many of my questions were answered, yet, as with any conventional archaeological investigation, the true meaning of what is uncovered will often require deeper analysis and interpretation; a more meticulous excavation than one that simply reveals the more obvious artefacts and stratigraphic layers. Certainly, this excavation had as its objective something more subtle, more sublime, than just the bare facts – being almost spiritual in its approach to the person whose past this was. It was implicitly embarked upon as an exercise in commemoration while also a personal journey of (self) discovery. I wanted to find him, the person, and to discover him at arguably the most difficult and stressful time of his life.

We all experience challenging emotional situations for a variety of reasons, and sometimes self-discovery can help us to cope with these situations by informing our experience and enabling a richer experience of the future. And the production of this volume was coincident with a need to dig into my own family history, to uncover a man of obvious courage and immense integrity, inner strength and fortitude, of loyalty and patriotism; a loving and caring man with an obvious sense of humour which helped him through tough times.

In the true interdisciplinary spirit of attempts to uncover the biographies of objects, and the ways in which they intersect people's lives, this personal excavation of a diary has achieved many ends. It has revealed traces of the campaign, my grandfather's experience of it, and his experience of war, but more significantly it has revealed the person, his family and, ultimately, something about myself and what I have inherited from a grandfather who until this point existed as nothing more than a photographic image, familiar for as long as I can remember, but only ever in two dimensions.

Such stories and accounts, however irrelevant and mundane they may appear to the author, prove invaluable as primary source material as well as displaying an intimacy and immediacy that other sources cannot provide. Once a war drifts away from popular memory, and the cultural and social landscape changes beyond recognition, what people wrote at the scene and at the time throw light on many complex issues. It reveals the conditions endured, the social interactions between people, and how they coped with stress and the physical exertion of marching, fighting – simply of living and 'being' a long way from home. Such words tell us, directly, what people were thinking when not fighting or preparing to fight.

My grandfather's interest in the cultural landscape around him was an obvious distraction, and some of his notes and photographs are of historic interest in their own right. His observations about people and their personalities tell us about those individuals, but also about himself, and how he saw the world and those around him. It is a biography of place (in this case a battlefield) and of the people inhabiting it at that time. Too often critical discussions of war diaries and first hand accounts focus on their accuracy and reliability as historical documents. Here, I argue that their real value is as artefacts from which the social commemoration of warfare, and an understanding of its conditions and character, and its personalities, can be pursued. Buried 'past time' is brought into the present for future benefit, and valued for contributing a personal view of the war.

So, by reading the diary, and my grandfather's handwritten comments on one of the official accounts (Candler 1919), as well as using that knowledge as the basis for conversations with my mother and my aunts, I now know my grandfather better than before. I have begun to understand what he was like, how he dealt with his year in Mesopotamia, how he coped with loss, in part what his motivations were, and how he acted with his company and the men with whom he served. He was mentioned in Dispatches three times during this campaign and the subsequent Palestine campaign, and was awarded the Distinguished Service Order (DSO) 'for conspicuous devotion to duty and gallantry'. This no doubt made him very proud, though it is only a small part of a story that in one short year in Mesopotamia directly influenced the course his life was to take, notably through the death of W.F. Garraway and the consequent relationship that developed with his sister.

Ultimately, though, my grandfather's closing comments in his diary of 1916–17, following the advance on Baghdad, says so much more about how (and who) he was: a caring man, conscious of the needs and concerns of others, and anxious that his men should share in any credit and praise that came the company's way.

> The thing that stands out is the magnificent conduct all through the regiment . . . A more charming crowd to serve with and a better lot of officers I shall not meet again. The regiment owes them a great debt.

For me, these are the main results of this excavation, results that imbue and inspire a sense of courage and responsibility in times of uncertainty. Excavation for inspiration almost.

Dedication

This chapter is dedicated to the memory of my grandfather, Harold John Hunter Davson (Lieut. Col. DSO), 1880–1961, according to his confidential report (May 1916) 'a capable, popular, self-reliant and energetic officer, popular with all ranks'. Also a devoted father to my mother and my aunts and uncle, and a grandfather who regrettably I never met.

Acknowledgements

I am indebted to my mother, Maureen Schofield, and my aunt Shelagh Davson for providing thoughtful comments on the text, and helpful advice and source material, enabling my 'excavation' to proceed in a more authentic and meaningful direction than would otherwise have been possible. Also Emily Morrissey and Nick Saunders, who helped this chapter to evolve, and made perceptive remarks and observations on earlier drafts. Finally, I am grateful to staff at the Imperial War Museum, London, for their help in accessing documents relating to Mesopotamia 1916–17, and for arranging for reproduction of the photographs.

Notes

1   By this account, diaries now in the public domain were produced by only 0.05 per cent of those involved, raising questions of how representative they are, but also highlighting their cultural value notwithstanding the personal attachments that form the main focus of this chapter. Diaries of this type perhaps aren't as ubiquitous as some might think.
2   See Winter (1995), chapter 3, for a full discussion of spiritualism and séances during and after the Great War.

References

Barthes, R. (2000) *Camera Lucida: Reflections on Photography*. London: Vintage. [Originally published in French as *La Chambre Claire*, by Editions de Seuil, 1980.]

Bourke, J. (1999) *An Intimate History of Killing: Face-To-Face Combat in Twentieth-Century Warfare*. London: Granta Books.

Briggs, C. (2000) 'Literacy, reading and writing in the medieval West'. *Journal of Medieval History* 26: 397–420.

Buchanan, Sir G. (1938) *The Tragedy of Mesopotamia*. Edinburgh: William Blackwood.

Candler, E. (1919) *The Long Road to Baghdad*. London: Cassell and Company Ltd.

Davis, P. (1994) *The Mesopotamian Campaign: Ends and Means*. Toronto: Associated University Presses.

Davson, Harold J.H. (n.d.) 'My Diary'. Unpublished document held at the Imperial War Museum, London.

Joy, J. (2002) 'Biography of a medal: people and the things they value'. In J. Schofield, W.G. Johnson and C.M. Beck (eds) *Matériel Culture: The Archaeology of Twentieth Century Conflict*, pp. 132–42. London: Routledge (One World Archaeology 44).

Moberley, F.J. (1925) *History of the Great War based on Official Documents: The Campaign in Mesopotamia 1914–18*, Vol. III. London: HMSO.

Moreland, J. (2001) *Archaeology and Text*. London: Duckworth.

Schofield, J. (2002) 'Monuments and the memories of war: motivations for preserving military sites in England'. In J. Schofield, W.G. Johnson and C.M. Beck (eds) *Matériel Culture: The Archaeology of Twentieth Century Conflict*, pp. 143–58. London: Routledge (One World Archaeology 44).

—— (2004) 'Memories and monuments in Berlin: a Cold War narrative'. *Historic Environment* 17 (1): 36–41.

—— (2005) 'Jessie's cats and other stories: presenting and interpreting recent troubles'. In M. Blockley and A. Hems (eds) *Heritage Interpretation: Theory and Practice*. London: Routledge and English Heritage.

Townshend, Sir Charles W.F. (1920) *My Campaign in Mesopotamia*. London: Thornton Butterworth.

Winter, J. (1995) *Sites of Memory, Sites of Mourning: The Great War in European Cultural History*. Cambridge: Cambridge University Press.

Woodward, Sir L. (1967) *Great Britain and the War of 1914–18*. London: Methuen.

15

POSTCARDS FROM THE PAST

War, landscape and place in Argonne, France

Paola Filippucci

During the First World War, the Argonne region in north-eastern France was one of the main battlefield areas, and suffered great devastation. In spite of post-war reconstruction, its surroundings today still bear the marks of this almost century-old wartime destruction and damage. Here I will address the issue of whether, and how, the present inhabitants of Argonne use these surroundings to formulate a sense of identity.

In France, as elsewhere in Europe and beyond, physical surroundings play a role in identity formation as the basis for the notion of 'place'. 'Place' refers to the implication of people and land through habitation, and typically refers to an enduring, stable presence (Casey 1996: 36). In a phenomenological sense, 'place' is not only spatial, but also a fusion of self, space, and time (Basso and Feld 1996: 9). In relation to the idea of place, therefore, physical surroundings are seen as supports for, or material correlatives of continuity, their materiality attributed a 'stabilizing function' (Young 2000: 154).

But what of areas, such as Argonne, that are physically marked by, and perceived as bearing the marks of discontinuity and interrupted presence? Can they also be the basis for a sense of place – can they too support a place-based identity?

In considering this question, I will draw on the idea that the materiality of surroundings is multilayered, and includes not only the surroundings themselves but also the representations made of them (Saunders 2001; Lefebvre 1991). In Argonne, a sense of place is constructed by using images of the local surroundings that materialize a particular link between space and time that helps to accommodate a history of discontinuity and destruction. In this way, a sense of place is formulated which is centred on the idea of tenacity in the face of adversity. This speaks as much to the area's past as to a present beset by the threat of economic and demographic decline.

This sense of place positions those who express it as 'local' by opposition to other appropriations of the Argonnais surroundings serving other projects of identity.

Taken together, these different and competing appropriations represent and encap-sulate the complexity of space–time at a former First World War battlefield, in the sense that it was not produced once and for all in 1914–18, but continues to be produced by and through all the subsequent history of material and symbolic appropriations (Saunders 2001; 2004: 7–13).

Old postcards

When questioned about the past, the people of Argonne, by and large, volunteered pictures rather than narratives, specifically old picture postcards depicting Argonnais villages around 1900. In today's Argonne, these pictures, and sometimes pictures of war-ruined villages dating from the First World War, are displayed in private and public buildings, shops, guest houses and private houses, as well as published in books, used in school history projects and, especially, collected (Figure 15:1). Some collectors own hundreds or even thousands of these photos, but, partly because of the potentially considerable cost, many more own just a few postcards of the village where they live and/or where they or relatives or spouses were born. Many collectors said that the postcards were family heirlooms, while others spoke of touring antique markets and shops 'all over France' to retrieve postcards 'sent away by soldiers in the war of "14"'. These photos are now cherished and shown because, as one collector put it to me, through them 'on retrouve les villages' (you can find the villages again).

Figure 15:1 Display of pre-First World War postcards in public buildings: the Mairie (town hall) at Neuvilly, Meuse. (© author's collection)

Whatever their actual date, these images are invariably said to date 'from before "14"', pointing to the First World War as a watershed. More generally, the photos are used to make 'before and after' comparisons, pointing out buildings that withstood the impact of war, and those rebuilt in a different location or style (Figures 15:2 and 15:3). Most of all, they would use these images to stress the accuracy of post-First World War reconstruction: 'Look at the picture and look at the village now: it was all rebuilt identically the only change is that now there are cars' or electric lights, or tarmac.

More broadly, people related the topography depicted in the photos to today's village topography: 'You see this building here? It's the same one you see over there'; 'This here is the same bridge that you drove over as you came just now'; 'That one is the road towards Verdun.' A sense of continuity between the time of the photos and today was also expressed by the familiar tone used to describe the scenes depicted: 'That's where we used to take the animals to drink as there was no water in the stables' (Figure 15:4). At the same time, many scenes prompted comments about change and discontinuity: 'That's the High Street, look how many people there were in the village then'; 'Look what crowds used to go to church.' Less or no commentary was instead offered about the more brutal discontinuity inflicted by war, graphically rendered in postcard pictures of ruined villages, sometimes displayed and collected alongside those of pre-war villages. With these images, people tended to fall silent or say 'That one speaks for itself.'

How should we interpret the circulation of these images in today's Argonne, and their role in presenting the region's past? It has been argued that photos can be a

Figure 15:2 'Before and after 1': A crossroads in Neuvilly, Meuse, before 1914. (© author's collection)

Figure 15:3 'Before and after 2': The same crossroads at Neuvilly in 2005. (© author's collection)

Figure 15:4 'That's where we used to water the animals.' Postcard showing pre-war (early 1900s) view of Malancourt, Meuse. The bottom line reads, *'regarde bien c'est grandpère qui est sur la carte'* (look closely it's grandfather on the card). (© author's collection)

means of self-fashioning, insofar as 'certain forms of representation presuppose certain forms of subject' (Pinney 2003: 11–12). In the modern Euro-American context, photography contributes to fashioning a subjectivity that detaches and controls the world, in Heidegger's words, 'as picture' (ibid.: 12). Landscape/builtscape 'views' such as those immortalized in postcards arguably are a manifestation of this perspective, distancing people from surroundings 'conceived as grasped as a picture' (Gregory 1994: 34; Hirsch 1996: 2).

However, in the case of Argonne, photographic views of pre-war villages are a means for bringing together subject and surroundings or, in other words, for accomplishing the fusion of space and time that may be called 'place' (Casey 1996: 36). Photography may play this role in Argonne because of its particular qualities that help formulate a sense of place at a location where space and time do not 'fuse' smoothly because, in Benjamin's memorable words, by 1918 'nothing remained unchanged but the clouds' (quoted in Gregory 1994: 215).

Argonne

Argonne is an area of forest and hilly farmland stretching for about 80 km along the administrative border of the two French regions of Champagne and Lorraine. It is dotted with villages,[1] but sparsely populated because of the weakness of the local economy, which is centred on cattle breeding, cereal farming and a little light industry. Most residents commute to work to nearby towns, such as Verdun, Châlons-en-Champagne or Reims. Emigration is not as dramatic now as it was historically (particularly between the 1950s and mid-1970s), but population loss remains steady, fuelled by the disappearance of shops and services (Hussenet 2000: 169). Economic and demographic decline began in Argonne in the mid-nineteenth century with the collapse of the proto-industrial production of glass and ceramics that had earlier employed nearly half of the local population. Competition from other industrial centres led to decline, and by the turn of the twentieth century Argonne was the agricultural backwater it is today (Hussenet 1982).

These negative economic and demographic trends have been exacerbated in the past century or so by wars: Argonne, a few miles west of the fortified site of Verdun, was a theatre of combat during the Franco-Prussian War of 1870–71, then most dramatically in 1914–18 and again in 1939–45. During the Great War, the front-line stabilized across the area in late 1914, and remained more or less fixed until 1918. The civilian population was evacuated in 1915; forest and farmland on either side of the frontline were devastated, and villages completely destroyed or severely damaged (Hussenet 1982: 311–39; Clout 1996: 19). To this day, areas of the forest are closed off as part of the *zone rouge*, the designation given to areas judged to be too contaminated by wartime debris and unexploded munitions to be safe for civilian use, and consequently expropriated by the state for permanent closure (Clout 1996: 24–5).

Parts of the forest, much of the farmland and most of the destroyed villages were reconstructed during the 1920s. Nevertheless, visible and audible traces of the war remain in the form of monuments, cemeteries, memorials and the remains of trenches, tunnels and bunkers, as well as in the discovery of bodies and the sudden explosion of old munitions – a multi-sensorial landscape from an 85-year-old conflict (see Saunders 2001, 2004: 7–10).

In spite of post-war reconstruction, only just over half of the pre-war population returned to Argonne after 1918, and much local capital and war reparations were reinvested elsewhere. The population never regained pre-war levels even where reconstruction brought new residents, many of them from abroad, whose descendants still make up some of the population today (Hussenet 1982: 339; HdA 1978). The war accelerated a trend of economic and demographic decline that has continued into the twenty-first century, so that today Argonne falls significantly behind the rest of France and neighbouring areas in terms of population, jobs, services and infrastructure, and is classified as an area of 'rural decline' by France and the EU.[2]

In line with EU and French directives about revitalizing such areas, public policy response has centred on the promotion of tourism, especially agritourism and 'green' and cultural heritage tourism. The forest, villages and a few pre-twentieth century/First World War historic and archaeological sites are targets of valorization, and there is some limited commercialization of *produits du terroir* (local products), but, to date, tourist facilities are scarce in Argonne.

The one exception is that of sites related to the First World War that attract visitors on battlefield tours centred on Verdun, and dominate Argonne's tourist profile today. Thus, public policy aimed at 'valorizing' the surroundings of Argonne characterizes them in two contrasting ways: one, which is centred on ideas of tradition and nature, highlights their 'unspoilt' quality; the other, centred on history and specifically on war, stresses signs of destruction. These images also carry two different renderings of the region's past, one stressing age and continuity, the other brutal discontinuity. These different ways of characterizing the region can be related to dominant perceptions of Argonne as a place.

A place of death

In 2001, I interviewed Olivier, a young public official, who had recently moved to Argonne from urban Lorraine. He was struck, he said, by the feeling that people here were 'in mourning': 'One realizes that something huge occurred here, and that since then they have kept their distance from it, they look upon it as if it were at once close, and far.' War was central in Olivier's perception of Argonne as a site of lingering trauma, with a population of survivors haunted by a past of death and destruction that remains a vague but overbearing presence just beneath the surface of things, a poignant counterpoint to the quiet beauty of the area.

Such a perception of Argonne is shared by many visitors, and is in fact explicitly promoted in and around the many Argonnais wartime sites and remains. These include monuments, ossuaries and cemeteries erected in the years following the war for mourning and commemoration by France and by the other countries involved in the war (Winter 1995; Sherman 1999). More recently, with the demise of the war's direct survivors, mourning and commemoration have partly given way to evocation, centred around the remains of trenches, tunnels and other installations (see Chapter 18). Especially since the 80th anniversary of the war (1996), such remains have become the object of archaeological excavations and conservation, and the foci of a style of tourist presentation aimed at recreating the 'experience' of war in its 'lived' authenticity through costume re-enactments and guided tours that invite visitors to get in touch with the 'real' experience of war (see Price 2004). This is evoked through walking tours around the sites and routes of combat, through narrative, through viewing and touching artefacts, and reliving physical sensations such as the sticky mud underfoot, the acrid smell of burning powder, the flavour of 'the soldier's dinner' cooked and served on site.[3]

This kind of activity strives to lend immediacy and vitality to the war, otherwise known only from the dry pages of history. In guided tours and re-enactments, a sense of authenticity is sought and valued by visitors and spectators, who commonly say that being in 'the actual sites' of combat 'brings to life' received family memories or classroom accounts of the war.

Authenticity is also a key concern for those inhabitants of Argonne who volunteer for the excavation and restoration of remains, in undertaking guided tours, by acting in costume re-enactments, and through collecting militaria. They too visit wartime sites. Efforts are made to reconstruct the sites 'exactly as they were' by using old photographs and plans, and to furnish them with period objects. Authenticity is also looked for and found in evidence of the presence and experience of individuals: so, for instance, a volunteer archaeologist voiced his team's emotion at finding 'a bottle with a parchment with the names of the soldiers that worked at a tunnel in 1916' – 'its sentimental value and historical value'.

More generally, authenticity is claimed as a distinguishing feature of the Argonnais sites: here 'one sees the war as it was', through its 'actual' remains and in its 'natural' milieu. This is contrasted with the 'formality' and 'artificiality' of sites at Verdun, implying a local pride in war remains and sites. In the same vein, today's inhabitants are proud of 'their' military cemeteries, said to be 'more handsome' than those of other locations. Many residents are also keenly interested in and knowledgeable about the military side of the Great War, and appropriate it as an asset, giving the area a unique (and marketable) character. The appropriation of Argonne's remains permits the construction of a war-centred image of place, and serves different but overlapping local concerns.

At the same time, the image of Argonne that stresses its role as a battlefield in the First World War is not strictly 'local'. Commemorative monuments, practices and evocations make little or no reference to the impact of war on local civilian life and property, but focus instead on the suffering of soldiers, mostly *not* 'local'. Now, as in the past, the narrative about the war in Argonne refers primarily to national history and suffering, so people visit war sites to view and get in touch with 'French' history (or British, or German, or European), not 'Argonnais' history. In this respect, war-linked sites and practices co-opt the Argonnais surroundings for a project of identity that goes beyond the local. In fact, since the mid-1990s, a concern with recapturing the immediacy of the war experience through re-enactments, excavations and reconstructions, has not been confined to Argonne but is found all over the Western Front, matching a surge of public interest in the First World War in all the countries in Europe involved in the conflict (Saunders 2001: 45–6; 2004: 20–1; Audoin-Rouzeau and Becker 2002). This may be part of a trend in present-day European societies towards seeking direct, unmediated (though often mass-mediated) connections with the past (Huyssen 1995).

More specifically, however, the current focus on experience and immediacy in relation to the First World War can be interpreted as a bid to revitalize and repersonalize the social memory of the war, which is fading with the demise of survivors, but still 'alive' in terms of its many unresolved and unaddressed aspects. As Audoin-Rouzeau and Becker (2000: 9) argue, the First World War has many aspects, such as its brutal violence and its devastating impact in terms of loss, grief, and mental and physical illness, that went relatively unrepresented and unmourned in the societies involved, making it hard to 'put away' the war as a distanced, objectified part of 'history'.

From this perspective, the current revival is a particular moment in the elaboration of the social memory of the war in the countries involved which co-opts the former battlefields into new forms of remembrance that arguably reinvest the event with affectivity and sentiment, and so keep it in the domain of memory. This is in turn a dimension of the construction of national and 'European' identities,[4] in which the Great War is still one of the key landmarks. In other words, around and through war remembrance in Argonne, a sense of place is constructed that uses local surroundings for a national or even supranational project of identity.

In this process, the wartime past is continually reinscribed onto local surroundings, renewing their association with that time and event. This influences public perceptions of the area as many in Argonne point out:

> For the French, Argonne is a cold country [pays]. [They recall] the war of '14': 'oh yes, the battle of Argonne, frozen feet, cold, damp'. It's a very unattractive image. People want sun. It's necessary to change this image that sticks to the feet [like mud] and that endures in all the stories that can be told or written by historians and by people who have narrated the war of '14', this image has endured of a cold region, where people have suffered enormously, it's difficult to make this image shift.

This comment was made by a tour operator who offers accommodation in his seventeenth-century mansion and takes tourists on forest hikes, horse rides, hunting expeditions, mushroom picking and visits to historic sites in the vicinity *not* including those related to the First World War; at dinner he serves local cuisine with farm and forest products. This presentation of Argonne bypasses recent history to focus on things and experiences that the French associate with '*la campagne*' (the countryside): age and tradition, '*produits du terroir*' (local products) and nature.

A place of roots

French public policy classifies Argonne as a rural area, and as such it is the target of policies of cultural and natural heritage valorization that centre on themes of age, continuity, tradition, nature, typicality and authenticity (Gasnier 1992; Bertho-Lavenir 1988). In practice, public officials working in Argonne invoke the area's history to suggest that the area is 'hard to valorize' because few 'authentic' villages or buildings survive, and those which have do not clearly meet established canons of typicality. As a heritage official put it:

> [In terms of its character] Argonne is a bit of a blur [*un flou*], maybe due to its impenetrable terrain, with the forest . . . its soil too is difficult, the *gaize* [a type of friable limestone] is a difficult material [to work and conserve]. Argonne is a bit enigmatic: there is a spirit that you don't find anywhere else.

Both the image of the impenetrable forest and that of an ill-defined character point to the area's past as a battlefield. First, Argonne forest was considered an 'impenetrable' barrier to enemy attacks before and during the First World War. Second, Argonne is commonly described as a '*région frontière*', a border region, because today the area is on the administrative boundary between 'two regions and three departments', but also because, as people invariably add, 'in the past it was the border between France and Germany'. This was in fact never the case,[5] so that we may hear this remark as a reference to Argonne's role as a battlefield in recent wars between these countries; indeed, the term '*frontière*' in French denotes a disputed area or a militarized borderland (Nordman 1986: 51). So, overall, the image of a war-torn place pervades heritage officials' perceptions of the area: in their view it interferes with its heritage value, which, in a rural area such as this, requires age, typicality and authenticity.

However, the image of Argonne as a rural place of roots and authenticity does possess some currency. Like the tourist operator cited above, many individuals reject the war-centred image: 'in Gruerie wood, all I think about is where the mushrooms are' says someone of an area of forest on the former frontline, still partially in the 'red zone' and riddled with wartime debris and remains. When I say that I am moved by war remains visible in the forest, a friend replies that it is only '*gens de l'éxterieur*' (outsiders) who always see Argonne through the filter of the war: 'for me, the remains are part of the landscape, I don't think "war of 14" when I see them'. In both cases, the signs of the First World War in the Argonnais surroundings are dismissed in favour of the region's natural beauty, and the war is said to be an obsession of outsiders.

The claim to 'insiderhood' and attachment to Argonne based on knowledge and appreciation of its 'real' (pre-war) historic and natural richness is also made against 'locals': this same woman showed me pre-war buildings in her neighbourhood, pointing out how 'locals' have ruined them by installing modern window frames or replastering ancient walls in excessively bright colours. Her own house in the village, by contrast, has been carefully restored and conserved respecting canons of authenticity, partly because, as a substantial eighteenth-century residence, it is a listed building. Her parents live in this house, while she visits it periodically, coming from Paris to 'enjoy the country life'.

Similarly, the first speaker is a professional from Paris who is a major collector of eighteenth- and nineteenth-century Argonnais ceramics, who retired to Argonne where he bought a nineteenth-century ceramic manufacturer's residence. Both informants therefore know and cherish the pre-war heritage of Argonne in a direct way as familial or personal property. The Argonne is also, for them, 'the countryside' in the sense of a place of recreation juxtaposed to the urban, metropolitan life of Paris. In relation to this, it may be suggested that they hold a selective view of the builtscape and landscape of Argonne which focuses on age, continuity and 'unspoilt' nature as a function of an identity that appropriates the rural character of the area as a repository of roots and ancestry.

This role is attributed to the countryside in French 'bourgeois' identity, constituted around a life divided between metropolitan life and modernity in Paris and ancestral roots (real or putative) in the country, as embodied by the historic house (inherited or bought) (Augé 1989; Le Wita 1994; Green 1992). In Argonne, this entails bracketing off the more recent past of the area as a battlefield. A concession to that past may be made when Argonne's heritage is said to be more 'hidden' than that of other areas in France, and that, in order to appreciate it, 'one must know where and how to look'. In practice this quality adds to its value for social distinction, marking it off from the more 'commonplace' quaintness of places like Provence (as the Parisian owner of one of Argonne's most spectacular historic houses put it to me).

In this respect, the particular history of the area and its association with war is incorporated into an appropriation of the countryside as an item of social and cultural capital by a specific group whose identity is not centred on the area, and so is not, strictly speaking, local: rather it co-opts the 'local' and local surroundings as repositories of roots. In this respect also, the idealized 'rural' image of Argonne, while associated with claims of insider-hood and attachment to place, is as unrepresentative of a local sense of place as the battlefield image.

A local sense of place

Many people in Argonne echo public officials in saying that there are no 'old stones' in the area:

> This is an area that was always open to enemies for this reason there are no scattered farms as for instance in the Massif Central, houses are clustered together. Here we are not as rooted [*enracinés*] as they are over there, there are no old stones because everything was destroyed and rebuilt, destroyed and rebuilt each time. I don't even know whether here we are Franks or Saxons!
> The only thing we are not is Saracens!

My informant, a farmer, sees instability and uncertainty both in the landscape and builtscape of Argonne, and in the identity of its inhabitants. At the same time, his own claim to identity is emphatic: he is 'a true Argonnais' who 'would never leave' because 'this is where the family is'. It is the family, he says, which makes us *resister* (resist) here, in the face of 'isolation' and 'loneliness' especially in the 'long winters, the endless rain, the cold and dark'. Another time, he says that 'here we live well' because 'we are in the countryside' with its tranquillity, fresh air, lack of crime and opposed to the noise, pollution and insecurity of the city. Such contradictory views, mixing uncertainty with fierce attachment, and misery with bliss, is common in Argonne, and strategically uses both of the dominant images outlined above to affirm or claim a local space and so points towards a 'local' sense of place.

Ambivalence is pervasive when residents speak about Argonne. They say that it is scenic but 'there is nothing to see', or the forest is 'beautiful' but it is also 'wild' and impenetrable, dangerous ('it is easy to get lost', 'remember that in the past enemy armies used to get bogged down in mud and caught their death from pneumonia'). Mud, cold and rain are also mentioned to explain why tourists don't come here: 'it rains all the time and they want sun', but at the same time people say that life here is good because of the beauty, tranquility and fresh air. In practice, both dominant images of Argonne are drawn upon to characterize the place: that of a miserable, muddy and inhospitable location more or less explicitly linked with war and battlefield imagery; and that of a quiet, beautiful rural haven.

Rather than ambivalence, this is a strategic use of different images. Specifically, the negative war-linked image is deployed to stake a claim to a 'local' space against the intrusion (or invasion) of outsiders. Today, these are identified mainly with tourists, stereotyped as 'people from the cities' who patronize locals treating them like country bumpkins ('they ask us whether or not we have credit cards!'). Tourists and urban people more generally (including the bourgeois 'Parisians' discussed earlier) are also accused of wanting the countryside to be 'pretty' and the forest to be 'like a city park' instead of being filled with the smells and dirt that make up a proper, working countryside and the 'mess' and confusion of the forest as part of 'nature a bit wild'. Finally they are blamed and resented for buying up village houses and then 'keeping them closed all year', suggesting that at the root of this anti-tourist feeling are fears raised by the current demographic and economic decline of the area.

This is described in terms of 'life' leaching from villages as shops close, jobs disappear and people of all ages are forced to leave daily in search of basic services and employment: in other words what is envisaged and feared is the disruption of domestic and village routines. The fear is expressed in terms of loss of control of village space, and negative imagery about Argonne is deployed to reclaim such control. This evokes a 'local' space, a space for 'locals' in the most literal and banal sense of people who value and cherish life here, rather than people who are 'rooted' here. So, not all outsiders are resented: newcomers are welcome if they settle down in Argonne or, if seasonal visitors, they spend enough time there 'to get to know people' and 'take part in the life of the village'.

Thus, a 'local' sense of place is not, or not only, centred on 'roots', i.e. on a past of uninterrupted presence, but present- and future-oriented, centred on ensuring the continuity of villages as living, functioning socio-spatial units. This may be because this sense of place addresses fears about a weakening hold over the spaces of settled existence and habitation, or also because many of today's residents have moved to the area in the relatively recent past.[6] Moreover, in most Argonnais villages, a combination of war damage, neglect, and the fragility of traditional housing[7] makes it hard to claim rooted continuity through the materiality of a centuries-old builtscape: a 'traditional' look which mainly resulted from post-war reconstruction, and which tended to replicate pre-war appearance (Clout 1996: 196).

These reconstructed surroundings are neither authentically old nor fully modern, so arguably are 'characterless anachronism[s]' (Saunders 2001: 43). However, I also wish to show that, in Argonne, such surroundings are implicated in a discourse about presence and place – and so, arguably, 'authenticated' – through the medium of images of them in the pre-war postcards already mentioned. These items are a material way of bringing together self, space and time in a distinctive configuration which captures the tension between continuity and discontinuity, and that is central to a local sense of place in today's Argonne.

Postcards from the past

The circulation of old postcard images of Argonnais villages in today's Argonne is not unique to this area. France was one of the earliest countries in Europe to produce picture postcards at the end of the nineteenth century, and a 'craze' for sending and collecting postcards had developed by the turn of the twentieth century (Parr and Stasiak 1986: 11; Staff 1966: 63). Across Europe, the writing and sending of postcards was at its height during the First World War. By then, postcards were available in French villages and soldiers may have appreciated them for their ability, at least partially, to replace words with pictures (Holt and Holt 1977: 59; Huss 2000). Since that time, postcard collecting has been a popular hobby in France; in particular, it has been and still is characterized by a passion for 'topographicals', postcards depicting geographical localities typically of the collector's hometown or home region (Schor 1992: 204).

In their focus on a home-place, French enthusiasts are not, or not only, driven by collectors' passions for seriality – the assemblage of diverse examples of the same type of object within an arbitrary and self-contained scheme. Rather, the scheme of their collection is set by 'a cultural or historical totality' external to it, a real-life locality evoked and immortalized by their collection (MacCannell quoted in Schor 1992: 200–1). As Schor argues, this preference expresses 'the French sense of *terroir* [territory/land]' corresponding to a national and personal identity rooted in a specific place of origin (ibid.: 204).

A link between postcards, *terroir* and home-place is also found in Argonne. As mentioned, the postcards collected or displayed there are of the local area and, more specifically, of the place of origin or residence of collectors or their relatives. This last aspect suggests that today in Argonne these postcards not only express a connection with geographical location, but also an overlap between geography and genealogy. This same connection is perhaps evoked or made when, as is common, the postcards are displayed in domestic interiors, in albums alongside family photographs or passed on as family heirlooms. Such a link between family and local surroundings speaks of place in its double meaning – spatial and temporal – as an instance of enduring presence and of continuity (Casey 1996; Crang 1996: 430). But why should photographs of surroundings be a better medium for affirming a sense of place and place-based belonging than the surroundings themselves?

Photography constructs and relates time and space in a particular way. For Crang (1996: 449), the structure of photography is to capture 'the moment when "now" becomes the past' and so in some sense to depict a world at the point of its disappearance. In this way, photos materialize the 'past-ness' of the past, and simultaneously they are also evidence of its having occurred (ibid.: 442). Photographs thus hold and embody the past, both as what has been and as what is no longer: they are perched between absence and presence, at 'the charged border between image and matter' (Stewart 2002: 349–50; Crang 1996: 449). This tension makes photographs privileged vehicles of longing and nostalgia. Both these sentiments rely on a binary ordering of time (now/then) in which past and present are generalized and typified terms, contrasted not to signify change or process, but to evoke an opposition between plenitude of meaning and its loss, fullness of presence and absence (Crang 1996: 441–2). Crang sees this particular structure of feeling as central to the constitution of urban modernity, linked with the idea of authenticity (ibid.: 436, 442; Williams 1973). Specifically, nostalgia may be seen as an instance of the fragmented temporality of modernity (see Gregory 1994: 216).

Photography fragments time by its structure. It renders the lineal flow of time into a series of 'instants clipped together one after another': thus it 'spatialises' or desequences time by materializing a past or pasts synchronous with the present against the grain of chronology (Crang 1996: 448–9). Conversely, spaces captured photographically are time-laden, but their temporality does not tie them into a cumulative, linear sequence (ibid.). Photographs represent and embody a non-lineal time–space, similar to that of personal memory, in which the past irrupts into and interrupts the present without regard for chronology. Perhaps, by this overlap with memory, photographs so effectively embody the evocative surroundings of one's home place (Crang 1996). It is also these qualities that may make photographs a particularly effective means for formulating a sense of 'home' in relation to surroundings such as those of Argonne, where the passing of time has not brought layered, orderly accumulation, but rather an unstable landscape described as repeatedly 'destroyed and rebuilt'.

The sense of a world caught in the moment of its disappearance is invested in the Argonnais postcards as soon as they are said to be from before '14', turning the war into a frame for these images that seem like 'glimpses of a poignant pause about to be broken and shattered' (ibid.: 444).[8] More broadly, nostalgia undoubtedly colours the way these postcards are viewed, when people compare the busy villages of the past with the present 'loss of life', and lament the lack of 'old stones' and the loss of 'authentic' surroundings wrought by war.

However, in relation to these old postcards, 'then' is not only contemplated nostalgically; nostalgic comparisons are voiced alongside a commentary that affirms continuity, as when images of the old villages are discussed familiarly, and correspondences sought and found between pre-war and post-war scenes, landmarks and buildings. In stating these continuities, people do not, or not only, single out the 'old stones' of a village, buildings or landmarks that have survived the conflict and thus arguably embody an authentic, 'unspoilt' local landscape as suggested by the discourse of heritage. They also single out the reconstructed buildings, highlighted as 'identical' copies of what went before, but no less valued for that; in fact, arguably, for that very reason, they are valued and proudly displayed as evidence of a capacity for returning, rebuilding and resettling.

The era of reconstruction is a period of local history, and of First World War history in particular, which is largely ignored in public narratives and commemorations of the war both locally and nationally (see Clout 1996: xiii). It may be suggested that through the display and collection of these photographs and their commentary on them, present-day residents of Argonne implicitly bring to mind – and into the present and future – that phase of the area's past. In this way, perhaps, the value and potential of place-making, and maybe a kind of authenticity, is bestowed on their reconstituted, ersatz surroundings.

Such value is denied both by the war-centred narrative, that valorizes military death and ruined surroundings, and by the heritage narrative that valorizes that which is 'unspoilt', untouched by war and history. Against both, the discourse that surrounds postcards draws attention to reconstructed surroundings, and refers to them in expressing a sense of place that combines a longing for stability and continuity with a pride in and claim to the ability to resist adversity. What they affirm is active staying power rather than passive 'roots'. This speaks as much about the area's past and the radical disruption of war as it does to its present and future, and the spectre of depopulation and decline.

In the current circumstances, what people feel is a longing for, rather than certainty of, place, and it may be this that makes these old photographs more compelling and expressive than their actual surroundings. Photography may provide a means of materializing this fragmented space–time, and also of reassembling it into a place, just as the postcards dispersed by soldiers 'all over France' are now brought back as if continuing the work of reconstruction begun in 1919 (see Chapter 4).

Conclusions

It has been argued that photographs block memory because of the way in which they fragment, objectify and distance time (e.g. Barthes 1984: 91; Connerton 1989: 73). Photographic views, moreover, have been said to fragment, objectify and distance the surroundings they depict, heralding the inception of space as opposed to place as a meaningful and embodied implication of people and surroundings (Pinney 2003: 12; Hirsch 1996: 2; Casey 1996). However, in this particular case, photographic views mediate a sense of place. In the 'context of circulation' of today's Argonne, old postcard photos of the villages are not 'simple objects of contemplation' but rather 'practically involved in a process of reconstructing the past and mapping out relations to it', and so are crucial tools for memory (Crang 1996: 434, 447; Lambek 1996: 240).

What is 'remembered' or related to in the past is a village full of life and activity, a 'recollection' which requires a recoding of the pictures to overlook the poverty and decline that was already visible in the early twentieth century (Pinney 2003: 4). The commentary on these images also brings to mind their reconstruction and resettlement after the First World War. This is 'remembered' alongside the fragility of those inhabited surroundings, silently evoked by framing these images by the start of the war, and by images of ruins shown without comment. So, as tools of memory, these photos 'recall' the recent past of the area as a battlefield and its reconstruction, moving into its present and future as a depopulated, declining area, drawing a link between past and present threats to settled presence at this location. They are thus used to affirm a longing, and a claim for the continuity of settled presence here, now and in the future. This claim defines a 'local' sense of place in the most literal sense that it is made by those committed to a life at this location. It is formulated against other constructions of place that draw on Argonne's surroundings for identity projects that do not have this 'local' focus or serve a 'local' interest in this sense.

These other projects charge the surroundings of Argonne with particular representations of place: that of a war-torn, ruined landscape, and that of a locale of age and roots. These emphasize, respectively, a radical discontinuity and the destruction of space by history and the passage of time, and a radical continuity and the virtuous implication of time and space encapsulated by the idea of tradition. These constructions of space–time are bound up with notions of how the nation state is imagined, and thus dominate people's imagination of Argonnais surroundings (including that of locals).

Perhaps because of this, an alternative material support, i.e. photographs, underpins the 'local' construction of place, centred on the idea of a space threatened by time but also tenaciously held, where continuity is resilience in the face of disruption and adversity. Photographs enable this construction of time–space, and as such their flimsy materiality is arguably a better foundation for a sense of place and local identity in Argonne than the massive materiality of its surroundings.

At the same time, these artefacts may be seen as aspects of the multiple, complicated materiality of landscapes, and specifically of battlefield landscapes. Because of the violent and contested nature of their past, the socially produced materiality of the battlefields includes not just the physical sites of combat, but also the many images and representations made of them at the time and since (Buchli 2002: 15; Saunders 2001; 2004). Such images display and enable shifting and diverse engagements required by that past, mediating successive and continuing material and symbolic appropriations that make up the battlefields as outcomes both of history and also of how this history lives on in society.

Acknowledgements

I would like to thank the participants in a seminar at the Department of Anthropology, University College London, in February 2004, and to those at the joint University College London/Imperial War Museum Conference entitled 'Conflict, Memory and Material Culture: The Great War, 1914–2004' on 11 September 2004 for their helpful comments; Paul Gough for recommending Crang's article; Nick Saunders for inviting me to the conference and to publish this paper.

Notes

1   Villages have between 30 and 200 inhabitants, a few have 500–1000 inhabitants. Population density is low (in 1999 it was16.8 inhabitants/sq. km, 12.7 inhabitants/sq. km excluding larger centres) (Hussenet 2000: 169).

2   The latest available data (1997) show employment levels in Argonne to be lower than the French average (35.7 per cent against 41.3 per cent) mostly in services and agriculture, some in industry (Triche 1997: 26–7). Most employed in the secondary and tertiary sectors must commute to work up to 50 km away.

3   I refer to a First World War guided walk in the Red Zone in Argonne entitled 'In the footsteps of the soldiers' that takes visitors along the route taken by soldiers from the rear up to the frontline then 'over the top' onto the battlefield where fallen and shattered tree-trunks, shell-holes, barbed wire and shrapnel are still visible; then 'behind enemy lines' to the remains of a German rest camp. An optional extra is a meal with 'soldiers' food' in a reconstructed hut at a rear rest camp. The commentary touches on events and chronology but centres on living conditions, the feelings of soldiers and the smells, sights and noises of the battlefield including graphic detail (e.g. powder extracted from a shell, 'authentic, not bought', is burnt so we can smell it, though the guide warns that 'of course then it was combined with that of corpses'.

4   For instance the war sites of Verdun have been used recently to affirm Franco-German friendship as the basis for a united Europe.

5   At different times it marked the border between Lorraine or the Duchy of Bar (both on and off part of the Holy Roman Empire) and the Kingdom of France (see Hussenet 1982).

6   There is no systematic study of immigration to Argonne since the First World War. My remark is based on anecdotal evidence collected during my fieldwork.

7   Pre-twentieth-century housing was built either of local limestone, which is very friable, or of a sort of wattle-and-daub.

8   Of a photo of the village of Vauquois, one of the most severely damaged in the war, a man said that two figures visible in the foreground are 'my grandfather telling his brother that the Germans are coming' at the first offensive of September 1914.

References

Audoin-Rouzeau, S. and Becker, A. (eds) (2002) *1914–1918: Understanding the Great War*. London: Profile Books.

Augé, M. (1989) *Domaines et Châteaux*. Paris: éditions du Seuil.

Barthes, R. (1984) *Camera Lucida*. London: Flamingo.

Basso, K. and Feld, S. (eds) (1996) *Senses of Place*. Santa Fe: University of Arizona Press.

Bertho-Lavenir, C. (1988) 'La géographie symbolique des provinces'. *Ethnologie Française*, XVIII, 3: 276–82.

Buchli, V. (2002) 'Introduction'. In V. Buchli (ed.) *The Material Culture Reader*, pp. 1–22. Oxford: Berg.

Casey, E. (1996) 'How to get from space to place in a fairly short stretch of time'. In K. Basso and S. Feld (eds) *Senses of Place*, pp. 13–51. Santa Fe: University of Arizona Press.

Clout, H. (1996) *After the Ruins*. Exeter: University of Exeter Press.

Connerton, P. (1989) *How Societies Remember*. Cambridge: Cambridge University Press.

Crang, M. (1996) 'Envisioning urban histories: Bristol as palimpsest, postcards, and snapshots'. *Environment and Planning A* 28: 429–52.

Gasnier, T. (1992) 'Le local'. In P. Nora (ed.) *Les Lieux de Mémoire. Vol. III, Les Frances 2*, pp. 463–525. Paris: Gallimard.

Green, N. (1992) *The Spectacle of Nature*. Manchester: Manchester University Press.

Gregory, D. (1994) *Geographical Imaginations*. Oxford: Blackwell.

H.d.A. (1978) 'Les étrangers dans nos villages'. *Horizons d'Argonne* 36.

Hirsch, E. (1996) 'Landscape: between place and space'. In E. Hirsch and M. O'Hanlon (eds) *The Anthropology of Landscape*, pp. 1–30. Oxford: Clarendon Press.

Holt, T. and Holt, V. (1977) *Till the Boys Come Home: The Picture Postcards of the First World War*. London: Macdonald and James

Huss, M.-M. (2000) *Histoires de famille: cartes postales et culture de guerre*. Paris: éditions Noêsis.

Hussenet, J. (1982) *Argonne 1630–1980*. Reims: Cendrée.

—— (2000) 'Le peuplement de l'Argonne en 1999'. *Horizons d'Argonne* 77: 169.

Huyssen, A. (1995) *Twilight Memories: Marking Time in a Culture of Amnesia*. New York and London: Routledge.

Lambek, M. (1996) 'The past imperfect'. In P. Antze and M. Lambek (eds) *Tense Past*, pp. 235–54. London: Routledge.

Le Wita, B. (1994) *French Bourgeois Culture*. Cambridge: Cambridge University Press.

Lefebvre, H. (1991) *The Production of Space*. Oxford: Blackwell.

Nordman, D. (1986) 'Des limites d'état aux frontières nationales'. In P. Nora (ed.) *Les Lieux de mémoire, Vol. II: la nation 2*, pp. 35–61. Paris: Gallimard.

Parr, M. and Stasiak, J. (1986) *The Actual Boot: The Photographic Postcard Boom 1900–1920*. Northampton: A.H. Jolly (Editorial).

Pinney, C. (2003) 'Introduction'. In C. Pinney and N. Peterson (eds) *Photography's Other Histories*, pp. 1–14. Durham and London: Duke University Press.

Price, J. (2004) 'The Ocean Villas project: archaeology in the service of European remembrance'. In N.J. Saunders (ed.) *Matters of Conflict: Material Culture, Memory and the First World War*, pp. 179–91. Abingdon: Routledge.

Saunders, N.J. (2001) 'Matter and memory in the landscapes of conflict: the Western Front 1914–1999'. In B. Bender and M. Winer (eds) *Contested Landscapes: Movement, Exile and Place*, pp. 37–53. Oxford: Berg.

—— (2004) 'Material culture and conflict: the Great War 1914–2003'. In N.J. Saunders (ed.) *Matters of Conflict*, pp. 5–25. Abingdon: Routledge.

Schor, N. (1992) '*Cartes postales*: representing Paris 1900'. *Critical Inquiry* 18 (1): 188–241.

Sherman, D. J. (1999) *The Construction of Memory in Interwar France*. Chicago: University of Chicago Press.

Staff, F. (1966) *The Picture Postcard and its Origins*. London: Lutterworth Press.

Stewart, K. (2002) 'Scenes of life/Kentucky Mountains'. *Critical Enquiry* 14 (2): 349–59.

Triche, S. (1997) *Pays d'Argonne: diagnostic et propositions pour le développement des ses activités économiques et touristiques*. Reims: Direction Départementale de l'Equipment.

Williams, R. (1973) *The Country and the City*. London: Chatto and Windus.

Winter, J. (1995) *Sites of Memory, Sites of Mourning*. Cambridge: Cambridge University Press.

Young, J. (2000) *At Memory's Edge*. New Haven and London: Yale University Press.

16

'CALCULATING THE FUTURE'

Panoramic sketching, reconnaissance drawing and the material trace of war

Paul Gough

Part one: the academies

Since the establishment of the training academies in the eighteenth century, the military have taught drawing as a navigation and exploratory tool. At Woolwich, Dartmouth and Great Marlow, gentlemen cadets and sailors were trained to analyse and record landscape and coastline as a means of neutralizing and controlling enemy space. Perhaps surprisingly, the practice is maintained today; the quality of drawing made by field gunners and reconnaissance scouts may lack the artistry of their eighteenth-century forebears, but it has in common the desire to schematize the act of looking, and to reduce drawing and note-taking to the essentials, using basic but tested methods of measuring and calibration by eye and hand.

Military drawing was an element of the curriculum at the first military academy set up at Woolwich in 1741. The rules and orders required the Drawing Master to 'teach the method of Sketching Ground, the taking of Views, the drawing of Civil Architecture and the Practice of Perspective' (Buchanan 1892: 33). Probably the most eminent artist associated with Woolwich was the watercolourist Paul Sandby, who served as Drawing Master from 1768 until 1796. Sandby was then at the height of his fame, and his appointment at a military academy reflects the importance of drawing in the training of the artillery and engineer cadets. Under his guidance the quality of observation and draughtsmanship was consistently high, and a number of his pupils went on to prove themselves as expert front-line draughtsmen, often making crucially important reconnaissance drawings and finely illustrated reports (Hardie 1966: 216).

During the Napoleonic Wars it was recognized that skill in drawing could be of immediate benefit in unmapped and unknown terrain. With the establishment of new Staff and Junior military colleges in 1801, drawing became firmly established as an essential element in the training of infantry and cavalry officers. At the height of the war period, the country was scoured for capable landscape draughtsmen to employ as drawing tutors. Even John Constable was interviewed in 1802 for the post of Drawing Master at the Junior Department in Great Marlow, but he later rejected the offer, arguing that had he accepted 'it would have been a death blow to all my prospects of perfection in the Art I love'.[1]

On mainland Europe, trained army officers were soon at work in the battlefield, exploring unfamiliar ground, making detailed sketches of its topographical features, and reporting back to their superior officers. The value of an accurate drawing, however hastily made, was often more useful than a verbal or written description, and the officer-draughtsman cadre played a significant part in Wellington's Peninsular campaign.

Constable's relief at turning down the military appointment is an important reminder of the disdain that many artists felt for topographic art. Whether for artillery or infantry use, military drawing puts a premium on producing an accurate report shorn of artistic and aesthetic trappings. For all its remunerative attraction, military sketching was regarded with some disdain, a process of 'tame delineation', of reducing the aesthetics of nature to something ordinary or (to borrow Thomas Gainsborough's dismissive phrase) something 'mappy'. For others, the task of 'breaking ground' and issuing a neutral report was (like the very term 'military intelligence') a contradiction in terms. Gainsborough wrote of the opprobrium cast upon artists who regarded themselves as 'topographers', rather than 'interpreters' of the landscape. Naturally, however, the military requires a factual, accurate drawing, however clumsy, rather than an idealized landscape picture.

Drawing for such purposes can be separated into two distinct fields of vision. These correspond approximately to the different arms of the military: on the one hand are those drawings made during mobile reconnaissance – usually by light cavalry patrols or units of advanced infantry – that are used to record intelligence about enemy positions and key terrain. On the other, there are drawings known as panoramas which are made from a static position, usually an elevated vantage point that commands an uninterrupted view of the enemy front. These are normally drawn by specially trained artillery or engineer officers and are vital for indicating targets and determining range and arc of fire.

The principle of panoramic drawing, when used in an artillery sense, developed from the role of the Forward Observation Officer (FOO) who was directing the fire of guns located much further back from his post on the edge of known and secure ground. Through close observation the FOO was able to engage targets very rapidly across the whole arc of view. If a number of targets had already been pre-registered and engaged to an exact point on the ground, that point could be marked on a drawn panorama. This drawing would also be copied to the gunners in the rear who would then be able to engage the same target number with greater speed and efficiency. In effect, the panorama became a surrogate view for the distant artillery blinded by dead ground or topographic barriers.[2]

Whereas the patrol sketch is often a collage of hasty impressions later rearranged to form a tactical narrative, the panorama is primarily concerned with scopic control and spatial dominance. The artillery panorama works on the same premise as military mapping; surveillance and graphic survey will eventually neutralize a dangerous terrain and assure mastery over it (Alfrey and Daniels 1990). In similar spirit, Foucault wrote of the system of permanent registration that operated in the plague town in the seventeenth century (Foucault 1977). On the septic terrain of the First World War battlefield, the panoramic drawing was an integral part in segmenting and immobilizing perceived space. The stasis of the battle line, however, meant that the panoptic ideal could never be attained: dead ground (space beyond or concealed from retinal view), camouflage and concealment were constant frustrations to retinal surveillance. Foucault's concept of a transparent space was constantly frustrated by the fissured and volatile landscape of the battlefield. The military sketch, though, provided the nearest graphic equivalent of Bentham's paradigm: it provided systematic observation 'in which the slightest movements are supervised, in which all events are recorded' (ibid.: 197).

Part two: 'The Drawing Manuals'

The different skills required for each type of drawing can be traced in the many official and commercial manuals that were published in the nineteenth century. During this period, proficiency in drawing was widely acknowledged as offering an advantage to boys competing for places at the military academies. Yet the varying qualities in the teaching of drawing across the 'public' and middle-class schools constantly under-mined the calibre of cadet applications to the military colleges. Both the Clarendon Commission of 1864 and the Taunton Commission four years later remarked on the erratic, often poor, quality of art teaching in schools, and the impact this might have on the quality of draughtsmanship in the professions and in the services (Sutton 1967: 88).

The unimaginative style of most military manuals of the late nineteenth century reflects the low status of drawing in the army's thinking. Invariably, freehand sketching was relegated to an item of 'special interest', and regarded as little more than an adjunct to map work. Manual writers leaned heavily on the conventional language and symbols of military cartography, transforming a single lesson in landscape drawing into little more than a matter of contours and geometric symbols.

Two manuals in *Rapid Field Sketching and Reconnaissance* of 1889 and 1903, for example, laid heavy emphasis on map and compass work, with only a cursory description of the merits of freehand drawing. Commercial manuals such as Major R.F. Legge's *Military Sketching and Map Reading* ignored observational work completely, concentrating instead on map co-ordinates, measurement of slopes, magnetic bearings and using the service compass (Legge 1906).

One of the first manuals to actively encourage freehand drawing was *The Active Service Pocket Book* written by 2nd Lt Bertrand Stewart and published in 1907. Stewart dedicated eight pages to freehand sketching, offering step-by-step advice on drawing in outline, using the pencil as a measuring instrument and mastering the challenging problem of perspective. The manual is clearly aimed at the novice. Stewart, for instance, recommends the construction of an oblong drawing frame attached to a stick with a pointed end. The frame is to be divided at regular six-inch intervals by stretched wire, thus forming a drawing grid that will help simplify any landscape seen through it. Drawing on squared paper, the soldier is encouraged to make an exact outline copy of the view through the frame, though conveniently the author skips over the difficult matter of situating the frame, piercing hard ground and avoiding enemy detection (Stewart 1907).

The hurried reissue of a number of drawing manuals at the outbreak of war in 1914 was followed, over the following four years, by the publication of training booklets. At least nine commercial and War Office books on topographical and panoramic sketching were made available to soldiers of all ranks. Through such publishing ventures tuition in freehand drawing and map-reading spread from being the preserve of the officer in the Regular Army to a craft capable of being learned by all. The Great War accelerated this development. Not only was the army able to draw upon a better educated and more intelligent workforce, but the static nature of the fighting on the Western Front called for highly accurate intelligence on enemy positions. Observational drawing became an integral element in surveillance work and was able to complement aerial photography as a method of scrutiny and surveillance.

Artistically talented soldiers of all ranks soon found themselves sought out to work in the Camouflage Corps or the Field Survey. Not all went willingly. Harry Bateman, having volunteered for service with the Royal Field Artillery, ignored a sergeant's request at their first parade for any artist present to make himself known.[3] He 'remained silent as he wanted to go and fight' (Brown 1978: 185). Others found that their skills were deemed inappropriate: the painter and poet David Jones, serving with the 15th (London Welsh) Battalion, Royal Welch Fusiliers, had five years' art school training to his credit when he was recommended to the 2nd Field Survey Company based at Second Army Headquarters at Cassel. But Jones appears to have lacked the requisite technical skills needed for map drawing, and was instead sent to one of the Company's four observation groups as a Survey Post observer. Having already been promoted sideways from 'Maps', Jones did not last much longer as an observer – 'Got the sack from that job because of my inefficiency in getting the right degrees of enemy gunflashes' (Hague 1980: 241; Chasseaud 1993: 19). Another artist failed in the simple task of 'breaking ground':

> From the OP (Observation Post) I saw a completely featureless landscape, save here and there a few broken sticks of trees. I made a pencil drawing of this barren piece of ground, but what use my superiors would be able to make of this sketch I could not imagine.
>
> (Roberts 1974: 27–8)

Thus ended the Vorticist painter William Roberts's first and only foray into reconnaissance drawing. In fact, surprisingly few of the other young 'moderns' serving in the armed forces during the Great War could subvert their artistic tendencies in the pursuit of technical objectivity.

Others advertised their skills quite freely. Adrian Hill – one of the youngest soldier-artists to eventually work for the official government war art schemes – combined his drawing abilities with his work in a Scouting and Sniping Section of the Honorable Artillery Company. After the war, he recalled a typical patrol into no-man's-land:

> I advanced in short rushes, mostly on my hands and knees with my sketching kit dangling round my neck. As I slowly approached, the wood gradually took a more definite shape, and as I crept nearer I saw that what was hidden from our own line, now revealed itself as a cunningly contrived observation post in one of the battered trees.
>
> (Hill 1930: 16)

Part three: malign space

As 'a palimpsest of overlapping, multi-vocal landscapes' (Saunders 2001: 37), the Western Front battlefield was a malign industrialized space where visibility was often a 'trap'. The military sketch was the spring in that mechanism. Concealment was the only antidote to the omnidirectional gaze of the trained eye.

Jay Appleton, developing Konrad Lorenz's thesis on the atavistic landscape, has proposed a habitat theory that categorizes any landscape into hierarchies of 'prospect, refuge and hazard' (Appleton 1975). The panoramic viewpoint is the paradigm of Appleton's system: military drawing systematized the graphic language so that trees became datum points, and fixed features of the land became the immutable co-ordinates of a functional terrain, a strategic field. Or, as Henry Reed phrases it in this poetic fragment, it is a domain where the temporal overlaps with the spatial:

> Not only how far away; but the way that you say it is very important.
> Perhaps you may never get
> The knack of judging a distance, but at least you know
> How to report on a landscape: the central sector
> The right of the arc and that, which we had last Tuesday
> And at least you know
> That maps are of time, not place, so far as the army
> Happens to be concerned – the reason being
> Is one which need not delay us. Again, you know
> There are three kinds of tree, three only, the fir and the poplar,
> And those which have bushy tops to; and lastly
> That things only seem to be things.[4]
>
> (Reed 1943)

As a piece of spatial interpretation, the drawn artillery panorama has clear areas of jurisdiction. The foreground is considered irrelevant. To the gunner, the near is already controlled. The middle distance and the horizon are the focal points. These, to borrow Appleton's phrase, are the prospect-rich domains and the most coveted.

Panorama drawings are predicated on trajectories and barrage lines. The horizon is the ultimate goal because it holds the promise of further territory for martial exploitation. During the First World War, the horizon took on special value when seen from the noisome mess of the front-line trench. Secreted in their observation posts, gunners described the green and unspoilt distance as 'The Promised Land' – perfect, but forever locked in an unattainable future.

These concerns, as W.J.T. Mitchell has observed, are the essential discourses of imperialism. Empires, according to him, move outward in space 'as a way of moving outward in time, the "prospect" that opens up is not just a spatial scene, but a projected future of "development" and exploitation' (Mitchell 1994: 16–17). The promise of control permeates every level of military drawing. In contemporary drawing manuals, the unmodulated pencil line is given the authority of military language: 'A line should be as sharp and precise as a word of command' (Newton 1916: 27).

Similarly, by ridding the page of ambiguity or doubt, the drawings aim to pre-ordain the future. This is also true of the written word, which uses the active and instructive tense of military command. It is a language where the passive or conditional tense does not function: 'Brigade will commence at . . . Objectives shall be taken by . . . reinforcements will be moved to . . . etc.' (Keegan 1976: 266). Maps and charts drawn up before offensives bear a similar code: barrage lines are clearly marked in minutes of advance; in June 1944, the objectives beyond the Normandy beach-head were marked out in time – D Day plus one, plus two, etc. – as well as in actual space.

Instruction manuals in military sketching equate clarity of line with clarity of purpose. Ambiguity and doubt are (quite literally) ruled out. The margins of failure (like the estimated casualty rate) are clearly prescribed and then codified. Any blank areas of the paper are not intended to be read as negative space, but as the area set aside for instructive wording. The panorama, though, could only make sense in a war where both sides were predominantly static, where a battle-scape was shared but where the zones of control were clearly demarcated. The view from the opposing emplacements might be radically different, but the contested ground was rationalized and systematized using a shared vocabulary of grid and line. In his analysis of the 'tourism' of war, Jean Louis Deotte has argued that the beachline of Normandy in 1944 constituted a common world, a shared objectivity for both defender (cooped in a concrete pillbox) and attacker (exposed in a metal landing craft). Both sets of adversaries experienced a 'reversibility of the points of view' because 'enemies share in common the same definition of space, the same geometric plane . . . they belong to the same world of techno-scientific confrontation, the substratum of which, here, is sight' (Diller and Scofidio 1994 : 116–77).

From a strictly operational point of view, the artillery panorama differed from a front-line or reconnaissance drawing in three respects. The artillery drawing reported a single view from a fixed Observation Post; it needed only to show a few prominent reference points drawn in a clear and unambiguous manner so as to indicate targets for observed fire; and it was drawn to maintain a record of artillery data on a particular battery front. The artillery panorama works on the same basis as military mapping, i.e. the act of surveying and transcribing a landscape helps neutralize the dangers of uncertain terrain and eventually assure mastery over it. The discipline of panoramic drawing reduced any landscape, however picturesque, into a series of immutable co-ordinates and fixed datum points.

Drawings made from reconnaissance patrols or from the lip of a trench are often less formalized than the artillery panorama. Seen through a trench periscope or pieced together from night patrols their descriptive language is less codified, they may combine a number of viewpoints and usually serve as visual elaboration for a longer written report. But they share with the panoramic drawing the same material fate: few images have survived, as they were intended for immediate, tactical use and were soon discarded.

Part four: Maze and Newton

One of the few front-line artists whose work did survive is the painter Paul Maze (IWMa). A French-speaking, self-confessed adventurer, Maze worked first as an interpreter to the Royal Scots Greys in 1914, and later as a liaison officer for General Sir Hubert Gough, Fifth Army commander. Gough would regularly send Maze on sketching sorties to the front line where the young painter would fearlessly record his impressions of the battlefield. One of his first missions, in May 1915, was to sketch the 7th Division's objectives around Festubert on the Somme, a task which required him to draw from the front line where he 'had to use a periscope and crane (his) neck over the sandbags quickly and peep'. This was Maze's preferred – if somewhat risky – method of drawing. In March 1916, ignoring all regard for his own safety, he drew in the line every day:

> My work was interesting. Bit by bit I dissected the ground with our field glasses, and I made drawings from every possible angle marking every obstacle which could hinder our advance.
>
> (Maze 1934: 130)

William Rothenstein, an official war artist working south of the Somme in March 1918, recalled seeing at Fifth Army headquarters 'drawings pieced together, showing a considerable view of the German front', made by Maze 'creeping, day after day, beyond our front lines . . . an act of rare courage and devotion' (Rothenstein 1932 : 334).

Maze supplemented his trench drawings with information gleaned from aerial photographs, and he also incorporated imaginary views taken as though from the enemy lines. Few of them have survived. Five held by the Department of Art at the Imperial War Museum must be considered typical of his style. A large sketch of the Somme battleground, dating from mid-1916 (Figure 16:1), has obviously been drawn from the lip of a trench. The parapet is broadly rendered in charcoal, a copse of trees in the middle distance is established with slabs of yellow paint, and its perimeter edge is clearly defined with a single pencil line. The names of two villages have been hastily scrawled in the sky. For all his abilities as an artist, the drawing is, in fact, heavily dressed in the idiom of map-making – the copse is given a clear perimeter line, the conifers are rendered in the conventional language of cartography, and houses are drawn as uniform blocks rather than as individual buildings.

Maze adopts further map conventions in an even larger drawing of the battlefield around the village of Hamel on the Somme, in which the British front line is drawn in blue and the German line in red. On this occasion, however, Maze was unable to finish this particular drawing: inscribed in the painter's hand at the bottom is the telling message 'could not go on through heavy shelling'. Maze was clearly excited by the dangers of drawing near the fighting line, and he relished his role as an explorer and recorder of the battlefield. His work earned him both injuries and decorations, and it gave him an unusual apprenticeship as a painter. Even at the front he occasionally forgot his military duty and became 'engrossed in form and colour' (Maze 1934: 138) but he was quite happy to be remembered as an artist who worked 'in shorthand'.

One artist who felt that it was not enough to entrust military drawing to adventurers or bemused avant-garde artists was subaltern William Newton of the Artist's Rifles. A trainee architect, Newton contended that it was possible to teach a novice how to draw a battle landscape after just one lecture and two days drawing in the field. This was an ambitious programme. By comparison, front-line infantry scouts took up to six weeks to train (Cameron 1916). Newton laid out his ideas in *Military Landscape Sketching and Target Indication* – a manual published commercially in 1916. In the introduction, Lieutenant Colonel H.A.R. May, commanding officer of the Artist's Rifles, applauded Newton's system.

> The test of each solution is whether a stranger can with ease and rapidity identify the exact place intended; and tested in this manner the results of his teaching have been most successful and many officers in the trenches have benefited by the care and devotion he has given to his work.
>
> (Newton 1916: 6)

Figure 16:1 Sketch by Paul Maze of the Somme battlefield in mid-1916. (© and courtesy Trustees of the Imperial War Museum)

In his opening definition, Newton clarified the function of a military sketch. It 'is a form of report, without the ambiguity of language. It is graphic information. For information clearness is essential, and clearness is attained by two avenues: a) thought, b) draughtsmanship' (ibid.: 8). In making this point, Newton distances himself from previous manual writers who opted for heavily annotated sketches and for a pictorial language rooted in the conventions of maps. But the real challenge, continues Newton, is how to simplify the visual chaos of a landscape, especially a landscape damaged by battle:

> It is therefore necessary to analyse, to bring order out of chaos. For this purpose there are three main methods of analysis – separation of planes, encircling or framing in, division of a whole into parts.
>
> (ibid.: 9)

Possibly the most interesting of these three methods is the first – the separation of planes. Newton suggests that the draughtsman should try to imagine a landscape as a series of horizontal (but not straight) bands that stretch from one side of the paper to the other. It might help, he suggested, to imagine the country as something like the scenery of an outdoor exhibition with each ridge, hill, wood cut out of sheets of wood and laid one behind the other. Having done this, a point can successfully be marked on the drawing and its approximate distance from the viewer clearly indicated by the number and density of horizontal lines representing fields, meadows, tree lines in between the draughtsman and the point.

Newton's manual is full of such pragmatic advice. He emphasized the draughts-man's duty in guiding the eye to salient points in the landscape by using key devices in the terrain – an isolated chimney, a single red roof amongst black roofs, three silhouetted bushes on a crest line – as so many 'labels' that indicate particular targets or tactically vital features. He avoids the tendency of other instructors to construct complex drawing frames, or string and protractor gizmos.[5] Instead, he argues for clarity of purpose at all times, for always using a sharp pencil and throwing the India rubber away: 'the aim should rather be to do a clear sketch from the first, because in the field opportunities of subsequent polish are limited' (ibid.: 27). He continues in fine style:

> A wavering line which dies away carries no conviction or information because it is the product of a wavering mind. Every line should be put in to express something. Start sharply and finish sharply. Press on the paper.
>
> (ibid.)

Such instruction may sound a little severe but it was born from a belief in the superiority of careful observational drawing as a method of study and analysis. Without the rigorous discipline advocated by Newton, military drawing can easily descend into a parody of itself – dull, repetitive diagrams in which trees have been reduced to a formula, producing a rather contrived landscape image that resembles 'nursery wall paper'. This was due in part to the consequence of drawing trees in outline which tends to make them resemble their cartographic equivalent – either bushy topped deciduous or 'Christmas tree' firs. It is also the consequence of drawing in outline alone and so accentuating the top line of trees and buildings with a minimum of shading and colour. The end results, however, had a curiously aesthetic appeal and many military drawings began to resemble the arts-and-crafts-style woodcut illustrations that were popular in the first decades of the century.

The Studio magazine was quick to note the similarity. In February 1916 an illustrated article applauded the army's work in broadening the education of the common soldier, noting with pleasure that 'instruction has been extended to the rank and file because the authorities recognize the immense value on active service of men who can use a pencil in making topographical sketches' (RFC 1916: 44–5). The writer marvelled at the short period of instruction, proof that 'one can just as easily be taught to draw the formation of objects in nature as to trace the design of the letters of the alphabet' but is most impressed by the unsophisticated aesthetic appeal of the drawings.

> These sketches are, of course, not intended to be artistic in their handling, but at the same time there is a certain charm in their simplicity, and the conventional method does not detract from their interest.
>
> (ibid.: 45)

The accompanying line drawings show a verdant landscape of rolling pastures and tidy villages – in truth, not dissimilar from the images on offer in the magazine each month. Similar pastoral scenery was uniformly used for target practice. One subaltern wryly noted the popularity of the rural idyll:

> Two fingers right, four o'clock from the haystack, at five hundred yards at the bushy-topped tree – fire! I don't think that a tree that was not bushy-topped existed in the picture, which at least saved any strain on the School of Musketry's vocabulary or inventiveness.
>
> (Mellersh 1978: 52)

To the military mind, though, such aestheticism was anathema. Though Major Pearson's manual of 1906 offered a wider range of tree types – pine, poplar, Scots fir, the banana – to wean his students from the tyranny of the 'bushy topped' formula, every drawing instructor warned the draughtsman to guard against 'artistic effect'. 'Indeed', argued the author of the 1912 manual, 'it is almost better that the artistic sense should be absent, and that instead of idealising a landscape it should be looked at with a cold matter-of-fact military eye' (War Office 1912: 75). A soldier-sketcher had to concentrate on the potential of the countryside for military purposes and not be distracted by 'its beauties of colouring or the artistic effects of light and shade' (ibid.).

To certain military artists, though, the call of landscape art would always overwhelm purely tactical considerations. Perhaps the least exacting type of military sketch is the conventional landscape painting that has been simply ruled off with vertical pencil lines to mark out the degrees of artillery fire. Wilfred de Glehn chose this method (IWMb). A professional artist, de Glehn served with the Royal Garrison Artillery on the Italian theatre of operations in 1917. From observation posts on the hills above the Isonzo Valley he painted a number of striking watercolour landscapes of the battlefield and the distant Austrian lines (Figure 16:2). Exquisitely painted and beautifully luminous, they are, however, rather limited as images of tactical information – important contour lines are lost in the refined brushwork, key points in the enemy line are sacrificed to the principles of aerial perspective, vaporous watercolour technique obscures hard military fact. Only the unwavering vertical lines remind us that this is a dangerous killing zone. Similarly, the sculptor Gilbert Ledward, who was stationed with the Royal Garrison Artillery on the Italian Front during 1917–18, made a panorama from a high vantage point above the village of Camporovere. His elegant watercolour captures something of the charm of the wide valley, but it relies almost entirely on dotted lines and numerical code to indicate the 'approximate location of hostile batteries'.[6]

Part five: legacy

Few of the innovations in battlefield drawing advocated by Newton seem to have survived the Great War. A sample panorama provided with the 1921 manual of map reading shows a wide tract of country either side of the Etaples–Verton railway in northern France. It was drawn on 3 July 1918 at 0900 hours by a Lieut. J. Smith, Royal Artillery, from an observation post some 15 metres high. It is a classic panorama – an endless vista of land described in a neutral outline. But as a piece of graphic information it relies almost entirely on annotations and graphic directions – arrows,

Figure 16:2 Watercolour landscape of the Isonzo Valley battlefield in northern Italy with the Austrian lines in the distance, painted by Wilfred de Glehn in 1917. (© and courtesy Trustees of the Imperial War Museum)

icons, symbols, etc. It premises literal description at the expense of pictorial invention.

In artillery and infantry training manuals between the wars, freehand sketching took a poor second place to the technical demands of map work. Panoramic work was regarded as an adjunct to map drawing and was afforded modest coverage in training texts. This trend continued after the Second World War. It seemed that the panoramic sketch as the material trace of war was now defunct.

In our era of photographic surveillance and computerized simulation, it would appear that we have achieved a perfection and totalization of surveillance technologies. Global Positioning System (GPS) satellites and digital technology can triangulate geographical location to within one metre, allowing a degree of precise digital time and space co-ordination that would have been unthinkable to the armed forces even 30 years ago (Graham 1999: 133). However, it may come as some surprise that freehand drawing is still practised in the British armed forces today. Light forward units of the British Royal Artillery rely on powerful binoculars, night sights and thermal imaging devices, but the skill of field sketching is still a part of their work, requiring little more than a pencil, paper and a keen eye. In concealed positions far ahead of their guns, operating from a known grid, Forward Observation Officers, normally captains, observe the ground to the front of their battery, determine targets and order fire. One such officer explained the value of drawing in this role.

Drawing is very important to the artillery, and to the observers particularly. We produce a panorama on a flat piece of paper, so that if we have to hand the position onto another party they have to be able to instantly pick up and identify features to the front. When we're drawing we look for key reference points – a prominent contour line, lone trees, buildings and so on.[7]

Carefully avoiding 'artistic effect', one of the observation party uses a felt-tipped pen to make a diagrammatic picture of the enemy terrain. But, unlike his predecessors' work, few of these images will be committed to history. As the observation post prepared to move position, the soldier took a damp cloth and, in one movement, wiped the drawing clean off the sheet of acetate. Material trace rendered immaterial.

Acknowledgements

I would like to thank Dr Nicholas Saunders and Paul Cornish for their support during the development of this paper. Colleagues at the University of the West of England, Bristol, Patricia Passes, Amanda Wood and Deanna Petherbridge offered valuable insights into the discipline of drawing, and to Abigail Davies I still owe a debt of gratitude for leading the team that produced many dozens of arts programmes for television in which I played such an enjoyable part.

Notes

1 John Constable to John Dunthorne, 29 May 1802. For a full account of Paul Sandby's tenure at Woolwich, see Hardie 1966: 16–222.
2 This is a fundamentally twentieth-century development. Indirect fire was only developed from the turn of the century, having been made practicable by the advent of quick-firing artillery. In British terms, serious developments of the techniques took place only after the outbreak of the First World War (Bidwell and Graham 1982).
3 Bateman's drawings are held in the Imperial War Museum (IWM) London, Department of Art nos. 6319–6338.
4 Henry Reed, Part II, 'Judging Distances' from *Lessons of the War*.
5 See for example the string and ruler contraptions suggested in the War Office Manual of Map Reading and Sketching (1912) and in Green 1908: 25. In summer 1994 a replica of a drawing frame was built according to the specifications laid out in a 1907 drawing manual. It was used during the making of an ITV documentary *Drawing Fire* to help train artillery officers in the rudiments of freehand sketching. Although useful as a drawing device it proved a large, rather unwieldy piece of equipment, difficult to camouflage and even more difficult to stick into the ground.
6 Ledward's only surviving panorama was made on 27 April 1918 from 94th Brigade Observation Post, at square H20. It is now housed in the Ledward Archive at the Henry Moore Institute, Leeds.
7 Quote from Captain Tim Henry, Forward Observation Officer with 266 (GVA) Battery, 7 Royal Horse Artillery, a recently converted parachute light gun battery. Henry described this method (to the author) as little more than 'fag packet gunnery'.

References

Alfrey, N. and S. Daniels (eds) (1990) *Mapping the Landscape: Essays on Art and Cartography*. Nottingham: Nottingham Castle Museum.

Appleton, J. (1975) *The Experience of Landscape*. London: Wiley.

Bidwell, S. and D. Graham (1982) *Fire-Power, British Army Weapons & Theories of War 1904–1945*. London: George Allen & Unwin.

Brown, M. (1978) *Tommy Goes to War*. London: J.M. Dent.

Buchanan. Lt.Col. H.D. (1892) *Records of the Royal Military Academy, 1741–1892*. Woolwich: Cattermole.

Cameron, Lt L.C.R.D.J. (1916) *Infantry Scouting: A Practical Manual for the Use of Scouts in Training at Home and at the Front*. London: John Murray.

Chasseaud, P. (1993) 'David Jones and the survey'. *Stand To! The Journal of the Western Front Association*, 39: 18–22.

Diller, E. and R. Scofidio (1994) *Tourism of War*. Princeton: FRAC: University of Princeton Press.

Foucault, M. (1977) *Discipline and Punish: The Birth of the Prison*. London: Allen Lane.

Graham, S. (1999) 'Geographies of surveillance'. In M. Crang and J. May (eds) *Virtual Geographies: Bodies, Space and Relations*, pp.131–48. London: Routledge.

Green, A.F.U. (1908) *Landscape Sketching for Military Purposes*. London: Hugh Rees.

Hague, R. (ed.) (1980) *David Jones, Dai Greatcoat*. London: Faber.

Hardie, M. (1966) *Watercolour Painting in Britain, Vol. 1: The Eighteenth Century*. London: Batsford.

Hill, A. (1930) *The Graphic*. 15 November 1930.

IWMa (n.d.) Maze, Imperial War Museum, Department of Art nos. 6070, 6072.

IWMb (n.d.) William De Glehn, Imperial War Museum, Department of Art nos. 270–277.

Keegan, J. (1976) *The Face of Battle*. London: Penguin.

Legge, Major F. (1906) *Military Sketching and Map Reading*. Aldershot: Gale and Polden.

Maze, P. (1934) *A Frenchman in Khaki*. London: Heinemann.

Mellersh, H.E.L. (1978) *Schoolboy into War*. London: William Kimber.

Mitchell, W.J.T. (1994) 'Imperial landscape'. In W.J.T. Mitchell (ed.) *Landscape and Power*. Chicago: University of Chicago Press.

Newton, W. G. (1916) *Military Landscape Sketching and Target Indication*. London: Hugh Rees.

RFC (1916) 'Topographical sketching in the army'. *The Studio*, February 1916: 44–5.

Reed, H. (1943) 'Judging distance'. *New Statesman and Nation* 25 (628), 6 March: 135.

Roberts, W. (1974) *Memories of the War to End all Wars: 4.5 Howitzer Gunner R.F.A. 1916–1918*. London: Canada Press.

Rothenstein, W. (1932) *Men and Memories: Recollections of William Rothenstein 1900–1922*. London: Faber and Faber.

Saunders, N.J. (2001) 'Matter and memory in the landscapes of conflict: the Western Front 1914–1919'. In B. Bender and M. Winer (eds) *Contested Landscapes: Movement, Exile and Place*, pp. 37–53. Oxford: Berg.

Stewart, B. (1907) *Active Service Pocket Book*. London: William Clowes.

Sutton, G. (1967) *Artist or Artisan? A History of the Teaching of Art and Crafts in English Schools*. London: Pergamon Press.

War Office (1912) *Manual of Map Reading and Sketching*. London: HMSO.

17

ARCHAEOLOGY OF THE GREAT WAR

The Flemish experience

Marc Dewilde and Nicholas J. Saunders

Archaeological interest in the First World War in Flanders, was, until recently, the preserve only of amateur archaeologists and collectors of Great War memorabilia. In these circumstances, it is clear that such activity could be termed archaeology only in very general terms, and certainly the investigated sites were neither excavated nor interpreted according to modern scientific archaeological methodologies.

In one sense, these activities emerged out of a long tradition of clearing and digging battlefields after 1918, in order to restore large areas to productive farmland, and to gather metal scrap for sale or transformation into battlefield souvenirs (a little investigated aspect of the relationship between people, objects and landscape). The post-war economy in the Ypres area depended to a considerable extent on battlefield tourism (see Blunden 1934; Ewart 1920; Lloyd 1998: 36–7), and many pilgrims and visitors purchased battlefield mementos of their visits (Saunders 2003: 145–7; Weixler 1938: 48–9). The origins of Great War archaeology in this region, while concerned with investigating the terrain of battle, are also intricately entwined with the contested landscapes of tourism and commemoration.

From 1918 until 2002, professional archaeological engagement with the First World War was sporadic. Belgium's wealth of more traditional archaeologies – from prehistory to the Gallo-Roman and medieval periods – was such that there was little time and fewer resources to explore the scattered remains of a war not yet a century old. There were exceptions, however. In 1989, a deeply buried dugout was identified and explored during the course of excavations by the Institute for Archaeological Heritage (IAP) of the remains of the medieval abbey at Zonnebeke near Ypres, which, during the Great War, was in the centre of the Ypres Salient battlefield (Dewilde 1991: 380). Wartime aerial photographs showed that Zonnebeke itself was totally obliterated during the war. At the request of the municipality of Zonnebeke, a second dugout – known as the Bremen Redoubt – was photographed and drawn to scale with the same professional attention to detail that was applied to more traditional archaeological structures (Figure 17:1). Both the Zonnebeke dugout and the Bremen Redoubt were exceptions – all other diggings of First World War sites were not carried out by professional archaeologists, a situation described by Saunders (2002: 103–4).

The situation changed dramatically in 2002 when Great War archaeology became an integral part of standard archaeological practice in Belgian Flanders. Interestingly, the impulse for this was political. It was due to a request by the then minister Paul

Figure 17:1 Interior of the Bremen Redoubt. This deep dugout (some 6 m below surface) accommodated up to 80 soldiers (wooden beds on three levels; each bed offered two sleeping-places). (© and courtesy VIOE)

Van Grembergen to the IAP (recently reconstituted as the Flemish Heritage Institute (VIOE)) to undertake an archaeological investigation along the stretch of a planned A19 motorway extension through the Ypres Salient, and to evaluate the possible impact on the archaeological heritage of the First World War (de Meyer and Pype 2004: 3). It is difficult to overestimate the significance of this political intervention, or its consequences for the archaeology of the war, and related heritage and tourism issues.

A year later, in November 2003, and partly as a consequence of the investigations carried out along the projected path of the A19, the same minister announced the formation of the Department of First World War Archaeology within the VIOE. This groundbreaking development was supported by the 'Flemish universities, the Belgian Army's Service for the Disposal and Demolition of Explosives (DOVO) and a wide range of international collaborators' (Dewilde *et al.* 2004). Later, the Association for World War Archaeology (AWA) was founded, mainly focusing on world war archaeology and the search for financial resources (de Meyer and Pype 2004: 45, 47–8; www.a-w-a.be). After some 85 years of amateur ad hoc digging and land clearance – and in the space of just over 12 months – a modern scientific archaeology of the Great War had arrived in a legally constituted and academically acceptable form.

Meanwhile, the professional discussion concerning the archaeological significance of the First World War was being vigorously pursued. These more far-reaching issues were problematized for the first time and formulated as key questions: Is Great War heritage really part of Belgian national archaeological heritage? Are Great War remains old enough to be archaeologically important and valuable? Should the archaeological record of the Great War be considered as equal to other, more traditional, kinds of archaeology? Is there an obligation to make an inventory of the complete heritage of the First World War and protect selected sites, as is the case with earlier archaeological remains? And, since there is such a wealth of documentary evidence available for the Ypres Salient area – maps, aerial photographs, letters, memoirs and regimental histories – can archaeological survey and excavation add anything meaningful to our understanding of the First World War? (See also Saunders 2002.) To what extent, perhaps, might the war's archaeological heritage expand the scope and social impact of archaeology more generally in Flanders? Crystallizing all these issues, was the A19 Project itself.

The A19 Project

The A19 excavation consisted of several trial digs to investigate the projected path of the A19 motorway extension which would run from Wieltje near Ypres, to Steenstraete at Langemark-Poelkapelle. This new motorway would traverse 7 kilometres of the northern section of the old Ypres Salient battlefield. This area has a rich and complex military history – especially in its role as a battlefield during the Battle of Second Ypres (April–May 1915) (Dixon 2003), and the Battle of Third Ypres (or Passchendaele), which began on 31 July 1917 (Steel and Hart 2000; Liddle 1997). In particular, this part of the Ypres Salient saw the first use of gas by the Germans on

22 April 1915 (McWilliams and Steel 1985), a significant technological development whose material traces were encountered during the excavations.

The investigations aimed to answer several critical initial questions for First World War archaeology in Belgian Flanders. What is the extent and state of preservation of the Great War archaeological record in this region? How widespread is the presence of uncovered human remains on the battlefield? What damage would be caused to the archaeological and human remains by motorway construction (Dewilde *et al.* 2004)?

It was decided to respond to the minister's request as if the A19 was one of the more usual medieval sites that the VIOE were regularly called upon to investigate. This approach, which involved substantial preliminary research, narrowed down the area to be investigated. Regimental archives, war diaries, trench maps, and contemporary and modern aerial photographs were all tools used to identify possible find spots (de Meyer and Pype 2004: 9–18). Associated with this was an intensive programme of fieldwalking which located concentrations of metal scrap, concrete and traces of a narrow-gauge (Decauville) military railway. Particularly useful, and an indication of the anthropological dimension of First World War archaeology, was 'the creation of a battlefield ethnography – contacts and interviews with local residents that proved very informative' (Dewilde *et al.* 2004).

The excavation of those areas that were chosen on the basis of this preliminary research proved extremely fruitful. The trial trenches at Turco and High Command Redoubt provided us with significant traces of the British and German positions. Moreover, it was possible to carry out an open-area excavation on the site known as Cross Roads, symbolically within view of the incomplete section of hanging A19 motorway (Figure 17:2). Excavations revealed, for example, part of the substructure of trenches, shelters, ammunition depots and gun emplacements (de Meyer and Pype 2004: 19–28). Where the front line outside Ypres stabilized between 1915 and 1917, significant evolution in trench-building techniques became clear. Straight-line trenches developed into a zig-zag system of trenches, communication trenches, connecting shelters, depots and gun platforms. Also evident were the changing methods of trench construction, and the introduction and different applications of such structural features as A-frames, corrugated iron, XP metal and sand bags that served to provide soldiers with safer and more comfortable conditions.[1]

The excavations also revealed a clear distinction between German and British structures. German remains are much more solidly built, with thick beams in contrast to the flimsier planks or boards used by the British. The German practice of revetting trenches with wattlework instead of the corrugated iron or expanded metal used by the British also proved to be much more stable. Protecting the common wooden shelters with concrete walls (sometimes made of concrete bricks) was another feature of German construction (Figure 17:3). This was archaeological evidence which supported the oft-mentioned point that German attitudes to trench construction (and trench warfare more generally) differed significantly (in military and cultural terms) from those of the British (see Fuchs 2002).

The Germans had the time and opportunity to choose and massively reinforce strategic locations (usually on higher ground), whereas the British and Allied forces

Figure 17:2
Aerial view of the excavation at the Cross Roads site, near Wieltje, in the Ypres Salient. (© and courtesy VIOE)

were constantly at a disadvantage – attempting to storm German positions from inherently weaker and inferior locations. German trenches were built to last, while British ones were conceived as temporary staging posts for the next attack.

The objects found during the excavations referred to daily life in the trenches – the portable material culture of war. Items of personal equipment (cap badges, buttons, shoes), tools, weapons and ammunition, rum jars and personal belongings (razor, wristwatch) were typical finds (de Meyer and Pype 2004: 28–42). The preservation of these items brought a personal element to the excavations in ways which are not usual for more traditional kinds of archaeology where analogous objects often do not survive. Regimental badges identified the presence of soldiers from the Royal King's Rifle

Figure 17:3 Remains of a wooden shelter, reinforced with walls of concrete building-bricks. (© and courtesy VIOE)

Corps and the Dorsetshire Regiment, amongst others, and a standard-issue spoon engraved with a soldier's service number was evidence of the personalization of belongings (ibid.: 28). Leather and webbing also survived, as did the more fragile mica eye-pieces from the earliest kind of gas masks used in 1915 (ibid.: 30) – a very personal and direct association between an individual soldier and the changing technologies (and moralities) of industrialized war.

Most poignant of all, however, and a reminder of what war is fundamentally about, were the human remains uncovered during the excavations (Figure 17:4). To date, the remains of five British, three German and five French soldiers have been discovered. At one location at Cross Roads, three soldiers were piled on top of each other, indicating perhaps that they had died during an attack – the presence on one of the men of a Webley handgun rather than a Lee Enfield rifle suggesting that he may have been a machine-gunner (ibid.: 38). More indicative of the effects of high explosive bombardment were the shattered and partial remains of soldiers found in shell holes (ibid.: 42).

With each discovery, another personal history came within reach, adding force to the realization that not only is this a very special kind of archaeology, but that it also involves a deeply anthropological dimension, intersecting the lives and memories of people today – those who are and those who feel they are directly connected to the soldiers of the Great War.

Figure 17:4 Remains of a British soldier found during the excavation at the Cross Roads site near Wieltje, in the Ypres Salient. (© and courtesy VIOE)

The significant results of the VIOE's excavations, and the international attention and television coverage that they attracted led to a unique development. The Flemish government and the ministers concerned decided not to go through with the A19 extension as it had originally been planned. Instead, the motorway extension would be diverted along a new course which completely avoided the front lines and the battlefields, with the only landscape damage cause by the necessary adaptation of the point at which the motorway ends – a situation which Flemish archaeologists considered as controllable. At a press conference on 12 August 2005 in Lo-Reninge, minister-president Yves Leterme confirmed this to be the final decision.[2]

This public announcement was a political acknowledgement of the importance of the First World War heritage in Flanders, and of the role of archaeology in identifying, investigating and interpreting this heritage for future generations. It brought Great War archaeology centre-stage, and demonstrated that modern scientific investigations of the traces of this conflict could provide vital new information for discussions about and evaluations of new developments, whether of motorway construction, the building or extension of industrial estates, or of private housing. In advance of such urban renewal projects, archaeological investigation must assess any potential threat to the region's First World War heritage. Great War archaeology was now recognized as being on the same level – and of the same importance – as Flanders' well known and longer established heritage of prehistoric, Gallo-Roman, and, mainly, medieval remains.

Wider aspects of Great War archaeology

The archaeology of the Great War in Flanders has many unique and distinctive features that are beginning to be addressed. Not least of these is its fundamental status as the 'archaeology of lethal behaviour' (Saunders 2004: 18). In order to ensure the personal safety of the excavators, it is necessary to maintain constant contact with, and briefing by, the bomb disposal team of the Belgian army (DOVO), based at Houthulst. DOVO's recognition and assessment of the origin, type and date of production of explosives can provide archaeologists with important information when interpreting particular features.[3]

Equally distinctive, particularly from the perspective of developing methodologies for this new kind of archaeology, is the recognition of features and artefacts not normally encountered in Flemish archaeology's more traditional kinds of investigations. Flemish archaeologists are used to excavating sites belonging to prehistoric and historical times, but are now confronted with shell holes as archaeological features, and (often volatile) bombs, bullets and grenades as archaeological finds. Learning to read and interpret this new kind of archaeological landscape is a major challenge for archaeologists specializing in the archaeology of the war.

These challenges – not least the vast quanitities and varieties of hitherto unfamiliar Great War matériel culture – have led Flemish archaeologists to actively seek co-operation with international specialists and institutions:[4]

> A unique feature of the First World War is that, in addition to military historians, it attracts a large and wide-ranging number of specialist groups. Together, they form a rich repository of specialised knowledge on such varied topics as trench and dugout construction, military maps, uniforms and equipment, armaments, munitions, and memorabilia.
>
> (Dewilde *et al.* 2004)

Not only did this wealth of outside expertise add immeasurably to the interpretation of excavated data, but, and importantly, the VIOE itself now acts as a legally constituted and professional scientific forum for this vast but heterogeneous mass of expertise.

Arguably the most significant difference between more traditional kinds of archaeology and that of Great War sites concerns issues of human remains. After recording the remains in the normal way, by drawing, photography and initial on-site examination by physical/forensic anthropologists, the local police take possession of the bones and the enclosed finds, which can include buttons, badges, miscellaneous military equipment and personal effects. These are then given to war graves authorities of the appropriate country, each of which then follows its own procedures that culminate in the formal reburial of the remains. This identification and reburial process is another distinctive feature of Great War archaeology, where human remains are placed back in the ground rather than put in storage boxes in a university or museum. In this sense, Great War archaeology shares a moral as well as a methodological set of concerns with indigenous communities across the world who seek to identify, repatriate and rebury their dead who have been kept in storage (or on display) in various international institutions (see Hubert 1989; Zimmerman 1989).

Another unique aspect of First World War archaeology is the media attention it receives, both internationally and locally. Newspapers from the United Kingdom, Canada, Australia, the United States and even Japan, regard this new kind of archaeology as particularly newsworthy. In addition, considerable numbers of the public visit the excavations – far more than would attend a more traditional excavation of, say, a Neolithic, Roman, or medieval site. School outings (from Belgium, France and the United Kingdom), tourists on battlefield tours and the simply curious all turn up on site, visiting the place where a relative fought or died. Such are the numbers that on occasion the excavation team was overwhelmed.

The presence of tourists often emphasizes the anthropological nature of First World War archaeology in terms of cultural memory and the emotional resonances that link generations by tying people to places. During the A19 excavations, at the location where the remains of a Northumberland Fusilier soldier were found, passing tourists covered the ground with poppies and remembrance crosses more usually associated with 11 November Armistice commemorations (Figure 17:5).

Figure 17:5
Poppies and remembrance crosses, left on the spot where a soldier fell, after a short ceremony was held.
(© and courtesy VIOE)

259

Archaeological activity is visibly extending the landscapes of remembrance, and connecting with wider notions of commemoration that were until recently focused almost solely on war graves and monuments to the missing, such as the Menin Gate and Tyne Cot cemetery.[5] In other words, archaeology is actively contributing to a better and more nuanced understanding of the Great War. Paradoxically, perhaps, it becomes clear that the closer the historical information comes to the present, the more people become interested. Faxes, emails, letters expressing appreciation, giving information or offering help flowed into the offices of the VIOE and to the team on site. More than any other kind of archaeology, excavations of Great War sites stimulate direct public participation.

Equally direct, if somewhat ambiguous, and certainly not without its problems, is the phenomenon of the 'television archaeology' of the war. Whereas in more traditional kinds of archaeology, television coverage focuses on dramatic new discoveries – in Egypt, Asia or South America – in the nascent archaeology of the First World War, television companies directly sponsor more excavations than official bodies can undertake through their restricted sources of funding. Television coverage, therefore, is less of discoveries made by archaeologists pursuing their professional activities, and more of investigations actively created and formulated by the television company itself, and driven by time, finances and broadcasting schedules rather than purely academic concerns. Recent excavations at Bikschote, 'Forward Cottage' and 'Caesar's Nose' have been sponsored by two separate Canadian television companies – YAP TV and Cream Productions. Contractual agreements with these companies do not allow publication of the information emanating from these investigations until after the programmes have been broadcast, and so any professional comment on this work will be in the future. It is clear that the practice of television-driven archaeological agendas at a time when First World War archaeology itself is still such a young sub-discipline is bound to be a double-edged sword.

Concluding thoughts

Although these are early days in the development of modern scientific archaeology of the Great War in Flanders, recent advances have been rapid and dramatic, and initial conclusions can be drawn.

There is no doubt that investigating the material culture of Flanders's Great War heritage is a worthwhile endeavour – indeed Great War archaeology is a prime example of the many and varied archaeologies of the contemporary past (Buchli and Lucas 2001). Archaeological data retrieved through excavation are more accurate and detailed than that gleaned from trench maps and aerial photographs. Archaeological fieldwork is able to identify sudden changes in the war situation, repairs made after heavy shelling, the presence of soldiers in a particular spot for a short period, and the emotive artefacts belonging to or made by individuals. Excavation can also reveal unexpected structures, such as the entrance to a deep dugout or an ammunition depot (Figure 17:6). A more detailed understanding of the evolution of trench construction can also be attained – the dimension of duckboards, for example, may indicate a date for their construction and that of the trench within which they are located (Figure 17:7).

Figure 17:6 Entrance to a small dugout (an ammunition depot), kept dry using a pump. (© and courtesy VIOE)

Figure 17:7 Duckboards of different shapes and thus probably of different date. (© and courtesy VIOE)

It is this fine-grained information, uncovered and interpreted by archaeologists and the many specialists referred to above, that has the potential to add new insights into the development of battles – to clarify degrees of ambiguity and indistinctness which are beyond the abilities of other kinds of investigation to recover. This point also highlights archaeology's ability to test the assumptions and interpretations of military history, the discipline which has hitherto contributed most to our understanding of the war.

Perhaps most important is archaeology's contribution to locating and recovering the dead. Archaeologists always take painstaking care when uncovering human remains, but in the archaeology of the Great War there is a unique and overriding imperative at work in such undertakings. Nothing, not even the smallest fragment of evidence can be neglected because it could contribute to the identification of the individual concerned. In other words, archaeology has the potential of reclaiming at least some of 'the missing', of identifying, perhaps naming, individuals, and bringing closure to the descendants after almost a century (see Chapter 18). Great War archaeology connects the past directly to the present, and in the most personal way.

There is a host of other issues associated with conducting modern scientific archaeological investigations of First World War heritage in Flanders, though they can only be briefly mentioned here. If the physical traces of the First World War are fully integrated into Flanders' overall archaeological heritage then a decree of 1993 can be enforced. This decree, issued by the Flemish government, deals with the management, research and protection of the archaeological heritage, and legally requires that archaeological finds are reported, that the granting of excavation permits is strictly controlled, and that the use of metal detectors is restricted to excavations in progress. However, this last item is bound to be adjusted.[6] The application of the act to Great War remains thus regulates and minimizes damage to sites by construction activities, and by those who engage in illicit digging (usually in order to collect military equipment for later resale in the local and international trade in war memorabilia; see Chapter 9). However, there is little doubt that the enforcement of this law needs to be strengthened.

Intellectually and historically, one of the most important advantages of excavating Great War sites is that it changes our perspective by redirecting attention away from the grand strategies of military history towards the everyday realities and experiences of the ordinary soldier. Furthermore, it has the power to associate particular events to a specific topography, linking the physical experience of landscape – a sense of changing heights and variable terrains – to perhaps more widely known (but incomplete) details of a battle or skirmish.

Archaeological research also contributes substantially to identifying and defining areas that require legal recognition as heritage locations. In 2004, in the framework of the Central Archaeological Inventory, an individual project was initiated, with the aim of documenting all Great War archaeological sites in western Flanders. Based on this inventory, it is increasingly possible to propose that certain areas be scheduled for protection as war landscapes (de Meyer 2005). The direct association between excavations and the public mentioned above could also lead to a heightened awareness of the cultural heritage value of such locations among local people who would then support the need for site protection. This in turn could lead to more financial resources and personnel being made available for investigations. Expert monitoring of the preservation of remaining structures will be introduced, though, once again, engaging a sympathetic local population would be extremely useful in this respect. In the past, subjective assessments of the decaying state of some structures have been repeatedly invoked by amateur groups in order to obtain permission to undertake the 'final dig' – a situation which would be rendered impossible with these new developments.

Finally, there are the implications for archaeology itself. There is little doubt that the unique and potentially dangerous conditions of excavating First World War sites constitute a significant methodological challenge. Great War archaeology requires innovative methodologies to be developed. For example, in basic archaeological prospection, the unequal clearing of the Ypres Salient battlefield after the war needs to be addressed. The reasons for this remain unclear, though they could be linked to individual landowner's decisions about such clearance activity – which in turn has implications for the degree of preservation of this heritage. Furthermore, we need to ask, for example, whether fieldwalking and tracing concentrations of mostly metal scrap is the best way of locating sites for excavation. What should be the role for metal detectorists in an archaeological landscape defined by its metallic nature? What, in such conditions, are the possibilities for geophysical research? How can we recognize and best excavate bomb craters, and can we identify telltale signs indicating the presence of human remains?

Perhaps the most reliable aspect of preliminary research is the analysis of aerial photographs – those taken during the war and its immediate aftermath, and more modern ones. The potential of aerial photography in archaeological research is well established, but here it can be combined with different kinds of information, such as that supplied by trench maps and documentary records. Interestingly and importantly, new techniques of analysing aerial photographs and integrating them with Geographical Information Systems (GIS) imagery that are being developed for Great War archaeology may also have significant consequences for archaeology more generally (Stichelbaut 2005a; 2005b; 2006; Stichelbaut *et al.* 2005; de Meyer 2005). In this way, methodologies developed for the archaeology of the First World War may significantly affect the parent discipline in years to come.

As First World War archaeology begins to mature, excavations such as the A19 Project play a crucial 'role in shaping a highly-focused methodology for First World War Archaeology' in Flanders (Dewilde *et al.* 2004). Beyond this technical development, the existence and practice of a professional archaeology of the war will attract a wider particpation in, and a deeper understanding of, the complex relationships between excavation, commemoration, heritage and tourism. From a more theoretical perspective, Great War Archaeology reveals how landscapes-as-artefacts preserve, define and redefine people through time, and how they are arguably the most contested of all the objects of war.

Notes

1   One can also consult IWM (1998).
2   Two headlines in Belgian newspapers were '*Akkoord Vlaamse regering spaart Pilkem Ridge*' (Agreement, Flemish government spares Pilkem Ridge) and '*A19 niet over slagveld Pilkem Ridge*' (The A19 will not cross the Pilkem Ridge battlefield).
3   Sergeant-major Tony Wittouck has been of particular help in this respect.
4   Peter Barton (Parapet Archives), Martin Brown (Ministry of Defence), Peter Chasseaud and Peter Doyle (University of Greenwich), Andrew Robertshaw (National Army Museum) and Laurie Millner and Nigel Steel (Imperial War Museum) have helped us through this initial phase of the research.
5   The following individuals have been working on this topic: Janiek Degryse, Mathieu de Meyer, Frederik Demeyere, Wouter Lammens, Pedro Pype and Franky Wyffels.
6   This decree states that archaeological heritage includes all remains, objects or other features of human existence that testify to eras and civilizations, for which excavations or finds are an important source of information. ('*30 juni 1993 – decreet houdende bescherming van het archeologisch patrimonium*' (This decree is operative as long as it does not contradict national laws), Belgisch Staatsblad, 15 September 1993).

References

Blunden, E. (1934) 'We went to Ypres'. In E. Blunden, *The Mind's Eye*, pp. 44–9. London: Jonathan Cape.

Buchli, V. and G. Lucas (eds) (2001) *Archaeologies of the Contemporary Past*. London: Routledge.

de Meyer, M. (2005) 'Houthulst and the A19-Project: inventory of World War I heritage based on wartime aerial photography and trench maps'. In J. Bourgeois and M. Meganck (eds), *Aerial Photography and Archaeology 2003: A Century of Information (Archaeological Reports Ghent University*, 4), pp. 87–99. Gent: Academia Press.

de Meyer, M. and P. Pype. (2004) *The A19 Project: Archaeological Research at Cross Roads*. Zarren: Association for World War Archaeology (AWA) Publications.

Dewilde, M. (1991) 'Opgravingen in de Augustijnenabdij van Zonnebeke'. *Biekorf* 91: 375–80.

Dewilde, M., P. Pype, M. de Meyer, F. Demeyere, W. Lammens, J. Degryse, F. Wyffels and N.J.Saunders (2004) 'Belgium's new department of First World War archaeology'. *Antiquity* 78 (301). Project Gallery: http://antiquity.ac.uk/ProjGall/saunders/index.html

Dixon, J. (2003) *Magnificent but not War: The Second Battle of Ypres 1915*. Barnsley: Leo Cooper.

Ewart, W. (1920) 'After four years: the old road to Ypres'. *Cornhill Magazine* XLIX: 734–41.

Fuchs, L. (2002) 'Baulust und Heimsinn: Gemütlichkeit im Schützengraben'. In Projektgruppe Trench Art, *Kleines aus dem Großen Krieg: Metamorphosen Militärischen Mülls*, pp. 84–101. Ludwig-Uhland-Institut für Empirische Kulturwissenchaft der Universität Tübingen. Tübingen: Tübinger Vereinigung fur Volkskunde.

Hubert, J. (1989) 'A proper place for the dead: a critical review of the 'reburial' issue'. In R. Layton (ed.), *Conflict in the Archaeology of Living Traditions*, pp. 131–66. London: Unwin Hyman.

IWM (1998) *Trench Fortifications 1914–1918: A Reference Manual*. London: Imperial War Museum.

Liddle, P.H. (ed.) (1997) *Passchendaele in Perspective: The Third Battle of Ypres*. London: Leo Cooper.

Lloyd, D.W. (1998) *Battlefield Tourism: Pilgrimage and the Commemoration of the Great War in Britain, Australia and Canada 1919–1939*. Berg: Oxford.

McWilliams, J. and R.J. Steel. (1985) *Gas! The Battle for Ypres, 1915*. St. Catharines, Ontario: Vanwell.

Saunders, N.J. (2001) 'Matter and memory in the landscapes of conflict: the Western Front 1914–1999'. In B. Bender and M. Winer (eds), *Contested Landscapes: Movement, Exile and Place*, pp. 37–53. Oxford: Berg.

—— (2002) 'Excavating memories: archaeology and the Great War, 1914–2001'. *Antiquity* 76 (1): 101–8.

—— (2003) *Trench Art: Materialities and Memories of War*. Berg: Oxford.

—— (2004) 'Material culture and conflict: the Great War, 1914–2004'. In N.J. Saunders (ed.), *Matters of Conflict: Material Culture, Memory and the First World War*, pp. 5–25. Abingdon: Routledge.

Steel, N. and P. Hart. (2000) *Passchendaele*. London: Cassell.

Stichelbaut, B. (2005a) 'Great War aerial photography: a contribution to the Flemish Battlefield Archaeology'. In J. Bourgeois and M. Meganck (eds), *Aerial Photography and Archaeology 2003: A Century of Information (Archaeological Reports Ghent University, 4)*, pp. 137–48. Gent: Academia Press.

—— (2005b) 'The application of Great War aerial photography to battlefield archaeology: the example of Flanders'. *Journal of Conflict Archaeology* 1 (1): 235–43.

—— (2006) 'The application of First World War aerial photography to archaeology: the Belgian images'. *Antiquity* 80 (307): 161–72.

Stichelbaut, B., D. Devriendt, R. Goossens and J. Bourgeois (2005) 'Reconstructing the past: the application of digital photogrammetry and GPS measurements for the study of the 1914–1918 wartime landscapes (Belgium)'. *Congresbundel AARG (Aerial Archaeology Research Group), Annual Conference*, pp. 43–4. Leuven.

Weixler, F.P. (1938) *Damals und Heute an der Westfront*. Berlin: Verlag Scherl.

Zimmerman, L.J. (1989a) 'Made radical by my own: an archaeologist learns to accept reburial'. In R. Layton (ed.), *Conflict in the Archaeology of Living Traditions*, pp. 60–67. London: Unwin Hyman.

18

'SLOWLY OUR GHOSTS DRAG HOME'

Human remains from the Heidenkopf, Serre, Somme, France

Martin Brown

In January 1917, the soldier-poet Wilfred Owen and his men occupied captured German trenches near Serre, on the Somme battlefield in France, which included an area known as 'The Heidenkopf' (or 'The Quadrilateral' to British troops). Coming under heavy shellfire they took cover in the enemy dugouts (Hibberd 2002: 208–12). During the barrage, several casualties were taken, including one man who was blinded, inspiring Owen's poem *The Sentry* (Stallworthy 2002: xxv–xxvi). This event was the focus of a BBC television programme broadcast in 2004 which, typical of the way in which First World War archaeology is developing, incorporated archaeological excavations in October 2004 by No Man's Land, a group specializing in Great War Archaeology (Figure 18:1).

The Heidenkopf was a salient projecting into no-man's-land from the German line. The feature was strategically useful because it possessed lines of sight along the allied line, as well as an ability to enfilade or split an attack. Its importance made the Heidenkopf a regular target for allied attentions (Horsfall and Cave 2003: 66–7). It was attacked repeatedly during the Battle of the Somme (1916) before falling in so-called 'Bite and Hold' attacks, designed to secure an area and expand control of the enemy line from the secure base (Griffiths 1994: 32–3).

Excavations examined two trench sections and an area immediately to their rear. One area of trench had been in-filled with thick deposits, including natural chalk. This is believed to relate to German mines blown to disrupt British attacks in 1916. The second area revealed traces of trench combat, including empty British Lewis gun magazines and a *chevaux de frise* (trench barricade) still blocking the trench. The entrance to a German mine was also observed (Brown 2005: 25–33).

Figure 18:1 General view of the no-man's-land excavations at Serre in 2003. (© author)

Finding the fallen

Three skeletons were found during the course of the week-long investigation. At the time of writing two have been formally identified, while a third remains 'Known Unto God', as the inscription on his tombstone in the Serre Military Cemetery Number 2, which lies adjacent to the field containing the Heidenkopf, attests. While the ascription of a name is a matter of interest, it is surely the attempts to give some form of identity to the skeleton that is of interest to the archaeologist who seeks to explore the past through its material culture.

Archaeologists are practised at investigating personal effects found with the dead. However, it is worth noting that Great War dead – the iconic 'Fallen' – come from a period which is very close to our own time – an era which still resonates strongly today (Saunders 2004: 15, 127–31). It is also worth remembering that the artefacts most commonly studied from more ancient archaeological contexts associated with the dead, at least in Great Britain, are from burial contexts. Unlike the formally buried body, the battlefield casualty who has been neither recovered nor reburied still lies undisturbed where he fell some 90 years ago.

Significantly, artefacts associated with such battlefield bodies are unlikely to have resulted from human agency within cultural norms associated with death rites or burial ritual designed to ease the passing of the soul, commemorate the body or equip them for the afterlife (Parker Pearson 1999: 9–11). In fact, the reverse is self-evidently the case. Instead of artefacts being deliberately added to the burial (for whatever personal or ritual reasons), a battlefield body may have been stripped of material considered useful or valuable, either by the enemy or by one's own side, and for a variety of reasons (see Saunders 2002: 104–5; 2003: 130–1). This is probably especially true in an area such as the Heidenkopf, where military action was prolonged and fierce.

Objects may have been removed to identify the casualty as missing, to collect personal effects to send home to kinfolk, or simply because the deceased would no longer have need of them. While cultural norms prevalent in industrial Europe may, by and large, have disapproved of the looting of bodies, the social dislocation provided by war and the long-standing tradition of looting (e.g. Urban 2003: 254–5) may have come into play (for the contemporary ethics of robbing corpses, see Chapter 1). While it may be possible to address issues of culture, identity or even of ethnicity when grave goods are present (Lucy 2000: 173–81), the unfiltered artefacts associated with battlefield casualties afford an opportunity to look much closer into the possible identity of the individual.

The objects carried not only afford an opportunity to say something about the soldier, but also, in at least one of our cases, about the way he presented himself to the world. It is possible for the archaeologist to consider the assemblage associated with a particular body and to try to say something about the fallen, beyond his military identity, as a member of an army or any subdivision thereof. One might call this process *re-membrance*, seeking, as it does to ascribe identity to the body. This process works alongside, but may subvert, the military process of claiming the body, and thereby the man, even in death. Remembrance seeks not only to ascribe some identity to the fallen, but also to create some focus for personal remembrance by humanizing the skeleton that is represented in turn by the sepia images of family photographs, or the film of Tommy eternally marching towards the front line. However, it is important to bear in mind that any such attempt at identification is tentative at best, and that emotional involvement with the bodies and their artefacts is inevitable in any such process (see Chapter 12).

Soldiers three

The individual who remains unknown was a British soldier from the King's Own Royal Lancaster Regiment (see Eastwood 1991: 88, 91). Unit identification was only possible because of the brass shoulder titles that survived with the skeleton. He lay on the chalk fills from the mine explosion. The 1st Bn The King's Own was part of the attack on the Heidenkopf on 1 July 1916, the first day of the Battle of the Somme. No immediate identification was possible as there was no trace of identity discs, and the lack of other personal artefacts raised the possibility that the body had been searched or looted shortly after death. The supine position of the skeleton raises the possibility that the body was given some form of inhumation – the screw picket may either have been equipment carried in the attack but may also have been reused as a rudimentary grave marker. Whether buried or not, he was not well covered enough to deter rats, whose burrows could still be seen in the abdominal area, underlining the gruesome realities of trench warfare and its aftermath.

The personal effects that remained with the body included a leather purse and coins. The identity of those involved in the burial remains unclear, but the failure to remove the small box respirator may indicate that they were German. The money was initially an unsurprising mixture of French and English coins of low denomination. However, there was also a penny from the States of Jersey dated either 1913 or 1915; the condition of the coin makes dating uncertain. This raises the possibility of the skeleton being that of a regular soldier, since the 1st Battalion were on garrison duty there before the war.

However, the fact that they had left the island in 1911 (Peter Donnelly, pers. comm.), raises the possibility that the individual returned to Jersey in his own time, perhaps because he was a local man, or because of some personal liaison formed during those years.

The cause of death was shell burst. Numerous shell splinters were found in and around the area of the skeleton (Figure 18:2). In addition, his upper right femur had been smashed, apparently a common injury associated with shellfire (Andrew Robertshaw, pers. comm.). This major injury and the resulting profuse bleeding probably resulted in the purse being left as it lay where a pocket would have been, close to the fracture.

Two Germans were also found. Careful excavation of the first individual revealed he had been wrapped in his rain cape before a burial so hasty that it is impossible to know if it involved anything more than lifting the body over the parados of the trench.

Figure 18:2 The femur of the British soldier showing potentially fatal trauma to the bone from shell burst. The purse and coins are visible toward the hip, indicating their location in his trouser pocket. (© author)

In addition to military equipment, a few personal effects and a badly corroded identity disc were discovered, and have since been treated by conservators at the Institute of Archaeology, University College London.

The only official information inscribed on identity discs was the regimental designation and number, the number of the company and the number of the individual on the company roll. This individual's disc showed that the man served with a reserve infantry regiment, but unfortunately the number was missing; he was in 7 *Kompanie* and was number 2 on their roll. It is known that 7 *Kompanie* of *121 Reserve Infanterie Regiment* were in the trenches at Serre from 10 to 13 June 1915. At this time there was heavy fighting with the French, and it was possible that the soldier had been killed during this engagement. They were not in this area on 1 July 1916, which was the other period of heavy fighting when one might expect unrecovered casualties. However, careful study also revealed additional details scratched onto the disc's surface. Perhaps the owner was uneasy about the lack of a name on his identity disc, and his personalizing graffito should be seen as a reassertion of his identity in the face of the literally regimented world of the state in arms. This was a widely practised habit, and is conceptually related to other kinds of artistic expression (see Saunders 2003: 93, 96).

Corrosion had removed some of the identity disc's legend, but it was possible to read the top line as 'Mun–', the second line as 'Hines', and the bottom line 'Jak–'. The difficulty was in deciding what this meant. The arrangement of the buttons on the cuff was of the 'Swedish' pattern, a style not uncommon in the Imperial German Army, but which, significantly, was used by a number of Württemberg infantry regiments. This sector was occupied from March 1915 to November 1916 by 26 Reserve Division, a Württemburg formation. It was discovered that the only regiment in 26 Reserve Division that wore Swedish cuffs was 121 Reserve Infanterie Regiment. A search of casualty lists for this unit in June 1915 revealed the loss of Jakob Hönes (the 'I' in 'Hines' on the disc actually being an 'ö'), a farm labourer from Munchingen near Stuttgart. His geographic origins were underlined by the lid from a polish jar (sold by a Stuttgart department store), which was associated with the skeleton (Figure 18:3). Further research revealed a Hönes family still living in the area, including Jakob's last surviving son. Skeleton 1, now reunited with family and name, rests today in the German military cemetery near Metz (Fraser 2004), a dramatic and poignant example of the intensely human aspect of First World War archaeology.

Other personal kit included a fragment of mirror, a manicure set and a comb, suggesting that this was a man who cared about his appearance (Figure 18:4). One might regard keeping one's nails clean in the muddy hell of the trenches as madness, but here was a man prepared to do it. Is it possible that Hönes adopted this action as his way of asserting his humanity as he had used his name to assert his individuality on his identity disc?

Jakob Hönes had been a labourer in a brick works, and worked his own small patch of land. He came from a family which had fallen on hard times (Alexander Brunotte, pers. comm.). Was his cleanliness perhaps a pre-war affectation borne partly of necessity through dirty, manual work, but which was perhaps also a way of adopting

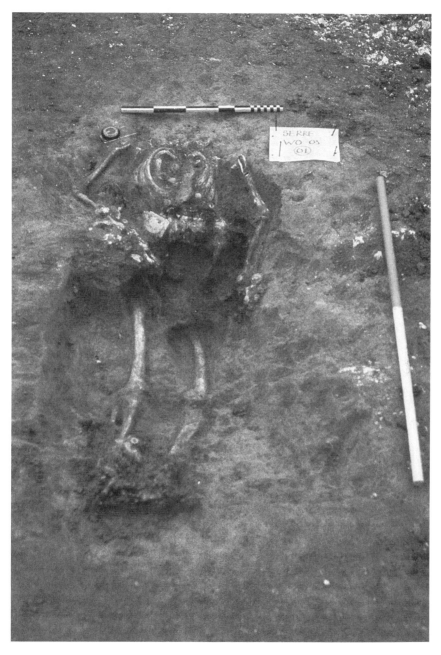

Figure 18:3 The body of Jakob Hönes during excavation. The buttons and the distinctive arrangement of the Swedish cuff can be seen. (© author)

Figure 18:4 The grooming kit of Jakob Hönes during excavation. (© author)

the habits of his wealthier forebears and asserting status? Taken together, these objects present a picture of a man concerned about his appearance and, perhaps, his position in the community, which, in a regionally based regiment would carry from the civilian world over into the military. Despite this consideration of the civilian world, it is important to remember that Hönes died in combat, something his equipment underlines. The ammunition pouches of his webbing were full, furthermore an extra charger of bullets had been jammed into the right hand pouch, where it would have been most accessible. The pouch was open, ready for him to reach down for the bullets. It appears that when he died he was expecting a busy day and one is tempted to see the extra ammunition as evidence that he was quite prepared for that. It has been reported that Hönes was killed by a French bullet found amongst the bones (Fabiansson 2000–5), whereas, in fact, the bullet was near the bones in the hollow where Hönes lay. He was actually killed by shell fragments that were scattered amongst bones and concentrated in the stomach cavity.

Skeleton 3 had also been the subject of minimal disposal, lying on one side, again in a shallow feature that may have been no more than a hollow in the battlefield (Figure 18:5). No attempt had been made to remove personal effects from the body, and his bread-bag, with its numerous contents, lay beside the skeleton. Examination of the contents revealed a pocket watch, razor, penknife, pipe and a roll of papers, which conservators identified as a bankbook from a bank in Halberstadt, a town in Sachsen Anhalt, eastern Germany.

Other contents of the bag had, perhaps, been edible and were certainly perishable. They had been eaten by maggots, as a compressed mass of blowfly casts was observed,

Figure 18:5
The body of
Alfred Thielecke
during excavation.
(© author)

a presence also associated with the soft tissue of the body. The corruption in the bag
may have preserved it from looting, or maybe the individual was killed at a 'hot'
moment when there was no time for such niceties, a view that the hasty method of
burial underlines. The bag also contained a prehistoric flint scraper, indicating, as has
been reported elsewhere, the curious nature of First World War archaeology which
incorporates strata and objects not just from the conflict itself, but also from deeper
and older levels of what is normally the remit of prehistoric archaeology – in other
words a unique mixing of the oldest and newest kinds of archaeological material
culture (Saunders 2002: 102–3) (Figure 18:6).

Figure 18:6 Alfred Thielecke's bread bag during excavation. The prehistoric flint lies near the left-hand side of the scale. Other items visible include a harmonica, a clasp knife and razor, and a pocket watch. (© author)

No identity disc was recovered for skeleton 3, suggesting that it may have been removed. However, available evidence for identification of the remains points to Alfred Thielecke, an NCO of 7 Kompanie, 121 RIR, who was killed in action on 11 June 1915. The NCO's buttons were located at the position on the body where one would expect the uniform collar to identify the rank. Fragments of piping from the uniform also suggested the rank of Vizefeldwebel, Thielecke's rank at death.

Alfred Thielecke is the only man of the correct rank in 121 or 119 RIR (both regiments were in the area in 1915–16) who had any known connection with Halberstadt, as the personnel of both regiments were predominantly from the state of Württemburg. Thielecke is known to have been an interior decorator and therefore perhaps a person who might have had a bank account. Unfortunately no bank records seem to survive because of two later twentieth-century tragedies, the 'Aryanisation' of the Jewish-owned bank by the Nazis, and its subsequent dissolution by the East German and Soviet authorities (Volker Hartmann, pers. comm.). The pocket watch may also indicate someone of slightly elevated social standing, again consistent with the small businessman. These suggestions have been deemed sufficient by the VDK (German War Graves organization) to accord the skeleton the identity of Thielecke, and this name has been inscribed on his tombstone in the Metz military cemetery.

The other contents of the bag reveal more insights into the man, irrespective of his actual identity. Indeed, the volume of material in the bag is of interest itself, since it shows a man carrying a small world around on his back. These personal artefacts perhaps reinforced his sense of self in the face of the depersonalizing horrors of the war. Some of the objects have no obvious utilitarian use, and one must ask why he carried them. A pipe is self-explanatory, but the action of lighting a pipe is more involved and personal than that of smoking cigarettes. Perhaps the pipe may be seen as a social indicator, like the bankbook and watch. A harmonica, the iconic musical instrument of the trenches, reveals someone with at least a modicum of musical talent. However, as archaeologists, it is perhaps inevitably the flint tool that spurs our interest.

This scraper is probably Bronze Age, and made of local Picardy flint. Perhaps the soldier picked it up during a march, on working party duty, in the trenches or while at rest in the rear areas. Whatever the truth, he chose to keep it. Conversations with soldiers and the reading of numerous accounts reveals the magpie nature of soldiers throughout history, but usually they pick up something they think might be useful or of value, if not at the time then later. Indeed, the author's own grandfather took a pair of door handles from the Station Master's office at Poperinghe Station in Belgian Flanders in 1917. Ancient archaeological artefacts might, in general terms, be said to be neither valuable nor useful to a modern soldier, particularly in the case of a flint tool. The collection of archaeological artefacts, however, is unusual but not unknown (Saunders 2002: 102–3), though the rare evidence which exists suggests that this was mainly an officer's pursuit, at least in the British Army.

For our German NCO, this flint not only suggests some degree of education, as well as an interest in the past, or of the place where he had found himself, but also underlines the concept of meta-archaeology identified by Nils Fabiansson (Fabiansson 2000–5). However, the flint itself crystallizes and personifies wider issues of identification, emotion and remembrance for the archaeologist, which are inherent in the study of the material culture of the conflict, particularly the personal effects of the dead.

Remembrance, politics and emotion

The object as focus of remembrance has been discussed elsewhere in the context of bringing the 'war' home to families with serving or fallen sons (Saunders 2003: 152–5). In this context it is possible to extend the discussion to include objects recovered with the fallen themselves. While these items may not carry the power associated with immediate emotion and, perhaps, continuing grief, they nevertheless emanate from the battlefield, and possess an equally visceral, if different kind of, potency.

The Great War has an enduring paradigm of butchered young men; sacrificed by generals in a war they did not understand or believe in (e.g. Holmes 2004; Fussell 1975). To subscribe wholesale to this paradigm betrays the diversity of personality and motivation in the armies, even in the British Army alone (Holmes 2004). By considering the man who is now but a skeleton, it is possible to individualize him as a human being who had, and in a sense still has, a life beyond the military. Although the No Man's Land group were fortunate in being able to identify two of the excavated skeletons, the possibilities of *re-membrance* – that is the process of ascribing identity and humanity to bones – have also been demonstrated. Such a process can only attempt to create narratives from artefacts – it would be rare indeed to find a body with associated objects and then to be able to fill in the data with a good collection of letters or a diary. However, this attempt to (re)create (*pace* Price 2004) a man from the objects sets itself against the enduring concept of 'The Missing' – the anonymous Tommy, Fritz, or poilu referred to above, eternally dwelling in the muddy Hell of the Front.

In a political sense, this (re)creation and *re-membrance* also stands in opposition to the eternal militarization of the body through its reinterment in a military cemetery, as has happened to all three of the Heidenkopf skeletons. These cemeteries, so often the focus of pilgrimage and remembrance, are of course also political landscapes (Winter 1998). They are official creations, and have an imposed order and style that preserves regimented order in perpetuity. The only individuality lies in the personal sentiments sometimes added to the headstones of those with relatives able to pay for the privilege (see Chapter 11).

The claiming of the body by the military, especially in a British context, is still an act of faith and remembrance by the Army. Wherever possible, burial is undertaken by the regiment or its successor unit, as was the case with the unknown British soldier, where the Queen's Lancashire Regiment, successors to the King's Own, provided a burial party (Order of Service, 2004). Through such ritualized action, their identity, so important in combat, may be reinforced, as modern soldiers come into direct contact with their traditions and the battle honours of their regiment (Holmes 2004: 112–5). Moreover, the modern soldier sees that he will be cared for and remembered, even in death, further reinforcing a kinship within the community. By ascribing an identity to the anonymous fallen soldier, society may be reminded that most were civilians, rather than professional soldiers, who had volunteered for the duration of the conflict. Nevertheless, the British casualty from the Heidenkopf at Serre appears to have been a regular soldier rather than a conscript, and that he had chosen a military life must also be acknowledged in considering his fate.

The burial reflects British tradition (ibid.) and underlines both the strength of tradition and the value of military power under civil control, whereby the soldier is inculcated in the history of the service and nation he upholds (Keegan 2001: 31–44). However, the issue of the permanent militarization of the body is more pertinent in connection with the German skeletons. Through burial in a military context they remain forever in the defeated army of 1918, they remain 'the vanquished' and, through association with war crimes, occupation and exploitation, the villains of the war. The demonization of the Imperial German Army was pursued in Allied propaganda during and after the war, and still appears in more recent works (Ferguson 1998). Perhaps attempts at personification can seek to counter this stigmatization by seeing a human being in the field-grey uniform worn by the Kaiser's men – surely one of the many important aims of the new field of First World War archaeology.

Whether German or Allied, the dead are remembered in official and personal acts of remembrance from Armistice Day to the individual fragment of family history. However, as veterans die and memories fade, this remembrance may become abstract, creating difficulties for a modern population in identifying with the 'Lost Generation' of the Great War. Perhaps a process of personification through artefact can join personification through image and document as a source of inspiration for study and remembrance, evoking identification and emotion in ways a monument cannot.

Despite aspirations to re-member the dead, the personification of human remains is a contentious issue. Apart from criticisms that might be levelled about the cultural assumptions of the personnel involved in the study, the reliance on material culture, and possible charges of blatant storytelling, there is also the issue of emotion. The traumatic shadow cast over the century following the Great War means that anyone involved in the study of these remains has an emotional reaction different to that encountered when excavating medieval monks or looking at Saxon grave goods (see Chapter 17).

The atmosphere amongst those involved in excavations at the Heidenkopf following the discovery of human remains was different to other projects that the No Man's Land group had undertaken. For some members of the team, the discovery of the flint tool crystallized the issues as it was tempting to see that body as 'one of us'. Here was a person with whom one had a point of contact – an apparent curiosity about the past. In addition, the contact with the Hönes family added a new layer of emotion unfamiliar to most archaeologists, whereby we saw someone like ourselves, someone with ancestors involved in the conflict, but someone from the other side of the line. Finally, the communication which informed us that Herr Hönes, the son of Jakob, had died, but that the discovery of his father had eased his passing was emotional beyond anything experienced in more traditional archaeology, and placed a moral responsibility on the team which no one expected when they became involved with First World War archaeology (see Saunders 2002: 107).

Conclusions

While the excavation at the Heidenkopf at Serre failed to find a dugout or any trace of Wilfred Owen, it illustrated the true value of archaeological investigation at a site which could have been written off simply as a pulverized battlefield. It was possible to explore military activity in the trenches, but, most importantly, the archaeological examination of human remains and associated artefacts has shown the potential for saying something about the men involved, not least as regards their identification.

This process can be seen as an act of remembrance, not only in the explicit act of respectful reburial, but also in attempts to give some identity and humanity back to the hitherto anonymous victims of the battlefield. Archaeology seeks to explore humankind through objects. While wider stories about the war are being written through other artefacts, the examination of the effects of war on otherwise unknown soldiers serves to bestow respect by restoring their individuality and humanity, offering other perspectives on their lives. In some cases, the careful archaeological excavation of the fallen can result in their formal identification. While this is valuable for families and military units alike, the wider story discussed above clearly matters as one seeks to work in the service of remembrance of the Great War.

The process of dealing with the dead in this way, however, raises issues of integrity with the evidence, of political perspectives connected to the war, and of the excavators themselves. Moreover, there are issues of emotional involvement. Objectivity may be impossible in the study of such contested ground as the battlefields of the Great War. Each and every one of these issues must be acknowledged as vital parts of the process of exploring this particularly violent area of European history. Finally, the sensitivity with which the fallen must be treated should always be borne in mind. These remains were once men, and deserve our respect as fellow human beings. Perhaps systematic study of the artefacts found with the fallen can recover something of a generation that might not be quite as lost as we had once thought.

Acknowledgements

I am hugely grateful to all members of the project team but especially to Luke Barber, whose initial work on the finds was invaluable. His work was developed by conservators at UCL and by Alistair Fraser and Ralph J. Whitehead. Further work in Germany was provided by Alexander Brunotte, of the Munchingen Stadtarchiv, and Volker Hartmann. Peter Donnelly of the King's Own museum was most helpful in respect of the British casualty. The efforts of all the No Man's Land team both at Serre and in later discussions and projects must also be acknowledged. Finally, to Nick Saunders for the opportunity to present these thoughts both at the joint University College London/Imperial War Museum conference entitled 'Conflict, Memory and Material Culture: The Great War, 1914–2004', held at the Imperial War Museum on Saturday, 11 September 2004, and in this volume.

References

Brown, M. (2005) 'Journey back to hell: excavations at Serre on the Somme'. *Current World Archaeology*, 10: 25–33

Eastwood, S. (1991) *Lions of England: A Pictorial History of the King's Own Royal Regiment (Lancaster) 1680–1980*. Great Addington: Silver Link.

Fabiansson, N. (2000–5) 'The Archaeology of the Western Front 1914–1918'. Unpublished paper, ex website: http://web.telia.com/~u86517080/BattlefieldArchaeology/ArkeologENG.html

Ferguson, N. (1998) *The Pity of War*. London: Penguin

Fraser, A. (2004) http://www.fylde.demon.co.uk/fraser.htm

Fussell, P. (1975) *The Great War and Modern Memory*. Oxford: Oxford University Press.

Griffiths, P. (1994) *Battle Tactics of the Western Front*. New Haven: Yale University Press.

Hibberd, D. (2002) *Wilfred Owen*. London: Weidenfeld & Nicholson.

Holmes, R. (2004) *Tommy: The British Soldier on the Western Front 1914–1918*. London HarperCollins.

Horsfall, J. and N. Cave (2003) *Serre, Somme: Battleground Europe*. Barnsley: Pen and Sword.

Keegan, J. (2001) *War and Our World*. London: Random House.

Lucy, S. (2000) *The Anglo-Saxon Way of Death*. Stroud: Sutton.

Order of Service (2004) Mimeo. Ministry of Defence.

Parker Pearson, M. (1999) *The Archaeology of Death and Burial*. Stroud: Sutton.

Price, J. (2004) 'The Ocean Villas project: archaeology in the service of European remembrance'. In N.J. Saunders (ed.) *Matters of Conflict: Material Culture, Memory and the First World War*, pp. 179–91. Abingdon: Routledge.

Saunders, N.J. (2002) 'Excavating memories: archaeology and the Great War, 1914–2001'. *Antiquity*, 76 (1): 101–8.

—— (2003) *Trench Art: Materialities and Memories of War*. Oxford: Berg.

—— (ed.) (2004) *Matters of Conflict: Material Culture, Memory and the First World War*, Abingdon: Routledge.

Stallworthy, J. (2002) *Wilfred Owen: The War Poems*. London: Chatto & Windus.

Urban, M. (2003) *Rifles: Six Years with Wellington's Elite*. London: Faber.

Winter, J. (1998) *Sites of Memory, Sites of Mourning: The Great War in European Cultural History*. Cambridge: Cambridge University Press.

19

GREAT WAR ARCHAEOLOGY ON THE GLACIERS OF THE ALPS

Marco Balbi

During the First World War, the Italian Front witnessed warfare with unique characteristics. This was industrialized conflict on high altitude mountainous terrain, and, even more extreme, on snowfields and glaciers. In this brief introduction to an unusual kind of conflict materiality, I will consider the ways in which the Italian and Austrian armies were forced to deal with the problems of survival for their soldiers in such hostile environments, and identify key issues and areas for the future development of battle-zone archaeology in this beautiful but unforgiving environment.

In recent years, the archaeology of the First World War has seen increasing interest and professionalization, particularly on the archetypal battlefields of the Western Front (e.g. Saunders 2002; Brown this volume; Dewilde and Saunders this volume; Price 2004; AGG 1999). The many issues with which archaeologists specializing in the investigation of twentieth-century battle-zones are confronted have required such work to be increasingly informed by the anthropology of material culture, as well as by military history (Saunders 2004). The result is the realization that this is a new kind of archaeology, which has to address many complex issues, as well as attempt to develop its own particular methodologies, and forge links with other cognate disciplines.

By comparison with the battlefields of France and Belgium, relatively little has been published in English on the war on the Italian Front, and even less on the beginnings of archaeology in this area (see Falls 1966; Wilks 1998; Schindler 2001; MacKay 2001, 2002). The extreme conditions under which the war was fought here, and the astonishing preservation of its material culture, makes it a unique landscape of conflict with many hitherto unacknowledged connections to broader issues, notably post-war Alpine tourism and its specialized technologies.

No other European front in the Great War had fighting taking place at altitudes as high as those between Italy and Austria. In fact, the front line ran through the Stelvio Pass – on the border between Italy, Austria and Switzerland – and down to the Adriatic Sea, traversing a number of the highest and most extensive mountain ranges in the central-eastern Alps, such as the Ortles–Cevedale, Adamello–Presanella, the Dolomites, and the Julian and Carnic Alps. Here are mountains over 3,000 metres in height, with several peaks approaching 4,000 metres. In these hostile environments, the main enemy for the soldiers was not human adversaries, but the prohibitive environmental and meteorological conditions that they were forced to endure for extended periods (Martinelli 1972; Viazzi 1976, 1981; Von Lichem 1983, 1995). The power of modern industrialized war to reconfigure the relationships between human beings, technology and environment was such that never before in history had so many people been forced to live at such high altitudes for such lengthy periods (Figure 19:1).

The commanders of the Italian and Austro-Hungarian armies had to solve problems never dealt with previously: combat at high altitudes, construction of shelters suitable for extreme conditions, and supplying a large body of soldiers with arms, ammunition, food and fuel for heating. This was complicated by the long ascents from valley floors to the mountain summits.

On all fronts, the First World War led men to great sacrifice as well as adaptation to every kind of environmental condition, but it was on the Italian front in particular that the struggle against the elements became top priority. More men lost their lives to the extremes of cold, frost-bite, illness and avalanches than to enemy action. Some estimates have calculated that two-thirds of overall mortalities were caused in this way (Von Lichem, 1995, 1: 65–6). Avalanches were probably the worst enemy, particularly

Figure 19:1 Austro-Hungarian soldiers on the Ortles front. (© author)

during the winter of 1916–17, which is on record as having had the heaviest snow-falls of the twentieth century (ibid.: 130). On the morning of 13 December 1916, for example, a massive avalanche hit the Austrian village of Gran Poz on the Marmolada, causing some 300 deaths (Andreoletti and Viazzi 1977: 220–1).

The conditions in which soldiers had to survive can be compared with those faced by modern-day mountaineering expeditions to the Himalayas or the polar regions, with but one significant (and technological) difference: the soldiers of the Great War were not supplied with the high-tech materials and equipment available today. There was no nylon or Gore-Tex, and no lightweight resistant alloys. At this time, soldiers were still using ropes made of hemp that went stiff in the cold, woollen sweaters that absorbed water like a sponge, and heavy iron crampons. In other words, the harsh landscapes of the Italian front highlighted the fact that while twentieth-century technologies for destroying human life had become increasingly sophisticated, those for saving it were literally and figuratively still in the Iron Age.

Nevertheless, both armies were studying avant-garde techniques and technologies that were to leave their mark in both sports (mountaineering and skiing) and cable transport in the years to come. The experience of the most famous mountaineers and alpine guides of the time was made available to the armies, and special mountaineering courses were organized for the alpine troops, such as the Italian *Alpini* and the Austrian *Kaiserschützen* (GA 1999). The Austrians in particular created specialized divisions composed exclusively of soldiers with expertise in mountains and mountaineering: the *Hochgebirgskompagnien* (high altitude companies) and the *Bergführerkompagnien* (companies of Alpine guides) (ibid.: 22–39).

Handbooks were published for distribution to the divisions, with explanations of mountaineering techniques on rock and ice, how to survive in the cold, and what to do in case of avalanches. These were the very first technical manuals in the history of modern mountaineering (ibid.: 26). Ironically, high-altitude war made a major contribution to both the development and spread of mountaineering and skiing skills as (post-war) leisure activities, and also introduced large numbers of people to the mountains, many of whom returned after the war for recreation and touring. The distinctive nature of the war in this region led to an equally distinctive relationship between conflict and tourism, quite different in many ways from that which developed along the old Western Front, first between 1919 and 1939 (Lloyd 1998), and again from the 1960s to the present (Saunders 2001: 45–6; Walter 1993).

The following section briefly looks at the ways in which the two armies dealt with the problems of war on the glaciers, focusing on three practical areas: clothing and equipment, transport and shelter.

Clothing and equipment

In addition to their standard uniforms, both the Italian and Austro-Hungarian armies needed to study, investigate and produce special clothing for troops fighting at high altitudes. In particular, they needed to find solutions to two primary needs: protection from low temperatures, and camouflage in places with abundant snow and glaciers where green, dark-coloured uniforms would make the soldiers stand out rather than conceal them.

Italian soldiers were usually issued with only a short cloak, but to combat the rigours of mountain fighting the Italian army provided padded woollen overcoats lined with fur – though, due to a lack of raw material, only for those on special duties, such as sentries – thick woollen socks instead of elasticized leggings, woollen gloves and woollen balaclavas (Viotti 1985: 87–97; NDO n.d.). Moreover, soldiers on sentry duty in high altitude forward positions were supplied with felt overshoes with wooden soles to prevent frostbitten feet. The Austrian version was made of straw.

Many civil associations, mainly women's groups, would send specially made woollen garments to the soldiers at the front: long thick socks, sweaters, waistcoats, balaclavas and warm waist belts (LPINS 1915). The Austrians provided their mountain troops with avant-garde style windproof jackets, and mittens, effective against frostbite (IRS 1995: 36–44). Both armies supplied their mountain troops with different types of non-glare sunglasses for protection against the blindingly reflective snow. Many officers, who had been mountaineers before they enlisted, used their own gear (such as boots) or arranged for them to be purchased in sports shops in the large cities. White camouflage suits, complete with hood and gaiters and worn over the uniform, were created for the troops who were to fight on the glaciers (ibid.: 17–23) (Figure 19:2). The Austrians often made use of white cloaks. The soldiers' accessories

Figure 19:2
Italian skiers with white camouflage suits on the Adamello front. (© author)

283

and matériel – from helmets to cartridge-boxes – were also often painted white, as were skis and even artillery in some cases.

Landscape and climate therefore had a profound effect on the relationships between men and the distinctive material culture of war with which they interacted, blending humans, skis and cannon equally into snowfields and glaciers. The specialized needs of soldiers fighting in such locations also produced a distinctive set of social relationships in the civilian domestic production of the special clothing and its movement to the front-line.

Transport

At the start of the conflict, both the Italians and the Austrians arranged for their high altitude troops to be supplied exclusively by shifts of men (old soldiers or prisoners of war) if not mules. But the commanders soon realized that the service was insufficient: it required too many men and, above all in winter – which saw bad weather, fog and avalanches – it was costing too many lives. Supply parties could not operate in adverse weather, and those divisions located at high altitude were often left for lengthy periods with no supplies.

Thus began the construction of mechanized cableways, a system used until then only in quarries and mines. Once again, a specialized technology was given a new role and underwent significant development in the process. It started with single-line cableways hauled by hand for supplying small military positions, but quickly developed into large-scale systems extending for several kilometres, climbing hundreds of metres, featuring twin cables (one for pulling, one for carrying the weight), and activated by an internal combustion engine or an electric motor (Figure 19:3). The technology used today for cable cars throughout the Alps was perfected during the First World War.

In the spring of 1917, the Austrians had 125 cableways operating in the South Tyrol region alone (excluding the Ortles region), with an average daily capacity of 1200/1400 tons of war matériél. It has been calculated that, between 1915 and 1918, the Austrians constructed 1,753 km of cableway on the Italian front (Benvenuti 1980: 405–11).

Animals were also used for transport across the glaciers. On the Adamello glacier in particular, the Italians used sledges hauled by dogs. The service began in the summer of 1916, and on the Adamello over 200 dogs were at work between 1917 and 1918. Each sledge could carry up to 150 kg and was pulled by three dogs, guided by a leader (Figure 19:4). The dog-runs went from the base at Passo Garibaldi to Passo della Lobbia, continuing through winter, even during blizzards (Viazzi 1981: 246–7). Donkeys were also used on the Adamello in the tunnel (see below) (ibid.: 238–41).

The soldiers themselves used skis, snowshoes and crampons on snow and ice. The use of skis underwent considerable development during the war, especially by the Italians who organized whole divisions (battalions) of skiers, who were deployed in all kinds of manoeuvres, particularly on the Adamello glacier (IRS 1995; Viazzi 1981). The Austrians on the other hand produced an unusual form of binding known as

Figure 19:3
An Austro-Hungarian
cableway station
(Dolomites). (© author)

Figure 19:4 Italian sledges hauled by dogs on Adamello glacier. (© author)

Bilgeri, for its inventor; it was the forerunner of modern bindings for ski-touring: it was hinged on the point, leaving the heel free, thus enabling soldiers to kneel down to shoot without having to remove their skis. Sealskins were also used, and a range of crampons for ice was invented (IRS 1995).

As with clothing, the relationships between soldiers and the material culture of transport were also reconfigured by the distinctive conditions imposed on soldiers by fighting at altitude – the repercussions of which extended far beyond the war itself. Not only were relationships between humans and animals redefined by war, but the shape of the multimillion dollar post-war skiing/tourism phenomenon – so important to the Italian economy – was also created at this time.

Shelters and tunnels

A full description of the types of high altitude habitation used during the war is beyond the scope of this chapter. Suffice it to say that prefabricated dwellings were used by both Italians and Austrians, the majority of which had wooden walls, with the exterior wall and roof being covered in tar, while insulation against cold and damp took the form of straw, wood shavings or fibreglass. In some cases, for larger buildings, the Italians erected sturdy stone structures.

On the glaciers themselves, huts would often be erected inside crevasses to better protect men and matériel from the cold, storms and enemy fire. Moreover, a glacier's internal temperature is constant, making such locations far more comfortable for human occupation. Making the most of this micro-climatic condition, Austrian soldiers constructed one of the most remarkable and unique projects of the entire war in the Marmolada glacier: the so-called 'City of Ice' (Bartoli *et al.* 1993; Andreoletti and Viazzi 1977: 157–62).

In the spring of 1917, Lieutenant Leo Handl, an engineer and commander of a platoon of Austrian alpine guides, thought of exploiting the crevasses within the Marmolada glacier, linking them up and hewing out artificial caverns in the glacier itself, thereby constructing shelters for men and matériel, and tunnels to connect the rear positions to the front lines. There were dormitories, canteens, storerooms and even a huge cave where Roman Catholic mass was celebrated – an icy counterpart to the similarly subterranean caves and altars carved from the chalk along the Western Front in France (e.g. AIPS 1996). The tunnels were excavated manually, with the use of pneumatic drills, and even using explosives. Over twelve kilometres of tunnels were excavated beneath the glacier in this way, allowing soldiers to be moved off the glacier's exposed surface in the autumn of 1916. For a short time, the tunnels were lit by electric light bulbs powered by a generating station. As with the trenches along the Western Front, the glacial tunnels and crevasses were given names, and wooden signposts were erected. There were thirty caverns in all, some as deep as 50 metres below the surface of the glacier.

For their part, in the summer of 1917, the Italians were responsible for an impressive tunnel on the Adamello glacier between Passo Garibaldi and Passo della Lobbia Alta: it was 5,200 metres long, two metres high, two and a half metres in width, and lit by 120 electric light bulbs powered by two generators. It had a total of 80 air vents, one every 60/70 metres, as well as bridges used to cross 25 crevasses. The tunnel was between 4 and 5 metres below the glacier's surface, and was used for the passage of supplies carried on sledges drawn by dogs and donkeys (Viazzi 1981: 249–50). Shorter tunnels were also excavated in the Ortles–Cevedale group, for the purpose of approaching objectives to be attacked under cover (Bertarelli 1923).

Glacier archaeology

The unusual climatic and environmental conditions on the glaciers have led to excellent preservation of the material culture of the war – especially (and importantly) in the case of otherwise perishable items made of wood, leather and fabric. Snowfall in the years following the war covered objects and structures with several metres of snow, successively transformed into ice. Immediately after the war, the natural downhill movement of the glaciers meant that much material (including human remains) came to the surface in the vicinity of the glacier's outlets. However, over recent years, with the rise in summer temperatures, this phenomenon has assumed sizeable proportions. Each summer, hundreds of different calibre artillery bullets appear, forcing the authorities to carry out regular cleaning-up operations to protect mountaineers, and, in the odd extreme case, even declare glaciers off-limits (Marseiler *et al.* 1998). In this respect, the high-altitude Great War battle-zones of northeast Italy are of a piece with the contested landscapes of France and Belgium, where munitions also rise to the surface on an annual basis, and access can be temporarily or permanently restricted (Saunders 2001).

In addition to human remains, there exist an astonishingly wide variety of objects that are preserved by the glacial conditions of this region – bullets and helmets, newspapers, books, letters, painted wooden plaques, skis, sledges, uniforms and headgear, and entire huts. Even complete artillery pieces emerge from the ice after 85 years, such as the remarkable case of the Austrian Skoda 105 howitzer freed from the ice below the Presanella, virtually intact and complete with its stand, protective camouflage roofing, store of ammunition and the sledge which transported it there (Balbi 2002; Ceruti 2002) (Figure 19:5). The quantity, diversity and often superb preservation of these items highlight the urgency of safeguarding the finds, and preventing collectors from removing them before they can be documented. It also raises the issue – frequently encountered in more traditional kinds of archaeology – of whether to leave objects in situ (despite the further deterioration they will inevitably suffer) – or remove them to a museum (equipped with the expensive technology of climate-controlled display cases for the more fragile items). Sometimes, as with the Presanella cannon, the latter option has been adopted, though this item is awaiting restoration and a suitable location for display.

As a scientific archaeology of the First World War emerges, and as the war's material culture is being recognized and valued, it is increasingly important that such objects be studied, identified and photographed in situ. One example of the connections between the archaeology and anthropology of such well-preserved objects

Figure 19:5 The Austrian Skoda 105 howitzer that emerged from Presanella glacier in summer 2001. (© author)

is the 'Kaiserschütze beret' found on the Presena glacier, intact with its feather and metal badges (Figure 19:6). One badge was not an industrial piece but handmade by the soldier from a section of thin corrugated iron and a bullet, and which bore the engraved name 'Presena'. This a remarkable example of material culture from the Great War (Offelli 2001: 166), and one which is firmly located in the corpus of objects known as trench art (Fabi 1998; Saunders 2003). It is particularly valuable as an artefact which ties together several important and crosscutting themes in the study of the material culture of war: military identification, recycled material, the association of an individual with a named place in the battlefield landscape, and the unique preservative conditions of high altitude landscapes. Few other handmade badges have been found in other front-line locations by excavators, indicating that, though this practice was geographically widespread, it was restricted to relatively few individuals (Todero 2003: 36–7).

The archaeology of the First World War – and of the Italian Front in particular – has only recently been seen as a worthwhile endeavour. As the rich potential of the war's material culture to throw new light on the individual's experience of conflict becomes evident, there is increasing professional and public interest in developing archaeological and anthropological approaches to a conflict hitherto known mainly from the perspective of military history. This brief overview of the Italian Front

Figure 19:6 Austro-Hungarian beret found on Presena glacier with a hand-made badge (far right). (© and courtesy Siro Offelli (Offelli 2001))

illustrates the potential for future research and investigation, across a range of issues as broad and distinctive as are the high-altitude battle-zone landscapes themselves.

Acknowledgements

I am grateful to the Museo della Guerra Bianca in Adamello, Temù (BS), and in particular to John Ceruti, for providing some of the photographs, and to my friends and colleagues of the Società Storica per la Guerra Bianca for suggestions.

References

AGG (1999) 'L'Archéologie et la Grande Guerre'. *14/18 Aujourd'hui, Today, Heute*. 2. (Revue Annuelle D'Histoire. Noêsis.)
AIPS (1996) *Les Carrières de Confrécourt: Soissonais 14–18*. Association pour l'inventaire et la préservation des sites. Vic-sur-Aisne: Imprimerie Lepigeon.
Andreoletti, A. and L. Viazzi. (1977) *Con gli alpini sulla Marmolada 1915–1917*. Milan: Mursia.
Balbi, M. (2002) 'Il cannone della Val Nardis: un esempio di integrazione fra osservazioni sul terreno e fonti scritte'. *Aquile in guerra*, 10: 100–4.
Bartoli, M., M. Fornaro and G. Rotasso (1993) *La città di ghiaccio : Guida agli itinerari e al museo della guerra 1915–1918 in Marmolada*. Trento: Publilux.
Benvenuti, S. (ed.) (1980) *La Prima Guerra Mondiale e il Trentino*. Rovereto: Comprensorio della Vallagarina.

Bertarelli, G. (1923) 'Le gallerie di guerra nei ghiacciai dell'Ortler'. *Le vie d'Italia*, 7: 760–74.

Ceruti, J. (2002) 'Importante ritrovamento storico alle pendici della Presanella'. *Aquile in guerra*, 10:105–7.

Editorial (1996) *Journal of Material Culture* 1 (1): 5–14.

Fabi, L. (ed.) (1998) *1918, la Guerra Nella Testa: Arte popolare, esperienze, memoria nel primo conflitto mondiale*. (Catalogue for exhibition held at Musei Provinciali di Gorizia, and Museo della Grande Guerra, Borgo Castello, Nov. 1998 to Feb. 1999.) Trieste: LINT Editoriale.

Falls, C. (1966) *The Battle of Caporetto*. Philadelphia: Lippincott.

GA (1999) 'Le guide alpine nella Grande Guerra'. *Aquile in guerra*, 7.

IRS (1995) 'I reparti sciatori 1915–1918'. *Aquile in guerra* 3.

LPINS (1915) *Lavoriamo per i nostri soldati*. Milano: Comitato centrale d'assistenza per la guerra.

Lloyd, D.W. (1998) *Battlefield Tourism: Pilgrimage and the Commemoration of the Great War in Britain, Australia and Canada, 1919–1939*. Oxford: Berg.

MacKay, F. (2001) *Battleground Europe: Asiago*. Barnsley: Pen & Sword.

—— (2002) *Battleground Europe: Touring the Italian Front 1917–1919*. Barnsley: Pen & Sword.

Marseiler, S., U. Bernhart and F.J. Haller (1998) *Memorie nel ghiaccio*. Bolzano: Athesia.

Martinelli, V. (1972) *Adamello ieri e oggi*. Brescia: Vannini.

—— (1980) *Corno di Cavento*. Brescia: Il Moretto.

NDO (n.d.) *Nomenclatore degli oggetti di corredo costituenti la serie vestiario invernale in distribuzione ai soldati delle varie armi e corpi*. Torino: Regio Esercito Italiano.

Offelli, S. (2001) *Le armi e gli equipaggiamenti dell'Esercito Austro Ungarico dal 1914 al 1918: Uniformi, distintivi, buffetterie*, vol. I. Valdagno: Rossato.

Price, J. (2004) 'The Ocean Villas project: archaeology in the service of European remembrance'. In N.J. Saunders (ed.), *Matters of Conflict: Material Culture, Memory and the First World War*, pp. 179–91. Abingdon: Routledge.

Saunders, N.J. (2001) 'Matter and memory in the landscapes of conflict: The Western Front 1914–1999'. In B. Bender and M. Winer (eds), *Contested Landscapes: Movement, Exile and Place*, pp. 37–53. Oxford: Berg.

—— (2002) 'Excavating memories: archaeology and the Great War, 1914–2001'. *Antiquity* 76 (1): 101–8

—— (2003) *Trench Art: Materialities and Memories of War*. Oxford: Berg.

—— (2004) 'Material culture and conflict: the Great War, 1914–2003'. In N.J. Saunders (ed.), *Matters of Conflict: Material Culture, Memory and the First World War*, pp. 5–25. Abingdon: Routledge.

Schindler, J.R. (2001) *Isonzo: The Forgotten Sacrifice of the Great War*. Westport, CT: Praeger.

Schofield, J., W.G. Johnson and C. Beck (eds) (2002) *Matériel Culture: The Archaeology of Twentieth Century Conflict*. London: Routledge.

Todero, R. (2003) *Kappenabzeichen*. Udine: Gaspari.

Viazzi, L. (1976) *Guerra sulle vette*. Milan: Mursia.

—— (1981) *I diavoli dell'Adamello*. Milan: Mursia.

Viotti, A. (1985) *L'uniforme grigio-verde (1909–1918)*. Rome: Ufficio Storico Stato Maggiore Esercito.

Von Lichem, H. (1983) *Der einsame krieg*. Bolzano: Athesia.

—— (1995) *La guerra in montagna 1915–1918*. Bolzano: Athesia.

Walter, T. (1993) 'War grave pilgrimage'. In I. Reader and T. Walter (eds), *Pilgrimage in Popular Culture*, pp. 63–91. Houndsmills: Macmillan.

Wilks, J.E. (1998) *The British Army in Italy 1917–1918*. Barnsley: Pen & Sword.

20

TRAINING FOR TRENCH WARFARE

The archaeological evidence from Salisbury Plain

Graham Brown and David Field

Introduction

After almost one hundred years, as the memories of those individuals who fought in the major conflagration of the First World War fade, film and documentary evidence remain to inform our views of trench warfare (see Chapter 12). The sites of these battles have invariably been levelled, cultivated and built upon – and evidence of and from them is seen mainly in museums where artefacts and uniforms are used to tell the story. For those in the United Kingdom, these places are on foreign soil and do not provide the kind of permanent landscape reminder that, for example, pillboxes or airfields do for the Second World War. Bereft of such sites, we have become accustomed to view such encounters as events that occurred elsewhere and, until recently, archaeology appears to have contributed little to their understanding (see Schofield 2004; Saunders 2002).

In recent years, however, there has been a tremendous increase in interest in the field evidence of battlefields of the First World War, which have become part of an integrated tourist circuit – the 'Western Front Experience' (Saunders 2001: 45). Many thousands of people, including school parties from England, go to gain first-hand knowledge of the warfare of those early years of the twentieth century. Places such as Beaumont Hamel and Vimy Ridge in France attract considerable numbers of visitors, while the areas around Verdun and Ypres in Belgium are widely visited (Coombs 1976: 144–56, 26–64). The earthwork remains of many of these battlefields, however, survive only in isolated pockets or in woodland, or as soil marks in the surrounding arable fields (Chippindale 1997: 506).

Earthworks of twentieth-century warfare, however, are not exclusive to the Western Front and the other foreign theatres of war, for in Britain they can also be found across large tracts of the military estates and other areas of the country where

291

they remain as testimony to how soldiers were trained in the art of warfare. Trench systems, often naturally silted up, or partially or completely backfilled, are increasingly being identified across the countryside. Some are small, disjointed examples, designed to provide soldiers with the merest familiarity with trench life, while others form more extensive, coherent systems that allow greater familiarization of tactics.

The extent of such systems is particularly striking on the Salisbury Plain Training Area, the largest military estate in the United Kingdom, where many have been preserved from cultivation, and where their comprehensive nature can be observed and appreciated. Notice of this was first made as part of a widespread investigation of extant archaeology on the military ranges when a number of systems were transcribed from aerial photographs (McOmish *et al.* 2002: 137–48). More recently, analytical surveys, interpretation and analysis of sites on the ground have enabled these systems to be placed within their landscape setting as well as their cultural context.

The earthworks

The northern part of Salisbury Plain in Wiltshire has been used as a military training area since the end of the nineteenth century (ibid.: 4) The extensive tracts of undulating downland were initially considered particularly suitable for large-scale cavalry manoeuvres, and pressure on ranges elsewhere (particularly at Okehampton on Dartmoor) meant that land for infantry and artillery training was required (see James 1987). The War Office took advantage of low land prices during the agricultural depression in the late nineteenth century and, with effect from 1897, began the process of buying up large estates on Salisbury Plain. As a result the traces of over one hundred years' of military activity have been engraved on the land: early small-arms and anti-tank ranges, observation posts and, rather bizarrely, impact areas all survive as earthworks to this day.

The most prolific military earthworks are the trench systems, many, but by no means all of which, dating back to the First World War. Some appear quite sophisticated, and, with many covering several hectares, must have provided a stage for large-scale military manoeuvres. Evidence of twentieth-century warfare is pervasive across the whole of the training area and, during a time of greater sophistication and rapidly changing tactics, it provides a fitting backdrop to research into the archaeology of modern warfare.

Many trench systems survive as extant earthworks, while others are revealed as levelled features on aerial photographs. Some are quite fragmentary and possibly reflect their temporary nature, rapid construction or the effect of shelling. Others, particularly those on Beacon Hill (which lies between the garrison towns of Bulford and Tidworth) and the area to the north of Tilshead, are well preserved, and are amongst the best examples of early-twentieth-century trenches seen anywhere in the United Kingdom.

By 1914, a typical military trench system comprised three main elements: a front line, a reserve line and a series of communication trenches connecting the two. In most cases, the front and reserve lines followed a castellated plan in order to give maximum protection against enfilade fire or shell-bursts, and this also allowed the projecting 'bastions' that formed the firing bays to give covering fire to other parts of the trench. Machine guns positioned at strategic points provided additional oblique fire, while saps were dug forward into 'no-man's-land' and allowed night raids, or acted as listening and observation posts. Along the zigzag communication trenches, shelter bays that fulfilled a number of functions – command posts, shelters or first aid posts – were constructed.

Trench systems vary enormously in area from perhaps as little as 0.25 ha up to 26 ha, and archaeological fieldwork shows that great care was taken in locating them within the landscape. Where situated on high ground, trenches were invariably placed just below the crest so that soldiers within them would not be sky-lined from below. A covered approach utilized hedgerows and other natural features so that troops could move to and occupy the reserve trench unobserved. Great ingenuity was used in adapting pre-existing features in the landscape to best advantage, not only in the location of systems, but also in the construction of trenches. On Chapperton Down, for example, a long communication trench was constructed on a slope along the line of an extant prehistoric 'Celtic field' lynchet, which would have provided additional cover and protection. Similarly, on Perham Down, some of the communication trenches extend from a hedgerow and tree shelter-belt on the low ground.

Although it is difficult to precisely date any particular system from the earthworks alone, aerial photographs and, on occasions, map evidence can be used to give a *terminus anti-quem*. For example, at least four trench systems are recorded on a military overlay of an Ordnance Survey map of the area to the north of Chitterne, and, although it is unclear when the overlay was actually made, the base map itself is dated to 1916 (Chitterne (North) 1:20,000 map GSGS 2748). On this map, a large trench system located to the south of Imber appears to have been abandoned and reused as a target since the artillery observation posts are positioned to the north and south of the system with their field of view directly towards the trenches (Figure 20:1).

The fieldwork

All systems visible on aerial photographs were plotted (McOmish *et al.* 2002) and checked on the ground during a programme of fieldwork carried out by the authors in order to ascertain the extent and condition of the features. Two of these have been analytically surveyed at large scale in order to attempt to understand their morphology and demonstrate how they fit into an already complex archaeological landscape.

The first survey was of a particularly well-preserved system in an area of scrub on Beacon Hill, a prominent ridge on the edge of the military estate and overlooking Bulford Rifle Ranges (Figure 20:2). The system is in fact part of a network of trenches along the summit of the hill and was probably one of the main trench training areas for the troops billeted in the vicinity of Tidworth and Bulford. Today, the area is rich in flora, contains many stands of juniper trees and is part of a Site of Special Scientific Interest (SSSI). It was during a programme of scrub management that the system was fully revealed.

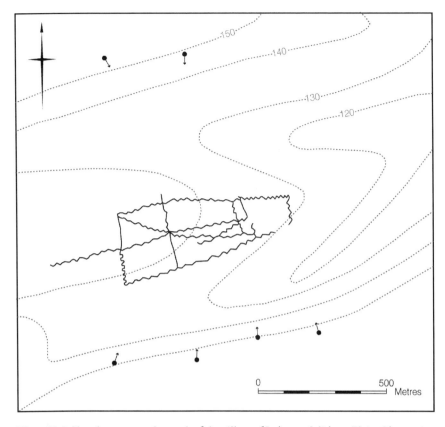

Figure 20:1 Trench system to the south of the village of Imber on Salisbury Plain. Observation posts are shown as black circles with arrows. (© authors, adapted from McOmish *et al*. 2002, Figure 6:6, with information from the Artillery Training map of 1916)

The system, covering some 7 ha and extending for 350 m, comprises two lines of trenches. It is situated on the southern slopes of Beacon Hill with the firing line on the lip of the summit, and a support trench 60 m further down-slope to its rear, the theory being that it should be difficult to shell positions on the rear slopes of hills (T. Crawford 1999: 33). While natural silting has occurred, both trenches survive to a depth of up to 1.5 m. The firing line is crenellated, with sides of 8 m, with each traverse encapsulating a small 'island', enabling troops to pass along the line without affecting those in their firing positions.

The cutting itself is 2 m wide, but the crenellations, islands and spoil heaps give considerable breadth to the trench amounting to some 12 m in all. These measurements partly reflect the result of collapse and the original proud, unweathered profile may have been rather different. Preservation is excellent in places, and one of

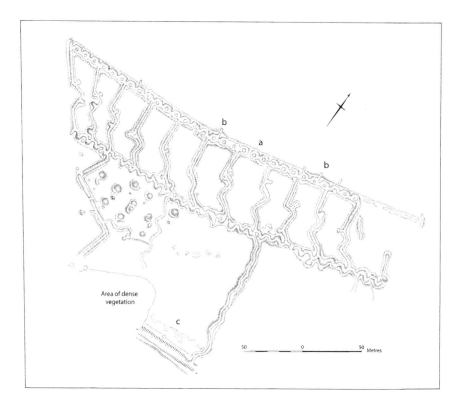

Figure 20:2 Survey of earthworks of a trench system on Beacon Hill. (© authors)

the crenellations ('a' in Figure 20:2) has a slight depression on the front edge that may have formed a 'rest' for a rifle. Slight linear depressions ('b' in Figure 20:2) projecting from the front edge of the firing line indicate the position of saps, and at the western limit a short slightly curving bay linked to a communication trench is perhaps an ideal location for a machine-gun emplacement. The eastern end of the front line appears unfinished, and is in a similar state on a 1920s' aerial photograph (National Monuments Record No: SU 2145/1) which indicates that it was never completed. In contrast, the support line is a simple zigzag trench. Here there are no 'islands', only a sinuous length of trench that would have enabled troops to pass relatively quickly along to a communication trench.

Linking the firing line and support trench are eleven communication trenches spaced at 25 m intervals. As with the support line, these are cut in a zigzag arrangement, but the final 20 m length leading to the firing line departs from this pattern and is straight, allowing a clear line of fire from the angle in the trench should the firing line be over-run and occupied by the enemy. Situated along the communication trenches are one or two, in one case three, T-shaped shelter bays, which could be used either for command and control or as small shelters or first-aid posts. To the rear of the support line are three longer communication trenches, which lead to a Bronze Age linear ditch, a hollowed depression some 10 m wide by about 1 m deep with a bank to the rear that led towards the valley floor below. The latter, with its bordering tree-line, provided additional cover which was fully incorporated into the trench system and may have been used as an additional reserve position.

Situated a few metres to the north of the Bronze Age ditch is a line of now silted and very shallow crenellated trenches ('c' in Figure 20:2) that may reflect an earlier phase of trench digging partially obscured by the construction of the main complex. In addition, there are a series of circular depressions and smaller, linear trenches immediately to the south of the support line. Some of these are more recent two-man battle trenches, though the function of others is less clear. Some were perhaps small dugouts, although only one appears to be linked to the trench system.

The second example is of a small section of a trench system located within the Bulford Rifle Range itself, which was initially surveyed to illustrate the relative chronology of the earthworks that can be observed, not only here, but on a number of trench systems across the plain (Figure 20:3). It is only a small part of a much more extensive system, most of which is at present covered in impenetrable scrub. The trench overlies a series of earlier, prehistoric landscape features, each of which is important in its own right, and which formed part of the terrain of the battle practice; then, in turn, the trench system was overlain by the earthworks of a later rifle range.

The earliest feature is part of a prehistoric 'Celtic field' system (rectilinear scarps, or lynchets) blanketing this part of the downs and probably dating to about 1500 BC, i.e. the middle Bronze Age ('a' in Figure 20:3). Overlying and cutting through this is a linear ditch of a type usually dated to some 500 years later, about 1000 BC, i.e. the later Bronze Age ('b' in Figure 20:3). As with the example on Beacon Hill, this is a massive feature, some 10 m wide and about 1 m deep, with a bank on either side that extends towards the northwest from the southernmost firing point where it has been levelled. The familiar First World War crenellated trench system ('c' in Figure 20:3) can be seen, almost centrally, cutting into the field system, with a front line comprising six firing bays, without, in this case, an 'island' to the rear. Two communication trenches are present: the northern example is of regular layout, while the other utilizes part of the Bronze Age ditch as cover. The final piece of the chronological jigsaw is provided by two of the rifle range firing points, each 100 m in length and 120 m apart ('d' in Figure 20:3); both overlie the linear ditch and field system.

Aerial photographs depict the extent and complexity of some trench systems that have long been abandoned and can now only be seen as crop marks. They also show how they were used in the contemporary landscape. On Orcheston Down, for example, a site at Shrewton Folly comprises a complex system of trenches of at least two phases (McOmish et al. 2002: 141). The most coherent part of this group consists of three lines of trenches, a firing line, support trench and reserve line, extending for about 1 km. Linking the front and support lines are 25 communication trenches, with a further ten that link reserve and support trenches. About 120 m in front of the firing

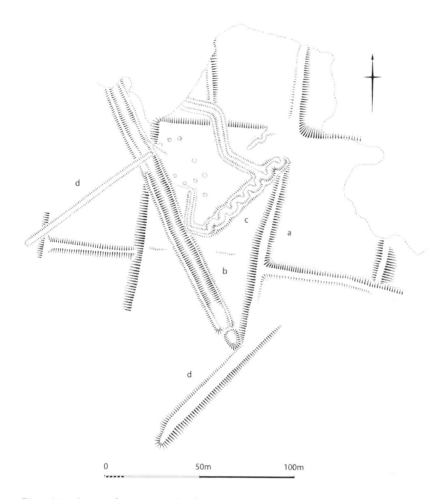

Figure 20:3 Survey of the earthworks of a trench system on Bulford Rifle Range. (© authors)

line is another continuous trench with eight smaller trenches (probably saps) leading from it. This latter trench was possibly constructed as a result of troops advancing from their initial front line and establishing a more advanced position. To the southwest of this coherent trench system is a more amorphous and disjointed scheme, which although incorporated, was probably initially unrelated to the larger system, but nevertheless provided practice in trench digging.

The largest concentration of trenches (which can now only be seen on aerial photographs, for example NMR: ALK 7418/74) is on Perham Down, which lies to the south of Tidworth. Here, they form a complex system that overlies an extensive area of prehistoric 'Celtic fields', and these in turn have influenced the layout. Two opposing firing lines were established up to 200 m apart. Each, along with their attendant support and communication trenches, extends for some 700 m over the undulating downs. As with the other systems, the firing lines are crenellated while the remainder are zigzag or sinuous. On both sides, communication trenches lead away from the support trench for several hundred metres towards a hedgerow, from where woodland, prehistoric earthworks and tracks provided shelter and covered 'entry points' to and from the system.

Training was also given in other aspects of warfare. Documentary references indicate that by 1916, 'trenching and mining of all kinds are practiced here' (Guy 1981: 1–2), and mine craters, some fortified, are depicted on the key of the 1916 Ordnance Survey map mentioned above. In places, deep craters can be observed across the downs, which may be the result of mining or practice in the use of explosives. In general, they are circular and measure about 10 m diameter and up to 2 m deep with no spoil around the perimeter. Some trench systems appear to have been shelled, for example the system at Chapperton Down is covered with shell holes, although it is not clear whether they are contemporary with trench use. Adjacent to a system of trenches in the southern limit of the ranges near the Iron Age hillfort of Yarnbury are hundreds of small craters, evidently the result of the Royal Flying Corps practice of dropping hand-held bombs or grenades from aircraft (O. Crawford 1924: 34).

Conclusions

The first use of military trenches on Salisbury Plain was recorded in 1902, when 'three 4 foot deep S-shaped Boer trenches, filled with standing dummies, were fired at both by guns and howitzers with fair effect' (Anon 1902: 23). This type of trench was used by the Boers during the South African Wars of the late nineteenth century, and was being investigated by the British army (zigzag trenches were certainly being dug on Okehampton, Dartmoor, by 1906; S. Probert, English Heritage, pers. comm.). However, having cleared the plain of fencing, and filled in rabbit holes and other obstructions in order to allow cavalry free rein, there was evidently reluctance to allow extensive trench digging, and consequently little work of this nature was carried out until 1914 (Crawford 1999: 11).

Military manuals indicate that British military thought on the use of trenches changed radically between 1877 and 1908 (compare military engineering manuals: School of Military Engineering, Chatham 1877, and General Staff, War Office 1908), and by the latter date the use of comprehensive trench systems were being widely advocated. Nevertheless, prior to the First World War, training in trench warfare was all but non-existent. The response to the commencement of hostilities in 1914 resulted in a piecemeal attempt at providing some idea of the processes, with trenches being dug wherever possible.

Evidence of practice trenches is not just confined to Salisbury Plain, but is widespread across many of the military estates in England: Penally, Pembrokeshire (Thomas 1997: 5–6; Brown 2004), Otterburn, Northumberland (Charlton and Day 1977: 137; Anon 1978: 155), Dartmoor (S. Probert, English Heritage, pers comm.) and Cannock Chase, Staffordshire (Welch 1997). Some of these date to the early twentieth century, although there are examples of earlier fortifications at Aldershot and Crowthorne Wood, Berkshire (English 2004; Smith 1995). In Crowthorne Wood, the Royal Commission on the Historical Monuments of England (RCHME) surveyed a complex of redoubts dating to the late eighteenth century as well as three sinuous trench systems that appear to date to the late nineteenth century (Smith 1995).

A series of military field manuals prepared between 1908 and 1917 established procedures in how to lay out and construct trench systems using a trace or template in order that symmetry and accuracy is maintained (General Staff, War Office 1908; Solano 1915; Anon. 1917, 1920). A perennial problem with ditch digging in gangs, as observed in many prehistoric monuments, is the variable nature of the result, and here it was essential that the overall plan was adhered to accurately in the field. Responsibility for layout initially rested with the Royal Engineers, and the purpose of the Cannock Chase model identified by the Royal Commission on the Historical Monuments of England (Welch 1997) was presumably to instruct their officers in trench layout.

Trench systems can be surprisingly uniform. On Lincoln Common, a crenellated front line extending for some 200 m can be traced as very shallow earthworks. The proportions of the crenellations are almost identical to a similar range of trenches on Swine Moor, Yorkshire (T. Pearson, English Heritage, pers. comm.). Once surveyed and marked out on the ground by the Royal Engineers, the soldiers are likely to have carried out the digging, and there are countless references to the practice of digging on Salisbury Plain (e.g. T. Crawford 1999: 37, 139).

The lack of emphasis hitherto placed on trench systems in the United Kingdom by both historians and archaeologists is probably a result of the perception of British wars being fought on foreign soil. Trench warfare is considered to be something that happened somewhere else. However, although forgotten, preparation for foreign wars has left its mark indelibly on the British landscape, with remnants of trench systems, redoubts and other features dating from the nineteenth century still visible.

Among these remains, trenches attributable to the First World War, either as fragments of front line or complete complexes, are more widely present than formerly imagined on the commons and open spaces across Britain. Some of the best preserved are those on the military training areas, and, when considered in detail, trenches located on, for example, Beacon Hill, and elsewhere on the Salisbury Plain Military Training Area, emphasise that by 1916 the training of soldiers in trench warfare was considered of the utmost importance. They help to indicate the variety of training that was given for designing and laying out the trenches, for planning tactics, and for those who would be engaged in the day-to-day activities of trench warfare.

Acknowledgements

We would like to offer out thanks to the military estate for allowing free access to the trenches on the Salisbury Plain Training Area over a number of years, and, in particular, to Jane Hallet, Ian Barnes and more recently Richard Osgood, who have all provided help and support, and to a number of successive Commandants who have all been extremely supportive. The penned illustrations are the work of Deborah

Cunliffe. Our thanks are also extended to the staff of the library at the Royal Engineers Museum, Chatham.

References

Anon. (1902) 'Annual report of the School of Gunnery: horse and field artillery at home'. Unpublished mss held at the Badley Library, Royal School of Artillery.

Anon. (1917) 'Instructions for construction of trenches and repairs of trenches'. SME Fortifications Circular, No 35, Chatham: Royal Engineers Corps Library 940.3 623.2/3.

Anon. (1920) *Military Engineering*, Vol. II. London: HMSO.

Anon. (1978) 'Otterburn'. *Current Archaeology* 64: 152–5.

Brown, M. (2004) 'A mirror of the apocalypse: Great War training trenches'. *Sanctuary* 33: 54–7.

Charlton, D.B. and J.C. Day (1977) 'An archaeological survey of the Ministry of Defence training area, Otterburn, Northumberland'. Unpublished manuscript (Copy in National Monuments Record Library, Swindon).

Chippindale, C. (1997) 'Editorial'. *Antiquity* 71 (273): 505–12.

Coombs, R.E.B. (1976) *Before Endeavours Fade: A Guide to the Battlefields of the First World War*, 6th edn. London: Battle of Britain Prints.

Crawford, O.G.S. (1924) *Air Survey and Archaeology*. Ordnance Survey Professional Papers, New Series, 7. Southampton: HMSO.

Crawford, T.S. (1999) *Wiltshire and the Great War*. Reading: DPF Publishing

English, J. (2004) 'Two late nineteenth-century military earthworks on Ash Ranges, nr Aldershot, Surrey'. *Landscape History* 25: 87–93.

General Staff, War Office (1908) *Military Engineering pt 1: Field Defences*. London: HMSO.

Guy, R. (1981) 'A history of Gunnery Wing, Royal School of Artillery 1929–1980'. Unpublished manuscript. Larkhill: Badley Library, Royal School of Artillery.

James, N.D.G. (1987) *Plain Soldiering: A History of the Armed Forces on Salisbury Plain*. Salisbury: Hobnob Press.

McOmish, D., D. Field and G. Brown (2002) *The Field Archaeology of Salisbury Plain Training Area*. Swindon: English Heritage.

Saunders, N. J. (2001) 'Matter and memory in the landscapes of conflict: the Western Front 1914–1999'. In B. Bender and M. Winer (eds) *Contested Landscapes Movement, Exile and Place*, pp. 37–53. Oxford: Berg.

—— (2002) 'Excavating memories: archaeology and the Great War, 1914–2001'. *Antiquity* 76 (1): 101–8.

Schofield, J. (2004) 'Aftermath: materiality on the home front, 1914–2001'. In N.J. Saunders (ed.) *Matters of Conflict: Material Culture, Memory and the First World War*, pp. 192–206. Abingdon: Routledge.

School of Military Engineering, Chatham (1877) *Instruction in Field Engineering, Vol. 1, Pt 1: Field Defences*. London: HMSO.

Smith, N. (1995) 'Military training earthworks in Crowthorne Wood, Berkshire: a survey by the Royal Commission on the Historical Monuments of England'. *Archaeological Journal* 152: 422–40.

Solano, E.J. (ed.) (1915) *Field Entrenchments: Spadework for Riflemen*. London: John Murray.

Thomas, R.J.C. (1997) Penally Training Camp. *Sanctuary* 26: 5–6.

Welch, C. (1997) *An Investigation of a Possible Trench 'Model' on the Site of the First World War Camp at Rugeley*. Staffordshire County Council Research Report No. 2.

INDEX